Language and National Identity

Impact: Studies in language and society

IMPACT publishes monographs, collective volumes, and text books on topics in sociolinguistics and language pedagogy. The scope of the series is broad, with special emphasis on areas such as language planning and language policies; language conflict and language death; language standards and language change; dialectology; diglossia; discourse studies; language and social identity (gender, ethnicity, class, ideology); and history and methods of sociolinguistics

General editor

Annick De Houwer
University of Antwerp

Advisory board

Ulrich Ammon
Gerhard Mercator University

Laurie Bauer
Victoria University of Wellington

Jan Blommaert
Ghent University

Paul Drew
University of York

Anna Escobar
University of Illinois at Urbana

Guus Extra
Tilburg University

Margarita Hidalgo
San Diego State University

Richard A. Hudson
University College London

William Labov
University of Pennsylvania

Elizabeth Lanza
University of Oslo

Joseph Lo Bianco
The Australian National University

Peter Nelde
Catholic University Brussels

Dennis Preston
Michigan State University

Jeanine Treffers-Daller
University of the West of England

Vic Webb
University of Pretoria

Volume 13

Language and National Identity: Comparing France and Sweden
by Leigh Oakes

Language and National Identity
Comparing France and Sweden

Leigh Oakes
Queen Mary, University of Londen

John Benjamins Publishing Company
Amsterdam / Philadelphia

♾™ The paper used in this publication meets the minimum requirements of American National Standard for Information Sciences – Permanence of Paper for Printed Library Materials, ANSI z39.48-1984.

Library of Congress Cataloging-in-Publication Data

Oakes, Leigh.
    Language and national identity : comparing France and Sweden / Leigh Oakes.
       p. cm. (Impact: Studies in language and society, ISSN 1385–7908 ; v. 13)
    Includes bibliographical references and index.
       1. Anthropological linguistics--France. 2. Anthropological linguistics--Sweden. 3. Ethnicity--France. 4. Ethnicity--Sweden. 5. Nationalism--France. 6. Nationalism--Sweden. I. Title. II. Impact, studies in language and society ; 13.
P35.5.F8 O18 2001
306.44'089--dc21   2001043496
ISBN 90 272 1848 X (Eur.) / 1 58811 116 4 (US) (Hb; alk. paper)

© 2001 – John Benjamins B.V.
No part of this book may be reproduced in any form, by print, photoprint, microfilm, or any other means, without written permission from the publisher.

John Benjamins Publishing Co. · P.O. Box 36224 · 1020 ME Amsterdam · The Netherlands
John Benjamins North America · P.O. Box 27519 · Philadelphia PA 19118-0519 · USA

Contents

Preface — vii
Acknowledgements — ix

1. Introduction — 1
   1.1 Aims of the book — 3
   1.2 Structure of the book — 5

2. Basic concepts — 9
   2.1 Ethnicity and the ethnic group — 9
   2.2 Nationalism and the nation — 11
   2.3 Language and linguistic variation — 18
   2.4 Language, ethnicity and nationalism — 21

3. Theoretical framework — 29
   3.1 Language attitudes — 29
   3.2 Social identity and ethnolinguistic identity theories — 33

4. Language and national identity: A general perspective — 49
   4.1 Linguistic consciousness — 49
   4.2 Language and identity in France: A historical overview — 53
   4.3 Language and identity in Sweden: A historical overview — 64
   4.4 French and Swedish attitudes to language change and spelling reform — 71

5. Language and national identity in the national arena — 79
   5.1 Ethnolinguistic minorities — 79
   5.2 Language and national identity in France: The national arena — 88
   5.3 Language and national identity in Sweden: The national arena — 104
   5.4 French and Swedish attitudes towards the teaching of minority languages and the Charter for Regional or Minority Languages — 116

6. Language and national identity in the European arena — 127
   6.1 The European arena: A new cultural battlefield? — 127
   6.2 English: The European *lingua franca*? — 131
   6.3 Language and identity in France: The European arena — 136
   6.4 Language and identity in Sweden: The European arena — 140
   6.5 France and Sweden in the European arena: Future challenges — 145

7. Language and national identity in the global arena — 147
   7.1 A new global culture? — 147
   7.2 English: A global language? — 149
   7.3 Language and identity in France: The global arena — 154
   7.4 Language and identity in Sweden: The global arena — 163
   7.5 France and Sweden in the global arena: Past and future challenges — 170

8. Language and national identity in France and Sweden: A survey — 175
   8.1 Aims of survey — 175
   8.2 Methodology — 177
   8.3 Results and comparative discussion of the survey — 185

9. Conclusion — 229
   9.1 Summary of findings — 230
   9.2 Future research — 235

Notes — 239
Appendix A: Questionnaire in French — 249
Appendix B: Questionnaire in Swedish — 257
References — 265
Index of subjects — 293
Index of names — 300

Preface

The aim of this book is to re-examine the relationship between language and national identity. Unlike many previous studies, it employs a comparative approach for a more comprehensive understanding of this relationship. France and Sweden have been chosen as case studies both for their similarities (e.g. both are member states of the European Union) as well as their important differences (e.g. France, at least in principle, subscribes to a civic model of national identity, whereas the basis of Swedish identity is undeniably ethnic; language is so obviously a core value of French identity, but at first does not appear to be so for Swedish identity). It is precisely differences such as these which allow for a more complete understanding of the ethnolinguistic implications of some of the major challenges currently facing France, Sweden and other European countries: regionalism, immigration, European integration and globalisation.

The present volume also differs from others on the market because of the variety of methods of inquiry used. Most previous studies of language and national identity are not reinforced by an empirical component, which adds weight to the investigation. This is the aim of the survey, which is the focus of Chapter 8. The book also uses a multidisciplinary approach that brings together materials from a range of fields (e.g. the sociology of language, sociolinguistics, social psychology, political science, history, economics) for a comprehensive examination of the role of language in national identity. Finally, it is worth noting that much of the French and especially Swedish literature reviewed in this book has traditionally been neglected by English-speaking researchers because of language barriers. All translations from foreign-language sources are those of the author, unless otherwise specified.

The origins of this book lie in a Ph.D. dissertation completed at the University of Melbourne, Australia, in August 2000.

Acknowledgements

The research on which this book is based owes much to many people. First and foremost, I would like to thank my friend and former supervisor, Monique Monville-Burston. For ten years, Monique has been an invaluable source of inspiration and encouragement. Monique's remarkable dedication and thoroughness will forever motivate me; in fact, so much of what I have already achieved, I owe directly or indirectly to her. For all this, I could never thank her enough.

Another person to whom I am greatly indebted is Kenneth Hyltenstam, of the Centre for Research on Bilingualism at Stockholm University. Kenneth kindly accepted to supervise my work from September 1997 until December 1998, when the Swedish Institute generously offered me one of their guest scholarships for overseas researchers. I am very grateful to others at the Centre as well: to Maria Wingstedt, Barbro Allardt Ljunggren, Christopher Stroud, Taija Nyborg, Anders Philipsson and Veli Tuomela; in essence, to everyone at the Centre, I thank you so much for giving me a home, and for making me feel welcome. I will always have fond memories of my time in Stockholm.

My Swedish experience was also shaped by the assistance of several others: Mikael Svonni, Annick Sjögren, Margareta Westman, François Aillet, César Ibanez, Agneta Karlsson, Birgitta Landström and Siv Wiss. There are many to thank in France too: Jean-François Baldi, Jean-François Battail, Maria Ridelberg-Lemoine, Monsieur Cicaronne, Monsieur Olsem, Monsieur Colpin, Monsieur Herlemont, Madame Rault, Madame Rebuffat, Philippe Audibert, Monsieur Rauch and Daniel Elduayen. From my time in Melbourne, I am indebted to Jane Warren, Tim McNamara, Catrin Norrby and Cathy Elder; in London to Itesh Sachdev, Luc Bougniol-Laffont, Per Sörbom and to Richard Bourhis, whom I met on a trip of his to the UK. This book also greatly benefited from comments made by John Edwards and Denis Ager, the examiners of the doctoral dissertation which preceded this work.

At my new home, the School of Modern Languages at Queen Mary, University of London, I am grateful to Jenny Cheshire, Jamal OuHalla and to my predecessor Hilary Wise, from whom I inherited the MA module Language and Nation, which allowed me to develop further the ideas on which this work is based. I would also like to thank Michael Moriarty and Marian Hobson for providing the necessary conditions for me to complete my research as promptly as possible. The incredibly warm welcome I have received from everyone in the School kept me going in the final weary stages of my research, and gave me a friendly working environment to look forward to at a UK university. An important part of this friendly environment was Jill Forbes, whose support, dynamism and intellectual acumen will be dearly missed.

In addition, I would like to thank my parents who spent many hours proof-reading and checking bibliographical references during a recent trip of mine to Adelaide. Needless to say that any errors or omissions remaining are entirely my own responsibility. Finally, I am especially grateful to Richard Cornes, without whose patience, emotional support and intellectual stimulation this book would not have been possible.

Leigh Oakes
London, summer 2001

Chapter 1

Introduction

> The year is 50 BC. Gaul is entirely occupied by the Romans. Well, not entirely... One small village of indomitable Gauls still holds out against the invaders. And life is not easy for the Roman legionaries who garrison the fortified camps of Totorum, Aquarium, Laudanum and Compendium... (Goscinny and Uderzo 1969: 3)

As any French comic addict will know, the 'one small village of indomitable Gauls' in Armorica is that of Astérix. For over three decades, this legendary comic figure has been granted heroic status and celebrated as a symbol of French identity because of his resistance against the Roman conquest. One element of Astérix's struggle was the maintenance of his Gallic language in the face of Latin, the irony being that had the Gauls not adopted Latin, the language so revered by a whole nation today would never have come into being. Nearly 2000 years later, in the 1974 Eurovision song contest, a Swedish pop group were about to become national heroes themselves. However instead of singing in Swedish, ABBA chose to make most of their career — and certainly all of their international career — through the medium of English. Astérix and ABBA constitute two extreme examples of the role played by language in national identity. While it has become somewhat of a cliché that the French place so much emphasis on their language, the Swedes, by contrast, have a reputation for readily embracing English as a global means of communication. Is this to imply that language is more important for French than for Swedish identity? This book seeks to examine this question by determining what role language has played and continues to play in the construction of French and Swedish national identities.

The re-examination of the relationship between language and national identity comes at an appropriate time. In the national arena, the phenomena of regionalism and immigration are causing many groups to rethink their identities. In Eastern Europe and elsewhere, such rethinking has even led to the redrawing of some political borders along ethnolinguistic lines. Within the European Union, processes of economic and cultural integration have also brought to the forefront issues of language and national identity. These same issues are occurring on the world stage too, due to increased internationalisation and globalisation. Phenomena such as these show that the relationship between language and national identity is neither static nor predictable, but rather varies over time and from one country to the next. In some cases, language is considered of the greatest importance for a nation's identity; in other cases, it is seemingly overlooked or taken for granted.

There are many factors which determine the role language plays in the construction of a nation's identity. By providing an introduction to some of these factors, Smolicz's (1981) notion of 'core values' serves as a possible point of departure for this study.

> Core values can be regarded as forming one of the most fundamental components of a group's culture. They generally represent the heartland of the ideological system and act as identifying values which are symbolic of the group and its membership. [. . .] [W]henever people feel that there is a direct link between their identity as a group and what they regard as the most crucial and distinguishing element of their culture, the element concerned becomes a core value for the group. (Smolicz 1981: 75–7)

Whether a language becomes a core value or not depends on various 'circumstances and challenges' (Smolicz 1981: 76) faced by a particular group, both at the present time and throughout history. Smolicz highlights the case of the Poles, for whom language has been considered a core value ever since it was banned in the nineteenth century, when Poland was partitioned amongst its three powerful neighbours: Austria, Prussia and Russia. It was forbidden to speak the language at school and parents who organised Polish classes for their children were threatened with deportation to Siberia. In this way, an 'indissoluble link' was forged between the Polish people and their language, which still exists today even if Polish is no longer an object of persecution.

Another example discussed by Smolicz is that of the Irish, who failed to revive their language following independence. In Smolicz's view, language is therefore not a core value for the Irish who found their identity on other elements.

> Bereft of their ancestral tongue, it was in Catholicism that the Irish found the refuge and shield behind which they could retain their identity and awareness of their distinction. (Smolicz 1981: 79)

What Smolicz seems to imply here is that a language can only be a core value if it serves as the regular instrument of communication. However, language has other important functions, such as acting as a symbolic marker of identity (Edwards 1977: 259; Fishman 1977a, 1997; Scherer and Giles 1979; Appel and Muysken 1987: 11–12; Clyne 1991: 3). For speakers of dominant languages, the communicative and symbolic functions co-exist: 'the language you do your shopping in is also that which carries your culture and history' (Edwards 1994: 114). But for many linguistic minorities, these same functions are divided between the dominant language, used for everyday communication, and the mother tongue, which remains a powerful force for group solidarity (cf. also Liebkind 1999: 143–4). Irish provides an excellent example of this symbolic function of language. Williams (1999: 271) notes that the number of people claiming knowledge of this language is actually on the increase.[1] While this increase does not so much translate into greater use of Irish, it does reflect the language's important constitutional status — it is the national language and first official language, with English as the second — and its role in the rhetoric and myth-making of political parties, not least in Northern Ireland (Ager 1997: 61). Yet even amongst the general public there is widespread support for Irish: 'the general population is willing to accept a considerable commitment of state resources to ensuring the language's continuance and even to support a considerable imposition of legal requirements to know or use Irish on certain groups within society, such as teachers and civil servants' (O Riagáin 1997: 279). Irrespective of how widely spoken the language is, it could be argued that Irish is an obvious core value of Irish culture, since it has a special place in the hearts of many Irish people.

That Smolicz has decided to neglect this symbolic value of language creates obvious problems for his core value theory. In his criticism of the model, Clyne (1991: 104–5) points to the increase in number of people who, in the Australian census of 1986, declared the use of Macedonian and Maltese as a result of heightened ethnic awareness. Similar observations were made by Fishman *et al.* (1985), who revealed huge percentage increases in the number of people reporting mother tongues other than English (such as Spanish, French and Norwegian) in the US censuses of 1960, 1970 and 1980 respectively. In both these cases, the reported increases did not reflect real language use so much as the symbolic importance attached to the languages. This distinction between the communicative and symbolic functions of language is of key importance in the field of language attitudes, the study of which constitutes one of the main aims of this book.

1.1 Aims of the book

The first aim of this book is to examine language attitudes in France and Sweden. It is due in part to this comparative angle that the study can be considered unique. As indicated by the examples in the opening paragraph, the choice of these countries is far from arbitrary. Not only are they both members of the European Union, France and Sweden also appear at first glance to represent two extremes *vis-à-vis* their attitudes towards the national language: while French is so obviously a core value of French identity, the importance of Swedish for Swedish identity is less evident. There is much to be learnt from contrasting language attitudes in different countries. In particular, a comparative approach allows for a better understanding of the link between language and national identity, as well as the ethnolinguistic implications of some of the major challenges currently facing France, Sweden, and other European countries: regionalism, immigration, European integration and globalisation. These challenges provide perfect conditions for studying language and national identity amongst groups for whom these concepts have traditionally been taken for granted. While many previous studies have focused on the attitudes of minority groups towards their own and the dominant language (e.g. d'Anglejan and Tucker 1973 for Québécois French; Baker 1992 for Welsh; Vassberg 1993 for Alsatian), very few quantitative studies have had as their object of study the attitudes of so-called dominant groups towards their own language (but cf. notably Flaitz 1988; Wingstedt 1998). The lack of studies of the latter nature can be explained by the fact that dominant groups were often considered as unmarked, even lacking in identity (see Section 2.1); similarly, attitudes towards dominant national languages were often considered irrelevant or at least predictable. Yet pressure from regional and immigrant languages on the one hand, and from more widespread languages such as English on the other, has meant that national languages now find themselves increasingly in positions similar to those normally associated with minority languages. It is in this context that the present study examines the attitudes of the French and the Swedes towards their respective national languages.

The second aim of the book is to go beyond simple description, to attempt to understand and explain the language attitudes of the French and the Swedes, and investigate the contexts in which these attitudes were and are being formed. As Edwards (1992: 134) believes, it is 'both unlikely and unparsimonious to assert that some groups value their language less. What is *more* likely is that some groups find themselves in different circumstances, requiring different adaptations'. Language attitudes are largely the product of strategies used to construct social identities, in this case ethnic and national identities. As the link between language and such identity strategies has traditionally been studied by a range of disciplines (e.g. sociolinguistics, the sociology of language, social psychology, political science, history, economics), a multidisciplinary approach is a necessary aspect of this study. It is important to stress that the author is nonetheless addressing the topic from the perspective of a linguist. This perspective does not preclude recourse to political science or history for a richer understanding of the relationship between a nation and its language, or to social psychology for a theoretical framework. Yet even if theories have been modified and developed for the purposes of this study, it is not the intention of the author to venture beyond his competence and contribute to theoretical debates in other disciplines. He seeks merely to benefit from the insightful, explanatory models proposed by other fields. When combined with the descriptive presentation of language attitudes, these models allow for a full picture of the relationship between language and national identity in France and Sweden, as revealed throughout the various stages of the book.

1.2 Structure of the book

Chapter 2 begins by introducing the basic concepts needed for a discussion of the role of language in national identity: ethnicity and the ethnic group, nationalism and the nation, as well as language and linguistic variation. Much confusion surrounds all of these notions, which are therefore examined in detail separately in the initial sections of the chapter. A final section discusses the ways in which ethnicity, nationalism and language interrelate.

Chapter 3 presents the theoretical framework which serves as a basis for the study: a combination of language attitude theory, social identity theory and ethnolinguistic identity theory. The examination of criticisms of the latter two theories leads to the proposal of a modified theoretical framework, which introduces communication accommodation theory, the distinction between linguistic and non-linguistic boundaries, as well as the concept of different arenas — national, European and global — in which national identity is constructed and can be studied.

Chapter 4 is the first of four societal analyses which compare language attitudes and national identity strategies in France and Sweden. While in later chapters, these analyses are conducted within the contexts of the particular arenas mentioned above (national, European and global), this chapter adopts a more general perspective. In particular, the notion of linguistic consciousness is used to present a historical overview of the relationship between language and national identity in France and Sweden. Any attempt to understand current language attitudes and identity strategies cannot neglect the social and political forces which have shaped the language-nation relationship throughout a particular nation's history (St Clair 1982). The final section of this chapter compares the linguistic consciousness of the French and the Swedes in a more contemporary context, by examining attitudes towards language change in general, and spelling reform in particular.

Chapter 5 consists of a societal analysis of language attitudes and national identity strategies in France and Sweden conducted in the particular context of the national arena. By 'national arena' is meant the territory delimited by the boundaries of a nation-state, which is usually dominated by one ethnic group, but which is also home to ethnolinguistic minorities. Like ethnicity, nationalism and language, the notion of minority is often misunderstood. This chapter therefore examines the concept in detail, before considering the specific role that both regional and immigrant ethnolinguistic minorities have played in the construction of French and Swedish national identities. A final section focuses on French and Swedish reactions to the particular issues of minority language teaching and the Council of Europe's Charter for Regional or Minority Languages.

The societal analysis of Chapter 6 is conducted within the context of the European arena which has come to the forefront because of the European Union. Despite efforts to forge a new European identity, the European arena can be considered as a 'cultural battlefield' (Schlesinger 1994) for the conflicting identities of EU member states. Following a discussion of the role of language in Europe, this chapter examines the language attitudes and identity strategies of France and Sweden as they exist in this arena, both from a diachronic perspective and in terms of challenges for the future. Of particular interest is the fact that French and Swedish can be increasingly considered as minority languages, faced with the *de facto* status of English as the European *lingua franca* (see Section 1.1).

Chapter 7 represents the final societal analysis, carried out within the framework of the global arena. As in the European arena, the increased contact between nation-states which has resulted from internationalisation has heightened opportunities for social comparison and competition between countries. Moreover, the process of economic, political and cultural convergence or homogenisation known as globalisation which has become particularly prevalent since the late 1980s–early 1990s has made it even more difficult for nations to attain psychological distinctiveness: myths of national superiority are less easily maintained in a world where national cultures become more similar. This loss of psychological distinctiveness often leads to identity crises for many nations, which are forced to consider new strategies for generating positive identities in the global arena. After considering the possible emergence of a global culture, and global language in the form of English, this chapter compares the language attitudes and national identity strategies of France and Sweden in the global arena, once again from both historical and contemporary perspectives. Even more so than in the European arena, French and Swedish can be considered as minority languages in the global arena, faced with the hegemony of English as a global language (see Section 1.1).

Chapter 8 focuses on an alternative method of examining language attitudes and national identity strategies: a survey which was carried out amongst 421 upper secondary school students in France and Sweden. Following a discussion of the aims, hypotheses and research questions of this survey, and the particular methodology used, this chapter examines the results of the students' language attitudes and national identity strategies. In accordance with the structures of Chapters 4 to 7, the results are considered first from a general perspective and then in the national, European and global arenas; in the final section, they are also summarised in terms of the hypotheses and research questions initially posed.

Finally, Chapter 9 brings together the findings of the two different forms of analysis in an overview of the current state of language attitudes and national identity strategies in France and Sweden. In particular, discrepancies are highlighted between the results of the empirical study, which focused on a certain sector of the general public, and those of the societal analyses, which concentrated more on the attitudes of official circles. Some key areas for future research are also identified.

This introduction has stressed the benefits of examining the role of language in the construction of national identity, both from a comparative and multidisciplinary perspective. One consequence of such an approach, however, is the need for a full understanding of the terminology required for a discussion of this nature. To mention but one example, the concept of nation is not necessarily perceived in the same way in France as it is in Sweden, nor need it have the same connotations for linguists or sociologists as it does for political scientists. Before focusing more specifically on the role of language in French and Swedish identities, it is therefore appropriate to examine more closely the basic concepts involved in the topic at hand.

CHAPTER 2

Basic concepts

This chapter examines the fundamental concepts used throughout this book. A discussion of the notions of ethnicity and ethnic group (Section 2.1) is followed by a parallel examination of nationalism and the nation (Section 2.2). The concepts of language and linguistic variation are then defined (Section 2.3) in preparation for the final discussion of the ways in which language, ethnicity and nationalism interrelate (Section 2.4).

2.1 Ethnicity and the ethnic group

The terms 'ethnicity' and 'ethnic identity' — the two are used here synonymously — are complex and employed with a variety of meanings. In everyday language, they are most commonly used with reference to culturally distinct minorities. For example, the adjective 'ethnic' is often associated with objects considered as 'exotic' or 'non-European' (Oxford English Reference Dictionary 1996: 481). In Australia, its meaning is even narrower — 'of or relating to members of a community who are migrants or the descendants of migrants and whose native language is not English' (Macquarie Dictionary 1997: 727) — and it may even be used as a noun. Many of the negative connotations of 'ethnicity' derive from those attached to the use of its Greek root. As used in the first Greek translation of the Bible, *ethnos* reflected a distinction made in Hebrew and served to denote non-Christian and non-Jewish outsiders (Fishman 1997: 328). Today, however, the concept of ethnicity is used more widely, especially by researchers, who refer to the ethnic identities of both insiders and outsiders, both majorities and minorities. Even if dominant groups prefer to speak of national as opposed to ethnic identity (Royce 1982: 3), these groups fulfil the same criteria for ethnic groups as do the ethnic minorities which live within their borders. While related, the concepts of ethnic and national identity are distinct: in some cases they may be coterminous, but in others they can express different realities. The distinction between ethnic and national identity as used throughout this book will be discussed in more detail in Section 2.2.

Ethnic groups — or *ethnies* to use the French borrowing (cf. Smith 1986) — can be defined by both objective and subjective characteristics (Edwards 1985: 7). On the one hand, a definition of ethnicity must include features such as a common origin, language, religion, culture and common values. On the other hand, ethnicity equally cannot be accounted for without reference to less tangible notions such as a sense of collective belonging, or the belief that members of the ethnic group share a common history. Another way of looking at ethnic characteristics is in terms of content and boundaries (Barth 1969). As well as constituting the essence or content of an ethnicity, the characteristics of an ethnic group also serve as boundary markers, distinguishing the ethnic group from other ethnic groups. It follows that there must be some minimum level of contact between groups for ethnicity to exist (Ross 1979: 4–5). In the words of one social anthropologist, 'ethnicity is essentially an aspect of a relationship, not a property of the group' (Eriksen 1993: 12). In the case of minority groups whose ethnic content has changed through acculturation, such as the adoption of the surrounding dominant group's language, cuisine, etc., it is the existence of boundaries which ensures minority group continuity over time. Along with the others so far discussed, the notion of boundaries is a key element in the formal definition of ethnic identity provided by Edwards (1994: 128):

> Ethnic identity is allegiance to a group — large or small, socially dominant or subordinate — with which one has ancestral links. There is no necessity for a continuation, over generations, of the same socialization or cultural patterns, but some sense of a group boundary must persist. This can be sustained by shared objective characteristics (language, religion, etc.), or by more subjective contributions to a sense of 'groupness', or by some combination of both.

A common explanation given for the persistence and intensity of ethnic loyalties is that they are 'primordial givens' (Geertz 1994), like gender or race. However, primordialist theories of ethnicity have been criticised for their failure to account for ethnic change and the development of multiple identities. By contrast, situationalist or instrumentalist theories (Cohen 1974a; Fishman 1977a; Brass 1991) view ethnicity as malleable, varying with the particular situation and dependent on how individuals wish to portray themselves at particular times. It is in this context that one should interpret the following words of Fishman (1977a: 31):

> 'Modern' man is not only viewed (perhaps exaggeratedly) as a shrewd calculator of membership benefits, but as a sensitive recognizer of alternative value systems and of the built-in (de)limitations in any ethnicity system.

Many young people of immigrant parents feel that they have multiple ethnic identities, which they under- and overcommunicate depending on the context. According to one version of situationalism, rational choice theory (Banton 1983; Hechter 1986), these contexts are governed by practical, utilitarian concerns, rather than sentimental, historical and cultural ones. In other words, by making 'rational' choices, individuals, and even whole groups, emphasise and suppress certain aspects of their ethnic identity or identities, in an attempt to maximise socio-economic advantages (wealth, power, honour, etc.). But while these advantages may once have been linked solely to majority group membership, many *ethnies* are returning to their minority identities which they now realise can provide them with similar advantages. This was the motivation behind the ethnic revival or 'new ethnicity' (Bennett 1975) witnessed in the USA in the 1960s and 70s amongst the third and fourth generations of immigrants. In some cases, such renewed ethnic awareness is purely symbolic and does little to reverse assimilation (Gans 1979). However, this cannot be said of the more recent ethnic upsurge observed from 1989 in Eastern Europe, and in particular in the former Yugoslavia. Far from being a case of symbolic ethnicity, the tragic events which took place there were the result of the powerful force of ethnic nationalism.

2.2 Nationalism and the nation

In their detailed study of nationalism around the world, Hettne, Sörlin and Østergård (1998: 78) point out that ethnic and national identity can be linked to each other by way of four scenarios:

a. ethnic identity is a subcategory of national identity;
b. ethnic identity is a historical predecessor, the raw material used to forge national identity of modern times;
c. ethnic identity is a competing identity to national (or rather state) identity;
d. ethnic identity is a supercategory of national identity, so that national identity is a specific type of ethnic identity.

All of the above scenarios show that there is an obvious link between ethnic and national identity, but that the nature of this link varies considerably. While the American research tradition has, according to Hettne, Sörlin and Østergård, awarded primacy to ethnic identity over national identity (scenario d), European history highlights the instrumental role of the state in forging a national identity (scenarios a, b and/or c). The key to understanding these different perspectives lies largely in whether a particular nation is of the ethnic or civic type. An examination of this dichotomy (Section 2.2.1) is followed by a discussion of when the nation first appeared (Section 2.2.2). A final section examines the different expressions or manifestations of the nation, phenomena which can collectively be referred to as nationalism (Section 2.2.3).

2.2.1 Ethnic versus civic nations

A traditional typology of nations distinguishes two fundamental types: ethnic and civic (Kohn 1955; cf. also Smith 1991: 8–15). An ethnic or organic nation, such as Germany or Sweden, can be considered as an extension of the ethnic group in so far as it is founded on *jus sanguinis* ('blood right'). Like the Greek *ethnos*, the Latin *natio* was used to refer to foreigners who were united by common blood ties. Medieval universities, for example, were divided into *nationes* which designated provenance either inside or outside the country (Kedourie 1966: 5). When introduced into English in the thirteenth century, the word was used with this sense of a blood-related human collectivity, but has since seen its meaning expanded to include people who share a common culture (Connor 1978: 381). It is this ethnic dimension of a nation which gives rise to the notion of nationality as opposed to citizenship (Taboada-Léonetti 1998: 30).

At the other extreme is the civic or political nation. In such countries as the USA, France, Australia and Mauritius, people are united around common laws and rights, regardless of their ethnic descent. Members of the nation are treated as individuals who freely, with authority and independently, make decisions regarding their own destiny (Hettne, Sörlin and Østergård 1998: 310). It is these civic principles which form the basis of a nation which is territorial in nature or founded on *jus soli* ('soil right'). The civic nation often brings together different ethnic groups which share a cause or interest, such as a common enemy. The latter was the case of the Swiss confederation which began as a military defence alliance in 1291 (Wardhaugh 1987: 212). Civic principles are thus said to transcend the ethnic reality of nations by having recourse to the notion of citizenship (Schnapper 1994: 49).

The ethnic-civic polarity has given rise to much conflict throughout history. While German Romanticists advocated the ethnic model of the nation, French intellectuals of the nineteenth century gave support to the civic model. Echoing Rousseau's notion of social contract, Renan claimed in his *Qu'est-ce qu'une nation?* (What is a nation?) of 1882 that, irrespective of its ethnic composition, a nation was defined by the will of its members to coexist through a 'daily plebiscite' (Renan 1990: 19). Indeed, this was the argument used by French authorities to justify their claims throughout history to Alsace: Alsatians are French because they want to be. This contrasted with the ethnic claims of German governments who maintained that Alsace belonged to Germany for linguistic and cultural reasons (Winock 1996: 8; Nguyen 1998: 23).

Despite the ethnic-civic dichotomy, it is rare that a nation finds itself at one extreme or the other (Smith 1991: 13; Østerud 1997: 27–8). On the one hand, it is not unusual for nations which are more ethnic in nature to implement policies normally associated with civic nations *vis-à-vis* their minorities (see Section 5.1.3). On the other hand, nations claiming to be at the other extreme frequently contain strong ethnic features obscured behind a civic façade. Recent proposals by the new Social Democrat-Green government in Germany, permitting guest-workers and their German-born children to obtain German citizenship, would greatly dilute one of the cornerstones of German identity: *jus sanguinis*. Obversely in France, the Pasqua-Debré law of 1993 represented a step away from civic or territorial principles, by making it more difficult for immigrants to obtain French citizenship (see Section 5.2.2). Moreover, the very nature of civic principles implies that they can never fully be realised without the emergence of a new, ethnic-like nation (Schnapper 1998a: 35).

> It appears inevitable that, to ensure its existence and vitality, the nation constructs and maintains elements of an ethnic nature. Paradoxically, in order to create a civic nation, which is based on rational principles (*dont l'ambition est rationnelle*), as rightly noted by Ernest Gellner, nationalists invoke ethnic arguments, race, language, religion or culture and contribute to their creation or maintenance. Nations have always reinvented a set of myths and ethnic values, they need a sacred territory, heroes and a golden age; in short, they give rise to a form of ethnicity, which generates amongst nationals the feeling of their belonging to the collective. Invention of tradition is a condition for the existence of all nations. (Schnapper 1994: 80–1)

The invention of ethnic tradition referred to by Schnapper manifests itself in the form of myths of origin, that is, the existence of an *Urfolk* or ancestral people, and symbols such flags, anthems, currency and language (cf. also Hobsbawm and Ranger 1984). The use of this '"ethno"-history' (Smith 1991: 26) is an essential part of guaranteeing the political legitimacy of nations, as is clearly demonstrated by the now famous words of Italian nationalist Massimo d'Azeglio following the Risorgimento in 1860: 'We have made Italy, now we have to make Italians' (cited in Hobsbawm 1992: 44). The discursive nature of national identity — the nation exists in so far as its citizens believe in its founding myths and act according to them (Hettne, Sörlin and Østergård 1998: 142 and 159) — has led many to declare the unnaturalness of nations:

> Nationalism is not the awakening of nations to self-consciousness; it invents nations where they do not exist ... (Gellner 1964: 168)

Others suggest that nations are no more invented than other forms of social organisation, since they usually derive their myths from those of the long-existing dominant ethnic core (Smith 1986; 1991: 39). However, such claims imply that ethnic elements are in some way more real or authentic than civic ones. Clearly all nations rely on ethnic and civic dimensions, albeit in different degrees, as demonstrated by Smith's (1991: 14) formal definition of the nation as:

> a named human population sharing a historic territory, common myths and historical memories, a mass, public culture, a common economy and common legal rights and duties for all members.

2.2.2 The emergence of the nation

The civic-ethnic dichotomy discussed in the previous section poses a particular problem for determining when the modern nation first emerged. On the one hand, those who view the concept of nation largely in civic or political terms declare that '[t]he true birth of a nation is the moment when a handful of individuals declare that it exists and endeavour to prove it' (Thiesse 1999: 11). Such was the case in Denmark, England, France, Holland, Portugal, Spain and Sweden. To take but one country as an example, William Shakespeare (1564–616) wrote of love for England in plays such as Henry V and Richard II, John Milton (1608–74) expressed his pride in England in his poetry and prose, while Henry St. John Bolingbroke (1678–751) demonstrated his 'secret pride' in being born a Briton, by collaborating in the writing of the anthem *Rule Britannia* (Snyder 1964: 79–84). On the other hand, those who view the concept of nation largely in ethnic terms point to the fact that these early expressions of national sentiment emanated from an élite only, and can therefore not be considered as truly national. Indeed, 'Montesquieu did not hesitate to declare in the middle of the eighteenth century, "*la nation, c'est-à-dire les seigneurs et les évêques*" — i.e. the nation, that is, the nobility and the clergy' (Schulze 1996: 104).

> A key problem faced by scholars when dating the emergence of nations is that national consciousness is a mass, not an élite phenomenon, and the masses, until quite recently isolated in rural pockets and being semi- or totally illiterate, were quite mute with regard to their sense of group identity(ies). Scholars have been necessarily largely dependent upon the written word for their evidence, yet it has been élites who have chronicled history. Seldom have their generalities about national consciousness been applicable to the masses, and very often the élites' conception of the nation did not even extend to the masses. (Connor 1990: 100)

Although heavily influenced by these earlier forms of political organisation, the modern nation is therefore regarded by most scholars to have developed in the late eighteenth century following the American and French Revolutions. In his discussion of nation-states in Europe, Kohn (1961: 573) claimed that 'before the [French] Revolution there had been states and governments, after it emerged nations and peoples.' Indeed in France, the struggle of the bourgeoisie against absolutism caused Louis XIV's famous *l'État, c'est moi* to give way to *l'État, c'est le peuple* (Connor 1978: 382).

However, as noted in the previous section, opinion differs as to which model of the nation — ethnic or civic — is the most appropriate. If, on the one hand, one adopts the ethnic view, it must be noted that in very few cases do nations completely coincide with the politico-administrative entity known as the state, to give what is called a 'nation-state'. Although the recent acquisition of statehood by many nations in Eastern Europe has certainly changed the geopolitical landscape, Connor (1993: 174) claimed that of some 180 states which existed in the early 1990s, no more than fifteen could be described as true nation-states (e.g. Iceland, and possibly Portugal and Japan). According to this ethnic definition of the nation, terms such as 'United Nations' and 'international relations' are clearly misnomers, since most of the states concerned contain several nations. Such terms are not problematic if, on the other hand, one adopts the civic, and notably French, perspective which equates nation and state. The possession of a state is of such importance for the French perspective that Corsicans, Bretons, Basques and Scots are considered merely as ethnic groups, and not as nations as they are according to the Anglo-Saxon research tradition (Schnapper 1991: 16). In order to distinguish this civic or political conception of the nation, some scholars prefer to speak of 'state-nations' (Fishman 1989: 130), that is those countries which have constructed the nation around the state (e.g. England, Spain, France, Sweden and Denmark). These countries contrast with 'nation-states' (e.g. Germany, Norway and Finland), where the formation of the state was itself a product of a growing sense of nationalism.

2.2.3 Nationalism

As an expression of the nation, nationalism can be said to have begun around the time which witnessed the birth of nations. While some scholars argue over when this occurred, even more dispute the cause of nationalism. For Kedourie (1966), nationalism is a result of social breakdown and the collapse of traditional values; it replaces religion as the key to salvation for a secular generation. Gellner (1964) argues that it was the exclusion of peripheral regions from industrialisation and the unequal diffusion of modernisation which led to the emergence of nationalist movements which demanded independence or autonomy for these regions. Alternatively, Anderson (1983) attributes nationalism to the rise of 'print-capitalism', that is the printing industry's search for new markets in the form of speakers of vernacular languages (see Section 2.4.1). But as the masses were on the whole illiterate, print-capitalism was a phenomenon which was largely confined to the élite. The ideas and images of the nation as promoted by this latter group of society constitute a form of official nationalism, which is to be distinguished from the folk nationalism experienced by the masses (Smith 1991: 102; Hettne, Sörlin and Østergård 1998: 425). The distinction between official and folk nationalism remains appropriate today, and can be used to explain the simultaneous existence of ethnic and civic types of nationalism on different dimensions.

In addition to the official–folk distinction, further confusion surrounding nationalism results from the various phenomena which the term describes: a movement, a sentiment and an extreme right-wing ideology (Winock 1996: 13; Nguyen 1998: 30–1). As a movement, nationalism prescribes that the boundaries of the state and the nation should be coterminous. This philosophy of a right to national self-determination was largely developed by Fichte and other German Romanticists (see Section 2.4.1), who extended Kant's idea of autonomy of the individual to the group. The resulting 'nation=state' equation or 'principle of nationality' was later established as the prevailing international principle at the Versailles peace agreement in 1919–20 (Hettne, Sörlin and Østergård 1998: 101). It is nationalism of this sort which has led to the emergence or re-emergence of nation-states in Eastern Europe.

Nationalism can also describe a sentiment, and as such can be considered synonymous with national identity. During the nineteenth century, this identity was sought in vernacular cultures. Epics (e.g. Lönnrot's *Kalevala* in Finland and the work by the Grimm brothers in Germany), historical novels (e.g. the works of Dumas in France), theatre (e.g. the works of Goethe in

Germany) and music (e.g. works by Sibelius, Verdi and Wagner in Finland, Italy and Germany respectively) were all used as expressions of nationalism. When referring to their own group, many individuals prefer to speak of 'patriotism' or 'loyalty to country' instead of nationalism, not least because of the images of extreme violence which this latter term has traditionally evoked.[1] However, nationalism need not necessarily entail violence: a good example of less aggressive forms of nationalist fervour can be found in international sporting events, which may be thought of as mock battles or 'metaphoric wars' (Eriksen 1993: 111).[2] Still more benign is what has been termed 'banal nationalism' (Billig 1995). This involves the everyday construction of a sense of national identity, the continual, often concealed, cultural and political reproduction of already established nations.

> Just as a language will die rather for want of regular users, so a nation must be put to daily use. (Billig 1995: 95)

Putting the nation to daily use is the purpose of the 'unwaved flags' flying outside the post office or stitched onto a uniform (Billig 1995: 40–1). Other inconspicuous symbols of the nation include national recreations, the countryside, popular heroes and heroines, fairy tales, forms of etiquette, styles of architecture, arts and crafts, modes of town planning, legal procedures, educational practices and military codes (Smith 1991: 77). These are taken for granted, but nonetheless serve as boundary markers, as continual reminders of the existence of the nation. Even the most mundane of everyday experiences, or 'habitus' to use Bourdieu's terminology (cf. Thompson 1991: 12), can be suffused with nationalist meaning. Linde-Laursen (1995: 1133–7) provides an entertaining example in the form of the different dishwashing practices which have developed respectively in Sweden and Denmark, but which ironically both stem from the same report issued by the Swedish Domestic Research Institute in 1946. This example shows that there is in fact nothing in the nationalist doctrine which prescribes how national boundaries should be ascertained. It is for this reason that nationalism can rely on ideologies as different as liberalism, communism, fascism and racism (Smith 1995: 150).

The pernicious side of these last two ideologies — fascism and racism–has resulted in many scholars identifying a third extremist type of nationalism, which can nevertheless be considered as an extension of nationalism as a sentiment. Although many left-wing ideologies are clearly nationalist in nature (Eriksen 1993: 107; Østerud 1997: 11–12), nationalism is frequently associated with extreme right-wing groups. These groups typically view national identity in terms of ethnicity (Barbour 1996: 31), while the nationalism they promote is often characterised as closed, in that it is pessimistic, hostile and protective of the nation from all forms of corruption (Winock 1982: 7). Extreme right-wing nationalists need not in theory have any enemies, when they are free from foreign oppression and live in an already established nation-state. However, in times of crisis when identities are insecure, the desire to assert the grandeur of one's nation and its superiority over others can lead to tensions or wars with neighbouring countries. More frequently, nations will seek to generate a more positive identity by designating internal enemies, in the form of autochthonous and immigrant minorities (Nguyen 1998: 31; see Chapter 5).

Despite the differences discussed so far, all nationalisms share some features. Like ethnicity, they all depend on subjective elements to construct the nation as an 'imagined community' (Anderson 1983).

> It is imagined because the members of even the smallest nation will never know most of their fellow-members, meet them, or even hear of them, yet in the minds of each lives the image of their communion. (Anderson 1983: 15)

As mentioned in Section 2.2.1, nations also justify their existence with the aid of objective characteristics, such as a shared religion, culture or origin. Of these characteristics, language is usually considered one of the most important.

2.3 Language and linguistic variation

As was noted in the introduction to this book, a language is more than just a means of communication. So powerful is its symbolic value that language is often perceived as an institution, an entity in its own right. The notion of what constitutes a language may at first seem straightforward: French, Swedish and English are all accepted examples of languages. However, this apparent clarity is easily upset when one considers linguistic variation.

Linguistic variation of a social nature refers to that which is conditioned by a speaker's socio-economic class, sex, age, ethnic group, etc. This variation often exists despite strong pressures to conform to a norm which is defined both in linguistic and socio-political terms (see Section 4.1). But while social varieties clearly challenge the homogeneity of a given language (cf. e.g. Ager 1999: 63–85), they rarely lead to the emergence of what can be considered as separate languages. This cannot be said of linguistic variation of a geographical nature, which is traditionally perceived in terms of dialects and regional accents.

Unlike 'variety', preferred by linguists for its neutrality, the term 'dialect' is very socio-politically loaded. It is often used by the dominant sector of a society as a deliberate means of reinforcing the inferior status of minority groups. In addition, 'dialect' carries a range of different connotations depending on the sociolinguistic context: in France, for example, there is a long tradition of referring to other regional languages and varieties of French as dialects or *patois* for specific political purposes (see Section 5.2.1). The problem is that one cannot rely purely on linguistic criteria (shared phonological, morphosyntactic, lexical, etc. features) to define a language. Swedish and Norwegian share many linguistic characteristics to the point that they are mutually intelligible in most cases; they are nonetheless accepted as separate languages. On the other hand, Mandarin and Cantonese are often perceived, especially by the Chinese authorities, as varieties of the same language, despite the fact that a speaker of one cannot understand a speaker of the other, unless communicating in writing through the use of a common script (Edwards 1985: 20; Coulmas 1999: 400). The key to distinguishing a language from a variety lies more often than not in socio-political conventions. Swedish and Norwegian are separate languages because Sweden and Norway are separate states. Conversely, Mandarin and Cantonese are considered varieties of one language to emphasise the unity of the Chinese people. These varying perspectives, which result in the use of different terms, are inextricably linked to questions of identity. Meän Kieli, spoken in the Torne Valley in the north of Sweden, is considered a dialect of Finnish by some, especially Finns. However by its own speakers, Meän Kieli is increasingly regarded as a separate language — translated literally, it means 'our language' — and constitutes an important element in a distinct Tornedalian identity (Hyltenstam 1999b: 130–1).

Another reason why the term 'dialect' is problematic in certain contexts concerns standardisation. Standardisation refers to the suppression of linguistic variation in favour of linguistic uniformity. According to Haugen's (1966a) model, a variety — usually that of the dominant ethnic core — is first *selected* as a norm, then *codified* or documented by linguists, grammarians, as well as writers, statesmen and women, and other personalities. The subsequent stages of *elaborating* the variety, so that it can be used in a wide range of domains, and promoting its *acceptance* amongst the speakers-to-be are often on-going processes. Some degree of standardisation appears to be necessary in distinguishing a language from a variety (Hyltenstam 1999b: 112). Australian English provides an example of standardisation in progress: since the late 1960s and early 1970s, an Australian norm started to replace the Received Pronunciation (RP) formerly used in public speaking and broadcasts made by the Australian Broadcasting Corporation (ABC) (Jernudd 1989: 13–16). Similarly, in terms of lexical development and orthographical conventions, there now exists a range of dictionaries which specialise in Australian English (e.g. Macquarie Dictionary 1997; Australian Concise Oxford Dictionary 1997). While the prospect of a separate Australian language may still be remote, it may only be a matter of time before the concept of a distinct American language is widely accepted. Indeed, the Swedes already buy *svensk-amerikanska* bilingual dictionaries, while the French take night courses not only in *anglais*, but also in *américain*. In both these cases, reference is made only to American, as opposed to American English.

Like 'dialect', the notion of 'regional accent' is also manipulated by the dominant sector of a society in order to discriminate against a minority group.

> [A]n Alsatian accent when pronouncing French usually produces very negative judgements of the speaker: 'an accent' is considered unrefined, ungraceful, crude, ridiculous, a mark of lower-class origins and a lack of education. (Vassberg 1993: 170)

Similar results were obtained by Paltridge and Giles (1984), who used the matched-guise technique (see Section 3.1) to find that a Parisian accent was rated more favourably than a Provençal one, which in turn was considered more prestigious than a Breton guise, which itself was evaluated more highly than an Alsatian accent. That an accent can be the source of prejudice highlights the simplistic nature of Anderson's (1983: 122) comment that:

> [l]anguage is not an instrument of exclusion: in principle, anyone can learn any language. On the contrary, it is fundamentally inclusive, limited only by the fatality of Babel: no one lives long enough to learn all languages.

The particular phonological and prosodic markers which constitute an accent serve as a means of emphasising a different identity (Giles 1979: 259). To a Swede unaware that there is a native Swedish-speaking minority in Finland, the *Finlandssvensk* (i.e. Finland Swedish) variety may be misinterpreted as a Finnish accent, in other words as that of a native Finnish speaker who has learnt Swedish. Such a misinterpretation would ignore the fact that Finland Swedes feel unique and clearly distinct from both their Finnish and Swedish neighbours (Herberts 1991).

The use, then, of the term 'language' is far from clear-cut. In particular, it is an abstract construct, based in part on purely linguistic criteria, but more importantly on socio-psychological factors: 'A speech community is made up of people who *regard themselves* as speaking the same language' (Corder 1973:

54). These factors are in turn linked to socio-political issues, such as ethnic identity and nationalism.

2.4 Language, ethnicity and nationalism

While language features prominently in most forms of nationalist rhetoric, the nature of the language-nationalism relationship varies according to the type of national model which dominates. After considering the rise of the vernaculars and their transformation into national languages, this section examines the context of nineteenth-century Germany as an example of the role language plays in an ethnic model of the nation (Section 2.4.1). The role of language in the civic model of the nation is then discussed in the present-day contexts of the USA, Switzerland and Belgium (Section 2.4.2).

2.4.1 Language and ethnic nationalism

Expressions of ethnolinguistic pride, that is those which linked language and ethnic identity, became common in Europe from the time of the Renaissance, when many writers and philosophers decided to use the vernacular instead of Latin. This celebration of vernacular culture owed much to what has been termed 'print-capitalism' (Anderson 1983). Once the market of Latin-speaking élites had been saturated, the printing industry looked to the speakers of vernacular languages, which were spreading throughout Europe as a result of the Reformation. These languages were standardised and promoted to positions formerly only held by Latin (Armstrong 1982: 257; Thiesse 1999: 69). For example, the publication of Luther's translation of the Bible unified High German and eastern Low German, while the translation of the Calvinist Bible helped to establish Dutch as a language distinct from High German (Armstrong 1982: 257). But this process was not confined to the field of religion: dictionaries, grammars and other literary works all served to document and fix the vernaculars. The emergence of such texts is part of what has been termed the 'first ecolinguistic revolution' in Europe, whereby vernacular languages encroached on domains formally dominated by Latin (Baggioni 1997). Nevertheless, as seen in Sections 2.2.2 and 2.2.3, one must remember that the majority of such works were written by the literate, who, like the speakers of Latin, belonged overwhelmingly to the élite of society. Not until the French Revolution can the idea of a truly national language begin to be entertained.

The notion of a national language was further developed and popularised as a result of nineteenth-century Romanticism. Originating in Germany, this movement was in part a reaction to the rationalism of the Enlightenment, but was also spurred on by the growing Francophobia felt by many Europeans. The numerous victories of Napoléon led to the imposition of French in countries across the continent. Although political in nature at the outset, this resentment quickly developed a cultural dimension, namely the rejection of the French language which, during the eighteenth century, had enjoyed the superior status of the language of literature and of polite society. Nowhere was this anti-French sentiment felt more than in Germany, where it gave rise to what is called linguistic nationalism. This was particularly evident in the work of philosophers such as Herder, Fichte and von Humboldt.

> Has a nation anything more precious than the language of its fathers? In it dwell its entire world of tradition, history, religion, principles of existence; its whole heart and soul.   (Herder 1881, vol. 17:58; trans. Berlin 1976: 165)

For Johann Gottfried Herder, language was the core value of a people's *Volkgeist* (national spirit), so that to speak a foreign language was to lead an artificial life, detached from one's own spontaneous and instinctive personality. In his poem *An die Deutschen* (To the Germans), Herder attacked the German obsession with things foreign, inciting his fellow people to be as proud of their language as other nations were of theirs.

> Look at other nationalities. Do they wander about
> So that nowhere in the whole world they are strangers
> Except to themselves?
> They regard foreign countries with proud disdain.
> And you German alone, returning from abroad,
> Wouldst greet your mother in French?
> O spew it out, before your door
> Spew out the ugly slime of the Seine
> Speak German, O you German!
> (Herder 1881, vol. 27:129; trans. Kedourie 1966: 52)

Herder's follower, Johann Gottlieb Fichte, demonstrated even greater jingoism in such works as *Reden an die deutsche Nation* (Addresses to the German Nation), written in 1807 as a direct reaction to Napoléon's victories over Prussia in Auerstädt and Jena in October of the preceding year. Fichte sought to overcome the humiliation of defeat, 'to bring courage and hope to the suffering' (Fichte 1968: 15). The key to regaining a sense of German pride lay in a reappraisal of the German language, its transformation from a source of shame into something even more prestigious than French. Fichte did this by creating a distinction between 'living' and 'dead' languages. Unlike German, other 'Teutonic' languages — roughly all neo-Latin languages and presumably also English–were considered dead, having been bastardised by the adoption of foreign, mainly Latin, elements.

> [T]he German speaks a language which has been alive ever since it first issued from the force of nature, whereas the other Teutonic races speak a language which has movement on the surface only but is dead at the root.   (Fichte 1968: 58–9)

Such 'ideological acrobatics' (Coulmas 1988: 8) allowed Fichte to claim the superiority of the German language and people over all others. Only Germans were true to their original linguistic identity and therefore worthy of being called a nation. Moreover, Fichte addressed all German speakers 'from all the lands in which they are scattered' (Fichte 1968: 3); the German language thus 'unite[d] within its domain the whole mass of men who speak it into one single and common understanding' (Fichte 1968: 59). Finally, in one of the first explicit declarations of the right to linguistic self-determination, the anthropologist and philologist Wilhem von Humboldt (1988: 153) later echoed the claims that 'the concept of a nation must chiefly be founded upon [language]', and that 'the *character of a nation* (. . .) is primarily disclosed in *language*' (1988: 158).

So strong was this tendency to link language and nation in the nineteenth century that Europe witnessed the advent of the *Sprachnation* (language nation), that is, a nation which uses language to justify its right to an independent state (Kloss 1969a: 21). Norwegian, Romanian, Bulgarian, Ukrainian, Finnish and Turkish were all used as grounds for the formation of new nation-states in what has been termed the 'second ecolinguistic revolution' in Europe (Baggioni 1997). According to this revolution, the vernacular or common languages were elevated in status to national languages. Nevertheless, it is more than likely that the average citizen still did not consider him- or herself as part of a nation, nor that he or she spoke a national language (Connor 1990). In this sense, national languages remained largely 'semi-artificial constructs' (Hobsbawm 1992: 54), instruments manipulated by intellectuals to create a collective consciousness (Safran 1999a: 82). This manipulation of language was not limited to ethnic nations, but was also common amongst the élite in civic nations.

2.4.2   Language and civic nationalism

The example of nineteenth-century Germany clearly demonstrates the importance of language for ethnic nations. Civic nations also claim that language is important, not because it is central to the *Volkgeist*, but because it acts as a unifying factor for citizens of various ethnic backgrounds. In true civic nations, all languages and ethnicities should in theory be respected as constituting essential components of national identity. Such is the case of the United States, where a clear distinction is made between nationality (or ethnicity) and citizenship (Safran 1991: 222). However as in ethnic nations (see Section 2.4.1), power imbalances usually result in the promotion of the language of the ethnic core, a phenomenon from which the United States is clearly not immune. Generally considered as forming part of a broader English-only movement, US English was founded in 1983 as a response to fears about the growing number of Spanish speakers. The organisation is against bilingual education in American schools on the grounds of 'identity confusion' and 'resegregation' (cf. Edwards 1994: 169); it also advocates the enshrining of English as the official language of the country and of individual states (Schiffman 1996: 245; see also Section 5.1.3). In particular, it is claimed that the official recognition of other languages, especially Spanish, would undermine the founding (civic) principles of the nation (Fishman 1988: 128). One cannot help but be sceptical about the real motives behind US English and similar movements.

> Clearly US English taps into concerns about immigration, eugenics, welfare reform, population and environment control, and political movements that wish to preserve America as a White English-speaking nation. (Schiffman 1996: 271)

It seems more likely that behind the civic rhetoric of the melting pot, there is a fervent ethnic nationalism in the USA which has its roots in White Anglo-Saxon Protestant (WASP) culture (Smith 1991: 150; Edwards 1994: 177–8). Calls to officialise English are concerned less with ensuring equality between all citizens than with alleviating the insecurities of a mainstream middle class fearful of losing its dominant socio-economic position (Fishman 1988: 133; Tollefson 1991: 128; Hettne, Sörlin and Østergård 1998: 418). Far from its initial unifying role, language is thus increasingly being used by the dominant group as a means of excluding minority group members from socio-economic benefits.

> The English Only movement, an outgrowth of the immigration-restrictionist lobby, has skilfully manipulated language as a symbol of national unity and ethnic divisiveness. Early in this century, those who sought to exclude other races and cultures invoked claims of Anglo-Saxon superiority. But in the 1980s, explicit racial loyalties are no longer acceptable in our political discourse. Language loyalties, on the other hand, remain largely devoid of associations with social injustice. While race is immutable, immigrants can and often do exchange their mother tongue for another. And so, for those who resent the presence of Hispan-

ics and Asians, language politics has become a convenient surrogate for racial politics. (Crawford 1989: 14)

Language in the USA has thus become 'an instrument for ethno-racial prejudice' (Safran 1992: 549). To be fair, although manifesting itself in official circles, this ethnic nationalism emanates largely from the grassroots level, and the federal government has a record of largely promoting pluralistic values. In what reflects the distinction between official and folk nationalism (see Section 2.2.3), two types of language policy have developed: overt and covert. While there is no explicit, formalised or codified policy promoting English in the USA, the dominant status of English is nonetheless accepted *de facto* at the grassroots level: it is the primary language in schools, business, in state, federal and local administration, in health care, in the media and in entertainment (Schiffman 1996: 14).

Other so-called multilingual nations also reveal the difficulties faced by the civic model in accommodating several languages. Switzerland and Belgium have traditionally been presented as models of multilingual nations that work (e.g. Haugen 1985; cf. Hettne, Sörlin and Østergård 1998: 30; cf. Wright 2000: 75). However, on closer examination, the situation in both of these countries actually confirms the strength of the link between language and ethnicity. As noted by Baggioni (1997: 32) on Switzerland:

> Indeed if quadrilingualism is inscribed in the constitution of the Confederation, it is nowhere present in social life, because monolingualism is the rule at the cantonal level and at the communal level in the case of bilingual cantons (such as Valais and Fribourg). Territorialised monolingualism and institutional multilingualism are thus only present at the federal political and administrative level.

When two or more ethnolinguistic groups in Switzerland do mix, respective attitudes towards the other group are anything but tolerant. The French-speaking (and Catholic) Jura, for example, separated from the German-speaking Berne only after a long period of tension stretching from 1947 to 1978, which even included the occasional bombing (Wardhaugh 1987: 214–16).

Tensions have also characterised relations between the Flemish and Walloon communities ever since the formation of the Belgian state in 1830 (Wardhaugh 1987: 203–11; Ager 1990: 87–8; Nguyen 1998: 185–93). As in Switzerland, territorial monolingualism is currently the rule, and has dominated since the introduction of linguistic borders in 1962–3 (Tabouret-Keller 1999: 345–7). Although the majority has traditionally not considered such proposals seriously, a small number of Walloons go as far as to favour unification with France on linguistic grounds (Nguyen 1998: 191). However, anyone visiting Belgium or Switzerland will notice that the Walloons and French-speaking Swiss have an ethnic identity and variety of French distinct from people across the border in France, or for that matter anywhere else in the *Francophonie* (cf. also Clyne 1991: 100–1). The Walloons and French-speaking Swiss *ethnies* can thus be considered distinct within the two entities to which they nevertheless belong: the wider French speech community and the Belgian and Swiss nation-states respectively (see Figure 2.1).

While the above observations may raise the question of whether Switzerland and Belgium constitute nations at all, any possible answer must take into account the definition of nation employed by the respective countries themselves. Switzerland has until now found creative ways of considering itself a nation (e.g. particular political structure, and a wide use of referendums). However, some researchers (e.g. Hettne, Sörlin and Østergård 1998: 31) believe that individual ethnic affiliations will in time outweigh any sense of 'national' or superethnic identity, resulting ultimately in the country's dissolution. Signs of this are beginning to show as a result of the debate surrounding the new school curriculum in Zurich (*Learning English, The Guardian Weekly*, 16–22 September 1999). By introducing English from year one in primary schools, Schools Project 21 has overturned one of the foundations of Swiss language education: all children must learn another national language of Switzerland as their first foreign language. Indeed, young Swiss people from different linguistic communities increasingly use English to communicate with one another, while at the cantonal level, it is more common to be exposed to English, in the context of tourism and business, than it is to observe any display of the country's other national languages. The increased use of English over other

Speech community (e.g. French-speaking world) — Ethnolinguistic group (e.g. Walloons, French-speaking Swiss) — Multilingual nation-state (e.g. Belgium, Switzerland)

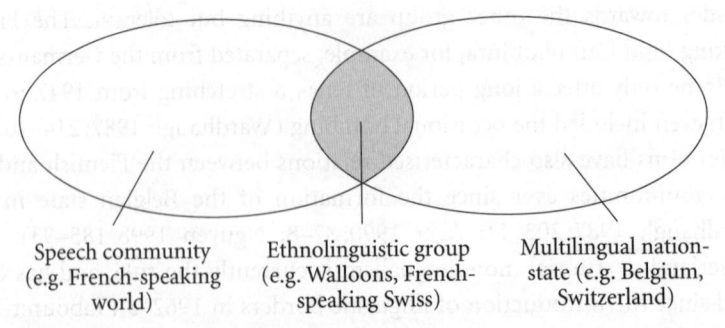

Figure 2.1 The participation of the ethnolinguistic group in both the wider speech community and the nation-state

national languages has provoked fears that the patchwork quilt of Swiss identity is in a state of decay.

> The debate in Switzerland over language has revealed that antipathy, not solidarity, between communities is the reality, and the much vaunted multi-lingual society has never existed. As one observer comments: 'The Swiss get on so well with each other because they don't understand one another.' (*Learning English*, *The Guardian Weekly*, 16–22 September 1999)

The examples of civic nations given above only seem to confirm the inevitable link between language and the ethnic, as opposed to civic, dimension of nationalism. Indeed in a 1981 survey of 73 identifiable *ethnies* in Europe from the Atlantic to the Ural mountains, Krejči and Velímský (1996) found that 60 of these groups could be classified by language.[3]

Amongst all the possible markers of ethnicity, one can wonder why it is language which so frequently becomes predominant (cf. Pool 1979: 19; Sachdev and Bourhis 1990: 216–17). Indeed the Sapir-Whorf hypothesis of linguistic determinism—whereby a group's thought patterns and culture are determined by the structure of its language — and linguistic relativity — whereby distinct languages give rise to distinct worlds — has proven very problematic (cf. e.g. Pinker 1994: 59–67). Nonetheless, 'the idea that language and society are closely linked; that language is a symbol of the identity of those making up society; and that a particular society is both unique and worth preserving, is widespread' (Ager 1997: 27). Indeed, so strong is the link between language and ethnic identity in some cases, that language even becomes the identity itself (Lafont 1968: 44–7). For example, the separation of language from Basque identity is impossible, not least because the Basques refer to themselves as *euskaldunak*, literally 'those having the Basque language'.[4] But while language may be the ethnic symbol *par excellence*, this is more likely due to its effectiveness as a rallying point, its ability 'to enact, celebrate and "call forth" all ethnic activity' (Fishman 1977a: 25). That some people are prepared to kill one another for the sake of their language has little to do with any inherent importance of language and everything to do with politics and questions of ethnic or national identity (Kedourie 1966: 55; Coulmas 1988: 2).

> At all events problems of power, status, politics and ideology and not of communication or even culture, lie at the heart of the nationalism of language. (Hobsbawm 1992: 110)

The problems mentioned by Hobsbawn stem from the interaction between different ethnic or national groups. As such, any examination of the relationship between language and national identities — such as that observed in France and Sweden — cannot ignore the field of social psychology and its theories concerning interethnic relations.

Chapter 3

Theoretical framework

The theoretical framework used in this book owes much to the field of social psychology, and in particular the social psychology of language. More specifically, the three theories which form the basis of the theoretical paradigm used here are language attitude theory (Section 3.1), and social identity theory and ethnolinguistic identity theory (Section 3.2).

3.1 Language attitudes

According to Baker (1992: 23), language attitude theory should have a strong grounding in general attitude theory. Following this tradition, an attitude is defined as 'a disposition to respond favourably or unfavourably to an object, person, institution, or event' (Ajzen 1988: 4). An attitude is also considered as comprising three sub-components: affect (feelings about the attitude object), cognition (thoughts or beliefs about the object) and behaviour (predisposition to act in a certain way towards the object) (Ryan, Giles and Sebastian 1982: 7; Fasold 1984: 148; Baker 1992: 12–13; Edwards 1985: 139; 1994: 97). The merging of these three components into the higher level of abstraction which constitutes an attitude is shown schematically in Figure 3.1.

An attitude directed specifically at language can thus be defined as 'any affective, cognitive or behavioural index of evaluative reactions toward different language varieties or their speakers' (Ryan, Giles and Sebastian 1982: 7).

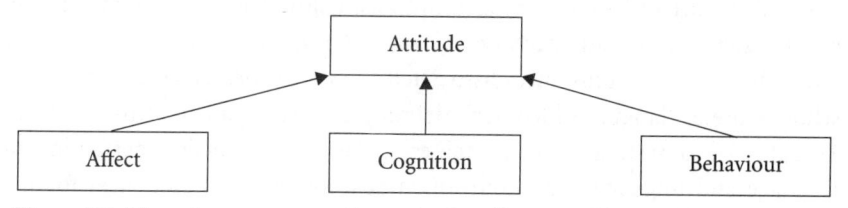

Figure 3.1 The subcomponents of an attitude: affect, cognition and behaviour. (Adapted from Baker 1992: 13)

The measurement of language attitudes is particularly difficult because there is often a lack of harmony between the three components mentioned above (Agheyisi and Fishman 1970: 150–1). While overt behaviour may be easily observable, this behaviour can deliberately conceal negative beliefs, especially if these beliefs are considered socially unacceptable (Baker 1992: 15–16). Even more difficult to measure than beliefs is affect. To take an example from the field of second language acquisition, a mother may encourage her child to learn French (behaviour), believing that it will be important for his or her future career (cognition), yet all the while possibly loathing the language herself (affect) (Edwards 1985: 140; 1994: 98). Doubt must be expressed as to whether these deep-seated feelings (affect) are truly elicited in attitude measurement (Baker 1992: 12). However, in studies of macro-phenomena, such as ideologies and national identities, it can be argued that it is more important to tap what people think are mainstream beliefs (i.e. cognition) rather than their actual innermost personal attitudes (i.e. affect) (Wingstedt 1998: 252). This point is discussed in more detail in Section 8.2.1.2 in the context of the empirical study which is also included in this book.

There are three main techniques used in the measurement of language attitudes (Ryan, Giles and Sebastian 1982: 7; Ryan, Giles and Hewstone 1987: 1068): content analysis of societal treatment, direct measurement and indirect measurement. Content analyses of the societal treatment of a language include 'observational, participant-observation and ethnographic studies; demographic and census analyses; analyses of government and educational language policies; analyses of literature, government and business documents, newspapers, and broadcasting media; and analyses of prescriptive language books' (Ryan, Giles and Hewstone 1987: 1068). It is important to realise that emphasis here is on the group as opposed to the individual. While 'language attitude' is the term used in this book to refer to group beliefs, some researchers prefer different terminology to reflect the broader orientation of their studies. In his study of France, India and the USA, Schiffman (1996: 5) speaks of 'linguistic culture' to refer to 'the set of behaviours, assumptions, cultural forms, prejudices, folk belief systems, attitudes, stereotypes, ways of thinking about language, and religio-historical circumstances associated with a particular language.' Other scholars prefer 'language ideology', defining this as a 'global attitude' (Baker 1992: 15) or 'a system of ideas, values, emotions and beliefs pertaining to language and linguistic behaviour, often at a low level of awareness for the individual' (Wingstedt 1998: 23). Examples of content analyses of the societal treatment of languages are Fishman's *Language Loyalty in the United States*

(1966), Bourhis' (1982) overview of language attitudes in the *francophone* world, and Carranza's (1982) similar study of Hispanic parts of the world.

Alternatively, language attitudes can be measured by means of direct methods in the form of questionnaires or interviews. Questions which respondents might be asked involve such topics as language evaluation and preference, reasons for learning a particular language, fear of language shift, protection of a certain language and the preservation of multilingualism. Finally, attitudes may be measured by means of an indirect method. Developed by Lambert *et al.* (1960), the matched-guise technique infers language attitudes from evaluations of speakers of different languages or language varieties. The details of this method will not be discussed here. As mentioned in Section 1.2, this study makes use of the societal treatment and the direct methods only. The decision to conduct a direct over indirect method for the purposes of the survey which is included in this book is explained in Section 8.2.1.

Early research (e.g. Jones 1949, 1950) considered language attitudes as one-dimensional (cf. also Baker 1992: 30–1). From the 1970s onwards, opinion changed amongst scholars who began to consider attitudes as consisting of multiple components. Although opinions vary, most contemporary researchers agree with Gardner and Lambert (1972) that there are at least two main dimensions: instrumental and integrative. On the one hand, instrumental dimensions of a language attitude reflect pragmatic, utilitarian motives, such as improving or maintaining socio-economic status through knowledge of a certain language. Instrumental attitudes towards a language are mostly self-oriented, concerning individuals rather than groups as a whole; they are implied in statements such as 'Knowledge of English will help me to find employment.' Integrative dimensions, on the other hand, reflect interpersonal motives, resulting from a sentimental desire to affiliate or identify with a certain language group (Baker 1992: 31–2). This integrative component of an attitude is expressed in statements such as 'I learn English because I like Americans.'

It must be noted, however, that the opposition between instrumental and integrative dimensions of an attitude is not without its problems. For example, Muchnick and Wolfe (1982) have shown that there is much overlap and that it is not always possible to separate the two dimensions, while Dornyei (1990) argues that integrative motivation is less relevant for learners of a foreign language than for those of a second language. This latter argument is of particular relevance for the present study, considering the claims that English has already become a second, rather than foreign, language in Sweden (see Section 7.4).

While the instrumental-integrative dichotomy is usually confined to the field of second language acquisition, it is linked to a similar distinction made in the broader context of language evaluation, which encompasses attitudes to foreign and second languages, as well as to one's mother tongue. The matched-guise technique developed by Lambert *et al.* (1960) and mentioned above identified two dimensions on which languages could be valued: status versus solidarity. When presented to a speaker of another language, a statement such as 'Knowledge of French will help me find employment' would seek to tap an instrumental motivation to learning French. However, when presented to a native French speaker, the aim of the same statement would be to determine if that person valued her or his mother tongue on a status dimension. Obversely, the aim of a statement such as 'We owe it to our ancestors to speak French' when put to a native French speaker would seek a judgement in terms of ingroup solidarity, that is a measure of one's sentimental or integrative attachment to the mother tongue. A similar instrumental-sentimental opposition has also been used to account for an individual's loyalty or attachment to the nation-state (Kelman 1972: 188).

Language attitudes can be considered as reflecting issues of group identity (Appel and Muysken 1987: 16; McNamara 1988: 70). When in a series of tests listeners were made to rate totally unfamiliar foreign languages and language varieties, it was found that no discrimination was made according to alleged linguistic or aesthetic criteria (Giles *et al.* 1974; Giles, Bourhis and Davis 1979; cf. also Trudgill and Giles 1978). In other words, listeners were unable to claim that one language was more beautiful, logical, clear, etc. than another. Rather than being determined by any inherent value of a particular language, language attitudes were shown to be formed predominantly by imposed societal norms. These societal norms are themselves the product of preconceptions about other ethnolinguistic groups (Fasold 1984: 148). Language is thus a metaphor for intergroup contact, a reflection of the attitudes of the Self towards the Other (Stroud and Wingstedt 1989: 5). When languages are described as vying for dominance, as indicated in the title of Wardhaugh's book *Languages in Competition* (1987), the real competition is between different ethnolinguistic groups, not the languages themselves. Similarly, when English is described as the world's most powerful language, it is English-speaking countries, and in particular the USA, which have been and still are powerful in relation to other countries, and not the English language *per se*. That language attitudes — both of the instrumental and integrative types — must be considered in the broader context of intergroup relations is also highlighted by Pennycook (1994:15), who uses the example of language attitudes in the Philippines.

> [W]e cannot reduce questions of language to such social psychological notions as instrumental and integrative motivation, but must account for the extent to which language is embedded in social, economic and political struggles. Arguing against the standard interpretation of the language situation in the Philippines, therefore, which tends to ascribe instrumental value to English while Philipino struggles to maintain a symbolic and integrative role, Tollefson [1986] makes it clear that 'consistent leftist opposition to English in the Philippines should not be viewed as an effort to adopt Philipino as a symbol of national unity and identity, but rather as a part of a program to change the distribution of political power and material wealth' (p.186).

Any examination of the link between language and the ethnic or national identity of a particular group can therefore not neglect the power relationships that exist with other groups. Social identity theory and the related ethnolinguistic identity theory are models designed to study the nature of intergroup contact; they thus provide suitable means for examining the role of language in the construction of French and Swedish identities.

3.2 Social identity and ethnolinguistic identity theories

Social identity theory and ethnolinguistic identity theory rely heavily on the notion of the Other. It is therefore with this concept that the following discussion begins (Section 3.2.1). The details of social identity theory and ethnolinguistic identity theory are then examined (Sections 3.2.2 and 3.2.3 respectively) before some of the major criticisms of both theories are considered (Section 3.2.4). A final section proposes a revised theoretical framework to be used throughout the book (Section 3.2.5).

3.2.1 The Other

As was seen in Section 2.1, it is difficult to speak of ethnicity in isolation, that is, without reference to other ethnic identities. This applies to all types of social identities, including national identity.

> [N]ational identity is produced through a process of negation, the creation of a coherent sense of self through explicit rejections and denials. It is a dynamic relationship, defined through the exclusion of groups deemed not to belong. [...]

> National identity is a fluid entity, where categorisation of 'self' or of 'other', inclusion and exclusion, is an arena of contest between competing groups and institutions within society.   (Evans 1996: 33–4)

In other words, national identity is constructed in contradistinction to that of other groups or Others (Kristeva 1988: 139; Bhabha 1990; Billig 1996: 189). So important is this Other for our identities, that it can even be considered as part of ourselves (Kristeva 1988: 9). For example, the particular view of the Far East known as Orientalism and propagated by French writers in the nineteenth century defined the West by reinforcing the latter's self-perceived superiority. The Orient was largely a 'European invention' (Said 1978: 1) in so far as it was constructed by the discourse of European intellectuals in a variety of fields, ranging from philosophy, history and anthropology to philology, linguistics and literary interpretation (Pennycook 1994: 60–1). Obversely, Europe was itself a product of its own colonial beliefs about the Orient (Pennycook 1998: 65).

The importance of the Other for the construction of Western identities is highlighted more recently by the collapse of the Soviet Union and Communist block. The loss of this major ideological Other has played its part in a wave of identity crises in many Western countries including France (Gildea 1996: 209; Jenkins and Copsey 1996: 114; see Section 7.5). Among the prerequisites for regaining confidence is the designation, if not outright construction, of new, less favourably-viewed Others.

> If foreigners with their knavish tricks did not exist, it would be necessary to invent them.   (Hobsbawm 1992: 174)

In the post-Cold War West, the main Other is played by Islam, which serves as a contradistinction in particular to American identity. Not only do Muslim countries represent external threats in terms of foreign policy, Muslim immigrants are also seen to threaten national identities from within (Schlesinger 1994: 323). The internal threats posed by immigrants is discussed in more detail in the context of France and Sweden in Chapter 5. What is of importance for the present discussion is the significance of this Other for social identity theory.

3.2.2   Social identity theory

Social identity theory (SIT) is a model developed within the field of social psychology of intergroup relations (Tajfel 1974, 1978; Tajfel and Turner 1986).

| Social categorisation | → | Social identity | → | Social comparison | → | Psychological distinctiveness |
| a. | | b. | | c. | | d. |

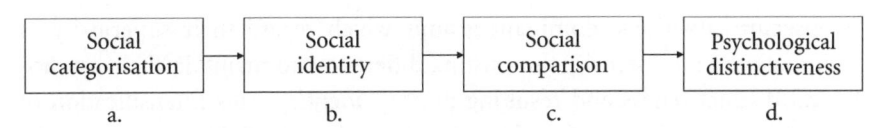

Figure 3.2 Causal sequence of the four main concepts involved in social identity theory

It relies on four main concepts, which are linked in a causal sequence shown in Figure 3.2.

From an early age, individuals categorise themselves and others into social groups (concept a), such as the ethnic groups or nations studied in this book. From the individual's perspective, people either belong to the same group (ingroup) or another group (outgroup). People's awareness of their own social group and the positive or negative values that are related to their membership in that group is known as their social identity (concept b) (Giles, Bourhis and Taylor 1977: 319). According to the theory, when comparing social groups (concept c), individuals will favour the ingroup and discriminate against outgroups. This ethnocentric behaviour, which relies heavily on the use of popular myths and stereotypes, such as those about neighbouring countries, seeks to generate or maintain a state of psychological distinctiveness (concept d), which itself leads to a positive self-esteem and social identity. A basic assumption of the theory is that social groups in Western societies strive to create and maintain positive identities.

Social identity theory also makes use of a distinction between 'secure' and 'insecure' identities (Tajfel 1978), which is essential for understanding identity strategies used to promote social change. Social comparisons and identities are said to be secure when the status relationship between the relevant groups is perceived as immutable: the dominant group remains dominant and the minorities remain subordinate. More frequently, however, social comparisons and identities can be considered as insecure. The existence of 'cognitive alternatives', which render other states of affairs conceivable, is what makes it possible, for example, for a minority group to strive for autonomy or outright independence. But insecure identities do not only apply to subordinate groups; they can also affect majority groups.

> Any threat to the distinctly superior position of a group implies potential loss of positive comparisons and possible negative comparisons, which must be guarded against. (Tajfel and Turner 1986: 22)

In insecure situations, dominant groups which regard their superiority as legitimate tend to intensify the existing differences to maintain their psychological distinctiveness and resulting positive identity. This intensification of differences is usually manifested by a heightened sense of identity amongst the dominant group, and increased discrimination against minority outgroups. As for these latter groups, an insecure identity implies that the group no longer accepts its subordinate status. Attempts are made to improve this status and generate a more positive identity by employing one or more of the following strategies (Tajfel and Turner 1986: 19–20): social mobility, social creativity and social competition.

Social mobility refers to assimilation to the dominant outgroup. Like the instrumental motives behind language attitudes (see Section 3.1), acts of social mobility are generally considered characteristic of the behaviour of individuals, albeit derived from group identity. However, there seems no obvious reason why social mobility cannot be extended to groups as separate entities. This slight modification to the theory would presumably have implications for the long-standing debate on whether group identity can be considered as a distinct phenomenon, as opposed to a mere component of the social psychology of the individual (cf. Turner *et al.* 1987: 1–18).

Social creativity takes three main forms. First, previously negatively-viewed symbols can be redefined in a more positive light. Such is the case of the use of the term 'black' in the slogan 'black is beautiful', and the rescue and reinterpretation of the term 'queer' in queer theory (McNamara 1997). Second, new, positively-viewed symbols may be created: marginalised groups find new ways to distinguish themselves, with the creation of new cultures (e.g. punk, skinhead) (Lange and Westin 1981: 367). Third, social creativity may involve the selection of an alternative, less favourable outgroup for comparison. For example, a minority may consider itself as the most dominant within a hierarchy of minorities in a given society. Alternatively, social comparisons can be made on other dimensions, such as class rather than ethnicity. Rosenberg and Simmons (1972) found that Blacks who made comparisons with other Blacks, rather than Whites, demonstrated a more positive social identity.

The third strategy used by groups to generate a positive identity is known as *social competition*. Unlike social creativity, which has as a goal the improvement of the group's subjective social location, this strategy involves the competition for scarce, objective resources. An example of such a situation might be Belgium, where rival Flemish and Walloon groups vie for socioeconomic superiority (see Section 2.4.2). As well as creating antagonistic group relations, social competition has the effect of reinforcing social categorisation, and can therefore be used as a strategy for generating a positive group identity.

3.2.3 Ethnolinguistic identity theory

As a highly visible symbol of ethnic and national identity, it is not surprising that language features predominantly in the three strategies mentioned in Section 3.2.2: social mobility, social creativity and social competition. It is out of this realisation that ethnolinguistic identity theory (ELIT) was formed by Giles and Johnson (1981) as an extension of SIT. ELIT is therefore based on the same principles as those mentioned in Section 3.2.2, with the addition of three factors which are claimed to determine the salience of ethnolinguistic identity: perceived permeability of boundaries, multiple group memberships and ethnolinguistic vitality.

ELIT states that the perceived permeability of intergroup boundaries influences social mobility. On the one hand, boundaries perceived as soft and permeable facilitate social mobility. Clément and Noels (1999: 248) give the example of White Anglo-Saxon Protestants from the Commonwealth countries, who would have few difficulties crossing ethnic boundaries to become part of the dominant group in the UK. On the other hand, boundaries perceived as hard and impermeable do not allow for social mobility and usually lead to heightened ethnolinguistic identities on both sides. ELIT also states that the strength of ethnolinguistic identity is determined by the number of social groups to which an individual belongs (e.g. professional, social class, age, etc.). In particular, it is claimed that the fewer groups an individual belongs to, the stronger his or her ethnolinguistic identity will be. Finally, ELIT introduces the notion of ethnolinguistic vitality (ELV) defined as 'that which makes a group likely to behave as a distinct and active collective entity in intergroup situations' (Giles, Bourhis and Taylor 1977: 308; cf. also Sachdev and Bourhis 1990). As the present study makes no specific use of the theory of ethnolinguistic vitality, the latter will not be discussed further here.

Unfortunately, ELIT does not explain why language is favoured by some groups more than others as a symbol of ethnic or national identity. As mentioned in Section 1.1, this book seeks to go beyond description and understand why language is valued by some ethnic groups more than others. For this purpose, the broader SIT proves to be a more useful framework, since it also allows for the consideration of non-linguistic factors which may result in an emphasis being placed on language. This is not to say that elements of ELIT are not also called upon in the societal analyses of Chapters 4, 5, 6 and 7. Before proposing a revised theoretical framework to be used throughout the remainder of this study, it is worth considering some criticisms of SIT and ELIT.

3.2.4 Criticisms

The criticisms which are relevant to the theoretical framework used in the present study are discussed below according to three main themes: motivation behind social identity constructions (Section 3.2.4.1), inability to deal with large-scale groups (Section 3.2.4.2) and monocultural-assimilationist bias (Section 3.2.4.3).

3.2.4.1 *Motivation behind social identity constructions*

According to SIT, the motivation behind the construction of social identity is a desire for a positive self-esteem (see Section 3.2.2). Many researchers claim that self-esteem is insufficient and argue the need to incorporate additional motives into SIT. Such alternative motives could include the desire for material wealth, power, control, psychological comfort or stability, security, self-efficacy, meaning and self-knowledge (cf. Abrams 1992: 66). For example, in a study of British and European identity, Cinnirella (1996: 265–6) found that desires to maintain autonomy and exert control over world affairs were more important motivations associated with British identity than was self-esteem.

As motivation can be defined as a desire to achieve a certain goal, it follows that these alternative motives correspond to alternative goals of wealth, power, control, etc. Yet whether people are aware of it or not, these goals can themselves be linked to higher self-esteem: 'we' have higher self-esteem than 'them', because 'we' are wealthier, more powerful, exert more control, etc. than 'them'. It is therefore important to identify different levels of goals (cf. Ager 2001: 7–8). One possibility is to consider desires to be wealthy, powerful or exert control as intermediate goals which constitute a first step to reaching the ultimate goal of high self-esteem (see Figure 3.3).

It may be that while most people are able to identify intermediate goals, very few can recognise the ultimate, often subconscious, goal of high self-esteem. Such a model would explain the results obtained by Cinnirella (1996: 265–6). More problematic, however, are such motives as security and stability. Brown *et al.* (1992) claim that these are important for 'autonomous groups', that is those which do not depend on frequent intergroup comparisons. While the very existence of such groups can be debated — SIT regards all

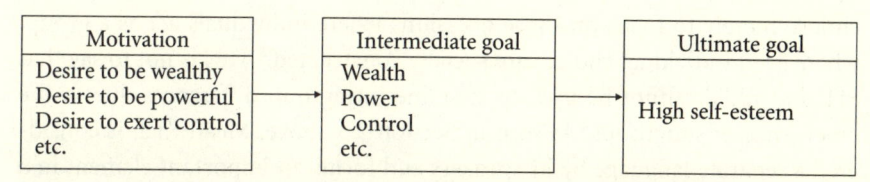

Motivation	Intermediate goal	Ultimate goal
Desire to be wealthy Desire to be powerful Desire to exert control etc.	Wealth Power Control etc.	High self-esteem

Figure 3.3 Motivation and the causal link between intermediate goals and ultimate goal in social identity construction

social relations as inherently competitive — the fact remains that motivations of security and stability are more difficult to link to self-esteem than wealth, power or control. One reason for this is that security and stability may better thought of in terms of needs, rather than goals (cf. Ager 2001: 8–9). Clearly, the motivation behind social identity construction demands closer examination and could benefit from the consideration of different types of needs, such as those distinguished by Maslow (1954). Nonetheless, self-esteem can still be deemed important for many groups, perhaps not so much as an initial motive, but rather as an ultimate, often subconscious goal.

3.2.4.2 Inability to deal with large-scale groups

SIT and ELIT were formulated to examine memberships of both small and large social groups. They have, however, been criticised for oversimplifying the latter, by considering them homogenous, when in fact they contain much variation, not least at the level of the individual. This makes the use of the term 'group' problematic for large-scale categories such as nations (Husband and Saifullah Khan 1982: 200; Cinnirella 1996: 255).

> [T]here is no such thing as 'national identity' in an absolute sense. Every nation has many national identities since each individual, in social context, negotiates what the meaning of his or her national identity is and can renegotiate moment by moment. (Breakwell 1996: 22)

As Breakwell suggests, national identity is for the most part an abstract concept, but this does not imply that it is not real. It may have originated from the social reality of a small group of élites, bureaucrats and policy makers; it may have been largely constructed by the ethnic core. Nevertheless, with the help of compulsory schooling and the media, it is propagated as the legitimate national identity and appropriated to varying degrees. As such, a nation is treated as a type of group for the purposes of this book.

SIT and ELIT do not specifically rule out the existence of individual variation within national identities. As theories of intergroup relations, they choose merely to focus on those occasions where individuals act as a group, where even individual choices are socially constructed.[5] This is not to say that SIT and ELIT cannot be used to examine intragroup differences due to the emergence of subgroups. As seen in Section 2.3 above, Meän Kieli is considered a separate language by its speakers and forms an important element in a separate Tornedalian identity (Hyltenstam 1999b: 130–1). Far from not being able to deal with this sociolinguistic variation, SIT and ELIT treat such groups as entities in their own right with separate ethnolinguistic identities.

Related to the criticism that SIT and ELIT cannot adequately deal with large-scale groups is the claim that the theories consider all groups alike, regardless of size or nature. In other words, it is claimed that the two theories neglect the specific meanings of social categories and flatten out different ways of representing the world (Billig 1995: 66–8).

> [G]rammatically similar statements of identity can have different meanings. 'I am a sociologist' uttered at [a] professional gathering of anthropologists carries a different meaning from the famous declaration of US President John Kennedy, 'Ich bin ein Berliner'. (Billig 1995: 68)

That Kennedy's declaration was more powerful than that of the sociologist is surely a function of the geopolitical stakes involved. While SIT may use the same framework for examining the identities of national and professional categories, its broad scope nevertheless allows for consideration of a variety of linguistic and non-linguistic factors which differ in perceived importance. There is therefore no reason why it cannot be used to study all types of groups, including large powerful ones such as nations.

3.2.4.3 Monocultural-assimilationist bias

By monocultural-assimilationist bias, Husband and Saifullah Khan (1982: 203) refer to the incapacity of the theoretical framework in question to deal with biculturalism and integration. ELIT may have introduced the notion of multiple group membership (Giles and Johnson 1981), allowing individuals to enjoy simultaneously different social identities (family, gender, age, sexuality, class, professional, ethnic, etc.); but this does not take into account those cases when an individual belongs to multiple groups *of the same nature*. Many second generation immigrant children have positive identities connected to their memberships both of the dominant *and* minority ethnic groups. A similar scenario characterises the lives of children raised bilingually and/or biculturally, often on account of the different nationality of one parent. And what of those French-speaking Canadians, for example, who do not have difficulty in reconciling their (minority) French-speaking and (majority) Canadian identities? Quite falsely, SIT and ELIT assume that one of these identities must be viewed negatively. Such situations need not necessarily lead to assimilation, or the abandonment of one of the identities to the benefit of the other. Various models of acculturation (e.g. Berry 1980) and bicultural identity (e.g. Hamers and Blanc 2000: 220–2) demonstrate that a minority can in fact share cultural features with the majority without compromising its minority identity (cf. also Liebkind 1996: 46). Integration and bilingualism clearly need to be incorporated into a revised version of the SIT/ELIT framework.

3.2.5 Social identity and ethnolinguistic identity theories revised

Although this book does not seek to contribute to theoretical developments within social psychology, some modifications have been made to the SIT/ELIT framework for the purposes of the study and are discussed below. First, the social mobility and creativity strategies discussed in Section 3.2.2 are reclassified in terms of the notions of convergence and divergence (Section 3.2.5.1). Second, a more in-depth understanding of the interaction between linguistic and non-linguistic boundaries is sought in order to take into account the negotiation process which takes place between different dimensions of national identity (Section 3.2.5.2). Third, the modifications made to the theoretical framework introduce the concept of different arenas — national, European and global — in which national identity is constructed and can be studied (Section 3.2.5.3).

3.2.5.1 *Convergence and divergence*

The notions of convergence and divergence have their origins in speech accommodation theory (Giles 1973; Giles, Bourhis and Taylor 1977; Giles and Coupland 1991). This later became known as communication accommodation theory in order to encompass non-verbal as well as discursive dimensions of social interaction (Giles *et al.* 1987). According to the theory, interlocutors may decide to accommodate each other through communicative convergence. This is defined as:

> a strategy whereby individuals adapt to each other's communicative behaviours in terms of a wide range of linguistic/prosodic/non-vocal features, including speech rate, pausal phenomena and utterance length, phonological variants, smiling, gaze and so on. (Giles and Coupland 1991: 63)

Members of a minority group may approximate the high-prestige language of the dominant outgroup in what is known as 'upward convergence'. The motivational assumption for this is a desire for social approval (Giles and Coupland 1991: 72). Alternatively, minority group members may wish to emphasise their own group's communicative style in a process known as 'divergence', which seeks to accentuate differences between the ingroup and the dominant outgroup along a salient and valued dimension (Giles and Coupland 1991: 80).

As far as SIT is concerned, divergence can be considered as a form of social creativity. Moreover, if the notions of convergence and divergence are expanded to include all forms of behaviour, not only communicative ones, they can be used to reclassify both the social mobility and social creativity strategies of SIT. The strategy seen in Section 3.2.2, whereby dominant groups intensify their differences in order to maintain a positive identity under threat, can thus be re-conceptualised as a act of divergence. As for those strategies available to subordinate groups, these are both of a convergent and divergent nature:

Convergence to dominant outgroup
- assimilation
- acculturation/integration
- overcommunication of dominant group's culture (in the case of bicultural individuals)

Divergence from dominant outgroup
- re-definition of previously negatively-viewed symbols
- creation of new, positively-viewed symbols
- selection of an alternative, less favourable outgroup for comparison
- undercommunication of dominant group's culture (in the case of bicultural individuals)

The term convergence is used here to refer to some form of cultural movement towards the majority outgroup. Unlike in the original formulation of SIT, this does not necessarily imply complete assimilation; intermediate states of acculturation and/or integration also involve movement to the dominant group, while at the same time allowing individuals to retain elements, if not all, of their original group identity. In the case of bicultural individuals — that is those who have both minority and majority identities — convergence refers to the overcommunication or emphasising of the latter at the expense of the former. This falls in line with the discussion in Section 2.1, where ethnicity was seen to be situational: individuals and even whole groups customise their identities, over- and undercommunicating them according to the context, often to seek socio-economic gains.

Unfortunately, minority groups or members of those groups who attempt to converge towards the dominant outgroup, be it through assimilation, acculturation or integration, are not always met with open arms. Dominant groups with insecure identities often harden their boundaries in an attempt to protect their socio-economic privileges. This is confirmed by Tocqueville's observations in certain states of the USA, where a sense of social distance was recreated along racial lines to compensate for a lack of institutionalised segregation.

> The prejudice of race appears to be stronger in the States which have abolished slavery, than in those where slavery still exists; and nowhere is it so intolerant as in those States where servitude has never been known.   (Tocqueville 1875: 364)

The very act of exclusion from the majority is often what causes a sense of self-awareness among a previously largely passive minority. Different divergence strategies are employed in an alternative attempt to generate a positive identity. To this end, symbols can be re-defined: an ethnic group may express a renewed pride in their language formerly considered a *patois*; an indigenous group may re-appraise its once considered 'primitive' lifestyle, highlighting its ecologically sound nature. New symbols may also be created from scratch: economically disadvantaged Blacks in the USA and Britain privilege success in sports, music and 'coolness', dimensions on which they score relatively well compared to more prosperous Whites. The Norwegians too, once a minority in the Danish and then Swedish kingdoms, managed to generate a positive identity by inventing symbols (see also Section 2.2.1), even appropriating those of other cultures.

> In many cases, the so-called ancient, typically Norwegian customs, folk tales, handicrafts and so on were neither ancient, typical nor Norwegian. The painted floral patterns depict grapevines from the Mediterranean. The Hardanger fiddle music and most of the folk tales had their origin in Central Europe, and many of the 'typical folk costumes' which are worn at public celebrations such as Constitution Day were designed by nationalists early in the twentieth century. [. . .] When Norway became independent, its first king was recruited from the Danish royal family. He was nevertheless named Haakon VII as a way of stressing the (entirely fictional) continuity with the dynasty of kings that ruled Norway before 1350.(Eriksen 1993: 103)

The choice of symbols used to glorify the ingroup are far from unpredictable. Löfgren (1989) shows how national identity is constructed by means of a 'doit-yourself' kit, which relies on internationally accepted symbols such as flags, anthems, monuments, currencies, etc. In the case of minorities aspiring to independence, these symbols increase the chances of recognition by other nations-states (Billig 1996: 190). Of particular importance is the claim to a distinct language, as was the case with New Norwegian and the more recent Bosnian. *Nynorsk* (New Norwegian) came into existence as the result of a standardisation process carried out by Ivar Aasen in the middle of the nineteenth century on a range of Norwegian dialects, especially that spoken around Bergen. By creating a truly Norwegian language, clearly distinguished from the heavily Danish-influenced Norwegian called *bokmål* (book language), the Norwegian people had further justification to their claim to independence (Haugen 1959, 1966b). As for Muslim Bosnians, national identity relies heavily on their distinction from Orthodox Serbs and Catholic Croats. An effective means of reinforcing this distinction is by progressively filling their language with borrowings from Arabic. Over time, this tendency may even spread to the introduction of the Arabic script (Baggioni 1997: 21). The formation of a separate linguistic variety is not only confined to such groups aspiring to nationhood. Halliday's (1976) notion of an 'anti-language' was designed to explain this same development, whereby a different linguistic variety symbolises an alternative or counter-reality, set up in opposition to mainstream society. Youth languages are typical examples of anti-languages: young Germans use Anglicisms, onomatopoeia and neologisms as a means of distancing themselves from dominant cultural patterns (Clyne 1995: 148), while young inhabitants of the *cités* which exist on the outskirts of large cities in France use slang, foreign borrowings, *verlan*[6] and other lexical innovations to create a language which reflects their bicultural identity (French-immigrant) and social misfortunes (Goudaillier 1998; de Saint Robert 2000: 59; cf. Méla 1997: 31–2 on functions of *verlan* in particular).

3.2.5.2 Linguistic versus non-linguistic boundaries

The examples in the previous section highlight the use of both linguistic and non-linguistic dimensions of interethnic comparison. This opposition is incorporated into Giles' (1979) model of linguistic and non-linguistic boundaries, which builds on Banton's (1983: 125–9) notion of hard and soft boundaries. While hard boundaries are not negotiable and render interethnic mobility impossible, soft boundaries allow for convergence towards the outgroup. The interaction of these two notions creates four types of category, as seen in Figure 3.4.

```
              Hard
          non-linguistic
               │
         A     │    B
               │
Hard   ────────┼────────  Soft
linguistic     │          linguistic
         C     │    D
               │
              Soft
          non-linguistic
```

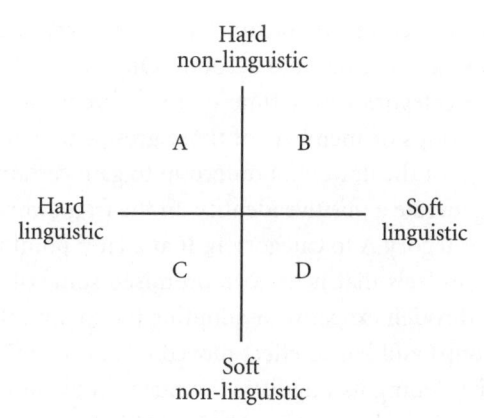

Figure 3.4 Matrix of hard versus soft, linguistic versus non-linguistic boundaries. (From Giles 1979:275)

The Hutterites and Amish in North America are examples of ethnic groups in category A: they have a distinctive language (hard linguistic boundary) and religion (hard non-linguistic boundary). Category B of Giles' model would include the Irish, who have adopted another language (soft linguistic boundary) yet retain other ethnic characteristics (hard non-linguistic boundary) which distinguish them from the English (see introduction). Loss of language need therefore not necessarily imply loss of identity (Edwards 1992: 134; Liebkind 1996: 45, 1999: 143–4); concerns about language loss may even have the effect of heightening ethnic consciousness (cf. Ross 1979: 4).

Since the Quiet Revolution, when Québec underwent a rapid process of liberalisation and modernisation, many French-speaking Québécois feel that the only thing that separates them from Anglophone Canadians either inside or outside Québec is their language (Sachdev and Bourhis 1990: 213; Taylor 1991: 54; Kymlicka 1995: 88). They thus fall into category C, having their own language (hard linguistic boundary) yet displaying cultural traits similar to those of other Canadians (soft non-linguistic boundary). Finally, French-speaking Swiss living in France can be thought of as belonging to category D: they share many cultural characteristics with the surrounding French majority (soft non-linguistic boundary), while their language does not differ greatly from standard French (soft linguistic boundary).

Giles (1979: 277) explains that his model is dynamic. On a micro-level, members of the same ethnic group can be put in different categories depending on how they perceive the softness or hardness of the boundaries in general or during specific interethnic interactions. In this respect, the heterogeneity of large-scale groups can be taken into account. On a macro-level, whole ethnic groups can move categories over time or in different circumstances. Many minority ethnic groups or members of those groups thus willingly learn and speak the language of the dominant outgroup to gain certain socio-economic advantages and generate a positive identity. In the framework of Giles' model, they move from category A to category B. If at a later point in time, however, the minority group feels that it has compromised some of its non-linguistic boundaries (e.g. through exogamy or adopting too many cultural traits of the dominant outgroup) and has in effect moved to category D, it may decide to compensate by hardening its linguistic boundary, thus moving into category C. Some groups may emphasise their ethnic speech style, with all its phonological, grammatical, lexical and prosodic particularities. This is the case in German-speaking Switzerland, where dialect serves as a '"protection" from the "outside world" and the identity marker to distinguish German-speaking Swiss from their powerful neighbours, the Germans' (Clyne 1995: 45). Other groups may go further and attempt to revive a dying language, such as Irish, or Basque and Breton in France. This movement from one category to another highlights the continual negotiation which takes place between linguistic and non-linguistic components of identity in order to maximise psychological distinctiveness. This negotiation process makes it possible, for example, for a group to converge linguistically to the dominant outgroup, yet still maintain a distinct identity through divergence on other, non-linguistic dimensions of intergroup comparison.

Majority groups, too, manipulate language as a means of creating social distance and guaranteeing their dominant status. Gibbons (1990) has shown how language is often used by members of the police force in Australia in a way which clearly disadvantages second-language speakers of English, thus reinforcing the power imbalance between the two parties. Miller (1982) makes similar observations regarding language myths in Japan. The Japanese are convinced that their language is difficult to learn and that very few *gaijin* (foreigners) succeed in mastering it. Unlike the general rule in other countries, a foreigner is praised for his or her efforts to learn Japanese at the outset, but encounters increasingly more resistance as progress is made.

> [T]he foreigner who is resident in Japan for any length of time finally realizes that Japanese society behaves in a fashion that is directly contrary to this general rule. Japanese society usually distrusts and dislikes any attempt by the foreigner to learn and use the Japanese language. The distrust and dislike grow stronger and show

themselves more and more stridently, the more the foreigner gains fluency in understanding and using the language. (Miller 1982: 154)

Miller's analysis is that the Japanese language is the last vestige of the myth that the Japanese as a people or 'race' are somehow special. Language is thus used as a defence mechanism. When foreigners demonstrate real signs of crossing the linguistic boundary, the Japanese express hostility in order to maintain their psychological distinctiveness and resulting positive identity. That language is frequently used as a defence mechanism in this way is seen in the particular context of Sweden in Section 5.3.2.

The use of linguistic boundaries to construct identities can in part be explained by having reference to language alone. The example of Polish discussed in the introduction of this book shows how the persecution of a language can result in it eventually being attributed greater symbolic importance. In a similar manner, it can be suggested that a large proportion of the ethnolinguistic vitality observed amongst Catalans derives from their language having been targeted by Franco. But the strength of linguistic boundaries is also determined by non-linguistic factors. In order to compensate for years of Soviet (predominantly non-linguistic) oppression, the newly liberated nation-states of Estonia and Latvia have hardened their linguistic boundaries, denying access to citizenship for members of their Russian minorities if they fail to pass a stringent proficiency test in the national language (Baggioni 1997: 25; Wingstedt 1998: 106–11). This negotiation process which takes place between linguistic and non-linguistic dimensions plays an important role in the construction of a positive national identity.

3.2.5.3 *Arenas for construction of national identity*

Not only can groups converge and diverge simultaneously on different dimensions (linguistic and non-linguistic), they can also do so within different arenas which act as construction sites for national identities. Those arenas recognised as particularly important for the construction of French and Swedish identities are the national arena, the European arena and the global arena.

On the one hand, these arenas can be considered as existing independently of one another, not least because the status of a group may differ from one arena to the next. While the French and Swedish *ethnies* may be dominant in their respective national arenas, France and Sweden can be considered as minorities in the wider contexts of European integration and globalisation (see Section 1.1). Since social identity theory takes into account the strategies of both dominant and subordinate groups, all three of these arenas can be examined with the help of the same theoretical framework.

On the other hand, the arenas also overlap in so far as the identity a nation constructs in one arena affects the construction of that same nation's identity in another arena. Difficulties in maintaining a positive national identity in the global arena may result in a strengthening of national identity within the European arena, or cause a dominant ethnic group to adopt a harsh line with ethnic minorities back home in the national arena. The way in which the national identities of different arenas combine to form an overall national identity is shown in Figure 3.5.

In the analyses of language attitudes and national identity strategies in France and Sweden that constitute the remainder of this study, reference will be made on occasion to certain elements of social identity theory and ethnolinguistic identity theory in their original form. However on the whole, the aim of the societal analyses of Chapters 4, 5, 6 and 7, is to examine past and present language attitudes and national identity strategies with the aid of the revised theoretical framework proposed here. To summarise, this modified framework makes use of the notions of convergence and divergence, advocates a broad perspective which considers both linguistic and non-linguistic factors, and introduces the concept of different arenas — national, European and global — in which national identity is constructed and can be studied. This same paradigm will be used to present and interpret the results of the survey in Chapter 8, and to draw overall conclusions in Chapter 9.

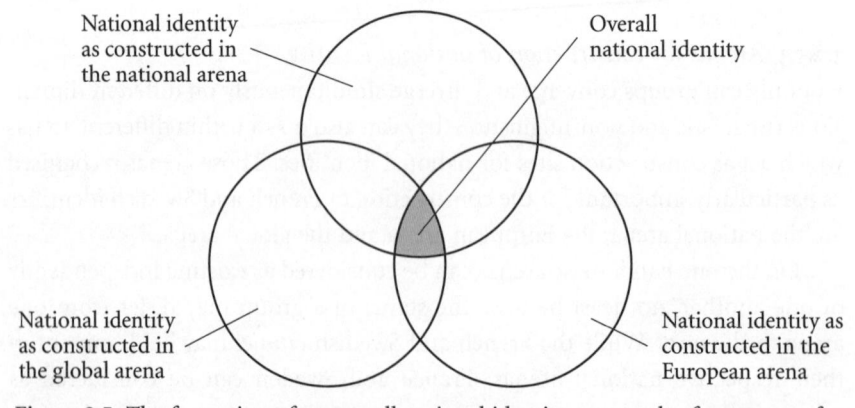

Figure 3.5 The formation of an overall national identity as a result of processes of identity construction in the national, European and global arenas

Chapter 4

Language and national identity: A general perspective

This book has so far highlighted many instances of the link between language and national identity, both in a range of contexts and in a variety of manifestations. Before examining the particular contexts of the national, European and global arenas, it is appropriate to examine French and Swedish language attitudes and national identity strategies from a more general perspective. A convenient point of departure for such an approach is the notion of linguistic consciousness (Section 4.1). As the concept of linguistic consciousness is particularly useful for a diachronic study of language and national identity, it is used as a framework to provide a historical overview of the role language has come to play in French and Swedish identities (Sections 4.2 and 4.3 respectively). A final section compares the linguistic consciousness of the French and the Swedes in a more contemporary context, by focusing on societal attitudes towards language change in general, and towards spelling reform in particular (Section 4.4).

4.1 Linguistic consciousness

Linguistic consciousness is not an easy concept to define. As a first attempt, one might describe a linguistically *un*conscious community as 'one where the population takes the prevailing language situation for granted and only expends effort on learning and using language as correctly as possible' (Vikør 1993: 179). In other words, there is no societal preoccupation with language or with the sociolinguistic climate. The five variables which Vikør (1993: 180–1) considers as important components of linguistic consciousness are: linguistic variation versus standardisation, spelling conservatism versus reformism, purism versus liberalism, assimilation versus non-assimilation of foreign words, and stylistic norms. All of these phenomena relate to the corpus or quality of language. In the opinion of this author, a comprehensive definition of linguistic consciousness should also include factors which relate to the status of a language. The present study therefore adopts a broader definition which includes the four following components: linguistic standardisation, linguistic prescriptivism or correctness, language myths and language purism.

As seen in Section 2.3, some degree of standardisation is usually a necessary element in distinguishing a language from a variety. If claims to a separate language are important to national legitimacy (see Section 3.2.5.1), then it follows that the degree of linguistic standardisation will often reflect the strength of a group's national identity. The link between standardisation and national identity has been studied by numerous researchers from various angles. In the context of West Indian creoles, Le Page and Tabouret-Keller (1985) show how groups with a strong sense of shared linguistic norms (i.e. a strong degree of standardisation) are usually also 'highly focused communities', that is, they feel a sense of common identity. In discussing the eventuality of a Tornedalian language distinct from Finnish (see Section 2.3), Hyltenstam also notes how ethnic (or national) identity and language standardisation reinforce each other.

> It is out of the feeling of ethnic differentiation and peculiarity that conscience of one's own language as an important carrier of culture stems, as does the will to cultivate and develop this language in counteraction to an existing standardised language. Conversely, the degree of standardisation, and the status which that language has gained because of this process, influences the strength of ethnic identity. This is illustrated by the ethnic consciousness of many minorities which have long literary traditions, for example the Catalans. (Hyltenstam 1999b: 115)

Yet standardisation is not only a reflection of group identity; it is also used as an active means of reinforcing a separate ethnic or national identity.

> The need for shared linguistic norms springs in part from pressures of functional efficiency (as with the adoption of a standardised system of weights and measures, e.g. the metric system in France at the time of the French Revolution): suppression of variation in language will ensure communication over longer distances of space and time with a minimum of misunderstanding. In addition, however, the needs of the group may call for a uniform language to act as a badge or symbol of group identity. [. . .] [T]he general point being made here is that standardisation of languages arises as much from subjective pressures (group identity) as from objective ones (functional efficiency). Language serves a demarcatory as well as communicative function. Individuals or institutions concerned with promoting the standard language in Britain and France are always insistent upon the importance of the latter function; they are often more coy about the role played by the former. (Lodge 1993: 23–4)

So while in some languages, standardisation occurs automatically for reasons of efficiency, it can also be the result of deliberate action, usually taken by state authorities. In this case, standardisation is a form of language planning. Language planning consists of two dimensions: corpus and status planning. Corpus language planning aims to modify the 'nature of the language itself' (Kloss 1969b: 81); in Haugen's model, it comprises the linguistic processes of codification and elaboration (see Section 2.3). Status language planning, by contrast, concentrates on the social standing of the language, thus involving Haugen's social processes of selection and acceptance. Despite this distinction, corpus and status planning cannot be separated from each other: language-planning policies are thus never exclusively corpus-orientated or status-orientated (Daoust 1997: 448). The example of Québec highlights how corpus planning often doubles up as status planning: the terminological work (elaboration) carried out on the corpus of Québécois French since 1961 by the *Office de la langue française* has at the same time sought to promote the status of the language in domains dominated by English (selection/acceptance).

Since the goals of language planning or explicit standardisation often stretch beyond those of communication, Garmadi (1981: 64–72) makes a distinction between *norme* and *sur-norme*. As 'the constraint which effectively guarantees the satisfactory functioning of any linguistic system as an instrument of communication', a *norme* is the result of an implicit linguistic consensus needed for communicative purposes, but which nevertheless allows for some degree of linguistic variation (Lodge 1993: 154–5). The notion of *sur-norme* is much stricter, prescribing as it does for socio-political rather than communicative reasons.

> It is a set of instructions defining what should be chosen if one wishes to conform to the aesthetic or sociocultural ideal of a social group enjoying prestige and authority, and the existence of this set of instructions implies the existence of forms that are banned. (Garmadi 1981: 65)

The banned forms to which Garmadi refers encompass all kinds of linguistic variation from the *sur-norme*: lexical, syntactic, phonetic and orthographical. That spelling reform has proven particularly difficult in France (see Section 4.4) is a result of an especially strong *sur-norme* in that country (Lodge 1993: 155).

Normative or prescriptive tendencies have been observed in many different countries, and may be triggered by a perceived threat to the identity and/or language in question. Such a motivation could explain the interest manifested by the Swedish-speaking minority in Finland towards the correct use of its language (Arnstberg 1989: 247); it might also account for the apparent lack of linguistic pride observed amongst the Dutch (Ager 1997: 32), who have the comfort of knowing that their language is dominant in the Netherlands and enjoys official status in the European Union. In light of the prescriptive dimension represented by the *sur-norme*, Milroy and Milroy (1985: 22–3) prefer to speak of standardisation as an ideology, and a standard language as 'an idea in the mind rather than a reality'. Such a view is reminiscent of Anderson's (1983) notion of an 'imagined community' used when referring to nations (see Section 2.2.3). Standardisation of language — especially when it includes linguistic prescriptivism — is thus an important element in imagining or constructing a national identity.

Another possible manifestation of a strong link between language and national identity is the use of language myths, which serve to claim the superiority of one language — or rather the group who speaks it — over another. The myth that French is inherently associated with clarity and logic dates back to the late-seventeenth and eighteenth centuries but remains widespread today (see Section 4.2). As pointed out by Lodge (1993: 186, cf. also 1998), this particular myth results from a failure, either deliberate or not, to distinguish between *language system* and *language use*.

> Claims are commonly made by guardians of usage about the superiority of the language *system* of standard French over those of non-standard varieties on the basis of the *use* made of that system by the community's most highly valued writers. Such writers may well produce texts of compelling clarity and logic, but these qualities in their writing spring not from the system itself, but from the use they make of the system. (Lodge 1993: 186)

Other language myths concern the perceived aesthetic value of certain languages. As seen in Section 3.1, tests conducted within the field of social psychology of language have revealed that judgements of the type 'Italian is a beautiful language' and 'Arabic is a harsh language' are not founded on inherent values, so much as on cultural norms, pressures and connotations which reflect broader social attitudes towards the speakers of those languages (cf. also Giles and Niedzielski 1998). Still other language myths relate to the claimed purity of a certain language from foreign influences. Indeed, such was the grounding of the 'ideological acrobatics' used by Fichte to claim the superiority of the German language and *Volk* over all others (see Section 2.4.1).

Language purism is therefore also a possible indicator of a strong link between language and ethnic or national identity, as further highlighted by Hobsbawm's (1992: 56) preferred term for the phenomenon: 'philological nationalism'. Intellectuals endeavour to rid their national languages of foreign borrowings, even if these had long established themselves and adapted to the host language (Fishman 1971a: 4, 15). As noted by Shapiro (1989: 28), language purism of all types is frequently triggered by a desire to strengthen national identity in the face of a perceived threat from the Other.

> Language purism is a move in the direction of narrowing legitimate forms of meaning and thereby declaring out-of-bounds certain dimensions of otherness. It is not as dramatic and easily politicized as the extermination of an ethnic minority or even so easily made contentious as the proscription of various forms of social deviance. But the Other is located most fundamentally in language, the medium for representing selves and other. Therefore, any move that alters language by centralizing and pruning or decentralizing and diversifying alters the ecology of Self-Other relations and thereby the identities that contain and animate relations of power and authority. (Shapiro 1989: 28)

However as Clyne (1991: 93-4) rightly points out, purism of the kind which seeks to rid a language of foreign influences need not necessarily indicate that language is a core value; it merely constitutes one response to a language contact situation. For many Italians in Australia, the English-influenced Australo-Italian acts as a source of identity and many call for it to be taught in Australian schools instead of standard Italian (Clyne 1991: 162). That language purists often target a certain foreign language but not others — Catalans struggle against the influence of Castilian, but readily embrace English words (Weinstein 1989: 54) — is further evidence that language purism is not an indication of language constituting a core value *per se*, so much as a by-product of a particular relationship with a particular group (in the case of the Catalans, the Castilians). Cases of this latter type show nonetheless that language purism can be an important component of linguistic consciousness, in addition to standardisation, linguistic prescriptivism and language myths as mentioned above. Aspects of all four of these phenomena will therefore be exposed in the following historical overviews of the role played by language in the construction of French and Swedish identities.

4.2 Language and identity in France: A historical overview

This section does not attempt to provide a detailed history of French linguistic consciousness. Such studies have already been carried out elsewhere to various degrees (e.g. Wartburg 1946; Brunot 1967; Chaurand 1969, 1999; Caput 1972; Balibar and Laporte 1974; de Certeau *et al.* 1975; Balibar 1985; Rickard 1989;

Cerquiglini 1991; Lodge 1993; Schiffman 1996; Baggioni 1997; Wise 1997; Perret 1998; Ager 1999). The aim here is to highlight some of the most important milestones in the development of the link between language and French identity. Particular attention will be paid to the specific components of linguistic consciousness which were discussed in the previous section.

The history of French linguistic consciousness is generally held to have begun around 813 AD with the declaration at the Council of Tours. While retaining Latin as the language of the Mass proper, this declaration allowed for the use of the vernaculars — *rustica romana lingua* and *teudisca lingua* — in sermons and homilies (Lodge 1993: 93). Such a decision was deemed necessary to spread the word of God amongst the masses. As a result of Charlemagne's attempts to reintroduce classical Latin, which he felt had deteriorated under the Merovingians, it had become increasingly clear that the language of the masses, especially in northern Gaul, had developed into something quite different from Latin. It is thus thanks to the Carolingian Renaissance that 'French became conscious of itself' (Wartburg 1946: 69).

The first surviving text in which this proto-French was used was the *Serments de Strasbourg* (Strasbourg Oaths) of 842. The Strasbourg Oaths embodied the agreement between two of Charlemagne's grandsons against the third: Charles the Bald was to take possession of *Francia occidentalis*, Louis the Germanic of *Francia orientalis*, and the third brother, Lothaire, was to be given Lotheringen/Lorraine (Balibar 1985; Cerquiglini 1991). A significant aspect of the document was the swearing of oaths by the two brothers in the vernacular of the other's realm: Charles in *teudesca lingua* and Louis in *lingua romana*.[7] The proposed division was enshrined in the Treaty of Verdun of 843.

The Council of Tours declaration and the Strasbourg Oaths reflect the separate linguistic consciousness which began to form from the ninth century in contradistinction to Latin (Lodge 1993: 92). For some researchers (e.g. Perret 1998: 36), the *Serments de Strasbourg* also signal the beginning of a French national consciousness. But the budding linguistic and national sentiment was felt only by an élite, in particular by clerics (Balibar 1985: 38; see also Sections 2.2.2 and 2.2.3). Indeed, it was the clerics who began to transcribe this 'new' language, or *roman* as it was called: the first literary work appeared in the form of the *Séquence de sainte Eulalie* (c 880), which is believed to have predated the famous *Chanson de Roland* by two centuries (c 1086). By the end of the eleventh century, a standard based on the vernaculars began to develop in the south. This common written language (or *koine*) of the *langue d'oc* region was used in administration and the literary works of the Troubadours

(Lodge 1993: 110–11). In the *langue d'oïl* region of the north, the extensive use of the vernacular in writing did not begin until the following century. Yet unlike in the south, the written form was characterised by a large degree of regional variation (e.g. *picard, normand, champenois*). Not until the twelfth-thirteenth centuries did one see the rise of a supra-dialectal writing system (or *scripta*), which was nevertheless based on the speech of Île-de-France (Cerquiglini 1991:118; Lodge 1993:114–15).

It was this northern vernacular (the King's French) which was to spread throughout the thirteenth to sixteenth centuries. Paris was not only the seat of the Capetian kings, it had also become an important commercial and administrative centre, and was home to the Sorbonne founded in the mid-thirteenth century. As territories were annexed, the Île-de-France vernacular, or *françois* as it became known, progressively challenged not only Latin, but also regional vernaculars. While the crusades against the Albigensian heresy in the south in the thirteenth century sought principally to remove a rival political power, they also had the effect of undermining the status of *langue d'oc*.

The next milestone in the construction of French ethnolinguistic identity was François I's Ordinance of Villers-Cotterêts (1539) which stated that:

> all legal decisions and all procedures pertaining either to the highest courts or to the lowest or inferior ones, whether they concern records, inquests, contracts, commissions, wills or whatever other legal acts or instruments or whatever is dependent thereon [...] should be pronounced, registered and delivered to the litigants in the French vernacular language (*langage maternel françois*) and in no other way.   (cited in Lodge 1993:126)

While the ordinance was directed primarily at the Other represented by Latin, there is much debate about whether *langage maternel françois* referred to local vernaculars in general (known as *langages maternels*) or to the King's French in particular (known as *françois*; cf. Lodge 1993:126–7). It is likely that the ordinance also had an implicit effect on the status of regional vernaculars, especially *langue d'oc*. The Ordinance of Villers-Cotterêts can thus be considered as reinforcing the social power imbalance, by bestowing on the élite surrounding the King the honour of being the bearers of the linguistic norm (Lodge 1993:127).

In the field of education too, French was encroaching on Latin: while the Sorbonne remained adamant that the latter should continue to be used as the language of instruction, the founding of the *Collège de France* (originally *Collège Royal*) in 1530 meant that French was used in the classroom for the first time (Walter 1988: 87). The courses given at this college by the mathematician Estienne Forcadel reflected how French was also making inroads in the field of science (Clerico 1999:185), even if Latin was still considered most appropriate. The importance of French increased even in religious domains: 1523 saw the publication of Lefèvre d'Étaples' translation of the New Testament, shortly followed by the rest of the Bible; French also became the language of the Protestant Church in all French-speaking countries from 1550 (Brunot 1967, vol. 2:21; Perret 1998:47).

As a sense of 'national' identity formed around the 'new' language, it became clear that the latter needed to be enriched through the processes of codification and elaboration (Haugen 1966a; see Sections 2.3 and 4.1). This was the goal of the many grammars and dictionaries of the time: the Latin-French grammar *Isagôge* (1531) by Jacques Dubois, the French-Latin dictionary (1549) and *Traicté de la grammaire française* (1557) by Robert Estienne, the *Tretté de la grammere françoese* (1550) by Louis Meigret, the *Gramere* (1562–72) by Ramus (Pierre de la Ramée), etc.[8] The literary value of French was also asserted, especially by those in the group of poets known as the Pléiade. The best known representation of the movement's ideas appeared in du Bellay's *Défense et illustration de la langue françoise* (1549). Although stressing that French was capable of treating any subject, this work nevertheless reflected the sense of inferiority felt by intellectuals with regard to their young, still undeveloped language.

The sixteenth century also saw the use of French as a means of strengthening French identity in contradistinction to other rival groups outside France. The economic and cultural prosperity of northern Italian cities had the result of releasing a flow of Italian loan words into French, which was well under way by 1560, when Henri II acceded to the throne with his Italian wife, Catherine of Medici (Walter 1988:95). In his famous *La précellence du langage françois* (1579), Henri Estienne denounced this form of linguistic 'betrayal' and asserted the superiority of French over Italian (Hagège 1987:17). The purported pre-eminence of the French language reflected the identity France sought for itself in the global arena. It comes as no surprise that the country was at the same time embarking on its first wave of colonial expansionism. Jacques Cartier had already taken possession of Canada; the rate of French settlement there, as well as in the West Indies, Guyana, Africa and India, was to increase throughout the seventeenth century.

The founding in 1635 by Cardinal Richelieu of the *Académie française* on the model of the *Accademia della Crusca* in Florence marked the beginning of linguistic prescriptivism or the *sur-norme* tradition (see Section 4.1) in France.

The Academy was entrusted with corpus work, in particular the publication of a dictionary, a grammar, a rhetoric and a poetics of French, in order to render the language 'pure, eloquent and capable of treating the arts and sciences' (cited in Caput 1972, vol. 1: 206). As director of the dictionary, it was perhaps Vaugelas (1585–1650) more than anyone else who was responsible for the codification or fixing of the French language. Vaugelas followed in the footsteps of Malherbe (1555–1628), who is often considered the first representative of French classicism. In the name of *clarté, précision* and *pureté* (clarity, precision and purity), Malherbe had previously reacted against the extensive efforts of sixteenth-century intellectuals to enrich the French language, condemning as he did the use of neologisms, archaisms, Italianisms, dialectal and technical words (Lodge 1993: 173–4; Hagège 1996: 58–61; Wise 1997: 221). In his influential work, *Remarques sur la langue française* (1647), Vaugelas defined *le bon usage* as 'the way of speaking of the most sensible part (*la plus saine partie*) of the Court, when that accords with the way of writing of the most sensible part of the authors of the day' (Vaugelas 1970: II.3; trans. Lodge 1993: 176). This work served as a sort of guide to linguistic etiquette for many financial and judicial office holders who, despite their legal standing, were nevertheless not accepted socially by the *noblesse de race* (Ayres-Bennett 1987: 194). Through their work in the Academy, Vaugelas and his colleagues had a profound effect on the role language was to play in French identity. It is in this sense that Battye and Hintze (1992: 24) view the Academy as 'an embodiment of the official recognition of the importance of language as a means of giving a sense of identity to a group of individuals.'

The political and military power of France during the reign of Louis XIV (1643–1715) was not without its linguistic consequences. French had become the preferred language for many writers across the continent, such as Bedford and Gibbon in England, Liebniz in Germany and Casanova in Italy (Perret 1998: 67). The prestige of the French language also stemmed from the exemplary works of writers and philosophers such as Descartes, Corneille, Molière, Pascal, Mme de Sevigné, Bossuet, Boileau and Racine. These works not only provided France with a great literary heritage which would serve as a model for future generations, they also gave currency to the belief that the French language had reached a state of perfection (Lodge 1993: 136, 178–9). During the second half of the seventeenth century, Vaugelas' notion of *le bon usage* as defined by the speech of a specific social group began to give way to the emerging myth that French was inherently associated with logic, clarity and elegance. Arnauld and Lancelot's *Grammaire générale et raisonnée* (a.k.a. Port-

Royal Grammar) of 1660, which applied Aristotelian logic to French, lay the foundations for a new, rational approach to the language which came to dominate in the eighteenth century.

The French may have lost a great deal of their empire to the English as a result of the Treaties of Utrecht (1713) and Rastatt (1714), as well as later on as an outcome of the Treaty of Paris (1763). However, these treaties signalled a success for the French language: the Treaty of Rastatt in particular marked the ousting of Latin and the official adoption of French as the diplomatic language (Hagège 1987: 207). French was also gaining ground in schools: as of 1762, French grammar and orthography were taught in all French colleges (Perret 1998: 49). In addition, French was fast becoming the language of the élite throughout Europe, not least because of the works of the great philosophers of the Enlightenment: Voltaire, Diderot and Rousseau. Perhaps more so than in most European countries, French was wholeheartedly embraced by intellectuals in Germany, as demonstrated by Voltaire's famous remark while visiting the Prussian court: 'I find myself here in France. Only our language is spoken. German is for the soldiers and the horses; it is only necessary for the road' (Voltaire 1953–65, vol. 18:188). It was also the Berlin Academy — or the *Académie de Berlin* as it called itself — which awarded Antoine de Rivarol a prize in 1783 for his *Discours sur l'Universalité de la langue française*, which proclaims the virtues of the French language.

> What distinguishes our language from the ancient and the modern languages is the order and structure of the sentence. This order must always be direct and necessarily clear. French names first of all the *subject* of the discourse, then the *verb* which is the action, and finally the *object* of this action: this is the natural logic present in all human beings [. . .] That which is not clear is not French; that which is not clear is still English Italian, Greek or Latin. (Rivarol 1998: 72–3)

Rivarol's work is a classic example of the role of language myths in the construction of national identity (see Section 4.1).[9] When successive French generations have recalled Rivarol's *Discours*, it has usually been neglected that the prize was also awarded jointly to a Professor Schwab of the Caroline Academy in Stuttgart, whose work was of a much more scientific nature (Caput 1972, vol. 2: 67–9). Forgotten too has been the fact that, while Rivarol clearly regarded French as superior in terms of logic, he nonetheless thought that other languages were better suited to music and poetry (Rivarol 1998: 73–4). Finally, it has been of little consequence that Rivarol's use of logic was essentially flawed, since many other languages demonstrate subject-verb-object word order. What has mattered is that Rivarol's work has provided a convenient argument for claiming French superiority. That this argument has made use of a language myth is not surprising considering the immense symbolic importance that language was to acquire for French identity in the decades following Rivarol's work.

If the founding of the *Académie française* was a milestone for French corpus planning, the Revolution must be considered a victory for French status planning (Schiffman 1996: 85). No longer was French to be considered the language of the King and his surrounding élite. As the language of the Declaration of the Rights of Man and the Citizen, it was now the property of the nation and was granted the status of national language. This is not to say that French was spoken by the majority of the population.

> [I]n 1789 50 per cent of Frenchmen did not speak it at all, only 12–13 per cent spoke it 'correctly' — and indeed outside a central region it was not usually habitually spoken even in the area of the *langue d'oui*, except in towns, and then not always in their suburbs. (Hobsbawm 1992: 60)

In the beginning of the Revolution, linguistic diversity was not considered a problem by the authorities; in 1790 the *Assemblée nationale constituante* ordered that all revolutionary decrees be translated and posted in local dialects and languages (Brunot 1967, vol. 9: 25; Hagège 1996: 76). The end of this tolerance of multilingualism was signalled by the Talleyrand report of 1791, which called for public instruction in French (Caput 1972, vol. 2:108; Picoche and Marchello-Nizia 1994: 31). Abbé Grégoire was also concerned about the poor knowledge of French throughout the country. In what was perhaps one of the first examples of a sociolinguistic study, he drafted a questionnaire which was sent to prominent people in the remotest corners of France to gather information on the linguistic situation there: the degree of use of French, the pronunciation, vocabulary and grammar of the various *patois*, how they varied from village to village, their use in religious life, their presence in texts and literature, as well as the ideas they expressed which were favourable or hostile to the Revolution (de Certeau *et al.* 1975; Hagège 1996: 84). Several researchers have pointed out a number of problems concerning Grégoire's methodology: many questions were politically loaded; not all regions in France were covered; some responses were later omitted by Grégoire, possibly because they did not reveal what he had hoped; and no details were given as to how the results were calculated, for example whether women and children were included (Lartichaux 1977; Walter 1988: 106; Schiffman 1996: 103). But Grégoire succeeded nonetheless in drawing attention to the linguistic situation in France. Presenting his report to the Committee of Public Instruction in 1793, he famously claimed that:

> [w]e can confirm without exaggeration that six million French people, above all in the countryside, are in complete ignorance of the national language; that a similar number is more or less incapable of holding a continuous conversation; that as a final result, the number of people who speak French does not exceed three million, and no doubt the number of those who write it correctly is even smaller. (Grégoire cited in de Certeau *et al.* 1975: 302)

Grégoire's observations resulted in the Convention[10] voting a law on 21 October 1793, which established state primary schools in every commune where children would learn French (Calvet 1974: 168). Teachers became known as *instituteurs* as their task was to 'institute' the nation (Schnapper 1994: 131). In this way, France could truly become *une et indivisible* (one and indivisible), in accordance with the predilection for centralisation which came to define Jacobin ideology.[11] But it proved impossible to apply the law which followed Grégoire's report, not least because of the absence of teachers in the provinces (Caput 1972, vol. 2: 114–15).

A few months earlier, another committee had been established. Although originally part of the Convention, the Committee of Public Safety came to wield great power under Robespierre, which resulted in a dictatorship known as *la Terreur* (the Terror). Robespierre and his colleagues 'hijacked' the work of the Committee of Public Instruction, considering issues of language a matter of public safety. It is in these circumstances that the deputy Barère de Vieuzac presented his report *Sur les idiomes étrangers et l'enseignement de la langue française* on 27 January 1794 before the Convention in the name of the Committee of Public Safety (Brunot 1967, vol. 9: 180–1).

> Federalism and superstition speak Breton; emigration and hatred of the Republic speak German; the counter-revolution speaks Italian, and fanaticism speaks Basque. Let us smash these harmful and faulty instruments. (Barère cited in de Certeau *et al.* 1975: 295)

Barère's report confirms a point made on numerous occasions throughout this book: the Other is located most fundamentally in language. Regional languages symbolised all of the enemies of the Revolution: the federalists who led internal insurrections in peripheral regions such as the Vendée in 1793; the non-juring clergy who were suspected of using local idioms to gather support for their opposition to the Republic; and the aristocrats who had fled abroad and who were now infiltrating the regions with their coalition of neighbouring European powers (Caput 1972, vol. 2: 105; Hagège 1987: 234). Against this background, Barère's report resulted in the decree of *8 pluviôse an II* (27 January 1794), which sought to appoint French-speaking school teachers within ten days in all areas where the language was not spoken. *La Terreur* became *la Terreur linguistique* (Balibar and Laporte 1974: 83), as attested by the theme of Grégoire's report which was read before the Convention on 6 June 1794: *Rapport sur la nécessité et les moyens d'anéantir le patois et d'universaliser l'usage de la langue française* (Report on the Necessity and the Means of Destroying the *Patois* and Universalising the Use of the French Language). Difficulties in implementing the ruling of *8 pluviôse* led to the decree of *2 thermidor an II* (20 July 1794). In what has been described as the second great language law after the *Ordonnance de Villers-Cotterêts*, French was to be used in all public and private acts.

> Any civil servant, public officer or government agent who, from the date of publication of the present law, draws up, writes or signs, as part of his functions, reports, judgements, contracts or other general acts in idioms or languages other than French, will be brought before the criminal court, sentenced to six months imprisonment and dismissed. (article 3, decree of *2 thermidor an II*, cited in Hagège 1996: 86–7)

But the fall of Robespierre only one week after the law of *2 thermidor* meant that it was suspended by the Convention from as early as *16 fructidor* (2 September 1974) and was subsequently never implemented (Brunot 1967, vol. 9: 291; de Certeau *et al.* 1975: 11; Hagège 1996: 150).

The difficulties in establishing language laws in no way implied a weakening of the link between language and nation in France. Indeed, it was the strength of this link which led to attempts to incorporate into the French state other French-speaking communities, such as those in Belgium in 1792 and Switzerland in 1798 (Lodge 1993: 215). France also attempted to impose its rule on non-French-speaking countries. As seen in Section 2.4.1, much of the Francophobia in Europe, and especially in Germany, was due to the expansionism of Napoléon Bonaparte, who came to power following a coup on 9 November 1799. Napoléon transformed the nature of French identity: no longer did sovereignty lie with the people, but rather with the state (Jenkins 1990: 41). In a return to the ways of the *ancien régime*, Napoléon consolidated the regal inspiration and administrative centralisation of the despotic state which had effectively existed since 1792 (Citron 1991: 253). Even after the fall of the Napoleonic Empire in 1815, French expansionism continued from the Restoration (1815–48) through into the Third Republic (1870–940): French colonies were established in North and West Africa, the Near East, Indochina and the Pacific.

Both Bonapartist and colonial expansionism reflected the very ethnic conception of the French nation which had stemmed from the initially civic principles of the Revolution (Safran 1991: 223; Thiesse 1999: 171).

> Under the Jacobins, for example, French nationalism was essentially civic and territorial; it preached the unity of the republican patrie and the fraternity of its citizens in a political-legal community. At the same time a linguistic nationalism emerged, reflecting pride in the purity and civilizing mission of a hegemonic French culture preached by Barère and the Abbé Gregoire. In the early nineteenth century French cultural nationalism began to reflect more ethnic conceptions of the nation, whether Frankish or Gallic; later these became validating charters for radically different ideals of France. (Smith 1991: 13)

The ethnic conception of French identity was further developed as a result of nineteenth-century Romanticism. The search for a myth of origin led to the selection of the Gauls as ancestors, giving rise to the famous maxim recited by all French school children after the introduction of the compulsory French history teaching in 1867: *nos ancêtres les Gaulois* (Walter 1988: 32; Citron 1991: 30–1).[12] As the French *Urfolk* (see Section 2.2.1), the Gauls were worshipped to the point that a statue was erected in 1867 in honour of Vercingétorix. Sometimes referred to as France's 'first patriot', this Gallic warrior fought against the Roman invasion, but was eventually taken prisoner by Caesar and later executed in Rome (Citron 1991: 44; Thiesse 1999: 128). Citron (1991: 181) highlights the 'paradoxical popularity of Vercingétorix and Astérix who hide from us the fact that we are an amalgam of peoples and cultures'.

French ethnic nationalism was also cultivated by the Third Republic (1870–1940), which was born in the aftermath of France's humiliating defeat in the Franco-Prussian War of 1870. Whereas previously the founders of the Third Republic had favoured decentralisation, once in power they merely continued the Jacobin tradition of 'cementing' the French nation from above, by stressing the necessity for internal (ethnic) cohesion (Jacob and Gordon 1985: 115; Østerud 1997: 34; Winock 1997: 13). 1881–6 saw the introduction of free, compulsory and secular education, as a result of laws by the Minister of Public Instruction, Jules Ferry. One of the major aims of the Ferry laws was to spread the French language, as is clearly apparent in the following citation from *Le Bulletin officiel* (1921), a publication issued by the Ministry of Education to all teachers in France.

> Our teachers [. . .] are well aware that the teaching of French is not only about working for the maintenance and spread of a beautiful language and literature, it is also about strengthening national unity. (cited in Désirat and Hordé 1976: 93)

Through the teaching of the national language, history and geography, the school sought to instil a sense of national pride and greatness. Instrumental in this construction of the nation were books like G. Bruno's *Le Tour de la France par deux enfants* (1878) and Lavisse's *Histoire de France* (1884), which was continually revised and used up until 1950 (Citron 1991: 15, 27–9; Smith 1995: 91; Thiesse 1999: 237; Wright 2000: 206–7). For the leaders of the Third Republic, France had become a 'religion' (Citron 1991: 17; Winock 1997: 13), which had as its aim the conversion of 'peasants into Frenchmen' (Weber 1977). The particular conception of French identity which was promoted was of a very ethnic nature, as crystallised in the Dreyfus Affair (1894–906).[13] As Jenkins (1990: 98) points out, '[t]he very concept of free and equal citizenship, on which the republican national ideal was based, was replaced in the thought of Barrès, Drumont, Déroulède and Maurras, by the themes of race, ethnic tradition, 'rootedness', and *la vieille France*.'

Despite their major differences, supporters of the ethnic and civic traditions both agreed that language was a key element in defining the French nation. By 1905, academic theses in France could be submitted in French, without the Latin translation which had previously been necessary (Walter 1988: 108). The benefits of learning the language of social mobility spoke for themselves, as demonstrated by increased literacy rates, which in 1906 had reached around 95 per cent (Lodge 1993: 224). Industrialisation and the construction of railways and roads lead to increased population movements which reinforced the use of French as a *lingua franca*; World War I had a similar effect, by bringing together soldiers from a variety of different linguistic backgrounds (Bonnemason 1993: 32; Perret 1998: 62).

> The situation in 1920 was just the reverse of what it had been in 1880: bilinguals were more awkward in patois than in French; the majority, and most important, the young were on the side of the national language.   (Weber 1977: 79)

The strong link which existed between language and the French nation at the time is manifest in the words of the linguist André Thérive (1923: iii): 'our linguistic consciousness is nothing less than our national consciousness.'

Following World War II and France's Vichy episode, which once again promoted a very ethnic, anti-republican form of French identity (Østerud 1997: 35; Jenkins and Copsey 1996: 108), the country enjoyed relative economic success during the *Trente Glorieuses* (mid-1940s to mid-1970s). Yet towards the end of this period, French identity faced a growing number of challenges: the difficult process of decolonisation, the events of May 1968, and the gradual decline of France in the global arena are but a few (see also Section 7.3). Perhaps the most significant blow to French national pride was dealt by the international economic and monetary crisis of 1973; until then, the country had enjoyed the prestige of having the fastest economic growth rate in Europe (Duhamel 1993: 103). By the mid-1980s, this economic crisis had compounded with other concerns relating to immigration and European integration (see Sections 5.2.2 and 6.3) to induce a more general *malaise* or identity crisis (Citron 1991: 7; Hettne, Sörlin and Østergård 1998: 26; Ardagh 1999: 709). It comes as no surprise that this crisis was to have a profound effect on attitudes towards the French language, the symbol of French national identity *par excellence*. In the words of Fernand Braudel, eminent historian and member of the French Academy:

> France is the French language. In so far as it is no longer pre-eminent, the way it was during the 18th and 19th centuries, we are in the midst of a crisis of French culture. (*Le Monde*, 24–5 March 1985)

The general crisis thus spilt over into a crisis of the French language, which reinforced the already prescriptive attitudes towards language change in France (cf. Gueunier 1985). These attitudes are examined in more detail in Section 4.4, which follows a historical overview of the role of language in the construction of Swedish identity.

4.3 Language and identity in Sweden: A historical overview

Swedish linguistic consciousness may not be as old as its French equivalent, but it is founded on a long history of a Swedish speech community. From around 1000 AD, a Swedish 'language' began to distinguish itself from the common tongue previously spoken in the Nordic region (Bergman 1984: 12). It is generally considered that the first book in Swedish was the *Västgötalagen* (West Gautish Law), dating from around 1250 (Bergman 1984: 30).[14] No language is mentioned by name in this document, and it is quite possible that the author would have claimed to have spoken Danish, despite the language's clear difference from that of Danish texts of the time (Janson 1997: 124). The first mention of Swedish as a distinct form of speech was not made until around 1300, at the end of poems translated into the *swænskæ thungo* by order of the Norwegian queen, Eufemia (Bergman 1984: 32). It is thus perhaps around the fourteenth century that one can speak of the beginning of a Swedish ethnolinguistic conscience.

Magnus Erikssons landslag (Magnus Eriksson's National Law) of 1347 was the first law which applied to several provinces, establishing a Swedish kingdom and giving official status to the Swedish language (Janson 1997: 128). Yet this language was far from standardised and the first impulses in this direction did not occur until the fifteenth century. The monastery of St. Birgitta at Vadstena in Östergötland became Sweden's literary centre, translating many religious writings into a heavily Latin-influenced Swedish (Bergman 1973: 88). Swedish did, however, benefit from this encounter with Latin, which served as a model for literature and a standard orthography (Janson 1997: 130).

Sweden is usually referred to as one of the oldest states in Europe, having been formed during the sixteenth–seventeenth centuries during what Baggioni (1997: 74) refers to as the 'first ecolinguistic revolution', when vernacular languages encroached on domains formally dominated by Latin (see Section 2.4.1). At this time, there were two main outgroups from which Sweden could distinguish itself in an effort to forge its own identity. The dominant Other in the region at the time was Denmark. Breaking Sweden free from the largely Danish-dominated Kalmar Union, which had linked it to the other Nordic countries since 1397, was therefore one of Gustav Vasa's immediate concerns when he ascended to the throne in 1523. Another of Gustav Vasa's priorities was to sever ties with the religious Other represented by Rome. Much more than in Catholic countries like France (see Section 4.2), the Reformation favoured vernaculars like Swedish, which became the language of the state Church. The first Swedish translation of the New Testament appeared in 1526, followed by the translation of the whole Bible (1540–1), known appropriately as the Gustav Vasa Bible. The latter had a great influence on the Swedish language, acting as a standard for Swedish grammar, vocabulary and orthography not only for the purpose of sermons, but also for other literary genres (Bergman 1973: 30–1).[15] Three decades after the Gustav Vasa Bible, the Church Ordinance of 1571 is considered as the starting point of language cultivation (*språkvård*) or language planning in Sweden: it was in this document that Archbishop Laurentius Petri first expressed a puristic approach to the use of foreign words in sermons (Dahlstedt 1976: 17).

During its time as a great power (1611–1718), Sweden established an empire around the Baltic Sea, and even had colonialist aspirations in Delaware on the American east coast and in Cabo Corso on the African west coast (Johnsson 1995: 40). The privileged position held by Sweden was not without its linguistic consequences; in particular, the belief that the Swedish language was as worthy as any other in Europe led to increased language purism regarding foreign influences. The best known of the country's seventeenth-century linguists, Georg Stiernhielm, attempted to purify Swedish of loan words, an agenda he applied in his didactic poem *Hercules* of 1648 (Bergman 1984: 126).[16] At the same time, King Karl XI encouraged the judiciary and other officials not to complicate texts with Latin words; in 1661, detailed guidelines were established regarding the use of language in diplomatic correspondence.

> [I]f the Emperor or other potentates, princes and states write to His Royal Majesty in their mother tongue, His Royal Majesty shall from his side reply back in Swedish (excepting the King of France). (cited in Bergman 1984: 125)

One can only assume that French was allowed due to its prestige as a *lingua franca* amongst the European aristocracy of the time (see Section 4.2). For all other purposes, Swedish had become the only acceptable language. It was therefore of no surprise that language was to play an important part in the policies of Swedification carried out in the regions of *Skåne* (Scania) and *Bohuslän*, which were ceded to Sweden from Denmark and Norway respectively, in the Peace of Roskilde of 1658 (Ohlsson 1978; Löfgren 1993: 82–5).

The extent of the growing linguistic consciousness in the second half of the seventeenth century is clearly witnessed by the elaborate language myth constructed by the scholar Olof Rudbeck. Rudbeck argued in his work *Atlantica* (1679) that the ancient languages had, in fact, all derived from Swedish, since Sweden was the former Atlantis, the country from which Antiquity had originated (Janson 1997: 149). While this myth focused predominantly on the status of Swedish, efforts also continued to cultivate its corpus, such as with Samuel Columbus' *En swensk ordeskötsel* (The Cultivation of Swedish Words) from around 1680 (Bergman 1984: 101). Four years later, the first Swedish grammar, *Grammaticae Suecanae specimen*, was published in Latin by Ericus Aurivillius. The first grammar in Swedish appeared in 1696: *Grammatica Suecana* by Nils Tiällman (Baggioni 1997: 164).

Swedish was to become more or less standardised by the eighteenth century (Hyltenstam 1999a: 31), the period which saw the beginnings of a great Swedish literary tradition, with writers such as von Dalin, Bellman and Kellgren. The first of these authors was the anonymous publisher of Sweden's first moralising periodical, *Then swänska Argus* (The Swedish Argus), modelled on *The Tatler* and *The Spectator* in England. With its first edition in 1732–4, this publication scorned foreign influences in its praises of the Swedish language.

> It is soft yet strong, pure yet rich, simple yet formal, brave yet delicate. It is melodious and lends itself to poetry and prose, to song and speech, to stories and

novels, to the serious and comical, to church and theatre, to sermons and Argus. Nothing more is needed other than that we care for and cultivate it; but despite all that, one prefers to speak and write foreign words, for the simple reason that they are foreign. (von Dalin 1910: 345-6)

Some 150 years following the French model, the Swedish Academy was founded by Gustav III in 1786. Even the statutes reflected those of its French equivalent: to work for the 'purity, strength and greatness of the Swedish language' (cited in Bergman 1984: 136). As in France, this was to be achieved through the writing of a grammar and dictionary.[17]

The Romanticist movement which swept across Europe in the nineteenth century gave great impetus to the linguistic component of Swedish identity. In what Baggioni (1997) has termed the 'second ecolinguistic revolution' (see Section 2.4.1), Swedish was transformed from the language of the state to the language of a nation. Swedish became a regular school subject from 1807, and while King Karl XIV may have spoken no Swedish and conducted all affairs of state in French (Lalanne-Berdouticq 1993: 75),[18] this did not mean that Swedish was any less important an element in the construction of a myth of origin. Unlike in France, where the Gaulish ancestors had spoken a language unrelated to French, the Swedes enjoyed a more or less continual linguistic link with their Germanic-speaking forebears. Like the Viking ancestors, the Swedish language was portrayed as strong, masculine and racially pure, an image which clearly emanates from *Language*, a poem by Tegnér from 1817.

> Language of honour and heroes! How noble and manly you move,
>   pure as ore is your ring, as sure as the sun's is your course.
> You dwell on the peaks, where the thunder and storms speak,
>   the lower pleasures of the valleys are not made for you.
> Behold the reflection of your face in the sea, and from the manly features
>   wipe clean the foreign make-up, soon it is perhaps too late.
> (Tegnér 1959: 198)[19]

Linguistic purism was seen as the answer to combating the 'feminine' influence of foreign loan words. Rydqvist wrote his grammar *Svenska språkets lagar* (Speech laws of the Swedish language) in 1850-74 with this goal; and in 1873, in an essay entitled *Tysk eller nordisk svenska* (German or Nordic Swedish), Rydberg criticised the Bible Commission's translation of the New Testament for containing too many words of foreign origin. In his view, the abundance of foreign borrowings rendered the situation of the Swedish language quite precarious.

> In the worse case, it seems to us that Swedish would sink into becoming a beggar's language, which lives on the charity of others, until it dies with no respect, dragging the people with it into death.   (Rydberg 1873: 530)

Following the example of the Icelanders, Rydberg Swedified his own language by replacing words and morphemes of foreign origin, especially Latin and German, with those of Nordic derivation.

The shift away from foreign influences was not limited to language, but also led more generally to the emergence of a *bondekultur* (peasant culture) by the end of the century. Museums dedicated to Swedish culture were built, while Swedish handicraft and folk dance became the object of increased interest. Regional dialects also became worthy of study, whereas they had been scorned in the past (see Section 5.3.1). Literature too played an important role. As Sweden's first internationally renowned author, Strindberg contributed to the creation of the heavily romanticised image of Sweden. Other important writers included Karlfeldt and Lagerlöf. The latter's *Nils Holgerssons underbara resa genom Sverige* (the Wonderful Adventures of Nils) of 1907 was used as a geography book in Swedish schools, as was the case in France with G. Bruno's *Le Tour de la France par deux enfants* (see Section 4.2). Somewhat paradoxically, the *bondekultur* movement was a construct of the growing upper class. Fearful of mounting class oppositions and social tensions around the turn of the century, this layer of society sought a more secure identity in a simple life of the past. But for the real peasants, the image of the past was not so positive, dominated as it was by memories of degradation, misery, poverty and starvation. Unable to recognise themselves in the *bondekultur* image put forward by the upper classes, many peasants were ironically accused of lacking the very culture which was supposedly their own (Löfgren 1985: 24–5). To use the words of Gellner (1964: 162), 'genuine peasants or tribesmen, however proficient at folk-dancing, do not generally make good nationalists.'

It is in this context that one must interpret the discourse surrounding the mass emigration of Swedes to the USA, which reached its peak in the 1880s, but which carried on into the next century. Gustav Sundbärg, the population statistician responsible for the *Emigrationsutredning* (Emigration Inquiry), attributed the great wave of out-migration to an absence of 'national instinct' on the part of Swedes (Sundbärg 1911: 31). This purported lack of national pride was due, in Sunbärg's view, to the country's remaining outside the nationalist movement that swept across Europe after the Napoleonic wars. A more likely explanation for Swedish emigration lies in the hardships suffered by many peasants at the time. Indeed, Romanticism had a great influence on

Sweden, which in many respects played a leading role in the movement through the work of Artur Hazelius. It was this ethnologist who created the Swedish pavilion at the 1878 international exposition, along with the Nordic Museum (1880) and *Skansen* (1891), the open-air museum, which all served as models for ethnographical museums in other European countries (Thiesse 1999:200). That there was certainly a Swedish 'national instinct' is further highlighted by the results of a survey of the time. When Gothenburg school pupils were asked which person they would most like to emulate amongst those they had seen, heard or read about, the Swedish 'hero king' Gustav II Adolf came in first amongst the boys (22 per cent) and second amongst the girls (11 per cent) (Andolf 1985:17).[20] Despite this clear sense of national pride, it was felt nonetheless that Swedish identity needed to be bolstered, not only because of emigration, but also because of the psychological effect of the union crisis with Norway[21] and the imminence of World War I.

With the school reform in 1905, Swedish became the central subject in education, finally ending the long struggle with Latin (Thavenius 1995:474). School children were also subjected to propaganda through history books and patriotic songs (Netterstad 1982:33–46). A passage from one school history book from the time clearly indicates the emphasis placed on Swedish culture, including language.

> And let us remember that our country is not just the beautiful countryside, not just our lakes and rivers, our valleys and mountains, our fields and meadows! Let us remember that our country is also the laws we have built up against violence and influence (*väld*), the freedom we have struggled for and gradually obtained, the language we speak! (Bergström 1907:170)

A mere three decades later, Swedish identity was to undergo a major transformation. The breakthrough of social democracy in Sweden in the 1920s–1930s, coupled with the racial theories developed by the Nazis, led to the discrediting of the concepts of national identity and nationalism (Østerud 1997:10). In short, it became more or less taboo to discuss Swedishness (Daun 1996:2). The belief that Swedes lacked national consciousness gained currency; that they somehow expressed a 'negative' or 'inverted' nationalism developed into a popular myth which is still present today (e.g. Herlitz 1995:54–6; cf. also Löfgren 1993:28; Lilliestam 1996:131). But even this idea must be interpreted in the social setting of the 1930s to 1980s. Hilton *et al.* (1996:293) suggest that in some cases an image of oneself in the past may serve as an Other for the purposes of constructing a positive identity in the present. The social democratic rejection of the nineteenth-century view of Swedish identity can thus be seen as a means of emphasising a new Swedish identity, founded in part on the ideologies of anti-traditionalism, rationalism, democratism and internationalism (Dahlstedt 1976). Any attempt to define Swedish identity in the twentieth century cannot avoid reference to these themes.

> If it is possible at all to discuss the core of national Swedish identity, that core would be this notion of modernity, of being part of modern Sweden, part of an advanced, highly developed, rationally organised country whose leading principles include justice and social welfare. (Daun 1996: 153)

The traditional view of Swedish identity may have been rejected, but there was nevertheless a certain irony in the playing down of Swedish nationalism in the 1930s to 1980s (Löfgren 1993: 28). Sweden exhibited a new type of nationalism, portraying itself as the world's conscience and a model for other countries to follow. Economic success and consequent high standards of living served only to reinforce this self-righteous and ethnocentric image. But the positive identity which Sweden had succeeded in constructing was to come to an abrupt end in the late 1980s–early 1990s, when economic recession swept across Sweden, France and most of the Western world (see Section 4.2). As the Swedish model fell into crisis, a major blow was dealt to Swedish national pride. The question which the country now faced was how best to rebuild a positive identity.

Social democratic ideals still dominate in Sweden at the time of writing. Unlike May Day, reserved for workers' demonstrations in the streets, the Swedish national day, June 6, is not a public holiday and certainly not celebrated as much as May 17 in neighbouring Norway. Nor do the Swedish authorities, unlike their Nordic and French counterparts, appear to show an overwhelming interest in their national culture or language: in particular, Teleman and Westman (1997: 5) note the absence of language from Swedish cultural politics.[22] Yet at the grassroots level, there are clear signs of a return to a Swedish identity of the type which existed in the nineteenth century. With hindsight, one notes that this traditional sense of Swedish identity was never too far away. While the Swedes may not celebrate their national day as lively as the Americans or the French, they have always been keen flag wavers, displaying the blue and gold colours on the front of buses, from apartment balconies and outside country homes. Swedish identity may have been toned down throughout the 1930s–1980s, but it existed nonetheless through different cultural registers (Löfgren 1993: 27, 72–3). In today's Sweden, one can thus speak of a revival of traditional Swedish identity. This identity went underground especially from the 1960s, but is now resurfacing to fill the identity vacuum caused by the challenges of a changing world (Lilliestam 1996: 135–6; Karaveli 1997: 74). In its most extreme form, the revival of Swedish nationalism is manifested through the rise of neo-Nazism. Like in many other European countries, Sweden has also seen the emergence of more mainstream extreme right-wing parties in recent years. These parties have, however, by no means enjoyed the level of popularity of Le Pen's *Front national* in France: *Ny demokrati* (New Democracy) failed to obtain the necessary 4 per cent threshold for a seat in the 1994 elections; the same fate was shared by *Det nya partiet* (the New Party) in the 1998 elections. More frequently, the revival of Swedish nationalism can be witnessed in less pernicious forms, such as a renewed interest in Swedish history and culture. Ehn *et al.* (1993: 9) note that more publications on Swedish culture appeared during the decade prior to their work than there had been published in the whole of the twentieth century up until then. Not only was it during the 1980s that Sweden finally received an official national day, this decade also marks the beginning of an era when Swedishness became a serious object of study (e.g. Phillips-Martinsson 1981; Alsmark 1984; Arnstberg 1989; Daun 1989). This revival of Swedish nationalism has continued into the 1990s. Herman Lindqvist's numerous books on Swedish history and character have become best sellers, while the music of Nordman, a group which combines rock with traditional Swedish folk music, found immediate appeal especially amongst young Swedes (cf. Lilliestam 1996).[23] The heightening of Swedish national consciousness witnessed at the time of writing may not be without its linguistic implications too, as will be seen in the following section.

4.4 French and Swedish attitudes to language change and spelling reform

Sections 4.2 and 4.3 have highlighted the close relationship which existed between the rise of national and linguistic consciousness in both France and Sweden. Linguistic standardisation and language purism *vis-à-vis* foreign influences proved to be key elements in reinforcing national cohesion in the two countries, while language myths were seen to serve as vital constructs for generating positive French and Swedish identities. This section focuses on the other element of linguistic consciousness mentioned in Section 4.1, namely language prescriptivism. Yet in this case, the use of a more modern perspective does not reveal similarities so much as differences between France and Sweden. Following a very brief presentation of the agencies involved in language planning in both countries, the discussion centres on attitudes towards language change, with particular attention paid to the issue of spelling reform.

Unlike in the past, in today's Sweden, 'the cultivation, planning or treatment of language [...] is not commonly the subject of decisions by official institutions' (Dahlstedt 1976: 33). The same cannot be said for France, where language planning quite clearly continues to be an affair of the state, as attested by the large and complex network of language planning agencies in that country.

> In 1966 President de Gaulle set up the Haut Comité pour la Défense et l'Expansion de la langue française, which had among other tasks that of ensuring that modern French vocabulary could match the requirements of a technological age. As this group changed its name, and to a certain extent its role, over the next few years, the task of managing terminology became ever more important, so terminology committees were set up in each ministry after 1970. The mechanism for implementing state 'interference' in the actual language was revised in 1984, again in 1989 and 1993 to give a somewhat complex range of committees, groups, associations and services which all felt they had a hand in managing French. The main ones at the national level now, apart from the Academy, are the Conseil Supérieur de la Langue Française (CSLF) chaired by the Prime Minister and to which the Délégation Générale à la Langue Française (DGLF), attached to the Ministry of Culture, reports. (Ager 1999: 147)

To be sure, language agencies exist in Sweden as well. *Tekniska nomenklaturcentralen* (TNC) (the Swedish Centre for Technical Terminology) founded in 1941 is concerned with collecting, initiating and disseminating technical terminology in Swedish and is partially funded by the state (Vikør 1993: 155–6). As the successor of *Nämnden för svensk språkvård* (Committee for Swedish Language Cultivation) founded in 1944, *Svenska språknämnden* (the Swedish Language Council) is responsible for 'following the development of spoken and written Swedish and carrying out language cultivation activities' (www.spraknamnden.se/SSN/stadgar.htm). It receives annual subsidies from the state, but also depends on other sources of income such as private funds and the sale of publications (Vikør 1993: 153). The Swedish Language Council is the primary source of advice for the general public. That a large proportion of the public have a keen interest in language cultivation is demonstrated by the continual popularity of books on language usage, such as those of the former head of the Swedish Language Council, Bertil Molde (e.g. 1992; 1997), and a weekly programme on national radio, *Språket* (Language).

Despite the presence of elements of a prescriptive tradition, language cultivation in Sweden has included the democratisation of language as part of an overall ideology of democratism which characterises Swedish society (see Section 4.3). The Swedish democratic approach to language has traditionally subscribed to three main principles (Dahlstedt 1976: 32–44). First, a belief in the majority principle advocates the acceptance of linguistic variation if it occurs amongst the majority of the population. Second, freedom and tolerance of dialectal and sociolectal variation should be promoted. While linguistic freedom must be balanced against a communicative need for standardisation, Dahlstedt (1976: 34) claims that Sweden has long abandoned the 'Darwinistic approach to language cultivation', whereby one set of linguistic forms survives at the expense of others (see Section 5.3.1). In a study of the use of dialect in two schools in the west of Sweden, Andersson (1979) noted that the school system still contributed, albeit mostly indirectly, to the disintegration of dialects. Nonetheless, the following citation from a course plan for the teaching of Swedish in (compulsory) lower secondary schooling, clearly highlights the more liberal approach to linguistic variation in Sweden, compared with that in France (see this section below).

> A person's language is closely related to her or his personality and circumstances. If that link is broken, the development of both language and personality is blocked. An important goal of the teaching of Swedish is therefore to strengthen the pupils' self-esteem, so that they are not afraid to express themselves and stand by their opinions. Work should therefore be based on the language and experiences the pupils have. All children must feel that their language is good enough and that they can use their experiences and words in learning to read and write. (Läroplan för grundskolan 1980, Allmän del, svenska: 133)

The third principle on which the Swedish democratic approach to language rests is a belief in social equality, which should be reinforced through language cultivation of several kinds: orthographical reform, lexical transparency, the simplification of Swedish officialese and the abolition of pejorative words. Yet since the last reform of 1906, there has been little interest amongst language cultivators in more far-reaching measures to regularise Swedish orthography (Dahlstedt 1976: 39): new proposals in the 1930s, 40s and 60s for phonetically-based spelling reforms found limited response (Vikør 1993: 189–90).[24] More success at democratising language has been observed through the promotion of lexical transparency, whereby less frequently used words of foreign origin are replaced by words which comprise well-known morphemes of Nordic derivation (e.g. *årtionde*=decade, literally 'year' + 'tenth', instead of the Latin loan word *decennium*). Yet the demand for lexical transparency often paradoxically favours language purism, which is inconsistent with another integral component of Swedish societal ideology: internationalism (see Section 7.4). Social equality has also been encouraged through calls, especially from the radical left, for a move away from officialese in favour of a more informal usage.

> The gulf between official Swedish and colloquial spoken Swedish causes a communication barrier between the authorities and the citizens, especially those who lack higher education and linguistic training. (Dahlstedt 1976: 42–3)

Specific efforts to undermine the use of 'officialese' include the *Skriv som du talar!* (Write as you speak!) campaign undertaken by the Swedish postal service in 1977 (Vikør 1993: 193). Finally, the use of words and expressions which carry pejorative connotations are avoided in an attempt to reverse the social inequalities of the past. The 1970s saw the replacement of Lapp and Lappish by *Sámi*, from the indigenous word *sábmi* or *sápmi* (see Section 5.3.1), while special female profession designations (e.g. *lärarinna*=female teacher) were increasingly replaced by generic (formally male) forms (e.g. *lärare*) (Dahlstedt 1976: 43).

Unlike in Sweden, there is strong opposition in France to the democratisation of language. This opposition rests on a long tradition of prescriptivism clearly demonstrated by the early work of the French Academy.

> [T]he Academy confirmed the existing bias towards an orthography reflecting the etymology of words (for example ruling in favour of the unpronounced *s* in words like *teste* and *mesme*). Their justification, that 'la Compagnie préfère l'ancienne orthographe, qui distingue les gens de lettres d'avec les ignorans et les simples femmes', is a reminder that, at the time, les gens de lettres would naturally be familiar with Latin [. . .], and that the Academy was in no way concerned with making the written language accessible to a wider public. (Wise 1997: 223)

The democratisation of language which did follow the Revolution was not so much concerned with accepting alternative linguistic realities as imposing the linguistic norm of the dominant group. This practice was to increase with the literacy programmes of the Third Republic which made 'spelling the touchstone of educatedness and a uniform spelling system the chief indicator of a uniform language, symbol of a united nation' (Lodge 1993: 164). For this reason, any attempt to reform orthography and the French language in general is considered as 'an attack on the fabric of (traditional) society and the identity of France' (Ager 1996a: 125) and ultimately results in failure. Such was the fate of the *tolérances* published by the Ministry of Education in 1901, intended to allow for some departure from the strictest norms in spelling, grammar and usage, as well as the minor orthographical changes proposed by the Academy in the 1975 edition of its dictionary (Ager 1996a: 120). The most recent attempt at orthographical reform occurred in 1989–90. In line with the majority principle seen above in relation to Sweden, the minor changes which were being proposed in France had already been largely adopted by the majority of the population (Schiffman 1996: 117 and 298). Nonetheless, the suggested reforms provoked outrage amongst some members of the general public and the media, who justified their views by evoking the 'imaginary decree of 1832–5'. It was this decree which supposedly authorised the spelling norms of the Academy as the state orthography (Catach 1991: 115; Schiffman 1996: 115–20).[25] The authors of the reforms were accused of equating orthographical rules with Fascism, of viewing so-called correct spelling as an 'instrument of social segregation' (cf. Ager 1996a: 124). Even the *Centre national de la recherche scientifique* (CNRS) found itself the object of criticism for merely attempting to study the effect of the proposed reforms: 'some of its questionnaires were defaced with right-wing slogans or soiled with excrement by people who found even the idea of *discussing* spelling reform to be a left-wing attack on the sanctity of the language' (Schiffman 1996: 298).

The failure of spelling reforms in France stems in part from a refusal to accept different usages and norms (Maurais 1985: 2).

> The Frenchman [. . .] does not consider his language as a malleable instrument, at his disposal to express himself and communicate. He sees it as an immutable institution, constrained in its traditions and practically untouchable. (Walter 1988: 18)

This unwillingness to accept linguistic variation or change in any form has prompted many traditionalists to allege that the French language is in a state of crisis (cf. Gueunier 1985; Weinstein 1989: 56). In particular, it is claimed that growing illiteracy and a deteriorating command of language amongst school children is having an adverse effect on French. De Broglie (1986: 114) claims that 'the school situation is verging on disaster', that there is a lack of 'linguistic morale'. He quotes one survey in which final-year primary school pupils made on average fourteen spelling mistakes in a text of 55 words, while pupils in the final year of lower secondary school (*troisième*) made on average sixteen mistakes in a difficult text of 150 words. However, most of the crisis perceived by de Broglie and others stems from their negative attitudes towards efforts to democratise language, for example through curriculum reforms.

> While in short the objective of the reforms is to break the system which makes the mastery of language, and especially of written language 'one of the most impor-

> tant axes of social differentiation in modern societies' (J. Goody [and Watt], 1963[:335]), everything indicates that a majority of speakers are attempting, against their interest, to protect this differentiation. (Gueunier 1985: 28)

The widespread view that 'orthography is a discipline' (de Broglie 1986: 115) which must be learnt is manifest in the French obsession with dictation exercises, including Bernard Pivot's annual televised dictation competition (Walter 1988: 251). Through the mastering of the complexities of language, and in particular of orthography, an individual can obtain intellectual and social worth (Ager 1996a: 125; cf. also Balibar 1985: 9, Lodge 1993: 225). So strong is this belief in France that in 1994 it was enshrined in the Toubon Law (see Section 7.3) which states that 'the mastery of the French language [. . .] is one of the fundamental goals of education' (article 11, paragraph II). The then Minister of Education, François Bayrou, also included an increased commitment to the teaching of French in his *Contrat pour l'école*, which has been progressively implemented from 1995 (Ager 1999: 65–7). A further example which contrasts with the democratisation of language observed in Sweden is that of the ill-fated proposals in 1986 to introduce feminine forms of professions, titles and positions (Ager 1996a: 179–82). The proposals provoked a lively debate in the media and a warning from the Academy, which considered them as 'an attack on the French language' (cited in Haut conseil de la Francophonie 1999: 44). The final recommendations of the terminology commission in charge of researching the issue were watered down from a decision (*arrêté*), which would have imposed their use in official language, employment advertisements and in school text books, to a circular (*circulaire*), which presented them as mere guidelines.

There is another reason for the language 'crisis' in France, namely the effect of the more general identity crisis mentioned in Section 4.2.

> The crisis, if crisis there be, is one of attitudes towards cultural identity rather than towards language alone. (Ager 1990: 238)

It is perhaps here that we might expect to observe more similarities with the Swedes, considering the identity crisis which they too appear to be undergoing (see Section 4.3). Throughout the 1930s–1980s, Swedes had a self-evident relationship with their language: '[t]he status of the Swedish language in Sweden has long gone without saying' (Teleman and Westman 1999). This is not necessarily to say that language was less valued in Sweden that it was in France. It seems more likely that the role of language in the construction of Swedish identity was merely different to that in France; it was an 'unwaved flag' (see Section 2.2.3) for the purposes of expressing Swedish identity. This observation provides further evidence for Clyne's (1991: 93–4) claim that the existence of language purism — or indeed other acts of corpus language planning — need not imply that language is a core value (see Section 4.1). Nonetheless, the current revival of Swedish ethnonationalism signalled in Section 4.3 does appear to be having linguistic implications, including the Swedish Language Council's programme for the promotion of the Swedish language (see Section 7.4). Another possible example of linguistic implications of the national revival is the comeback amongst young Swedes of the formal second-person pronoun *ni* (you) (Mårtensson 1986; Norrby 1997). In the same way that the use of *tu* increased in France following the anti-establishment demonstrations of May 1968 (Ager 1999: 160), the pronoun *ni* all but disappeared in Sweden in favour of the informal *du* — the so-called '*du* reform' of the 1960s — which better reflected social democratic ideology (Daun 1996: 211). With the weakening of this doctrine from the 1980s (see Section 7.4), the pronoun *ni* lost most of its negative associations with social distance, thus opening the way for a return to the use of both pronouns.

As the Swedes continue their search for a new positive identity, it is still unsure which course they are likely to take: one which stresses a traditional, nineteenth-century identity, or one which continues the modern, rational, international image which emerged especially from the 1960s. There is no reason why Sweden will not decide to head down both of these paths simultaneously. Which aspect of Swedish identity is stressed at a given point in time will depend on the particular context in question. It thus seems appropriate to examine the different arenas which serve as 'construction sites' for national and linguistic identities, beginning with the national arena, which is the focus of Chapter 5.

CHAPTER 5

Language and national identity in the national arena

By 'national arena' is meant the territory delimited by the boundaries of a nation-state. As seen in Section 2.2.1, the identity which characterises this arena is usually founded on that of the dominant ethnic core. This ethnic core relies on the presence of internal Others to act as contradistinctions, a role which has traditionally been played by regional minorities; in more recent times, it has also been assumed by immigrant minorities. This chapter first examines the notion of minority as used in the terms 'minority language' and 'ethnolinguistic minority' (Section 5.1). The specific roles that ethnolinguistic minorities have played in the construction of French and Swedish national identities will then be considered (Sections 5.2 and 5.3 respectively). A final section will compare the identity-generating strategies of France and Sweden in the national arena by focusing on the particular issues of minority language teaching and attitudes towards the Council of Europe's Charter for Regional or Minority Languages (Section 5.4).

5.1 Ethnolinguistic minorities

Before discussing the different types of ethnolinguistic minorities, it is necessary to understand fully the notion of minority, which is the object of much terminological confusion (Section 5.1.1). Only after this can one consider the separate cases of regional minorities (Section 5.1.2) and immigrant minorities (Section 5.1.3).

5.1.1 What is meant by 'minority language' and 'ethnolinguistic minority'?

The definition of a minority language rests on two essential criteria: numerical weight and status. A first attempt to identify a minority language might therefore lead one to consider the number of the language's speakers. However, some so-called minority languages have a large number of speakers (e.g. Catalan with 6 million speakers); others are spoken by a majority within their respective regions (e.g. Faroese on the Faroe Islands and French in Québec). While the numerical dimension is clearly an important consideration in the definition of a minority language, there is another, even more important element to consider: the language's political status.

> [W]hether or not a language is a minority one has nothing to do with the language, but everything to do with the situation in which it finds itself.
> (Simpson 1981: 237)

The political status of a minority language is largely a reflection of the standing of the ethnolinguistic minority which speaks that language. Ethnolinguistic minorities typically 'lack the political, institutional and ideological structures which can guarantee the relevance of those languages for the everyday life of members of such groups' (Nelde *et al.* 1995: 1). In other words, ethnolinguistic minorities are not free to use their language in certain domains, which typically include administration, commerce and education (Ross 1979: 6). To understand the relationship between numerical weight (or quantum) on the one hand, and issues of power or access to power on the other, Srivastava (1984: 101) suggests the use of the two-dimensional matrix shown in Figure 5.1.

Although the term minority is often used loosely to refer to any dominated group, Srivastava claims that a real minority is one which lacks both power and numerical weight (category D). Similarly, a real majority in Srivastava's view, is one that is marked '+' for both the power and quantum dimensions (category A). Alsatians, Basques, Bretons and other regional groups in France are thus true minorities, lacking as they do the political power and numerical superior-

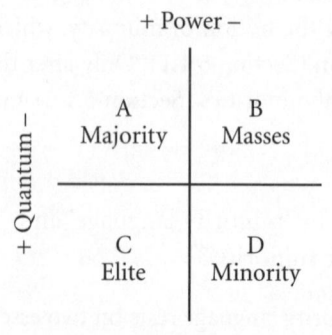

	+ Power −	
− Quantum	A Majority	B Masses
+ Quantum	C Elite	D Minority

Figure 5.1 The interaction between the two dimensions of numeric weight (quantum) and power which are involved in the definition of an ethnolinguistic minority. (Adapted from Srivastava 1984: 101)

ity of the overall ethnic French majority. However, it is often the case that the general masses (category B) are dominated by a small group of powerful élites (category C). This was the predicament of indigenous populations in French and other European colonies; or the Blacks in apartheid South Africa, who despite constituting a numerical majority, were dominated by the White élite. Two dichotomies thus result from Srivastava's framework. While the majority-minority dichotomy is common to industrialised, Western countries which are home to many different ethnic groups, the élite-masses opposition is characteristic of colonial situations (Hyltenstam and Stroud 1991: 22).

5.1.2 Regional minorities

By regional minority is meant an ethnolinguistic group which has its homeland in a certain region of a state (e.g. Bretons in Brittany, Basques in the Basque country). A distinction is sometimes made between regional languages, which are spoken within a certain geographical region, and territorial languages, which are spoken within a legally defined political area (Breton 1994: 47). Regional languages like Breton, Occitan, Catalan and Basque in France do not enjoy the same status as the territorial languages Catalan, Basque and Galician in Spain, or French in the Italian autonomist region of Val d'Aoste (Aosta Valley). Following the special status which was accorded to Corsica in 1991 (Huguenin and Martinat 1998: 24; Ager 1999: 61), linguistic and administrative borders on the island now coincide, thus also making Corsican a territorial language (Breton 1994: 47).

Relations between the state and regional minorities in Europe have historically been characterised by a mixture of pluralistic and assimilationist policies. In the fifteenth and sixteenth centuries, at the time of the emergence of the first states (i.e. England, France, Spain, Portugal, Holland, Denmark and Sweden), a *laissez-faire* attitude towards minorities prevailed: regional identities were free to flourish as long as peace and prompt taxes were assured (Gellner 1983: 10; Grillo 1989: 28; Edwards 1994: 131). In practice, cultural homogenisation did take place, but this was an unintended consequence of the consolidation of central control (Smith 1991: 100; Tilly 1994: 251). Not until the eighteenth century did explicit assimilationist policies emerge, largely as a result of the ideals of the Enlightenment. With their 'irrational' and 'primitive' sources of identity, regional minorities were considered direct challenges to the success of the modern, rational state. This belief was strengthened with the advent of the nation-state during the French Revolution (see Section 4.2). In order to survive, the state had to justify its existence as the defender of the nation. This required that the boundaries of the state and the nation be coterminous.

> To be legitimate [...] a nation-state must show that its citizens are sharply differentiated from 'foreigners', but equally undifferentiated from each other internally, as far as possible. In other words legitimation in a world of 'nation-states' requires a measure of internal homogenisation. (Smith 1991: 169)

With the help of compulsory education and military service, states embarked on overt or covert programmes of ethnocide and linguicide.[1] What can be considered from one perspective as 'nation-building' can be regarded from another as 'nation-destroying' (Connor 1972).

The nineteenth and early twentieth centuries saw a first wave of ethnic nationalism amongst regional minorities in Europe. As seen in Section 2.4.1, this 'ecolinguistic revolution' led in some cases to the formation of new nation-states in Eastern Europe, Turkey, Finland, Norway and other parts of Europe. What before constituted minority languages were now idealised and promoted as national languages (Edwards 1994: 130). Yet other regional minorities were not so fortunate in their struggles against central bureaucracies, nor did many wish to separate from the state into which they had been incorporated. Moreover, the newly formed nation-states did not always look favourably upon ethnic minorities themselves. Such was the case of Hungary, which after the creation of the Austro-Hungarian empire in 1867, promoted the assimilation of other ethnolinguistic groups (Ager 1997: 38).

The events of the nineteenth and early twentieth centuries were the product of a trend of liberalism favoured by theorists such as John Stuart Mill. According to this tradition, freedom required cultural homogeneity; regional minorities therefore needed to be 'dealt with by coercive assimilation or the redrawing of boundaries, not by minority rights' (Kymlicka 1995: 52; cf. also May 2001: 20–1). This was not to say that all liberals agreed with this reasoning: a competing liberal tradition argued for rights for regional minorities on the grounds that 'the combination of different nations in a state is a [...] necessary condition for civilised life' (Acton 1967: 150). While the two trends disagreed, they nonetheless both felt it necessary to address the minority issue. This issue was to disappear from liberal discourses after the Second World War, when the focus shifted to a preoccupation with universal human rights (Kymlicka 1995: 2–3; 56).

> [T]he general tendency of the postwar movements for the promotion of human rights has been to subsume the problem of national minorities under the broader

problem of ensuring basic individual rights to all human beings, without reference to membership in ethnic groups. The leading assumption has been that members of national minorities do not need, are not entitled to, or cannot be granted rights of a special character. The doctrine of human rights has been put forward as a substitute for the concept of minority rights, with the strong implication that minorities whose members enjoy individual equality of treatment cannot legitimately demand facilities for the maintenance of their ethnic particularism. (Claude 1955: 211)

It was in this climate that a second wave of ethnic nationalism occurred amongst regional minorities in Europe in the 1960s and 1970s (Allardt 1979). As Smith (1991: 125) explains, the earliest manifestations of this wave might possibly be found in Canada, amongst the Québécois, and in the United States, amongst the Southern Blacks and, in time, amongst the Indians and Hispanics as well. Spurred on as they may have been by the situation in North America, many of the European regionalist movements nevertheless had origins reaching back into the late nineteenth century. But unlike earlier attempts at revival, the regionalism of the 1960s–1970s was essentially left-wing in nature, led as it was by intellectuals, teachers and students. From the Basque Country and Wales, to the Jura and Occitania, newly formed or reformed political parties advocated autonomy, if not outright separatism. Their goals often included efforts to revive regional languages.

At a time when many former colonies were gaining their independence from European powers, it became popular to speak of 'internal colonialism' with reference to ethnolinguistic minorities within European states (Lafont 1967: chapters 2 and 3). This concept was developed further by Hechter, in his *Internal Colonialism: The Celtic Fringe in British National Development, 1536–1966* (1975). Internal colonialism relies on a distinction between the dominant core or centre and the subordinate periphery, as well as on the theory of economic underdevelopment.

> In the theory of underdevelopment great weight is attached to the operation of the economic order, or rather to the inner logic of the capitalist mode of production. In this order there are 'core' or 'central' places which in predatory fashion seek to incorporate and exploit resources, labour, markets in other areas which then become socially, economically, politically and geographically their 'dependent periphery'. (Grillo 1989: 81)

In particular, it is claimed that internal colonialism leads to a greater sense of nationalism in underdeveloped peripheral regions. But the concept of internal colonialism has been the object of much criticism (e.g. Edwards 1985: 73–4;

Grillo 1989: 82; Smith 1991: 125; Giordan 1994: 48). As Hechter (1975: 207) himself recognised, internal colonialism fails to account for the decline of regional languages in Britain, where according to the theory, these languages should thrive as a result of economic deprivation in the regions where they are spoken. Nor does the theory seem to be able to explain the secessionist desires of economically *developed* regions such as Flanders or northern Italy. As Grillo (1989: 82–3) summarises, regional nationalisms cannot be accounted for simply in terms of economic arguments. Moreover, it seems likely that economic factors *per se* do not cause ethnic revivals; rather they are used as further evidence to claim a separate regional identity (Giordan 1994: 48).

As a result of these regional pressures, and in line with a wave of cultural and linguistic pluralism which was sweeping the world (cf. Clyne 1991: 18–19; Kymlicka 1995: 14; Hyltenstam 1999a: 12), many European governments began to grant rights to ethnolinguistic minorities within their territories from the late 1960s–1970s, and in some cases from as early as the 1950s (e.g the Deixonne Law in France, see Section 5.4). Regional languages became visible on street signs and outside town halls and post offices; they could also be heard, albeit usually for short periods only, during broadcasts by local radio stations. But a more accepting stance towards cultural and linguistic diversity was not only the product of pressures from regional minorities; it was also seen as a means of dealing with the increasingly difficult circumstances of growing immigration.

5.1.3 Immigrant minorities

Immigrants have long constituted outgroups for the construction of national identities. Jews have throughout history found themselves the targets of anti-Semitism, for example during the Dreyfus Affair in France (see Section 4.2) and in Nazi Germany. As for Gypsies, for centuries their nomadic life-style resulted in their persecution in France, Prussia, the Netherlands, Italy, the Scandinavian countries, and in Hitlerian Germany as late as the twentieth century (Ager 1997: 70). Yet the Jews and Gypsies represent special cases: with long histories of settlement in most European countries, these ethnic groups clearly differ from recent immigrants. Indeed Yiddish and Romani are included in a recent survey of autochthonous — as opposed to immigrant — languages in Sweden (Hyltenstam 1999a: 27). Geographically dispersed as they are, Jews and Gypsies nonetheless also differ from regional minorities. While they are treated in this book along with recent immigrants, it is nonetheless recognised that these groups effectively constitute a third category of minority which is autochthonous but non-territorial in nature.

In its consideration of the role of immigrants in the construction of national identities, this book focuses predominantly on those ethnic groups which arrived after World War II. Far from being considered a strain on national economies, the first wave of immigrants in the 1950s was heralded as the key to economic success. Losses suffered during the war had left northwestern European cities — as well as those in Australia, Canada and the USA — without the supply of low-skilled labour needed for economic expansion. This need was met by large-scale immigration, in particular from Yugoslavia, Italy, Greece, Spain and Portugal (McNeill 1994: 302). When recruitment expanded further afield to attract Turks, Algerians, Indonesians, Pakistanis and West Africans, hopes of assimilation were abandoned and it was envisaged that immigrants would one day return permanently to their countries of origin. Such was the reasoning behind the *Gastarbeiter* status of immigrants in Germany and Switzerland, which gave rise to what has been termed 'denizens' (Hammar 1990).[2] That the majority of immigrants decided to stay posed a direct challenge to national identities: not only were many immigrants nonwhite, they also had radically different cultures and religions from those of the dominant ethnic group, not to mention the regional minorities as well. These perceived differences have only been heightened with the arrival from the late 1970s–1980s onwards of asylum seekers and refugees typically from places of ethnic conflict (e.g. Iran, Iraq, Turkey, former Yugoslavia).

A solution to the 'problem' of ethnic diversity was sought in cultural pluralism or multiculturalism. Many countries attempted to celebrate their ethnic differences and forge a new supra-ethnic or polyethnic 'national' identity (Eriksen 1993: 116–18). While it might at first appear that these pluralistic policies are most characteristic of nations founded on civic principles — and that assimilationist policies are typical of ethnic nations — a two-dimensional diagram illustrates that the situation is far more complex.

Figure 5.2 represents the interaction of the model of the nation with the model of integration promoted at the official level. Section A represents the civic nation which has embraced multiculturalism and actively supports ethnic diversity. Such is generally considered to be the case of Mauritius, Australia and Canada, for example. Mauritian nationalism composes two complementary trends: the state openly 'celebrates' the ethnic diversity of the island, at the same time as it emphasises the common history which the ethnic groups are in the process of building together (Eriksen 1993: 116–17; cf. also Eriksen 1990).

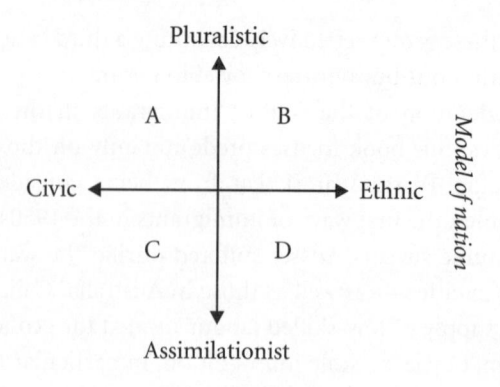

```
                    Pluralistic
                        ▲
                        │
              A         │        B
                        │                    ┌
      Civic  ◄──────────┼──────────►  Ethnic │ Model of nation
                        │                    └
              C         │        D
                        │
                        ▼
                  Assimilationist
```

Model of integration

Figure 5.2 The interaction of the model of the nation (civic versus ethnic) with the model of integration (pluralistic versus assimilationist) promoted at the official level

Multicultural ideology has also been instrumental in defining a truly Australian identity (Castles *et al.* 1992), while Canada was the first country in the world to adopt a multiculturalism law, in 1988, in order to protect and promote its immigrant languages and cultures (Driedger 1996).

Some may prefer to place Australia and Canada in section B, arguing that the model of integration in these countries is best described as Anglo-conformity, and therefore tantamount to assimilationism (Edwards 1994: 177–8; Kymlicka 1995: 14). A similar argument can be made for the USA: even if some ethnic minorities have not succumbed to the melting pot effect of American society (Glazer and Moynihan 1963, 1975), there nevertheless exist strong, covert assimilationist policies grounded in White Anglo-Saxon Protestant (WASP) culture (Smith 1991: 149–50). While the Bilingual Education Act of 1967 provided federal government subsidies for certain bilingual programmes in public schools, the specific goal of these programmes was not to promote minority languages so much as to facilitate the transition of immigrant minorities towards assimilation (Safran 1992: 548). More recently, in 1986, voters in California approved Proposition 63, amending the state constitution to make English the official state language. This was followed in 1988 by similar moves in Florida and Colorado (Schiffman 1996: 270–2). While scholars may disagree as to how best to describe the models of integration in Australia, Canada and the USA, all would no doubt agree that France belongs in section B. This country has traditionally considered itself a civic nation, yet the French model of integration is undeniably assimilationist, since ethnic diversity is considered incompatible with the ultimate goal of national unity (see Sections 5.2.1 and 5.2.2).

Section C represents nations which consider their identity in ethnic terms and implement assimilationist policies towards their minorities. Such is the case of Germany *vis-à-vis* the *Gastarbeiter*, one could argue that Québec belongs in this quadrant too, since there is a fairly strong expectation for Anglophone and *allophone* immigrant minorities to adopt the language and culture of the Francophone majority (Breton 1988: 95–6; Richard Bourhis, personal communication).[3] Finally section D encompasses ethnic nations such as Sweden, which has been experimenting with pluralistic policies since the late 1960s and 1970s (see Sections 5.3.1 and 5.3.2). That Swedish government policies, at least towards regional minorities, were on the whole assimilationist before this period highlights the dynamic nature of this model both in space and time: nations implement different ideological policies towards different minorities (regional and immigrant) at different points in time (cf. Kymlicka 1995: 10).

The pluralistic policies which many governments (e.g. in Australia, Canada and Sweden) have introduced since the 1960s–1970s have not been without their problems (see Section 5.4 for specific examples). In particular, they have traditionally suffered from a tension between a preference for individual rights on the one hand and collective rights on the other (see Section 5.1.2). For example, the liberal-minded former Prime Minister of Canada, Pierre Trudeau, opposed self-government rights for Québec because he favoured 'the primacy of the individual' and thought that 'only the individual is the possessor of rights' (Trudeau 1990: 363–4). While this remains the view amongst many liberals today, there is a movement to find a new way forward, to 'supplement traditional human rights principles with a theory of minority rights' (Kymlicka 1995; cf. May 2001: 110–26).

Another problem which faces countries which have adopted a multicultural ideology is that the latter does not necessarily filter down to the grassroots level. Indeed, in many cases (e.g. Sweden; see Sections 5.3.1 and 5.3.2), the introduction of pluralistic policies from above is thwarted by a rise in ethnic nationalism from below, creating a situation whereby *ethnos* threatens *demos* (Schlesinger 1994: 325). Some researchers claim that multiculturalism is itself destructive, the cause of neo-nationalism and ultimately the decline of the nation-state (Schnapper 1994, 1998a, 1998b; Karaveli 1997: 96–113; Nguyen 1998: 97–102; cf. Kymlicka 1995: 4; see Section 5.2.2). However, the majority of researchers argue that multiculturalism is essentially positive, but that if it is not accompanied by structural measures aimed at alleviating inequalities on ethnic grounds, it can lead not to a healthy integration, but to ghettoisation, *de facto* segregation (Castles *et al.* 1992: 146; Rex 1996: 243). Civic principles of equality can actually have the same effect as overtly discriminatory policies (e.g. policies of apartheid): in many cases, they deny special rights to socioeconomically deprived groups, thus creating or perpetuating *de facto* inequalities (Rouland 1991: 224; cf. Kymlicka 1995: 110). These *de facto* inequalities play an important role in the maintenance of a positive identity on the part of the dominant ethnic group, especially in times of economic recession and high unemployment, or when this identity is otherwise perceived as threatened. However, if segregation is a deliberate attempt to reinforce inequalities, it can also be regarded as the reverse side of the assimilationist coin: segregation and assimilation can both be used as strategies of control by means of divide-and-rule and unite-and-rule respectively (Wingstedt 1998: 55). That language has traditionally been employed as a means of overtly or covertly reinforcing inequalities between the dominant ethnic core and ethnolinguistic minorities is clearly seen in the specific cases of France and Sweden.

5.2 Language and national identity in France: The national arena

The French Revolution undeniably marked a milestone in the development of human rights. Yet as was seen in Section 4.2, it was not long before these new rights, particularly when applied to ethnolinguistic minorities, clashed with the construction of the French nation-state. *Liberté* did not entail a freedom to express one's cultural difference, but was rather an invitation, at least in theory, to free oneself of a 'primitive' ethnicity and adopt a 'universal' culture (cf. Kymlicka 1995: 50–4). The unwillingness of many to accept this invitation provided the nation-state with important outgroups or Others against which to consolidate French identity. This section examines the construction of French national identity in relation to the country's ethnolinguistic minorities, both of the regional (Section 5.2.1) and immigrant (Section 5.2.2) types.

5.2.1 Regional minorities

With reference to regional languages alone, France is the most multilingual state in Europe (Jacob and Gordon 1985: 107). Excluding both the languages of the overseas departments and territories (DOM-TOM) and those of immigrant populations, no less than seven regional languages are spoken in metropolitan

France, albeit to varying degrees: Alsatian/Lorrain,[4] Basque, Breton, Catalan, Corsican, Flemish and Occitan. These languages, along with a range of *langue d'oïl*/Franco–Provençal dialects, have traditionally acted as significant Others in the construction of French identity in the national arena (Figure 5.3).

The reason for such linguistic diversity is found in the history of the French state. The expansion of royal power from Paris led to the gradual annexation, be it through marriage, inheritance or simply conquest, of ter-

Figure 5.3 Regional languages and dialects in France. Langue d'oc refers to Occitan with its own array of dialects. (Adapted from Battye and Hintze 1992: 357)

ritories in the west and south from the thirteenth century, ending with the incorporation of Savoy and Nice in the nineteenth century (Figure 5.4).

As seen in Section 4.2, the expansion of royal power to these territories also implied the spread of French. Yet the gradual penetration of this language was in the beginning merely a consequence of annexation, rather than an explicit goal: in sixteenth and seventeenth-century France, the state was not interested in which languages were spoken by the masses (Lartichaux 1977: 68–9; Achard 1987: 40; Grillo 1989: 2).

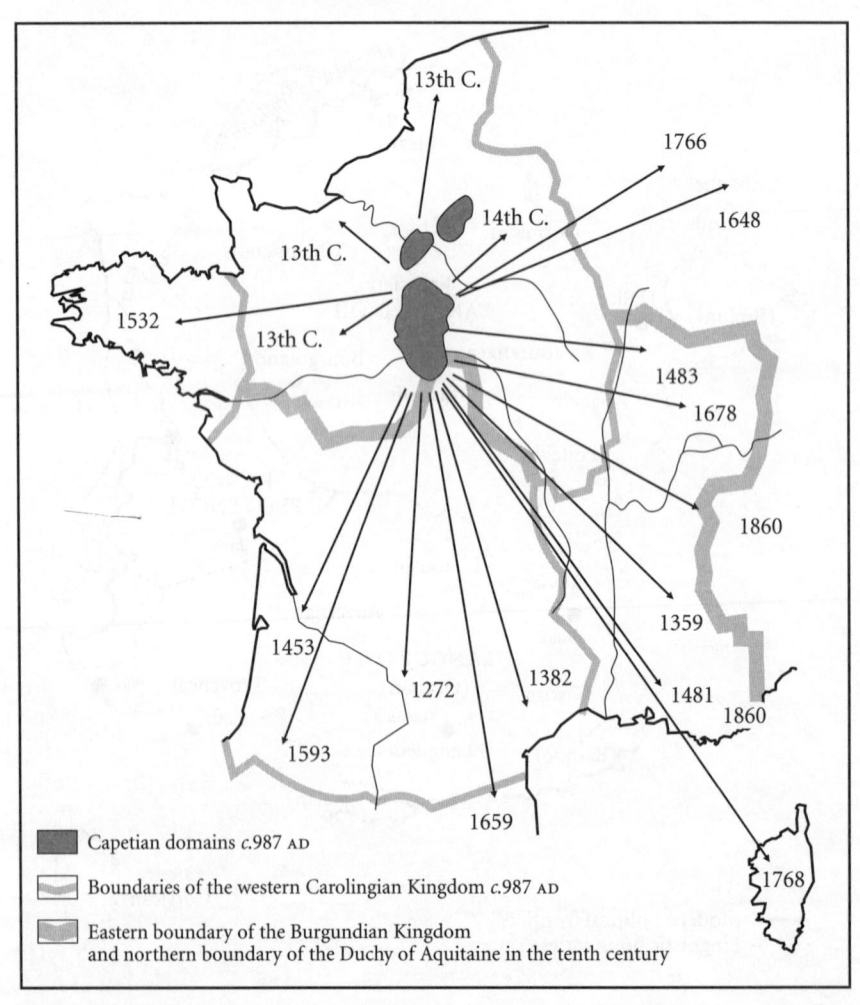

Figure 5.4 Territorial annexations in France. (From Lodge 1993: 121, but originally adapted from Citron 1991: 219)

> What the king demanded above all was loyalty [...] It mattered little then, up to a certain point, that custom and usage differed from one province to another. (Peyre 1933: 16)

Indeed the explicit aim of the Ordinance of Villers-Cotterêts (1539) was to undermine the status of Latin, not regional languages and dialects (see Section 4.2). Not until the Revolution did regional languages and dialects become a matter of state concern. While linguistic diversity had been of little relevance to purely administrative unity, it became significant when regional languages and dialects presented a threat to the new, national ideology which was propagated in the later years of the Revolution (Weber 1977: 72; Grillo 1989: 2; Giordan 1994: 24; see also Section 4.2).

For the regional élite who already favoured the language of Paris, the Revolutionary policy of linguistic unification offered a chance for further social mobility, a means of further developing a positive identity. In Bourdieu's terminology, a new sense of 'symbolic power' was bestowed upon the regional élite.

> The members of the local bourgeoisies of priests, doctors or teachers, who owed their position to their mastery of the instruments of expression, had everything to gain from the Revolutionary policy of linguistic unification. Promotion of the official language to the status of national language gave them that de facto monopoly of politics, and more generally of communication with the central government and its representatives, that has defined local notables under all French republics. (Bourdieu 1991: 47)

The opportunities for the regional masses were not so positive. While in theory the ideals of the Revolution offered the chance of social mobility to everyone, this possibility was strictly controlled. The masses were given some education, but not enough to allow for social mobility or convergence to the dominant group (see Section 3.2.5.1). Nor were they free to generate a positive identity through social creativity or divergence from the dominant group. Not only had the masses lost to the dominant group much of their élite, who might ultimately have led an ethnonational movement,[5] the ideology propagated by the dominant group which denigrated all regional languages and dialects also discouraged the re-evaluation of these important symbols of ethnic identity in a more favourable light. Giordan (1992b: 130–2) argues that the efforts of Grégoire, Barère and the like (see Section 4.2) did not so much seek to eradicate regional languages and dialects as serve a more insidious, discursive function of perpetuating the power imbalance between the dominant centre and the regional minorities.

> In fact, regional languages and cultures were able to survive because they fulfilled a specific function in the cultural hegemony of the dominant classes. (Giordan 1992b: 131)

In Giordan's view, the denigration of regional languages and dialects helped the dominant group to maintain a positive ethnolinguistic identity for around 150 years, from the time of the Revolution until the outbreak of World War II. This strategy relied heavily on the use of pejorative terms such as *dialecte*, *patois*, *idiome* and *jargon* to refer to regional languages and varieties of French (Grillo 1989: 26). While the use of linguistic criteria might understandably lead one to consider Picard and Gallo for example, as *dialectes* of French (see Section 2.3), Breton and Basque, for instance, are undeniably separate languages belonging to non-Romance language groups. The choice of *dialectes* to refer to all of France's regional languages is therefore incorrect. Unlike dialects, which allegedly possess a written form and a higher level of standardisation (Hudson 1980: 31; Lodge 1993: 5), *patois* are purely spoken languages and therefore viewed with even more contempt. For this reason, the designation *patois* was used indiscriminately especially in the late eighteenth century to refer to any language system which was not French (Lartichaux 1977: 67). Even more abusive still was the term *baragouin* (jabber), which is believed to have originated from Breton *bara ha gwin* (bread and wine) (Gordon 1978: 32; Grillo 1989: 26). The use of all of these terms reflects negative attitudes towards ethnolinguistic minorities, and in particular the power relationships which exist between these groups and the dominant *ethnie* (Ager 1990: 31).

As seen in Section 5.1.2, much of the disdain expressed towards regional minorities in the eighteenth and nineteenth centuries stemmed from the ideals of the Enlightenment, which viewed these groups as primitive obstacles to reason and modernity. This backward and uncultured image of rural peasants and their languages was also constructed in French art and literature of the nineteenth century, as the works of Balzac, Flaubert, Maupassant, Sand, Stendhal and others demonstrate (cf. Jacob and Gordon 1985: 115; Wright 2000: 186). Even prominent figures of regional origin contributed to the denigration of regional languages and culture, by relegating them to museum pieces, to non-functional objects of study. For example in 1889, Renan (see Section 2.2.1) had the following words to say about his native Breton language.

> Throughout one's life, one likes to recall the popular song in dialect which one enjoyed in one's childhood. But one would never conduct science, philosophy, political economy in *patois*. (cited in Hagège 1996: 126)

Paradoxically, the nineteenth century also witnessed a renaissance of regional cultures and languages as a result of the albeit minimal effect of the Romanticist movement in France compared with Sweden (see Sections 4.2 and 4.3). The poet Frédéric Mistral founded *Félibrige* in 1854 to preserve and encourage Provençal, while later years saw the formation of political parties such as the *Union régionaliste bretonne* in 1898 and *Vlamsch verbond van Frankryk* in the 1920s (Ager 1990: 65 and 79–80). Such efforts were however not sufficient to combat Jacobin ideology which was intent on denigrating regional languages and cultures. The well-known practice of tying a wooden clog or *symbole* around the neck of school children caught speaking Breton and other regional languages was widespread throughout the nineteenth century (McDonald 1989: 47; Laroussi and Marcellesi 1993: 96) and may even have persisted as long as the mid-twentieth century (Wardhaugh 1987: 108).

The vehemence of opposition to regional languages and cultures in France can be explained by the key role these languages and cultures played as Others for the purposes of constructing a positive national identity based on that of the dominant ethnic core. Perhaps more than any other region, Alsace/Lorraine had long been considered a security risk on account of its linguistic and cultural ties with neighbouring Germany. In a fashion reminiscent of the Terror (Brunot 1967, vol. 9:190–1; Schiffman 1996: 136–8; see Section 4.2), the use of German was banned or restricted in 1919, following the return of Alsace and Lorraine to France after World War I (Ager 1990: 54).[6]

> Autonomist newspapers were suppressed, separatists put on trial, and in 1924 French was made the exclusive language of instruction at the University of Strasbourg. (Jacob and Gordon 1985: 117–18)

Further concern about internal enemies developed during World War II, when some extreme political parties in other regions (e.g. the *Parti national breton*, the *Vlamsch verbond van Frankryk*) openly collaborated with the Nazis (Ager 1990: 66 and 79–80). As for Alsace and Lorraine, the overall process of denazification and degermanification which was carried out from 1945 led once again to the prohibition of German, which was not re-introduced as an optional subject and foreign language until 1952 (Ager 1990: 54).

The 1950s witnessed some degree of tolerance towards regional languages, namely in the form of the Deixonne Law, which allowed for optional teaching in these languages (see Section 5.4). Nonetheless, these measures did little to stave off the claims of political and especially economic marginalisation made by many regionalists in the 1960s–1970s (see also Section 5.1.2), as manifested in works such as Lafont's *La Révolution régionaliste* (1967) and Jean-François Gravier's *Paris et le désert français en 1972* (1972). In the most extreme cases, terrorist groups were formed (e.g. *le Front de libération de la Bretagne, le Front de libération de la Corse, Iparretarak* in the Basque Country) which demanded outright independence from France (Nguyen 1998: 110).[7]

The economic and political demands of regionalists sought strength in cultural and linguistic arguments. These arguments formed the basis of a strategy of social creativity, which re-appraised regional languages and exploited their symbolic power.

> The function of language changes. It is no longer only the guarantee, the proof of an identity, it also becomes a propaganda tool, a lever of cultural change. Rejected, scorned, oppressed by *bourgeois* culture, sociologically reserved for the subordinate classes, it becomes in a sense revolutionary by nature, a sign of the rejection of the dominant ideology. Hence the blossoming of a new, minority literature, with a new form and content: song, street theatre... (Martel 1987: 134)

Despite the multiplication in the 1970s of private schools which provided tuition in regional languages (e.g. *ikastolas* in the Basque Country, *bressolas* in Catalan-speaking Roussillon, *calandretas* in Occitania, and *diwans* in Brittany), there was a lack of real institutional support for these languages. The prospect of a Socialist president in 1981 brought hope that there would be a change in this situation; indeed before the regional convention of the Socialist party in Brittany on 14 May 1981, Mitterrand declared:

> For the Socialists, it is clear: to strike a people in its language and culture is to wound it in the deepest part of its being. We proclaim the right to difference. [...] The time has come to open wide the doors of the school to these languages and cultures, to create regional radio and TV companies allowing for their broadcast; to accord them the full status which they merit in public life. (cited in Jacob and Gordon 1985: 128)

Following Mitterrand's election to the presidency, some degree of decentralisation occurred as promised in the form of the Defferre Law of 1983 (Safran 1989: 124). However, these measures did nothing to change the administrative divisions of France (Winock 1997: 58), in particular the 96 mostly arbitrarily formed departments which date back to the Revolution (Ardagh 1999: 296–197). According to Giordan (1992a: 16; 1992b: 138–9), the lack of a real political framework for regional minorities highlights the Socialists' exclusively cultural treatment of regional demands. In particular, he notes how his own report, *Démocratie culturelle et droit à la différence* (1982), had been put under the authority of the Minister for Culture, Jack Lang. Neither the Prime Minister nor the Minister of the Interior and Decentralisation were concerned with Giordan's recommendations, which remained on the whole largely unheeded.

Central to the construction of French identity in the national arena since the Revolution has been the rejection of the notion of minority group: 'In France, the logic of citizenship is opposed to that of minorities' (Schnapper 1994: 189). At the 1918 conference of Versailles, a diplomat representing France claimed with conviction that: 'France had not signed any minorities treaty because she had no minorities' (cited in Jacob and Gordon 1985: 117). The International Covenant on Civil and Political Rights (1966), the annex to the United Nations Universal Declaration on Human Rights, was not ratified by France until 1980. Even then, this was only done on the condition that article 27, which guaranteed the right of minorities to practise their own language, religion, etc., would not apply to France (Grau 1992: 110–11). Before the Senate, the French Foreign Minister stated that:

> [a]rticle 27 only applies to states where minorities exist. Now such is not the case of France, since the principles of our public law, notably in article 2 of the Constitution, forbid distinctions amongst citizens on the grounds of their origin, their race and their religion.   (cited in Grau 1992: 110)

Article 2 — which later became article 1 — was also evoked by the *Conseil constitutionnel* in 1991, when it rejected article 1 of the National Assembly's proposed bill on the status of Corsica which spoke of a 'Corsican people, a constituent part of the French people' (Nguyen 1998: 98–9). The Toubon Law of 1994 (see Section 7.3) also entailed a rejection of the notion of minority. As Ager (1996a: 167) points out, much of the parliamentary debate surrounding the law notably created a new understanding: 'regional languages were part of French heritage, and many terms and expressions from them (for example culinary and gastronomic specialities) were accepted by the minister as being in effect French.' The idea that regional languages were the property of France as a whole, as opposed to the regional minorities which spoke them, was in fact already evident in 1975, at the time of the Bas-Lauriol Law (see Section 7.3). During similar parliamentary debates, it was proposed that words from regional languages should not be considered foreign, as were those from English, thus reducing the potential grounds for regionalist demands (Giordan 1992b: 140). The same assessment was to reappear in 1999, in the context of the debate surrounding the European Charter for Regional or Minority Languages (see Section 5.4).

At the time of writing, the issue of regional minorities and languages has again found itself on the political agenda as a result of Prime Minister Lionel Jospin's suggestion to grant a limited degree of autonomy to Corsica. One of the measures which has been proposed is to provide teaching of the Corsican language to all students in nursery and primary schools, except in the case of parental objection (Propositions du government soumises aux représentants des élus de la Corse 2000). The bill has led to in a lively debate in political circles and in the media, with many commentators (e.g. Kessel 2000) claiming that the French Republic and its founding values are under severe threat. The Socialist government's determination to get the bill passed has already resulted in the resignation of the Jacobin-minded Interior Minister, Jean-Pierre Chevènement (*Libération*, 30 August 2000). President Chirac is still trying to hinder the bill from becoming law and the issue of Corsica looks set to become a key factor in the 2002 presidential elections (*Libération*, 22 February 2001).

Regional minorities may well have been traditionally denied their existence by the French state; but this is only a reflection of the important role they have played in the construction of French national identity. Few people could seriously disagree with Hagège's (1987: 236) claim that regional languages no longer constitute a danger for French, that they no longer can be considered as rivals for the national language. Yet it is not these languages themselves which are a threat so much as what they represent. Founded on civic principles, the French conception of the nation does not claim to emanate from any one part of the country, but rather to represent the whole. At the time of decolonisation, France and many other European powers had to come to terms with losing part of their identity, which until then had been associated with the whole of their empires. In a similar fashion, quite apart from the question of independence, what would be left of French identity if its regions developed their own, distinctive identities? What would be left of French identity if it was no longer associated with the whole?[8] Indeed, according to the Anglo-Saxon research tradition, France is itself denied the very notion which it claims to have invented: 'France and many other continental countries are clearly not nation-states, containing as they do many groups' (Edwards 1985: 15). It is difficult to reconcile Renan's notion of a 'daily plebiscite' (see Section 2.2.1) with the many forced territorial annexations which have resulted in modern-day France. Equally difficult to accept is Renan's (1990: 16) claim that: '[a]n honourable fact about France is that she has never sought to win unity of language by coercive measures.' For this reason, Citron (1991: 8) stresses the need for a re-conceptualisation of the French nation, which rejects 'the too easy recourse to Renan's definition.' Such a major reconsideration of French national identity is all the more desirable since it would also alleviate many of the ideological problems concerned with immigration.

5.2.2   Immigrant minorities

The area which corresponds to present-day France has a long tradition of immigration. While in the beginning, this immigration often took the form of invasions, from the twelfth century onwards, it was economic, political and religious factors which resulted in the arrival in France of many different ethnic groups (Bernard 1998: 14–15). This immigration was to take on enormous proportions from the second half of the nineteenth century, when neighbouring countries provided the vast pool of unskilled labour which France needed during the industrial revolution. At a time when the Third Republic was embarking on policies of national homogenisation spurred on by the threat from Germany (see Section 4.2), Belgians, Luxemburgers, Italians and even Germans were arriving *en masse* in France to complement the local workforce which was suffering from a falling birthrate (Bernard 1998: 16). In later years, it was the turn of groups from further afield, such as the Poles who arrived around the turn of the century and between the two World Wars (Ager 1990: 154). The presence of Poles and other ethnic groups was not without its problems: the themes of invasion, unassimilability and barbarianism appeared frequently in the literature of the time (Bernard 1998: 19). Yet these groups did eventually assimilate, often with the help of the Catholic Church, workers' parties and trade unions (Nguyen 1998: 94).

The assimilation of the next wave of immigrants was to prove significantly more difficult. As in previous years, the immigrants of European origin, notably Portuguese, who arrived following World War II, eventually blended into the amalgam of ethnic groups which constitute the French nation (Bernard 1998: 21). This was not the case of those originating from the Maghreb countries, from Sub-Saharan Africa and from Asia, who were clearly distinguished from the dominant French ethnic group by their physiognomies, cultures and religions (Nguyen 1998: 94). In many cases, assimilation was rendered all the more difficult, or rather undesirable, by the fact that many had migrated from former French colonies, bringing with them a tradition of conflict and humiliation (Bernard 1998: 128).

With the oil crisis beginning in 1973 and the subsequent end of the *Trente Glorieuses* (1945–74), immigration was officially suspended in 1974 (Ager 1997: 71). As Safran (1991: 231) notes:

it was beginning with that period that the Maghrebi presence insinuated itself fully into the consciousness of the French population in general, as it became clear that the overwhelming majority of the immigrants would remain in France permanently.

Faced with the claimed inassimilability of Maghrebi immigrants in particular, and in line with international trends, a solution was sought in cultural pluralism (see Section 5.1.3). Through his celebration of *le droit à la différence* (see Section 5.2.1), presidential candidate Mitterrand pledged to abolish the 'discrimination affecting immigrant workers', to ensure 'the equality of rights', and to grant local election voting rights to foreigners who had resided in France for at least five years (Bernard 1998: 84). On the question of voting rights, Mitterrand met continual resistance amongst the French public. Yet many of his other pledges were realised following his election in 1981, such as the previously denied opportunity for immigrants to form associations (e.g. local sports clubs and charities) along ethnic lines (Safran 1989: 131; Ardagh 1999: 227). In effect, many associations formed along ethnic lines existed even before this date, but they increased in number dramatically thereafter: for example, in the Portuguese community, the number of associations jumped from 101 in 1975 to 900 in 1982 (Varro 1992: 149).

In particular, the Left attacked the ethnocidal nature of the Jacobin tradition, rejecting the notion of assimilation, which implied the absorption or negation of the immigrant Other. As a replacement, the term 'insertion' became widespread in the early 1980s to designate the acceptance of immigrants without the confiscation of their own identities (Bernard 1998: 130). However, following the *affaire du foulard islamique* (the 'Islamic headscarf affair')[9] in 1989, emphasis was placed on the concept of 'integration' in order to stress that immigrants as well as the host society had to respect the integrity of the whole (Bernard 1998: 131; cf. also Schnapper 1998b: 407–8). The notion of integration was more precisely defined in 1991 by the *Haut conseil à l'intégration*, which affirmed that the French conception of integration 'should obey a logic of equality and not a logic of minority' (cited in Bernard 1998: 132).

This conception of integration is a product of the uniquely French model of the civic nation or what has also been termed the French 'myth of inclusion' (Ager 1999: 86–7). In accordance with this model or myth, a distinction between the private and public spheres is of key importance. In the private sphere, individuals are free to express their ethnic, religious and/or linguistic identities, while in the public sphere, unity, equality and universality of citizenship should be observed (Schnapper 1998b: 186–7). Schnapper (1998a:

37) admits that the distinction between the public and private spheres is not always straightforward. For example, to which sphere belong the issues of forced marriages, excision and education? Nonetheless, the French conception of integration is seen as a unique principle which should be upheld, not least because it contributes to a positive French identity *vis-à-vis* certain Others. In particular, the French model is opposed to the multiculturalism or *communautarisation* of the 'Anglo-Saxon' approach, which is said simply to reinforce social inequalities, such as those which lead to the formation of ethnic ghettos (Schnapper 1994, 1998a, 1998b; Nguyen 1998: 97–102; cf. also Ager 1996a: 99). For this reason, the notion of 'affirmative action' is staunchly rejected in France (Schnapper 1998b: 411): in accordance with article 1 of the Constitution, there should be no discrimination — either positive or negative — on the grounds of origin, race or religion (Grau 1992: 99; Section 5.2.1).

There are nevertheless a number of theoretical and practical problems inherent in the French model of integration or myth of inclusion. Some critics highlight its abusive association of equality with the arbitrary demand for national unity (Giordan 1992a: 16). Others point out that civic models of the French type often conceal *de facto* inequalities (Rouland 1991: 224; Varro 1992: 143; see also Section 5.1.3). Others still emphasise that the French state's denial of a minimum degree of non-French ethnicity in the public domain may in fact encourage groups to stress their particular ethnic identities all the more (Bernard 1998: 134). The French model of integration is also faced with a number of practical difficulties. Ager (1999: 86–7) points out that the French myth of inclusion today does not respond to the conditions of modern society, one characteristic of which is mass immigration. And while the French civic ideology or myth of inclusion may still have supporters at the official level, this is not necessarily the case at the grassroots level, where French identity is often conceived in ethnic terms. Ardagh (1999: 225) gives the example of the '*de facto* discrimination practised by white residents of HLMs, who will try to move out of a block if it becomes too full of immigrants. This has tended sometimes to create Maghrebi or black ghettos, which the official French policy of integration expressly seeks to avoid.'[10] He summarises the situation as follows:

> The State promotes an integration which the public then obstructs; the public stresses cultural differences which the State refuses to recognize. [. . .] On the one hand the State regards all citizens as equal, with the same full rights, and turns a blind eye to any distinctions between them of race or culture. But the French public, in its mass, does *not* regard immigrants as fully or equally French, and will constantly remind them of their otherness.   (Ardagh 1999: 225)

Not only is French identity usually conceived in ethnic terms at the grassroots level, this is also often the case at the official level. When Schnapper (1994:98) and other defenders of the French model of integration struggle in the name of national unity against the '"ethnisation" of public life', they forget that the public sphere in France is already founded on the ethnic identity of the dominant group. Citron (1991) examines the very ethnic version of French history taught in schools, and offers the following reply to the question 'Can Mohammed be a good Frenchman?' posed by *L'Évènement du Jeudi* (13 June 1985): 'Surely not if we are content to impose a Gaulish past upon him!' (Citron 1991:177).

The inability of the theoretically defined French model to manage the ethnic reality of life in France in the 1980s–1990s only exacerbated the French identity crisis which began in the 1970s (see Section 4.2). Opinion was divided on how best to overcome this problem: while orthodox Gaullists and most Communists favoured traditional Jacobinism, the majority of Socialists and many centrist-progressive Giscardists advocated a new ethnic pluralism (Safran 1989:144–5). This ideological cleavage was reflected in intellectual debates. In its *L'Identité française* (1985), the left-wing *Espaces 89* political club pushed for a pluralistic France which distinguished between citizenship and nationality (or ethnicity). At the other extreme, the right-wing *Club de l'Horloge* attacked the notion of multiculturalism in its *L'Identité de la France* (1985), arguing that 'the "difference" of young immigrants constitutes the very negation of France' (Harouel 1985:206).

As attested by the breakthrough of the extreme-right *Front national* in the mid-1980s, the immigrant Other was clearly perceived as a threat by many in France. To be sure, the rise in racist discrimination and violence observed from the 1980s has also been directed at other ethnic groups, such as the Jews (e.g. the bombing of a synagogue in Paris in 1980, and the desecration of Jewish graves in Carpentras in 1990 and in Perpignan in 1993; cf. Gildea 1996:137). But as argued in Section 5.1.3, the Jews — along with the Gypsies and Armenians — constitute specific cases as there is nothing new about their presence on French soil: Jews were present in France from the fourth century, Gypsies from the fifteenth century and Armenians from the 1920s (Ager 1990:144, 148, 152). More threatening for French identity are the Maghrebis who, by settling in France, have overturned the spatial relations between the centre and the periphery established by colonialism (Evans 1996:46).

> The more those who were formally subordinate tend towards assimilation, the more those who dominated attempt to recreate a distance founded on nature.
> (Bernard 1998:170).

The dominant group hardens its boundaries in order to protect its socioeconomic privileges. Maghrebis have thus become the scapegoats for unemployment, criminality and the ailing social welfare system (Safran 1991: 231), while the notion of *droit à la différence* has been reformulated by the extreme right to claim that immigrants are inassimilable and therefore needed to be deported (Bernard 1998: 86–7 and 130). Much of the fear on the part of the dominant group has stemmed from a perception that France was being 'invaded' by immigrants. Yet analysis of statistics from the last three decades reveals a high degree of consistency in the percentage of the population with non-French citizenship: 6.5 per cent in 1975, 6.8 per cent in 1982 and approximately the same in 1997 (Ager 1997: 71). Nonetheless, the Pasqua laws of 1993 demonstrated a clear desire to harden the boundaries of French identity, by tightening immigration, increasing police checks of immigrants and reforming French citizenship legislation (Bernard 1998: 93).

French citizenship laws have always demonstrated a mixture of *jus soli* and *jus sanguinis* principles (see Section 2.2.1). The former stem from the ideals of the initial years of the Revolution, when France even adopted foreigners such as Friedrich von Schiller, Tomas Payne, Jeremy Bentham, George Washington and William Wilberforce (Hettne, Sörlin and Østergård 1998: 248). As for *jus sanguinis* principles, they were encompassed especially in the civil (or Napoleonic) code of 1804.

> After the revolutionary wars and confrontation with foreign powers, filiation ('*jus sanguinis*') is considered as the best guarantee of national unity. (Bernard 1998: 27)

The laws of 1851 and 1889 expanded the *jus soli* dimension for military purposes, that is to allow for the recruitment of children born in France to foreign parents (Schnapper 1994: 67). But the ethnic conception of French identity was to resurface in the Pasqua-Debré law of 1993 which required children born in France to foreign parents to make a formal request for French citizenship between the ages of 16 and 21 (Nguyen 1998: 29). Not until 1997, with the new Socialist government, did the *jus soli* principle again come to dominate, granting automatic citizenship for these children at 18, or from 13 years of age upon request. Yet the acquisition of French citizenship, even that founded on *jus soli*, seldom suffices to be truly considered as French (Taboada-Léonetti 1998: 31). Bernard (1998: 174) highlights 'the ambiguity of the French situation which claims to not take ethnic categories into account, while at the same time accepting to manipulate them without limitation or restriction (*sans cadre ni sanction*).' This exploitation of ethnic differences has become all the more frequent because the *de facto* hegemony of the ethnic core has been disrupted by the refusal of immigrants to accept the lack of official recognition which has traditionally sought to lock them into an inferior status.

As a potent symbol of ethnic and national identity, it comes as no surprise that language plays a key role in reinforcing these differences, in maintaining a boundary between immigrants and the dominant ethnic core.

> Even when he is legally and administratively accepted, the foreigner is not for all that accepted into [French] families. His untoward usage of the French language discredits him, consciously or not, in the eyes of the natives who identify themselves more than in other countries with their polished and cherished speech.
> (Kristeva 1988: 58)

Kristeva's reference to 'polished and cherished speech' evokes the *sur-norme* tradition which has dominated in France since the seventeenth century (see Sections 4.1 and 4.2). Of course many immigrants in France, especially those from Sub-Saharan Africa and the Maghreb, already speak French, but often a variety which is at odds with the ethnocentric, prescriptive conception of the norm which prevails in France. This prescriptivism offers a convenient shield for the dominant ethnic group, a means of discriminating against immigrants. In the same way as language use amongst some members of the police force reinforces the inferior status of immigrants in Australia (Gibbons 1990; see Section 3.2.5.2), the particular variety of French taught in French schools serves as an obstacle for children of immigrant or even lower-class backgrounds.

> School French, highly standardised (*normé*), disadvantages children from (French or foreign) families where the parents do not speak this type of French.
> (Varro 1992: 143)

In addition, there are those children who were born in France, whose mother tongue is standard French, but whose parents are immigrants. In this case, the frequent reference to second- or third-generation immigrants, when these children are clearly not immigrants, is a means of excluding this category of individuals from the dominant ethnic group, of 'locking them into a largely artificial cultural difference' (Bernard 1998: 170; cf. also Varro 1992: 138–9). As a counter-reaction, many young people in this situation have turned to social creativity, transforming their bicultural 'predicament' into a new, positive *Beur* identity.[11] What is important to remember is that the linguistic differences between *Beur* culture and French culture are predominantly symbolic. Indeed *Radio Beur* addresses itself to those young people who speak little Arabic or Berber (Jerab 1988: 47).

Much of the discrimination on the part of the dominant ethnic group stems from a lack of information in France about the use of languages other than French. No language questions were included in the censuses of 1975, 1982 or 1990, although questions on synchronic and diachronic language use were planned for a 1999 census amongst 400,000 people to study the history of the family (Haut conseil de la Francophonie 1999: 324). While they may not be founded on any real knowledge, the opinions which do circulate about other languages spoken in France serve an important discursive function for the construction of French national identity.

> The general ignorance of the language situation in France has generated ideas concerning different language or varieties of languages and their speakers which can only be analysed in terms of categorisation or discrimination. (Varro 1992: 141)

In the context of newly arrived immigrant children, these language attitudes sometimes take the form of a devaluation of bilingualism. While the term bilingualism is reserved for more prestigious languages and for children of more favoured socio-economic classes, school heads and teachers often speak of 'semilingualism' to refer to what they consider to be an insufficient command amongst immigrant children of both the home and host language, despite being unqualified to judge the children's competence in their mother tongue (Varro 1992: 141; see also Sections 5.3.1 and 5.3.2).

The inability of the theoretically founded French model to manage alternative ethnolinguistic identities has prompted calls for France to adopt a more realistic approach (e.g. Giordan 1992a: 11; Bernard 1998: 134). Such a major change of perspective would not be easy and would eliminate one of the cornerstones of French identity, at a time when the *exception française* is already suffering from further globalisation and European integration (see Sections 6.3, 6.5, 7.3 and 7.5). Fears that the French model is in crisis are no doubt responsible for some of the racism observed in France: only 29 per cent of those surveyed in a Louis Harris opinion poll released in March 2000 declared themselves to be 'not racist' (*The Guardian Weekly*, 22–8 June 2000). But other surveys have led to more optimistic results: while in 1991, 44 per cent of respondents agreed with the statement 'I think one is more comfortable amongst French people', this figure had dropped to 28 per cent by 1998 (*Le Monde*, 15–16 August 1999).

There are some signs that ethnic diversity is gradually being incorporated into the French national myth through recognition rather than denial. Immigrant cultures and languages are already closely associated with aspects of French culture which touch the lives of young people, such as French youth language and rap music (Hagège 1996: 164–7; Goudaillier 1998: 18–22). Another example is the French football team which won the World Cup in July 1998. Recognised as the most ethnically diverse in the competition, this team included players from West Africa, the Maghreb, Armenia, the French overseas departments and territories (DOM-TOM) as well as from the numerous regions within the *Hexagone*. Calls were even heard from supporters for one player, Zinedine Zidane, originally of the Kabyle minority in Algeria, to become President of France (Ardagh 1999: 220). More recently, France's victory in the Euro 2000 championships provoked similar reactions, as attested by one French journalist's claim that there now exists a 'cosmopolitan patriotism' in France (*Le Nouvel Observateur*, no. 1861, 6–12 July 2000). Such examples of overt recognition and acceptance of the ethnic diversity of France may well signal the decline of the French model, but this need not entail the end of the French nation as some scholars would have us believe (e.g. Schnapper 1994: 11). Indeed, the very future of the French nation in the twenty-first century may well lie in its creative ability to incorporate the ethnic reality of all French citizens — from both ethnic minorities and the dominant group — into the civic myth of French identity. Perhaps as a first step to overcoming the 'unconscious immigrant country' syndrome (Schnapper 1991: 13), France would benefit from remembering the words of the late François Mitterrand, pronounced during an address at the Sorbonne in 1987:

> We are all a bit Roman, a bit Germanic, a bit Jewish, a bit Italian, a bit Spanish and more and more Portuguese. I wonder if we are not already a bit Arab. (*Le Monde*, 20 May 1987)

5.3 Language and national identity in Sweden: The national arena

As in France in the years following the Revolution, the consolidation of the Swedish nation-state which began in earnest during the Romanticist movement (see Section 4.3) led to the disregard, if not outright denial, of the ethnolinguistic Others which had for centuries inhabited the country (Hyltenstam 1999a: 12). Sweden considered itself one of the most ethnolinguistically homogenous states in Europe: indeed, in the Swedish census of 1930, less than 1 per cent of population was of 'foreign stock', and this figure included the Sámi and Finnish-speaking regional minorities in the north

(Runblom 1995: 313). Yet just as it was in France, this myth was challenged by the arrival of significant numbers of immigrants from the 1950s. This section examines the construction of Swedish national identity, and in particular the role played by language in that process, first in terms of the two main regional minorities in Sweden (Section 5.3.1), then in relation to immigrant minorities, especially those which arrived following World War II (Section 5.3.2).

5.3.1   Regional minorities

The territory which is today known as Sweden has long been home to two other languages spoken in the north: Sámi and Finnish. The division of the world into nation-states resulted in the dispersal of the Sámi nation — or *sápmi* to use the indigenous term — over four states: Finland, Norway, Russia and Sweden. Similarly, it was geopolitical factors which divided the inhabitants of the Torne Valley or Tornedalians from their Finnish-speaking brethren, namely when the border was drawn between Sweden and Russia following the war of 1808–9 (see Figure 5.5).[12]

From the early seventeenth century, attempts were made to control the Sámi homelands or *lappmarkerna*. Missionaries endeavoured to drive out the Sámi religion through assimilationist education policies which remained nevertheless largely unsuccessful. In 1606, 16 Sámi boys were sent to Uppsala to train as priests, with the intention that they would return and preach amongst their people. The story goes that the majority fled during the journey there, and that of the few who arrived, none became a priest (SOU 1990: 72). In 1632, the *Skytteanska lappskolan* was founded in Lycksele with a similar purpose of producing *kateketer* or peripatetic teachers of Sámi origin, whose main responsibility would be to convert other Sámi to Christianity (Ruong 1975: 386). Although the school was active for two hundred years (Ruong 1982: 59), the initial decision to establish fifteen schools in the *lappmarkerna* appears never to have been implemented (Uppman 1978: 61; cf. also Wingstedt 1998: 38). In a country where the Church and the state had been associated since the Reformation, it was only natural that the two were to collude for common purposes (Salvesen 1995: 122; Hettne, Sörlin and Østergård 1998: 223–35). Religion thus played an important role in the Swedish authorities' attempt to gain supremacy in a region rich in natural resources and where borders had not yet been formerly established.

Although the Swedish language soon came to dominate in this region, the attitude of the Swedish authorities towards Sámi as well as Finnish was

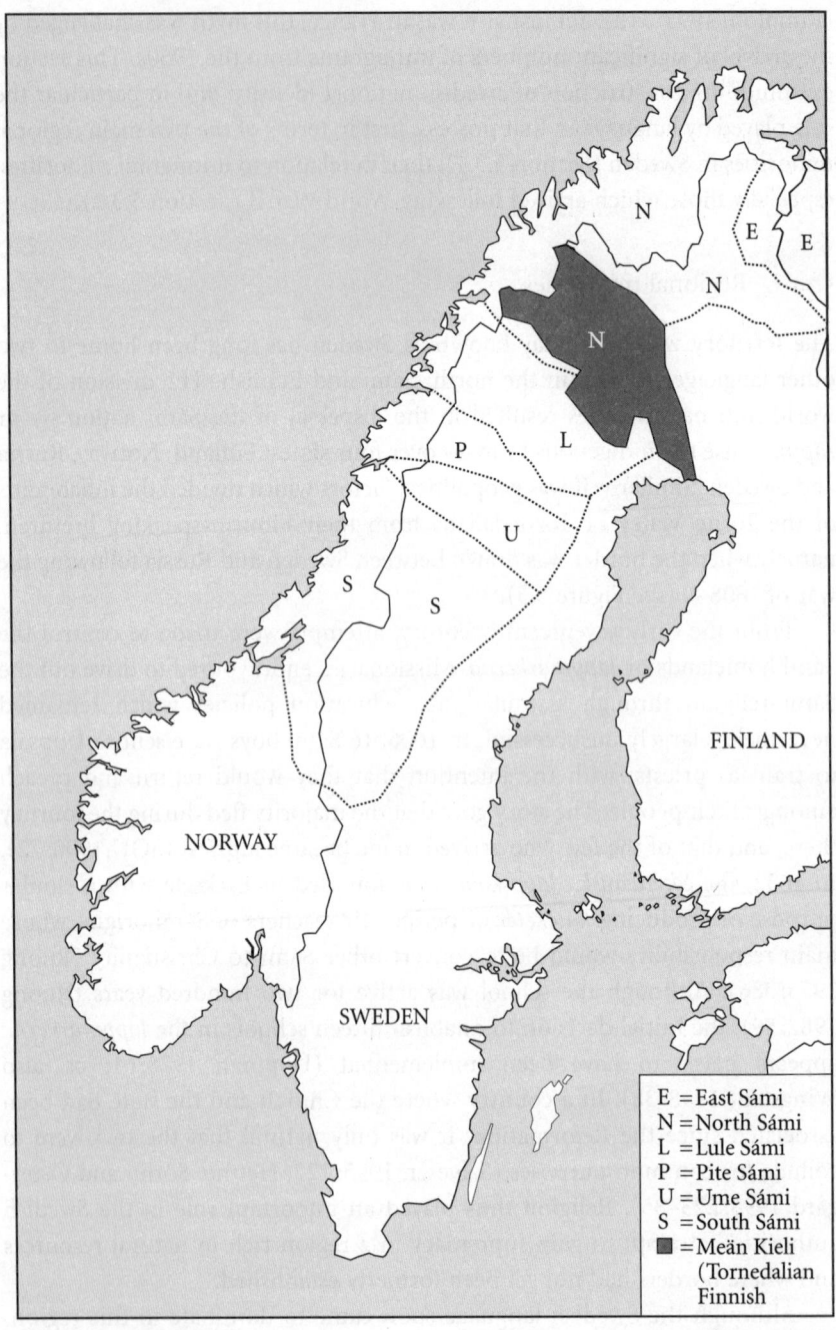

Figure 5.5 Regional languages of Sweden. (Adapted from Westergren and Åhl 1997, no page given)

one of 'indifferent tolerance' (Wingstedt 1998:78). Both these languages were readily employed by the Church, for example in the so-called 'Lapp schools' which came into being with the Royal Ordinance of 1723 (Hyltenstam, Stroud and Svonni 1999:65). Interpreters and translators were also provided in various public domains (e.g. legal courts). Yet the recourse to bilingualism was not so much an end in itself as a means of controlling the Sámi and the Tornedalians of ensuring loyalty to religion (Christianity) and to the state (Wingstedt 1998:75).

By the end of the nineteenth century, attitudes towards language were no longer the result of pragmatic or instrumental considerations, but rather reflected the symbolic role which Swedish had come to play as a factor unifying the nation. The 'second ecolinguistic revolution' had transformed Swedish from a state language into a national language (see Section 4.3). With the development of Swedish linguistic and national identity came a more clearly defined assimilationist policy, in particular for the Tornedalians. This minority not only posed an economic threat, competing as it did with Swedish settlers in the region; but like the Alsatians in France (see Section 5.2.1), the Tornedalians were also considered a security risk on account of their linguistic links with Finns on the other side of the border, who were under Russian control from 1809 (Arnstberg and Ehn 1976:97 and 99; Wingstedt 1998:67). Concerning the language of instruction in Tornedalian education, the translation method of the past, which employed a mixture of Finnish and Swedish, was now replaced with the direct method, which advocated instruction totally in Swedish (Wande 1988:403).

While the Tornedalians suffered from assimilationist policies implemented out of nationalist concerns, the Sámi were subjected to segregationism in line with the racial-biological thinking of the time: social Darwinism regarded the Sámi as unsuitable for modern life and claimed that they would only fall into drunkenness and poverty if attempts were made to modernise them (Wingstedt 1998:53). A good example of the 'Lapps should be Lapps' mentality of the time was the establishment of nomad schools in 1913. While these peripatetic schools were suited to the nomadic lifestyle of the reindeer herding mountain Sámi, they excluded other non-reindeer herding Sámi and therefore cannot be regarded as an overall positive experience for the teaching of Sámi language and culture (Hyltenstam, Stroud and Svonni 1999:65–6). The reasons for the different treatment of the Sámi and the Tornedalians were also of an economic order: it was in the interest of the Swedish state to promote the survival of reindeer husbandry, since it provided an added source of fiscal revenue (Wingstedt 1998:76). Yet even this industry would find it difficult to survive growing industrialisation and urbanisation. Mining, forestry and in time hydroelectricity were to attract great numbers of ethnic Swedish settlers to the north and increase the control of the dominant core over the periphery (Hyltenstam, Stroud and Svonni 1999: 60–1). The dominance of the Swedish language also increased: in 1925 it became the official language of instruction in Sámi schooling (SOU 1975: 178). Sámi children were also forbidden from speaking their language at school (Wingstedt 1998: 77), in the same way that the Tornedalians had been from the latter part of the previous century. An obvious parallel also exists with efforts to stamp out regional languages in schools in France (see Section 5.2.1).

The attitude of the dominant group towards regional minorities, and in particular the Sámi, thus wavered between segregation and assimilation. However, it should be noted that both these approaches had the same goal of preserving the ethnic homogeneity of the dominant group, of preventing minority group members from gaining access to the centre of power (Wingstedt 1998: 81; Hyltenstam 1999a: 54–5). At first glance, it may appear that this ethnocentric stance clashed with the notion of democracy, which spread throughout Sweden in the nineteenth and twentieth centuries. However, as in France, democracy assumed more of a theoretical than practical dimension in the context of ethnolinguistic minorities. The segregationist policies implemented towards the Sámi can be compared with Giordan's (1992b: 130–2) claim in France, that the language policies of the Revolution did not so much seek to eradicate regional languages as reinforce the inferior status of their speakers (see Section 5.2.1). As for the assimilationist policies directed towards both the Sámi and the Tornedalians, these offered real chances for social mobility only in theory. In the same way that the French model of integration conceals *de facto* inequalities behind a superficial homogenous front (see Section 5.2.2), the Swedish conception of equality is associated with similarity or uniformity, as indicated by the Swedish word *jämlikhet* ('equality', literally 'even' + 'sameness') (Daun 1996: 181). Of course being the same meant being the same as the dominant group. By associating political loyalty and reliability with the assimilation and homogenisation of citizens, democracy was thus used as an instrument for strengthening national identity: 'responsible citizens presupposed a process of homogenisation where countrymen [and women] learnt to speak the same cultural language' (Löfgren 1993: 54). A good linguistic example is a report from 1939 entitled the *Gothenberg Dialect and the School*, in which practical advice was given to rid dialectal features from the speech of pupils (Andersson 1985: 150–3).

The link between democracy and nationalism became particularly potent with the arrival of social democracy in Sweden in the late 1920s–1930s (see Section 4.3).

> However paradoxical it may sound, the social democratic hegemony and class struggle has been a double-edged sword for minorities. Democratic principles have often taken on the formulation *the same treatment for everyone*, while minorities need *the same possibilities* for everyone. The latter principle takes into consideration the characteristics and needs of minorities, the former assumes the perspective of the dominant group. (Lainio 1999: 158)

Central to maintaining this apparent 'equality' in Sweden has been the role of the welfare state. Following Baldwin (1990), Hettne, Sörlin and Østergård (1998: 213) note that the social democratic welfare state is not a product of a conscious social democratic policy during the 1930s and the 1950s, so much as a continuation of the paternalistic and conservative thinking of the latter part of the nineteenth century (Hettne, Sörlin and Østergård 1998: 213). So integral a part of the nation-building process was the Swedish welfare state that one can even speak of a 'welfare nationalism' with its own myths and heroes (Löfgren 1993: 57; see also Section 4.3).

The late 1950s signalled a change in attitude on the part of the dominant ethnic group towards a more humanitarian view of ethnolinguistic minorities. Through the *Nomadskoleutredning* (Nomad School Inquiry) of 1957, Sámi children now had a choice between nomad schools (later Sámi schools) and general comprehensive schools (Hyltenstam, Stroud and Svonni 1999: 66). By the 1960s–1970s, there had been a definite shift towards more pluralistic policies. The ban on speaking Finnish and Sámi in schools was lifted (Wingstedt 1998: 76), and it was at this time that the concept of ethnicity was first used to define the Sámi nation, so that all members of this group — not just reindeer herders — could benefit from protective legislation (Hyltenstam, Stroud and Svonni 1999: 55).

1968 witnessed the publication of Nils-Erik Hansegård's *Tvåspråkighet eller halvspråkighet?* (Bilingualism or semilingualism?), in which it was claimed that Tornedalians suffered from double semilingualism. By this, Hansegård meant that assimilationist policies had obstructed the Torndedalians from acquiring full competence in their own language, while education policies unsuited to speakers of other languages had led to their learning Swedish in a superficial and insufficient way (cf. also Skutnabb-Kangas 1981). The notion of semilingualism was to receive much criticism throughout the 1970s and 80s on both empirical and theoretical grounds (e.g. Loman 1974; Wande 1977; Stroud

1978; Hyltenstam and Stroud 1982; Stroud and Wingstedt 1989). Looking back on the debate sparked by his observations, Hansegård (1997) claims that he was greatly misunderstood, that the notion of semilingualism was not intended to be a scientific term, but rather a means of drawing the attention of the dominant group and of the Swedish authorities to the plight of the Tornedalians, and by extension to that of the Sámi. Yet Hansegård's intention was quickly overshadowed by an issue which was clearly of greater importance to the Swedes: immigration. Not only was the semilingualism theory 'hijacked' by both sides of the immigration debate (see Section 5.3.2 below), it was largely only because of the presence of immigrants that children belonging to regional minorities eventually gained the right to learn their own language at school through the Home Language Reform of 1977 (Huss and Lindgren 1999: 313; Hyltenstam 1999a: 12; see Section 5.4 below).

To be fair, some positive measures have been taken to protect the rights specifically of regional minorities and attempt to put a halt to language shift to Swedish which was well advanced (Hyltenstam and Stroud 1991). For example, two official inquiries concerning the Sámi, *Sameutredningen* (SOU 1975a; 1975b) and *Samerättsutredningen* (SOU 1990), led to the establishment of a chair in Sámi at Umeå university in 1971, increased support for the Sámi school board to develop teaching materials and methods, as well as the founding of the *Sametinget* or *Sámediggi* in Sámi (Sámi Parliament) in 1993 (Hyltenstam 1999a: 13–14). It was the *Sametinget* which resulted in language becoming one of two key elements in the definition of a Sámi, in particular for the purposes of identifying those eligible to stand for membership (Svonni 1996: 105). This definition, which has become widely accepted today, includes all those who consider themselves Sámi and who have Sámi as a home language, or whose parents or grandparents were Sámi-speaking (Hyltenstam 1999a: 53; cf. also Svonni 1996: 113–14).

Much of the progress made especially over the last decade has been the result of pressure by regional minorities, who from the 1970s have demonstrated an increasing degree of ethnic awareness (Huss and Lindgren 1999: 301). Both the Tornedalians and the Sámi have turned to social creativity to generate a positive identity: while the Tornedalians are demanding that Meän Kieli be considered a language in its own right (Hyltenstam 1999b: 30–1; see also Section 2.3), the Sámi are re-evaluating elements of their culture and history, for example through the modern, joik-based compositions of Marie Boine,[13] or the films of Paul Anders Simmas (Hyltenstam, Stroud and Svonni 1999: 83; cf. also Lainio 1999: 143).

Such efforts certainly serve to generate a positive identity for regional minorities themselves, but it is debatable how much effect they have on the attitudes of ethnic Swedes towards regional minorities and their languages. For example, the dominant group does not hesitate to exploit expressions of Sámi culture for its own purposes (e.g. to attract foreign tourists). Multiculturalism may well have become the new catch phrase in Sweden from the 1960s–1970s, but on the whole it has amounted to little more than the mere recognition of Sweden's ethnolinguistic diversity (Hyltenstam, Stroud and Svonni 1999: 56). This conception of pluralism is identical to the purely cultural treatment of *le droit à la différence* observed in France and criticised by Giordan (see Section 5.2.1). Even the more recent attempts at real, structural pluralism in Sweden have had little success in engendering a truly pluralistic, multilingual ideology amongst a wider public, where an assimilationist, monolingual ideology still appears to dominate (Sjögren 1996: 22; Wingstedt 1998: 81 and 341; Huss and Lindgren 1999: 311). Much of the problem can be explained in terms of the ethnic grounding of Swedish identity. As seen in Section 5.1.3, the imposition of multicultural policies from above does not imply that these will be incorporated into the national myth as constructed at the grassroots level. Indeed, observations at the time of writing point to a revival of Swedish ethnonationalism (see Sections 4.3 and 4.4), much of which is a reaction to the presence of a growing number of immigrants.

5.3.2   Immigrant minorities

Like France, Sweden has a long tradition of immigration. As far back as the twelfth century, German merchants established themselves on Gotland, an island off the east coast of Sweden. By the fourteenth century, predominantly as a result of the Hanseatic League,[14] the albeit relatively small German presence in Sweden had become very powerful, with a number of positions in government held by Germans. German was on the way to becoming the official bureaucratic language in Stockholm when calls were heard for the country to be run by Swedes (Arnstberg and Ehn 1976: 19). The sixteenth century saw the migration of a large number of Finns from the eastern part of the kingdom to work in the mines and forests (de Geer and Wande 1988: 94). As the forests were opened up for exploitation, most Finns were assimilated so that today toponyms are the only linguistic traces of their presence (Vikør 1993: 86). In the seventeenth century, it was the Walloons who came to work in the foundries, threatening their Swedish co-workers with better paid jobs, high literacy rates and the ability to speak the same language (i.e. French) as the foundry owners (Arnstberg and Ehn 1976: 33). In the eighteenth and early nineteenth centuries, it was the turn of Estonian peasants (both Estonian and Swedish-speaking) who were fleeing German oppression to find their way to Sweden (Raag 1988: 58). After this time, immigration all but ceased; for nearly a century Sweden was a country of emigration (Johnsson 1995: 21).

During the interwar period, Swedish attitudes towards immigration were far from positive. Much talk centred on the desire to preserve ethnic homogeneity, as witnessed by slogans such as 'Sweden for the Swedes' (Runblom 1995: 293). Not until the mid-1940s did these attitudes begin to become more favourable. As a non-aligned country during World War II, Sweden welcomed Estonian refugees following the Soviet invasion of Estonia in 1944 (Raag 1988: 59),[15] while the activities of Swedish diplomat Raoul Wallenberg in Budapest allowed for the immigration to Sweden of tens of thousands Jews in 1944 and 1945 (Runblom 1995: 294). Sweden's neutral status also had the advantage of protecting the country's production machinery. Swedish industry was prepared for economic expansion, and Sweden was consequently one of the first countries to open up its borders to immigrant labour at the end of World War II (Runblom 1995: 286). Unlike the immigrants of the past, who on the whole were not substantially culturally distant from the Swedes, the Yugoslavs, Turks, Greeks and others who arrived in the postwar years constituted a major challenge to Swedish identity. As was the case in France (see Section 5.2.2), these immigrant groups were from cultures with very different values concerning religion, the role of the sexes and child upbringing (Runblom 1995: 314). Even more of a challenge was the stream of refugees which began to arrive in the 1980s and 1990s from places and cultures still further afield (e.g. Iran, Iraq, Ethiopia/Eritrea and Central America).

As mentioned above (Section 5.3.1), the new immigrant situation in which Sweden found itself was largely responsible for the abandoning in the 1960s–1970s of official assimilation policies in favour of an official policy of multiculturalism. Indeed in 1975, the Swedish parliament adopted a bill which established three official objectives for immigrant (and by extension regional) minorities (Municio 1993: 116; Paulston 1994: 67; Runblom 1995: 316):

- equality between immigrants and Swedes (i.e. in terms of rights, duties and opportunities);
- cultural freedom of choice for immigrants (i.e. to retain the culture of the homeland, to adopt Swedish culture, or to blend traits from the two);
- cooperation and solidarity between Swedes and ethnic minorities.

It is quite appropriate that these three objectives mirror almost perfectly three principles which have formed the foundation of the French civic myth since the Revolution: *liberté, égalité* and *fraternité*. However the Swedish objectives reflect more contemporary conceptions of these notions; for example, rather than offering to free minorities from their ethnicity (see Section 5.2), *liberté* here offers a genuine cultural freedom of choice, comparable to the more recent notion in France of *le droit à la différence* (Section 5.2.1). This is not to say that the Swedish objectives were not dogged by ill-conceived policies which largely escaped discussion by the legislature (Runblom 1995: 316; 1998: 1–2). Such policies include the Home Language Reform of 1977 (see Section 5.4 below) and the appointment of an ombudsman against ethnic discrimination, who in reality lacks the authority to bring prosecutions or to act through the courts (Runblom 1995: 317).[16]

In addition to such implementation problems, multicultural policies in Sweden have to contend with the resistance of an ethnic backlash at the grassroots level. It is certainly exaggerated to speak as some do (e.g. Karaveli 1997: 106) of an 'invasion' of immigrants, since the rate of immigration in Sweden has actually been low in comparison with other European countries: 4.6 per cent of the population in 1986 were foreign citizens, as opposed to 6.8 per cent in France (Runblom 1995: 284–5). However, Sweden does have a large proportion of foreign citizens in comparison with other Nordic countries: in 1986, 2.6 per cent in Norway, 2.4 per cent in Denmark, 1.5 per cent in Iceland and only 0.4 per cent in Finland (Runblom 1995: 285). Moreover, the arrival of even a relatively small number of immigrants drastically changes the cultural fabric of a country, such as Sweden, which is strongly grounded in ethnic principles. Religion serves as a good example of these changes: in contrast to the high degree of religious homogeneity of the past, as witnessed by the association until recently of the state and (Lutheran) Church, Sweden is now home to 140,000 Catholics, more than 100,000 Muslims, approximately 16,000 Jews, around 3,000 Buddhists and a similar number of Hindus, as well as a substantial number of Greek Orthodox worshippers (Johnsson 1995: 28). In light of such visible changes, it is not surprising that postwar immigration to Sweden has contributed to a heightening of ethnic consciousness amongst the dominant group, which had in a sense lost contact with its own identity since the 1960s (see Section 4.3; cf. also Tägil 1995: 26).

> By being different and 'un-Swedish', the immigrants define what is Swedish.
> (Ehn 1993: 263)

Language has always constituted an important element in the relations with the immigrant Other. In his 1975 study of Yugoslav immigrants in a paper mill community in Dalsland, Ehn noted that language was an important criterion for acceptance by the dominant group.

> Certain people felt threatened by the newcomers, by their traditions and customs, and thought that they should adapt as quickly as possible to the Swedes and do as they did. The Swedish language became the all encompassing metaphor for that demand for Swedification. All other differences were manageable, if only the immigrants learnt Swedish. (Ehn 1993: 239)

Over two decades on, it is difficult to test the veracity of this claim. Ehn's (1986) later study of a daycare centre in Botkyrka, an outer suburb south of Stockholm with a large immigrant population, seemed to confirm his initial results: speaking Swedish had become an integral part of being Swedish. However, the two studies may well represent different perspectives: that in Dalsland, the perspective of the dominant group, and that in Botkyrka, the view of ethnic minorities. What is sure, however, is that language does not play a unifying role today, despite calls from Ingvar Carlsson, a former Prime Minister, for it to become the basis of a new 'united multiplicity' in Sweden (Sjögren 1996: 19); rather it has become divisive, a means of maintaining a distinction between immigrants and ethnic Swedes. In the beginning, distinction could be made simply between Swedish speakers and non-Swedish speakers. To further reinforce this distinction, there is a widespread myth amongst Swedes, like that amongst the Japanese (see Section 3.2.5.2), that their language is difficult to learn, too difficult for immigrants to master (cf. Wingstedt 1998: 216). Yet once immigrants began to learn Swedish, a new 'defence mechanism' (Sjögren 1996) was sought in the notion of *Rinkebysvenska* (Rinkeby Swedish), that is, the Swedish spoken by immigrants in the Stockholm suburb of Rinkeby (cf. Kotsinas 1992). Despite a lack of empirical evidence (cf. Paulston 1994: 70–1), it has become a popular belief that Rinkeby Swedish, and indeed other varieties of Swedish spoken by immigrants, pose a threat to standard Swedish, in terms of influencing the latter's pronunciation, syntax and vocabulary. Reference is also made to 'good Swedish' (Sjögren *et al.* 1996) or 'perfect Swedish' (Lainio 1999: 147) in order to re-establish psychological distinctiveness, to re-distinguish ethnic Swedes from Swedish-speaking immigrants. Such tactics serve as further evidence against Anderson's (1983: 122) claim that language is not an instrument of exclusion (see Section 2.3).

Also employed as a defence mechanism by the dominant ethnic group is the notion of semilingualism (see Section 5.3.1). Edwards (1994: 58) notes that this concept has been 'extended from a solely linguistic description to a catchword with political and ideological overtones relating to majorities and minorities, domination and subordination, oppression and victimization.' Not only has the semilingual debate served as rationale for Finnish groups in their demands for monolingual Finnish schooling in Sweden, it has also been exploited by the dominant ethnic group to justify the need for better resources for teaching immigrants Swedish (Wande 1988: 407). The use of such psychological arguments to conceal nationalistic concerns is also noted by Paulston (1994: 71), who gives the example of ethnic Swedish parents in Södertälje, a satellite town south of Stockholm known for its high immigrant population, who did not want Assyrian children in the same classes as their own children.

> It is preferable to segregate children on the basis of preventing harm, i.e. semilingualism, than on the basis of racial discrimination, at least in Sweden.
> (Paulston 1994: 71)

In a country where nationalist rhetoric has been played down since the 1930s (see Section 4.3), language offers a convenient means of discrimination against immigrant outgroups, when criteria such as race or skin colour are not deemed politically correct.[17] Language attitudes in Sweden thus serve as a metaphor for interethnic relations (see Section 3.1).

> In our opinion, the public discussion surrounding immigrant languages does not concern language *per se*, which one might think at first glance. Comments about language function instead mainly as so-called *metaphors* for intercultural relations in general. The claims we make about 'Rinkeby Swedish' or 'semilingualism' are in actual fact claims which reflect our way of relating to immigrants and our own Swedishness in a broad sense. (Stroud and Wingstedt 1989: 5)

In a similar fashion, Kotsinas (1992: 60) claims that 'behind fears about "foreign" linguistic features may lie the question "Are we going to lose our Swedish identity?"' It is thus in a metaphorical framework that one should view the claimed link between criminality amongst immigrant adolescents and problems concerning their learning of Swedish (Wingstedt 1998: 82), or the unrealistically high language requirements set for menial jobs (e.g. cleaning) often sought by immigrants (Kenneth Hyltenstam, personal communication).

The societal analysis of Swedish identity strategies in the national arena thus reveals two competing ideologies: multiculturalism and assimilationism (Wingstedt 1998: 341; Huss and Lindgren 1999: 316). As in the case of the ideological cleavage observed in France (see Section 5.2.2), official pluralistic policies are challenged by an assimilationist, monolingual ideology at the grassroots level, which is only reinforced by a revival of Swedish ethnonationalism. In light of the strong, social democratic tradition in Sweden, it seems unlikely that this ethnonationalism will express itself through overt forms of racism amongst anything more than a small minority of Swedes. Whereas the National Front in France has 'liberated' verbal expressions of racism, transforming 'I am not racist but ...' into 'I am racist because ...', only 2 per cent of Swedes (compared to 48 per cent of French respondents) claimed to be 'very racist' or 'quite racist' in a 1997 Eurobarometer survey (Bernard 1998: 168 and 172). It thus seems likely that language will become increasingly important for the construction of Swedish identity in the national arena. Indeed, the new extreme right-wing party in Sweden, *Det nya partiet* (The New Party), has already proposed as one of its 'common sense policies for immigration' that a good knowledge of Swedish be a prerequisite for Swedish citizenship.[18] However, as will be seen in the following section, such proposals are for the moment still at odds with an official policy of cultural and linguistic pluralism.

5.4 French and Swedish attitudes towards the teaching of minority languages and the Charter for Regional or Minority Languages

The comparison of Sections 5.2 and 5.3 reveals that, in sixteenth- and seventeenth-century France and Sweden, the state was not interested in which languages were spoken by the masses. Of greater concern was that those in the peripheries were loyal to the state and its religion. However, from the eighteenth and nineteenth centuries, the situation changed, and ethnolinguistic minorities began to play an important role as Others for the purposes of constructing national identity in both France and Sweden. But while the Swedish state changed its approach again, officially embracing multiculturalism from the 1960s–1970s, the authorities in France continued to regard ethnolinguistic minorities as a major challenge for the French model of integration. This fundamental difference in attitudes at the official level is clearly apparent in how successive French and Swedish governments have responded to two issues in particular: the teaching of minority languages in the state school system and attitudes towards the Charter for Regional or Minority Languages.

The teaching of regional and immigrant languages in state schools in France is governed by two separate provisions. Regional languages are covered by law 51–46 of 11 January 1951 relating to the teaching of local languages and dialects (a.k.a. Deixonne Law). In the beginning, this law applied only to four languages, but at the time of writing includes Basque, Breton, Catalan, Corsican, Gallo, Occitan (Auvergnat, Gascon, Languedocien, Limousin, Nissart, Provençal and Vivaro-Alpin), Alsatian and Lorrain, Tahitian, and four Melanesian languages (Aijé, Drehu, Nengone, Paicî) (Ager 1996a: 68–9).[19] Immigrant languages are predominantly covered by programmes for teaching languages and cultures of origin (*enseignement des langues et cultures d'origine* or ELCO). These programmes are financed by foreign governments and established through bilateral agreements: Portugal (1973), Italy and Tunisia (1974), Spain and Morocco (1975), Yugoslavia (1977), Turkey (1978) and Algeria (1982) (Varro 1992: 146).[20] By contrast, regional and immigrant languages are both taught in Swedish schools as a result of the Home Language Reform of 1977 already mentioned in Sections 5.3.1 and 5.3.2. This reform made it the responsibility of municipalities 'to provide home language instruction for all students who desire it and for whom the home language represents a living element in the child's home environment' (Hyltenstam and Arnberg 1988: 488).

An initial indication of the role minority languages and their speakers play in the construction of national identity in France and Sweden is provided by an analysis of the terminology used in the context of these programmes. In France, in the beginning, the Deixonne Law referred very cautiously to 'local languages and dialects'. Not until the 1960s was any mention made of 'regional languages', while the notion of 'regional identities' did not appear until the 1980s (Tabouret-Keller 1999: 343). Use of terminology is also revealing in the context of ELCO programmes: despite the official reference to 'languages and cultures of origin', overuse is often made of 'immigrant languages' (Varro 1992: 140), a notion which only reinforces the artificial cultural difference imposed on many children who were actually born in France (see Section 5.2.2). In Sweden, the term 'home language' was criticised by immigrant groups, who claimed that it emphasised the inferior status of their languages which were limited to the home environment (Wande 1988: 407–8). The term 'mother tongue instruction' was subsequently introduced, despite attention being drawn to the fact that Swedish too was considered a home language, as implied by the phrase 'home languages other than Swedish'. However, 'home language instruction' still remains the most popular term in unofficial contexts, and is consequently the one used in the questionnaire discussed in Chapter 8.

Further understanding of the role played by minorities in the construction of French and Swedish national identities is provided by a more detailed analysis of the structural problems which have dogged all of these minority language education programmes. The Deixonne Law was criticised for being merely 'permissive' (Ager 1996a: 68, 1999: 31): no additional resources were made available for the teaching of regional languages which were considered as optional subjects only, and which did not count towards the students' overall grade at school. Lessons were often assigned at inconvenient times, and no measures were made in the beginning for teacher training (Gordon 1978: 100; cf. also Jacob and Gordon 1985: 121).

> Every teacher who so requests will be authorised to devote each week, one hour of activities to the teaching of elementary notions of reading and writing in the local idiom and to the study of selected texts from the corresponding literature.
> This teaching is optional for the pupils.
> (article 3, Deixonne Law, cited in Grau 1987: 161)

Despite an expansion of the law in 1975–6, which included allowing for three hours of teaching per week, many at the official level remained opposed to any active promotion of regional languages (Ager 1999: 32; cf. also Boulot and Boizon-Fradet 1987: 168–9).

Beginning in the 1980s with the arrival to power of the Socialists, numerous circulars have sought to reactivate the Deixonne Law. Such measures included special provisions made in 1994 which enabled the state to pay for teaching staff in Basque and Breton immersion schools, thus giving rise to a new cataegory of education between the public and private sectors: the 'associative' sector (Ager 1996a: 69; Judge 2000: 54, 57 and 67). In the public sector, regional languages are today offered at primary level at the request of parents, either in the form of three hours per week, or in the framework of more intensive bilingual classes which are proving increasingly popular. At secondary level, regional languages may be taken as either optional or compulsory subjects (sometimes depending on the type of stream). The number of secondary students studying regional languages is increasing for most languages (but not Gallo and Occitan): 154,686 students or 3 per cent of secondary school population in 1996–7 (Délégation générale à la langue française 1999: 143–5). Yet despite these enrolments, it is doubtful whether official measures such as the Deixonne Law, bilingual signs and subsidies to cultural activities actually translate into real use of regional languages.

> Timid and purely symbolic, reticently implemented, they have little real effect on language use (the use of regional languages is in constant decline, even in Corsica), when they do not accelerate their decline through the folklorisation of their public use. (Baggioni 1997: 35)

As discussed by Varro (1992: 146-7), more serious structural problems have dogged the ELCO programmes for immigrant languages. One major problem concerns the segregationist nature of the programmes: when the programmes are integrated into the school timetable, students often have to miss out on other important subjects in order to attend; alternatively when they are run outside school time, their optional and marginal nature is stressed, all the more since they are not financed by the French state. Another problem relates to the choice of language taught, which is often the official language of the country in question, and not the actual language spoken by the students at home (e.g. classical Arabic instead of vernacular Arabic or Kabyle, and standard Italian instead of Neapolitan or other geographical varieties). In addition, there is no way of checking the teaching qualifications of foreign teachers who have little contact with French teachers and often use authoritarian teaching methods similar to those used in their country of origin. Furthermore, Arabic classes in particular are sometimes used for proselytising means. As Ager (1993: 79) notes, this also applies to children from West Africa, 'who often gravitate to the Arabic — and Islamic — teaching if their own languages are not on offer.' Little provision is made for continuation in secondary school especially for Arabic, resulting in only a few students with an ELCO background undertaking university studies in this language. To these, many other criticisms have been added: oversized classes, poor language learning material, and the non-recognition of student work in ELCO by the official assessment system (Ager 1996a: 87-8).

The segregationist approach to ELCO programmes which dominated from the 1970s until the mid-1980s shifted to assimilationism thereafter, when it was realised that immigrants would not return to their respective countries of origin (Varro 1992: 147-8). This transition only provides further evidence for the claim made in Section 5.1.3 that assimilation and segregation are often two sides of the same coin. Not until recently was there a move to a more 'intercultural' approach (Ager 1993: 81). This was the result of substantial official criticism of ELCO in 1994 (Ager 1996a: 88), and then again in 1997-8, much of which was acted upon in 1999 (Délégation générale à la langue française 1999: 102). The self-gratifying claims of the French government that the numbers of ELCO students are increasing demand closer examination. In fact, only enrolments in Italian and Portuguese are rising (cf. Délégation générale à la langue française 1999: 102). That these languages are also official languages of the European Union could imply that students are choosing them out of instrumental rather than identity-related integrative concerns for which the ELCO programmes were originally intended. Indeed, enrolments in Italian include non-Italians who desire early foreign language teaching (Ager 1996a: 87).

The same structural criticisms as in France are also heard in the context of home language/mother tongue instruction in Sweden. In addition to limited teaching time and the fact that students often have to leave their normal classes to attend home language classes, the programme suffers from a lack of clear and realistic guidelines concerning content, planning and teacher competence (Hyltenstam, Stroud and Svonni 1999: 58 and 68). The right to home language classes was tightened in 1985 to include only those children for whom the language was in daily use in the home. In 1987, Sámi, Tornedalian and Gypsy (or Rom) children were exempted from these cutbacks in recognition of their autochthonous status (Wande 1988: 404).[21] Yet despite these modifications, the teaching of a large number of languages — 78 in 1986/1987 (Wande 1988: 404–5) — is not viable in remote places throughout the country. Moreover, the decentralisation of the 1980s–1990s has only made it more difficult for municipalities to offer instruction in a range of languages from Afrikaans and Albanian to Xhosa and Yoruba (Lainio 1999: 151). Consequently, Sweden has lost the exemplary position it once held in minority language education (Hyltenstam 1999a: 12–13).

Another, more recent example of dominant group attitudes towards minority languages is offered by the Council of Europe's Charter for Regional or Minority Languages (1992). The aim of the Charter is to protect and promote the use of European regional languages in particular, but may also be applied to non-territorial languages. The Charter is not, however, intended for recent immigrant languages, or for dialects of the official language of a state (article 1). Neither France nor Sweden signed the Charter at its adoption on 5 November 1992. Yet it was the Swedish government which made the first move to do so, by appointing a committee (known as the Minority Language Committee) in May 1995 to investigate the desirability of a Swedish signature and eventual ratification. In October 1996, the Committee was given the added task of evaluating Swedish adhesion to a second document, the Council of Europe's Framework Convention for the Protection of National Minorities (1995). Rather than granting rights to languages as does the Charter, the Convention gives active support to national minorities, although the emphasis is not so much on collective as individual rights granted to those belonging to such groups (SOU 1997b: 39).

In its deliberations (SOU 1997a; 1997b), the Committee suggested that Sweden sign and ratify both documents. In respect of the Charter, it was proposed that the languages to be covered should be Sámi, Finnish and Romani Chib in all its varieties.[22] The decision not to treat individual varieties as separate languages (e.g. Meän Kieli or Tornedalian Finnish) was intended partly to avoid some varieties not meeting the numerical requirements to be covered by the Charter, and partly out of practical and economic concerns (SOU 1997a: 123, 132–7). As for Yiddish, this was not judged to have been spoken during a sufficiently long period in Sweden to be considered autochthonous (SOU 1997a: 148). The unique identity of Tornedalians and Jews was however recognised by including these groups in the list of national minorities identified for the purposes of the Framework Convention (i.e. Sámi, Tornedalians, Swedish Finns, Roms and Jews).[23] Amongst the proposals was a constitutional amendment (SOU 1997b: 85), which would name and recognise these groups as national minorities. In particular, an alteration was suggested to chapter 1, section 2(4) of the Instrument of Government, which is concerned with the protection of ethnic, linguistic and religious minorities, and their efforts to maintain and develop their own cultural associations and activities.

In response to the Committee's deliberations, the bill proposed by the government (1998/1999: 143), entitled National Minorities in Sweden, went one step further, by including not only all five of these groups, but also five corresponding languages: Sámi, Finnish, Meän Kieli, Romani Chib and Yiddish. Following the adoption by parliament of the government proposals on 2 December 1999, Sweden ratified the Charter and Framework Convention on 9 February 2000. Two subsequent laws, which came into effect on 1 April of the same year, guarantee the right to use Sámi, Finnish and Meän Kieli in certain northern municipalities, in relations with the authorities and in the courts. The new legislation also includes the right to pre-schooling and old age care completely or partly in these languages (Kulturdepartementet, press release, 31 March 2000, cf. www.kultur.regeringen.se).

In France, the decision to consider the Charter for Regional or Minority Languages was made a year later than in Sweden, namely in 1996 during a visit to Brittany by President Chirac. Prime Minister Jospin was even more positive than Chirac, declaring before the Council of Europe that:

> [r]egional languages are one of the treasures of our cultural patrimony. The time is indeed gone when the State could consider the teaching of these languages as threatening for national unity. (cited in Haut conseil de la Francophonie 1999: 36)

In October 1997, the government appointed Nicole Péry, Member of Parliament for the Pyrénées-Atlantiques, to investigate France's regional languages and cultures. This task was later taken over by Bernard Poignant, Mayor of Quimper (Brittany) and Member of the European Parliament, who presented his conclusions in what is commonly referred to as the Poignant Report (Poignant 1998). This report advocated the development of regional languages in the fields of education and the media; it also suggested that the region be recognised as responsible for matters of language and culture, and that France sign and ratify the Charter. Prime Minister Jospin subsequently appointed Guy Carcassonne, a professor of public law, to evaluate the constitutionality of such a ratification. The resulting report claimed that the Charter was in itself not contrary to the constitution, 'since, on the one hand, the aim of the Charter is to protect languages, and not necessarily to grant imprescriptible rights to their speakers, and, on the other hand, that these languages belong to the undivided cultural patrimony of France' (Carcassonne 1998: 128). Nevertheless, this was not the view of the *Conseil constitutionnel* (Constitutional Council), which considered the Charter contrary to articles 1 ('France is an indivisible Republic') and 2 ('The language of the Republic is French') of the Constitution (Decision No. 99–412 DC of 15 June 1999; cf. www.conseil-constitutionnel.fr/decision/1999/99412/99412dc.htm). By making reference to linguistic rights in the *public* sphere for certain *groups* within the *territories* where the languages in question were spoken, the preamble and certain provisions of part II of the Charter clashed with three cornerstones of French identity. First, the French model of integration and conception of the nation hold that minority identities should be confined to the private sphere (see Section 5.2.2). Second, there should be no positive discrimination in favour of any one group in France (see Sections 5.2.1 and 5.2.2). Although the Charter seeks to grant rights to languages, some mention is made of the groups which speak them. The French model of integration presumably also explains why there has been no mention whatsoever in France, unlike in Sweden, of the Framework Convention for the Protection of National Minorities. Third, the principle of territoriality, as expressed through the notions of social contract and *jus soli*, implies that regional languages are the property of France as a whole and not of individual regions (see also Section 5.2.1). This belief has characterised the conceptual framework of even those who are in favour of ratifying the Charter.

> [T]here are no people of Breton, Catalan, Corsican 'stock'. Blood right should not exist in our regions any more than it does in the nation. Otherwise, culture becomes ethnic. (Poignant 1998: 38)
>
> Languages, and the fact that they may be spoken in certain areas, are a product of

history, not of nature. They are therefore linked to people, possibly to their institutions, not to soil — no-one has ever heard a clod of earth speak French — any more than to blood — a newborn child has no language: she or he is merely the holder of a capacity for language, characteristic of the human species, which makes him or her apt to acquire whatever mother tongue this may be.
(Carcassonne 1998: 6)

This conceptual framework is so ingrained in the French psyche that it is by no means limited to politicians and legal experts. The linguist Bernard Cerquiglini (1999) may have highlighted that France had 75 languages which could benefit from the Charter, a far cry from the mere seven or so regional languages traditionally cited (see Section 5.2.1); yet some minority language activists have taken a more cynical view of the Cerquiglini report, claiming that the recognition of so many languages would dilute the effect of the Charter and limit the linguistic demands which could be made (cf. Wright 2000: 178). Moreover, even Cerquiglini did not hesitate to claim that 'the Corsican and Basque regional languages are not the property of the Corsican or Basque region but of the nation' (*Le Nouvel Observateur*, no. 1808, 1–7 July 1999). Cerquiglini may genuinely subscribe to republican ideology, as do many French intellectuals (e.g. Schnapper); alternatively, he may be toeing the political line, considering his position as director of the National Institute of the French Language (INaLF), part of the state-run National Centre for Scientific Research (CNRS). It may therefore not be coincidental that his views concur more or less with those of the government: in France, senior civil servants such as de Broglie, Deniau, Guillou, Lalanne-Berdouticq and the like generally wield greater power in state-run language initiatives than do trained linguists. Hagège (1987: 170–1) notes that, since the mid-nineteenth century, only two people worthy of being called linguists — E. Littré and G. Paris — have been members of the *Académie française*; nor were any linguists to be found at the time of Hagège's writing in what was then the *Haut conseil de la Francophonie*, the *Commissariat général de la langue française* and the *Comité consultatif pour la langue française*.[24] This scenario is symptomatic of a lack of dialogue between linguists on the one hand, and government officials and defenders of French on the other (cf. Shelly 1999: 308).[25]

> Faced with [the] multilingualism of France, the political authorities legislate, enact laws and regulations. But unlike in other countries, this political activity operates essentially without contact with the scientific community which focuses precisely on these languages. There is a divide between scientists and politicians which is not found in countries like Québec, for example, where the results of research fuels political actions and decisions. To hear or read the rare parliamentary

debates on these issues in France, one might think that there are no scientific works on languages. (Vermes and Boutet 1987: 23)

Despite having signed on 7 May 1999, France has therefore still not ratified the Charter at the time of writing. Prime Minister Jospin's call for a revision of the Constitution which would enable the country to do so was rejected by President Chirac, whose opinion was nevertheless that 'the place of regional languages in the cultural patrimony can be recognised perfectly well without necessarily modifying [the] Constitution and calling into question the unity of the nation' (Presidential communiqué, *Le Monde*, 25 June 1999). Such recognition will surely be limited and not offer regional languages 'the symbolic rehabilitation which is indispensable for their survival' (Catherine Trautmann, Minister of Culture and Communication, *Le Monde*, 31 July 1999). In so far as the Charter and Framework Convention represent important contributions to the protection of human rights, it can be seen that France still has a very limited and traditional view of this notion (see Section 5.2), which contrasts with the more contemporary conception of liberalism which prevails in Sweden (cf. e.g. SOU 1997b: 26).

Along with the issue of minority language teaching, the question of the Charter for Regional or Minority Languages highlights the fundamental difference which exists between official policies in the two countries. In France, there is a reluctance to grant any form of overt recognition to ethnolinguistic minorities, both of the regional and immigrant type. Caldwell (1994: 300) argues that it is the former which remain the greatest threat to the official view of French identity, since they challenge the integrity of the territorial principle in a way that intergovernmental agreements regarding immigrant language education do not. Yet the immigrant question extends far beyond the domain of language teaching: immigrant groups pose a major challenge to the French model of integration which constitutes an integral part of the *exception française*, of what it means to be French. To be fair, there are some signs that the French model is becoming more tolerant, at least of regional languages: for example, the *Délégation générale à la langue française* now has the added responsibility of enhancing the status of regional languages or what has become known as the *langues de France*, as witnessed by the latter's inclusion in some of the *Délégation*'s programmes to promote language learning as part of the European Year of Languages 2001 (cf. www.culture.fr/culture/dglf/AEL/points-accueil.html).

By contrast in Sweden, the attitudes of the authorities towards ethnolinguistic minorities have been more obviously positive since the 1960s–1970s, even if the official goodwill has not always been translated into well thought-out policies. But this multicultural ideology has not filtered down to the grassroots level, where there has emerged a new folk nationalism which has resulted in some negative attitudes especially towards immigrants (see Section 5.3.2). As a consequence of decades of social democratic ideology, many of these negative attitudes rely on the use of language as a metaphor. Yet it is not only in relation to immigrants that a greater emphasis is being placed on language; Swedish is also becoming an increasingly overt symbol of Swedish identity in other contexts, such as in the European arena.

CHAPTER 6

Language and national identity in the European arena

For nearly half a century, a new arena has been developing in Western Europe in the shape of the European Union. On the one hand, European integration has entailed a certain degree of convergence, predominantly economic in nature, but which may over time spill over into cultural and linguistic convergence. On the other hand, by bringing member states together and stressing unity, the EU paradoxically also encourages divergence: the reinforcement of individual national — not to mention regional — identities becomes all the more important in order to maintain psychological distinctiveness. This chapter examines first the nature of the European arena (Section 6.1). To what extent can a European identity be said to exist? And how is the arena used for the construction of individual national identities? This is followed by a discussion of the role language plays in the European arena (Section 6.2). The specific cases of French and Swedish ethnolinguistic identities as they exist in the European arena are then examined (Sections 6.3 and 6.4 respectively). A final section focuses on the future challenges for French and Swedish identity strategies in the European arena (Section 6.5).

6.1 The European arena: A new cultural battlefield?

While such organisations as the Council of Europe (CoE) have long encouraged a broad sense of Europeanness, the existence of a European arena has come to the forefront as a result of the establishment of the European Union (EU).[1] Albeit a mere economic forum at the outset, the organisation had ambitious goals and the spill-over theories of neo-functionalists predicted an automatic progression from an economic to a political, legal and cultural union (Hettne, Sörlin and Østergård 1998: 237). The notion of a European identity was first mentioned in the EEC/EU context in the Declaration on European Identity adopted in Copenhagen in December 1973. It reappeared in the Treaty on European Union (TEU), where the Common Foreign and

Security Policy (CFSP) was said to 'reinforce the European identity'; 'to assert its identity on the international scene' was also advanced as one of the objectives of the EU under article B of the TEU (Bainbridge 1998: 212–13).

Despite these efforts, any notion of a European identity represented little more than an official construction. In the eyes of the average European, the then EEC remained an élite-driven bureaucracy, far removed from everyday concerns (García 1993: 3; Østerud 1998). The resulting 'democratic deficit'[2] proved increasingly problematic as the decision-making powers of the EEC expanded into other, non-economic domains. By the 1980s, popular apathy had become so disturbing that the Commission engaged in a drive to create a more tangible European identity which involved the people. As with the construction of national identities, accepted symbols were used to this end, and the EEC soon found itself with a flag, an anthem, even a European day. Similarly, the founding of European educational institutions, the launch of new European newspapers, and the setting up of programmes to promote contact between citizens, such as student exchanges and foreign language programmes, all had the goal of reinforcing this new European identity. In 1993, the Treaty on European Union (TEU) introduced the notion of European citizenship which, it was hoped, would further reinforce the budding European identity.

There do exist some broad cultural patterns on which to found a European identity, although these are difficult to characterise (H. Wallace 1991). Smith (1991: 174) highlights in particular 'the heritage of Roman law, Judeo-Christian ethics, Renaissance humanism and individualism, Enlightenment rationalism and science, artistic classicism and romanticism, and, above all, traditions of civil rights.' However, the people of Europe are also divided on many dimensions: religious, economic, linguistic and ethnic (Smith 1995: 133–41). Moreover, the history they have shared, for example wars, has tended to highlight their differences, rather than their similarities. This has led one commentator to claim that northern Europeans have on the whole more in common with New Zealanders than with southern Europeans (Pocock 1991); another points out that if Europeans share some cultural characteristics, they are ironically those of American mass culture (Blackburn 1992: 32).

European identity as it exists today has been described as 'vacuous and nondescript' (Smith 1995: 131). For the most part, it is usually only experienced by geopolitical default: 'individuals consider themselves as Europeans because they are citizens of countries which are part of the EU' (Chryssochoou 1996: 307–8). Any real sense of European identity will require fundamental changes in the way Europeans perceive themselves and other member states. If these changes are not legitimised by the slow formation of common European memories, traditions, values, myths and symbols (Schlesinger 1994:321), any concept of a European identity risks being compromised by local nationalisms, which offer security and perceived stability in a modern world full of uncertainties.[3] Whereas the Italians consider the European project compatible with national identity, the British are claimed to regard the two as mutually exclusive (Cinnirella 1996:258-9). Some scholars claim that a European identity can be reconciled with national identities by limiting the former to a civic dimension. This is the idea behind Habermas' (1996:238) notion of 'constitutional patriotism', conceived initially as a new form of German identity but later extended to the European context. Others (e.g. Schnapper 1998a:35) claim that a purely civic concept of European society is not sustainable, presumably because ethnic elements are needed if it is to command the same sort of loyalties as national identities. Whatever the view, one point is clear: only by recognising the possibility of multiple identities can one come to terms with the concept of a European identity.

At the time of writing, however, the EU is undeniably more intergovernmental than supranational in nature; it has become a 'new cultural battlefield' (Schlesinger 1994), 'an arena [. . .] for conflicting identities and cultures' (Smith 1995:131). Competing ideologies and political views resulted in the inability of EU member states to act as one entity in the Persian Gulf crisis and in ex-Yugoslavia. Fish wars between the Spanish and the French in the Bay of Biscay, and the English and Icelanders in the North Sea led to an economically provoked nationalism (Hettne, Sörlin and Østergård 1998:410).[4] Examples abound of the ability of European integration to reinforce nationalisms. In the context of the prolonged import ban on British beef, the British shadow agriculture minister referred to the French and Germans as 'our competitors' (*The Guardian*, 9 October 1999). And calls by the EU for a seat on the United Nations Security Council are not expected to be backed by the United Kingdom and France out of fear that this would lead to an eventual erosion of their roles in this forum (*The Independent International*, 24-30 November 1999). Far from uniting Europeans, the European arena has hitherto mainly highlighted national identities and strengthened the nation-state (Hutchinson and Smith 1994:12; Chryssochoou 1996:308; Hettne, Sörlin and Østergård 1998:219). Some scholars even claim that far from intending to undermine the role of the national governments, European integration aimed specifically to reinforce and 'rescue' the nation-state (Milward 1992).

What makes the European arena such an interesting object of study for identity-construction strategies is that the power relationships between competing nation-states are still in the process of being determined. Paris and Bonn have traditionally formed the axis of the EU, as witnessed by the special relationship which existed between Chancellor Kohl and President Mitterrand. This centre of power now risks being displaced due to the new policy of engagement with Europe in the United Kingdom, coupled with the special relationship of the so-called 'New Left' ideological bedfellows Prime Minister Blair and Chancellor Schröder. But member states do not only vie for dominance with one another; they also compete with the European bureaucracy as a separate outgroup. With its far-reaching policies, this bureaucracy encroaches on the national arena and calls into question the role of the nation-state. While it is well-known that the EU has substantially limited the jurisdiction of national governments from above, many claim that the organisation also undermines the sovereignty of the nation-state from below by supporting regional minorities. Not only does European integration entail 'massification' at the supranational level, it is also characterised by 'diversification' at the subnational level (Fishman 1971b: 285). Some (e.g. Héraud 1993) welcome this action as a means of reversing centuries of oppression. Others deplore the formation of Euroregions — such the Working Community of the Pyrenees which brings together the regions/departments of Catalonia, Midi-Pyrénées and Languedoc-Roussillon — fearing that even the predominantly economic nature of these cross-border working communities may encourage a regional identity to challenge that of the national authorities (Nguyen 1998: 115–18). In this respect, the Treaty on European Union was perceived as all the more threatening, since it introduced the notion of subsidiarity[5] and lay the foundation for a new Committee of the Regions in 1994, the competences of which were expanded in the Treaty of Amsterdam which came into force on 1 May 1999.

That many national governments feel threatened by the EU is one matter; whether European integration has given rise to a European identity is another issue. If a European identity is ever to flourish, this will depend especially on the existence of Others (see Section 3.2.1). The Union has traditionally defined itself somewhat innocuously in contradistinction to the economically powerful USA and Japan (Schlesinger 1994: 318). Further outgroups were provided by the divisions of the Cold War, but these disappeared with the political changes which swept through Eastern Europe in the late 1980s and 1990s (Smith 1991: 174). It is probably the search for new outgroups in Europe which has led to an outbreak of racism towards immigrants.[6]

> Racism is thus not only something which appears like a mysterious undercurrent: it forms part of the definition of Europe and differentiation from 'the other'.
> (Hettne, Sörlin and Østergård 1998: 315)

The notion of the Other is likely to become increasingly problematic for the EU. While Brussels may prefer to stress such 'enemies' as terrorism, pollution, drugs and urban crime to justify European cooperation and reinforce a sense of European identity, questions of immigration and further enlargement will increasingly force the EU to take a more definite stance on what is meant by 'European'. For example, should immigrants have access to European citizenship?[7] And is Turkey a European country or not?[8] Not only could these issues affect the construction of identities in the national arena, where immigrants have long acted as outgroups for the purposes of generating positive identities (see Section 5.1.3); they could also have a profound influence on the future acceptance of any European identity, for which, whether it pleases Brussels or not, immigrants and especially Muslim ones have already become *de facto* Others. But the question of the Other is not the only problem likely to face the EU: efforts to forge a European identity will almost certainly also be hindered by issues of language.

6.2 English: The European *lingua franca*?

The EU is involved in language issues in two main respects. First, it regulates the use of languages within its institutions. Second, economic integration entails linguistic consequences in the Union at large. These two aspects of European language policy form the basis of discussion for this section.

> [T]he rules governing the languages of the institutions of the Community shall, without prejudice to the provisions contained in the rules of the procedure of the Court of Justice, be determined by the Council, acting unanimously. (Treaty of Rome, article 217)

That the founders of the EEC gave the task of deciding on the use of languages to the Council of Ministers, the most intergovernmental of European institutions, is surely an indication of their awareness of the thorny nature of the language question. Adopted on 15 April 1958, Council Regulation No. 1 therefore established the Community's internal language policy by declaring that '[t]he official languages and the working languages of the Community shall be Dutch, French, German and Italian' (Council of Ministers 1958: 385).[9] In line with different waves of enlargement, this regulation has been amended on four occasions to grant official status to Danish and English in 1973, Greek in 1981, Portuguese and Spanish in 1986, and to Finnish and Swedish in 1995.[10]

The policy of adding an official language with every new membership has not been without reason. For the sake of accountability and precision, there is a legal need to understand laws which directly apply in member states. There are also concerns regarding democracy and legitimacy, issues of crucial importance to the EU.

> [I]t would ill become the Community as a democratic organization to make regulations which some of its citizens cannot understand because they are phrased in a foreign language. [...] [In particular,] any language requirement for membership in the European Parliament would be tantamount to a social selection of members in some countries and not in others. Also as a directly elected assembly the European parliament has a representative function which is to say that every citizen should be able without qualification to stand for the Parliament and to follow its proceedings. (Coulmas 1991a: 6–7)

This latter point was also made by the Nyborg report (1982), which noted that the only proceedings to be made public were those of the Parliament, as opposed to the Commission or the Council.

While the official language policy was manageable with only four languages at the outset, the situation is more difficult today when the EU has more official languages than any other international organisation: despite bringing together 189 states, the United Nations has only six official languages (Arabic, Chinese, English, French, Russian and Spanish), while the Council of Europe has only two (English and French) for 43 member states (www.un.org; www.coe.fr). Ensuring the 72 possible translation and interpreting combinations which existed in 1991 accounted for 40 per cent of the EU's administrative budget or 2 per cent of the overall budget (Coulmas 1991a: 22; Haberland and Henriksen 1991: 90). These percentages are likely to have increased in light of the 110 combinations which exist at the time of writing. Maintaining this language policy following further enlargement could entail severe economic consequences for the EU.

> One must not hide the fact that the large number of national languages could, if poorly managed, go as far as compromising the economic efficiency and political coherence of our society. Neither Japan, nor the United States has this type of obstacle to overcome. (Giordan 1994: 7)

While no clarification is given in Council Regulation No. 1 as to the difference between official and working languages, the fact is that a limited number of languages *are* used, especially in informal contexts. For example, English, French and German play a greater role in the Commission's bureaucracy, while the European Court of Justice relies on French alone for its internal workings (Hyltenstam 1996: 29; Wright 2000: 167-71). However, the question of whether the EU should *formally* designate one or several working languages has been raised on several occasions. English is often claimed (e.g. by Minc 1992: 217-19) to be best suited to the role of the EU's official working language, either alone or in addition to one or two other languages. Much to the indignation of the French, it has already taken over as the main language used by young Eurocrats (Haselhuber 1991: 49; cf. also Melander 2000b: 21). German speakers are not content with the current *de facto* linguistic situation either. German and Austrian officials recently boycotted certain meetings under the Finnish presidency of the Council of Ministers, on account of a decision made by the Finnish authorities to confine translation at informal meetings to English, French and Finnish (*The Guardian*, 2 July 1999). In justifying its action, the German government pointed out that native German speakers are by far the most numerous, representing 25 per cent of all EU citizens, as opposed to only 16 per cent English speakers (Eurobarometer 1995). Numbers increased as a result of German reunification in 1989, and then again with Austrian membership in 1995. Any further enlargement of the EU to include countries in Central and Eastern Europe can only increase this figure, due to the large number of German-speaking minorities in these regions.

While the EU has no official competence in language issues outside its institutions, it is nevertheless developing a covert language policy for the EU at large due to the linguistic consequences of economic integration (Phillipson 1999: 98). This indirect impact on language issues became especially apparent as a result of the Treaty on European Union.

> The treaty, without saying so expressly, establishes the principle of free language use in transactional economic activity. When this linguistic freedom is limited by national rules on language use, a conflict may arise, which, owing to the principle of supremacy of Community law, is to be decided in favour of the EC rules, unless Community law itself recognizes a valid reason for maintaining the restrictions. (de Witte 1993: 157-8)

Finding the right balance between free language use in transactional economic activity and national rules on language protection is difficult, as is clear from the labelling of goods example. While the interests of the nation-state call for the use of the state language, usually out of concern for consumer protection, article 30 of the Treaty of Rome stresses that a product should have free access to local markets, irrespective of the language used on the packaging. Other linguistic consequences of European integration involve the free movement of persons, and state support for certain industries. Should an EU citizen be allowed to work in another EU member state without knowledge of the state language?[11] And should the EU stop national governments from supporting threatened cultural industries (e.g. national film and music industries) on the grounds that this reduces competition? The EU is thus faced with the dilemma of having to reconcile two of its principal objectives: the promotion of a free market and the protection of the cultural diversity of its citizens.[12]

> Accommodating diversity becomes tantamount to asking how much efficiency is the Community [sic] prepared to sacrifice, and, in a period of economic recession and increased global competition, how many efficiency losses can it [sic] afford to bear? (Boch 1998: 387)

The unwillingness of the EU to define any real overt language policy outside its institutions has left the decision largely to market forces. As a result, economic considerations have favoured larger languages and in particular English. EU-funded student exchange programmes (e.g. Erasmus, Lingua, Comett and Socrates) contribute to the free movement of persons by directly or indirectly encouraging the learning of languages (cf. Melander 2000b: 23–5). But of the 85,000 young Europeans who benefited from the Socrates programme in 1997–8, the majority chose to study in the United Kingdom (*Le Figaro*, 27 January 1999). To cite one example, more than twice as many French students (5,175) chose this country over the second most popular, Spain (2,042). English has also become by far the most studied language amongst European school children: 26 per cent of non-Anglophones in the EU learn English in primary school, while this figure rises to 89 per cent in secondary schools. The corresponding percentages for French, the second most widely taught language, are 4 per cent in primary and 32 per cent in secondary schools (Eurostat 1998).

Combining the number of native speakers of a language, with that of its foreign language speakers, Eurobarometer (1995) seeks to provide an 'indication of use and potential of the official Union languages'. Once again, English tops the list with 49 per cent, followed by 34 per cent for German and 31 per cent for French. Finally in a more recent study, respondents were asked to select the two languages they considered most useful to know besides their mother tongue. 69 per cent claimed that this was English, as opposed to 37 per cent for French and 26 per cent for German (Eurobarometer 1999). In the same survey,

English also came out on top as the most widely spoken language in all non-Anglophone EU member states. If this trend continues, English may not only find itself the official language of the institutions as well as in the EU at large, it may also become the linguistic component of an emerging European identity (cf. Wright 2000: 214). Again the work of Minc (1992: 218–19) comes to mind:

> Europe will not exist until the day when, legitimately or effectively, English is truly its language and when Europeans live with two natural languages; their own, and English. [...] The omnipresence of English will come about in any case and, as with any inexorable phenomenon, the choice is between submission or anticipation. Submission means forever fighting a rearguard action and creating for oneself innumerable handicaps within the Community. Anticipation means an enforced process of adaptation: making the study of English obligatory from a primary level; only allowing the choice of another language once English has been mastered, reinforcing teaching resources; making knowledge of this language a prerequisite for further studies, similarly to mathematics and spelling.

Minc's approach is of course that of an economist who favours linguistic efficiency. As ruthless as this rationalistic approach may be, it does highlight how the identity strategies of certain groups are often best explained in terms of economics. Language can be considered as capital within a linguistic market (Bourdieu 1991). Because of its high degree of economic value, English is often used as a means of generating a positive identity. Certain countries like Sweden have 'anticipated' the rise of English and exploit their knowledge of this language to attain psychological distinctiveness in the European arena (see Section 6.4). Other countries such as France do not see the prospect of English as a European *lingua franca* in such a positive light (see Section 6.3).

In addition to the threat to their national languages they perceive from above, many governments of EU member states have begun to express concern about attacks on their national languages from below, that is from regional languages. Although language policy concerning the institutions only recognises state languages, the European Parliament in particular has on numerous occasions called for the promotion of regional languages.[13] The Arfé Resolution (European Parliament 1981) led to the founding with EU finances of the European Bureau for Lesser Used Languages (EBLUL) (Labrie 1993: 237). Of the many activities of the EBLUL was the vehement campaigning for the inclusion of linguistic rights in the Charter of Fundamental Rights of the European Union, which was signed and proclaimed at the European Council meeting in Nice on 7 December 2000 (European Bureau for Lesser Used Languages, date not specified). Other European Parliament resolutions (e.g. European Parliament 1983, 1987, 1991, 1994) have also sought to improve the status of minority languages and their speakers by supporting initiatives like the on-going Mercator project, the aim of which is to collect data on the status of the EU's regional and minority languages in the areas of education, legislation and the media (cf. www.troc.es/mercator/index.htm). A similar project worthy of mention is Euromosaic (Nelde *et al.* 1996), a study of minority language groups in the EU carried out for the Commission. Finally, the efforts of the Council of Europe should also be considered, even if it is not an EU institution. The European Charter for Regional or Minority Languages (1992) and the Framework Convention for the Protection of National Minorities (1995) seek to improve the status of regional languages and linguistic minorities respectively. As seen in Section 5.4, some countries like Sweden have welcomed these documents; others have had difficulty reconciling them with their national identities. Such is the case of France.

6.3 Language and identity in France: The European arena

> To be French and to be European are today the same thing. (Pierre Moscovici, Minister for European Affairs, *Dagens Nyheter*, 3 January 1998)

To listen to the words of Pierre Moscovici, one could think that national identity is ceding to European identity in France. Such an inference could not be further from the truth. A recent Eurobarometer survey (1999) confirms that the French view themselves predominantly in national terms, albeit within a greater European context: 49 per cent of those questioned responded that they felt 'French and European', 35 per cent 'French only', 9 per cent 'European and French' and 7 per cent 'European only'.

While the French have traditionally stood out as the foremost advocates of European integration, this position can be viewed as an extension of French official nationalism, as part of the construction and strengthening of the French nation-state (Hettne, Sörlin and Østergård 1998: 26). It is in this light that one can understand the immense French support for the Common Agricultural Policy (CAP) for example; agriculture no longer employs a large percentage of the work force in France, but it remains a core value for French identity, symbolising the true French identity of *la France profonde* (Hettne, Sörlin and Østergård 1998: 198). Indeed, de Gaulle favoured a *Europe des patries* (Europe of nation-states) under French moral leadership and vehemently opposed further integration which was at the expense of national sovereignty: in 1954, the *Assemblée nationale* refused a European Defence Community that would have created a joint command structure for French and German troops; while in 1965, the 'empty chair' crisis entailed the French withdrawal from the Council of Ministers until de Gaulle's condition for a national veto provision was met in the Luxembourg Compromise in January 1966 (Bainbridge 1998: 336–42).

Faced with a decline of its role in the global arena (see Section 7.3), France therefore looked to Europe as a new source of positive identity, as a means of rescuing a sense of former grandeur.

> Never separate the grandeur of France from the building of Europe. (President Mitterrand in 1994, cited in Ardagh 1999: 679)

Perhaps more so than for other EU countries, being European for the French expresses itself in opposition to the Americans (Chryssochoou 1996: 307). Not only does the European Union offer protection from American political, military and economic hegemony (Duhamel 1993: 269–70), cooperation between EU member states also facilitates competition with the United States in fields upon which France has traditionally prided itself, including research and cultural industries such as film-making (Hagège 1987: 164). That Europe offered benefits in fighting American domination was clear to de Gaulle when he vetoed the United Kingdom's application for EEC membership in 1963 and 1967 (Jenkins 1990: 177). The view that the United Kingdom is a Trojan horse for American interests is still very much a concern amongst some French commentators today.

> Having become the loyal servant (*chevalier-servant*) of the United States, England is endeavouring to infiltrate Europe. (Lalanne-Berdouticq 1993: 115–16)

Nowhere do the French perceive the degree of this infiltration more than in the field of language (Gordon 1978: 68). It is not surprising that they find little comfort in the prospect of English becoming the language of the EU (see Section 6.2): French was the sole *de facto* working language of the then EEC until the entry of the United Kingdom along with Ireland and Denmark in 1973 (Phillipson 1992: 34).[14] British Prime Minister Heath purportedly agreed with French President Pompidou that French would retain its eminent role and that all British civil servants in Europe would use French (Ager 1996b: 168). Nevertheless, the British recognised the economic conditions which would favour the role of English in Europe. Indeed, the British ambassador to France at the time declared that 'language is like water, it flows where it wants' (cited in Deniau 1995: 93). Such statements only served to heighten the resolve of the French to actively promote their language in Europe through the work of organisations such as the *Comité international pour le français, langue européenne* (Gordon 1978: 67) and the *Haut comité pour la défense et l'expansion de la langue française* (Balous 1970: 180–6). In the then EEC at large, concerns regarding the free movement of goods led to the Bas-Lauriol Law of 1975 (see Section 7.3), in particular the language requirements it imposed on the labelling of products imported from other member states. However, these measures were attacked by the Commission, and the Bas-Lauriol Law was suitably modified by ministerial circulars in 1976 and 1982 to conform with European law (Ager 1996a: 44).[15] Efforts to protect French in the EEC were to no avail, especially in the institutions. While it still remained the *de facto* official language, French progressively lost ground to English over the following decade.

> Today, English holds important positions in some sectors such as foreign relations, scientific research, EURATOM, energy, and in so far as we could quantify this importance, the proportion can, in those cases, reach 50 per cent. But all other sectors, beginning with the Secretariat General of the Commission, use French for 70 per cent against more or less 85 per cent beforehand. (Fosty 1985: 100)

Advocates of French both as the official language of the EEC and as the foundation of an emerging European identity tried hard to justify their cause (cf. Ager 1996b: 172). Even linguists became involved in the debate, claiming the non-viability of English as the language for Europe.

> French seems to be today at Europe's disposal [...], as a language fairly well placed to give voice to a great shared design, all the more since, despite the presence of Great Britain which renders the situation complex, the adoption of Anglo-American as the principal language of Europe would remove much of the persuasive force from the European Community's efforts to build an independent identity. (Hagège 1987: 301)

More radical commentators engaged in less plausible ideological acrobatics worthy of Rivarol (see Section 4.2) in order to exclude the possibility of any other language for the role.

> The assets of French as a language of reference for Europe were and remain evident. This language needs to be European, which obviously excludes Arabic or Japanese, but which also removes a specifically European characteristic from those languages of which the great majority of speakers live on the other side of the Atlantic: English, Spanish, Portuguese. This language needs also to have excelled as a recognised vehicle of civilisation, which, despite their merits, eliminates many languages of a local nature. It must also have proven itself in our time in the

fields of science and economics, which for example, despite its past glory within the field of culture, would not be the case of Greek. Finally, the learning of this language, at least to some degree of fluency, should not pose too many difficulties, which excludes Russian. (Lalanne-Berdouticq 1993: 207; cf. also Lavenir de Bouffon 1995)

Nevertheless, the position of French in what later became the EU continued to decline. Some would claim that this was in part due to the adhesion in 1995 of Sweden and Finland, countries which favour the use of English as an international language (Délégation générale à la langue française 1998: 16; see also Section 7.4). Indeed it was in 1995 that French lost its role as the language used in dealings with the press; thereafter, any one of the official languages could be used with interpretation provided in English, French, German and occasionally other languages (Délégation générale à la langue française 1998: 13).[16]

1994–5 signalled a change of tactics with regard to the construction of French linguistic identity in Europe (see also Section 7.3). In particular, there was a shift from the largely defensive French language protection to the use of the more discrete networking abilities of diplomats (Ager 1996a: 109). To be sure, the active promotion of French continued: civil servants of EU member states and soon-to-be member states were and still are offered French courses by French cultural representations in their respective countries (Délégation générale à la langue française 1998: 28–31). Another example is the interministerial work group on French in the EU, which was founded in 1996 and which led to the publication in 1998 of *Le Français dans les institutions européennes* (www.france.diplomatie.fr/europe/fran_euro/index.html). Intended for all those having dealings with EU institutions, this guidebook serves as a reminder of linguistic rights and especially responsibilities concerning the use of French. To set the tone, Prime Minister Jospin stresses in his preface that the protection of French in Europe is 'indispensable to the preservation of our identity'. Nevertheless, from 1994 to 1995, the French authorities began to embrace a policy in favour of linguistic diversity and pluralism in Europe (Ager 1996a: 26). This position was reinforced by an official EU declaration made during the French presidency of the Council of Ministers on 12 June 1995. This declaration stressed that linguistic diversity carries with it important democratic, cultural, social and economic stakes. It also stipulated that the respect of linguistic diversity and the promotion of multilingualism should be taken into consideration in all community policy, including the teaching of European languages, consumer information, new communication technologies and the Union's external relations (www.culture.fr/culture/dglf/pluril.htm).

While this was the first time that such a policy had so overtly become part of the official government rhetoric, calls for multilingualism had been heard by defenders of French during the previous decade. At that time, the multilingual line was heavily criticised as disguising the real aim of promoting French as Europe's official language, which would ultimately have the same 'glottophage' effect as that attributed to English.

> [I]f Spanish, Portuguese, German, Dutch, Danish etc. disappear to the benefit of English, this will of course be a catastrophe, which must be averted at all cost; but if, on the other hand, these languages are just as radically destroyed to the benefit of French, it will be a triumph for pluralism and victory of Europe. (Chiti-Batelli 1987: 116)

Indeed, it is not difficult to find inconsistencies in the French multilingual argument today. Commenting on the unlikelihood that Irish Gaelic will ever fully recover from the imposition of English, Lalanne-Berdouticq (1993: 172) claims that '[m]oreover this is not desirable as far as the spread of the French language is concerned. An English-speaking Ireland learns French as a first foreign language. A Gaelic-speaking Ireland would learn English out of economic necessity.' In light of statements like this, one can only fear that the French government's new policy on European multilingualism will not genuinely be concerned with the status of all languages in the EU.[17] As an example, Ager (1996a: 140) points out that this new multilingual policy has not been extended to include regional languages in France. The words of President Pompidou uttered in 1972 are thus still very present: 'There is no place for regional languages in a France destined to make its mark on Europe.' (cited in Ager 1990: 30). Nor do the EU's lesser used official languages seem to benefit from this supposed multilingual policy. During its presidency of the Council of Ministers, France proposed to reduce the EU's working languages to five. This was followed by inevitable protests from the governments of smaller EU member states: the Dutch voiced their concerns *vis-à-vis* this 'French attack', while on a visit to Paris, the Swedish Prime Minister insisted on speaking Swedish (Ager 1996a: 109).

6.4 Language and identity in Sweden: The European arena

> When we become Europeans to a greater extent, we will also become more Swedish. (Bildt 1991: 318)

In his book *Hallänning, svensk, europé* (Hallander, Swede, European), the former Prime Minister and Moderate Party leader Carl Bildt (1991) challenged

Swedes to recognise their complementary multiple identities: regional, national and European. After nearly a century of Sweden remaining in the European political periphery, Bildt was encouraging his fellow citizens to turn once again to Europe in search of a positive identity. A renewed emphasis placed on the European context would hopefully compensate for the weakened position in which Sweden found itself on the global stage (see Section 7.4).

In the lead up to the referendum on EU membership in 1994, Sweden's main political parties joined forces for the purposes of ensuring a 'yes' vote. Both were in favour of further engagement with Europe, albeit for different reasons: the Social Democrats out of economic necessity; the Moderates (Conservatives) as a means of setting Swedish identity free of the social democratic 'strait-jacket' which had restrained it for over half a century (Karaveli 1997: 14–15; see Section 4.3).[18] The governmental literature which was distributed in letter boxes (e.g. Sekretariatet för Europainformation 1994; Utrikesdepartementet 1994) spoke of what Sweden had to offer its European neighbours. Just as in the past Sweden had prided itself on being a model country for the world, it now hoped to become the new European 'intellectual force' (Karaveli 1997: 76), teaching the Union about such issues as political transparency, equality between the sexes and ecological concerns. Nevertheless, it would prove difficult to convince the electorate that EU membership would not entail the loss of certain Swedish institutions — e.g. Sweden's policy of neutrality, the welfare state, *allemansrätten* (the right to roam) and even *snus* (chewing tobacco) — which had traditionally provided psychological distinctiveness from other European countries and indeed much of the world. This explains the high proportion of the 'no' vote in the referendum on 13 November 1994: 46.8 per cent as opposed to 52.3 per cent who voted in favour of EU membership (Svensson 1994: 1).

When Sweden joined the Union in 1995, the Swedish authorities quickly realised that their hopes had been ambitious.[19] Not only did the country encounter problems with European bureaucracy, it also had to contend with increased competition from other member states. The failure to compensate for the loss of Swedish prestige in the global arena and the attempt to use Europe to generate a new, positive national identity can in part be considered responsible for the heightened awareness of Swedish identity observed especially at the grassroots level from the 1980s (see Section 4.3). Along with the immigrants (see Section 5.3.2), the EU increasingly became a scapegoat for the economic problems Sweden was experiencing. Anti-EU sentiment has no doubt also increased as a result of Sweden's comparison of itself with its Nordic neighbours. While the Finnish economy has benefited from EU membership and the former Finnish President Martti Ahtisaari was praised for his diplomatic efforts as EU negotiator in Kosovo, the economic success enjoyed at the time of writing by Norway because of its oil reserves is reinforced by the country's remaining outside the Union.

The anti-European backlash in Sweden has even resulted in calls for the country to leave the EU. In a survey in December 1997, 61 per cent of Swedes claimed that they would vote no if a referendum on European Union membership were held on that day (*Dagens Nyheter*, 27 December 1997). It is difficult to predict the future state of Swedish identity within the European arena, not least because any enlargement of the EU will necessarily entail bureaucratic streamlining which may have implications for the balance of power between member-states.[20] In the same way that France looks to *la Francophonie* as a new arena where it is sure to dominate and which may increase its chances of remaining a major player on the world stage (see Section 7.3), the Swedish Prime Minister, Göran Persson, has turned towards the Baltic states, promising to support the applications for EU membership of Estonia, Latvia and Lithuania.

> Persson made a point early on to emphasise the great importance for Sweden of the Baltic region. He declared that 'the Baltic States are our business', and emphasised that an increased and deepened Baltic cooperation would give us increased weight within the context of European cooperation. After having sought to win international influence during the inter-war period by being the protector of small African and Asian states, Sweden now wants to achieve the same goal by being the sponsor of the Baltic states. (Karaveli 1997: 75)

If Sweden's entry into the EU has influenced Swedish identity, it has also had its effect on how Swedes perceive their language. On the one hand, the Swedes can be proud that their language has for the first time been granted official status in an international organisation, that it can now be used in an additional arena (Melander 2000a: 9; 2000c: 101). On the other hand, the Swedes are aware that the linguistic reality of the workings of the EU institutions does not favour the use of their language (Hyltenstam 1996: 28–9; Melander 2000b: 20). Moreover, proposals such as those of the French government in 1995 (see Section 6.3) only serve to highlight the precarious position of Swedish in a Union which is increasingly moving towards a working-language policy involving a few widespread languages.

> In Sweden as in other European countries, one can count on the formation of an élite with a European identity and weak national allegiance, an élite where Swedish is reduced to a spoken language, a private language. (Teleman 1993: 139)

Hyltenstam (1996: 113) draws a parallel between Swedish spoken abroad and within the EU. At home, the language has vitality (see Section 3.2.3) on account of Sweden's autonomy, but within the EU, it could well risk the same fate it met as a minority language in Estonia, North America and perhaps soon even Finland.

> In short, the EU implies that Sweden is incorporated in a further political administrative entity where Swedish is not useable in all contexts. This is a typical framework for language shift. (Hyltenstam 1996: 29)

Whether language shift reaches the critical stage will depend on the degree of political autonomy Sweden will enjoy in the future (Teleman 1993; Hyltenstam 1996): further integration and expansion eastwards will necessarily result in more power being transferred to Brussels, which may in turn entail a reduction in number of the EU's official languages.

Considering the state of affairs at the time of writing, Swedish is in no immediate danger (Hyltenstam 1996: 18). Indeed, in a study amongst members of the European Parliament, the Economic and Social Committee and the Committee of the Regions, Melander (2000c) found that there was widespread use of written and spoken Swedish, especially in official contexts. The responses he obtained to a question regarding whether it was important to use Swedish as much as possible in the EU included the following:

> Yes. In order to preserve national identity, so that Swedish does not deteriorate into an 'impoverished' language without the capacity to express itself in important areas. If Swedish cannot be used, the Swedes will no longer accept the EU.

> Yes, Swedish is an official language. Linguistic pride. Greater possibilities for nuances. Everyone else makes frequent use of their mother tongue, we do not need to be the 'best in the class', but can also be proud of our language. (cited in Melander 2000c: 125)

In addition to the political delegates mentioned above, Melander (2000c: 126–36) also distributed a questionnaire amongst civil servants working with EU-related issues in ministries in Stockholm. It was found that, out of claimed necessity, English was the language most frequently used by the respondents, but that a majority would use Swedish more if they could. Despite the differences between politicians and civil servants, Melander's results clearly show the linguistic pride felt amongst many Swedes who work in the European arena. The strategies of convergence which Sweden favoured for constructing national identity when it first joined the EU — as represented by the 'best in the class' mentality evoked by one respondent in Melander's study — appear to be giving way to new strategies of divergence.

The potential threat that European integration poses to the national language is therefore not going unnoticed by Swedish authorities and researchers. In 1996, notably two years before something similar appeared in France (see Section 6.3), guidelines were published on how the status of Swedish in the EU could be promoted (EU-sekretariatet 1996). Two years later, the plan of action to promote Swedish proposed by the Swedish Language Council (see Section 7.4) included several measures grounded in concerns which directly stem from Sweden's EU membership. The first recommendation stressed the need to guarantee the official status of Swedish in the EU. Another measure pointed to the need to consider possible legislation imposing the use of Swedish in the case of safety instructions, patent specifications, operating instructions, and product information and standards. On this matter, the Swedish Language Council was clearly inspired by the concerns of French language-planning agencies regarding the free movement of goods, even presenting its arguments under the same guise of consumer and worker protection (see Section 7.3). Similarly, the suggested need to impose a requirement that permanently employed school teachers demonstrate a complete mastery of Swedish evokes the case of Anita Groener regarding the free movement of workers throughout the EU (see footnote 11 in Section 6.2).

It was also recommended that resources be increased for the training of better qualified interpreters and translators. Such action would not only be an example of status planning, helping to ensure the presence of Swedish in the EU in the future, it would also constitute an indirect act of corpus planning: better qualified interpreters and translators would hopefully reduce the amount of stylistic interference (e.g. lexical, syntactic) which has been observed in Swedish translations of official EU documents originally written in English, French and German (Svenska språknämnden 1998). In particular, the Swedish Language Council suggests that better training of translators would help to avoid the stylistic oddities which often occur in the Swedish versions of EU documents as a result of the *punktregel* (point or full stop rule). This rule stipulates that one sentence in the original text should be rendered by one sentence in the translated text, and stems from a need to be able to identify with ease corresponding parts of texts which exist in several languages (Melander 2000a: 7–8). No-one denies the existence of so-called 'EU Swedish', which has already become an object of study (e.g. SOU 1998; Ekerot 2000). However, some (e.g. Edgren 2000) reject the fears of the Swedish Language Council on the grounds that only a relatively small number of Swedes (translators, politicians and civil servants) will ever come into contact with EU Swedish. Others (e.g. Melander 2000a: 9–10) point out that the effects of translations on Swedish are not new phenomena, but have made significant contributions to the historical development of the language (see Section 4.3 on the effects of translations from Latin). Nonetheless, despite some disagreement amongst scholars as to the real nature of the threat at hand, it is quite possible that legislation may well be the eventual result of at least some of the Swedish Language Council's proposals. Indeed at the time of writing, a parliamentary committee is investigating these proposals further, including those which relate to Sweden's engagement in the European arena (see Section 7.4).

6.5 France and Sweden in the European arena: Future challenges

In their relationship with the EU, France and Sweden have traditionally represented two extremes. As one of the larger founding members, France quickly became one of the centres of gravity for the EU. At a time when the country's influence was beginning to decline on the world stage (see Section 7.3), the European arena offered a new context in which France and its language could dominate. This use of dominant group strategies merely followed on from the way in which France had for centuries generated a positive identity in other arenas. For Sweden, however, there was never any question of employing such dominant group strategies. The country had long accepted its minority position in the global arena, even turning it to its advantage (see Section 7.4), and sought to exploit its small nation-state status similarly in the EU. Today Europe is a different place, at least from what it was when France helped found it nearly a half century ago. While France is struggling to maintain the dominant status which has traditionally served as a source of positive identity, Sweden is having its own difficulties finding success with the convergence strategies it had previously employed in the global arena. France and Sweden are therefore today faced with the same dilemma: how best to generate a positive identity in Europe?

For France, Europe will certainly prove a difficult source of positive identity in the future. While the success of the EU as a counterweight to American hegemony in the global arena now depends largely on the organisation's ability to integrate its members further, such action would seriously undermine one of France's other major positive identity-generating strategies, namely its policy of national independence (Hoffmann 1987). The fear that French national sovereignty might be compromised is felt by many French politicians, who now openly campaign on anti-European platforms. A virulent anti-Europeanism was notable in the lead-up to the 1995 Presidential elections (Ager 1996b: 176) and key defenders of the French nation-state in Europe have emerged in the likes of Philippe Séguin, Jean-Pierre Chevènement, Charles Pasqua and Philippe de Villiers (Nguyen 1998: 87).[21] As for the extreme right, Bruno Mégret, the leader of the National Front's splinter party, the *Mouvement national*, seems likely to be more ruthless with his anti-European stance than Le Pen, who has traditionally expressed hostility towards European integration as part of a policy of *préférence nationale* which favours ethnic French people (Ardagh 1999: 244–5).

Unlike in France, the political establishment in Sweden shows little sign of right-wing anti-EU sentiment. While the Left Party (former Communists) have from the beginning opposed Swedish membership of the EU, anti-European policies do not appear to have played a part in the manifestoes of Sweden's two recent extreme right-wing parties: the now defunct New Democracy and the The New Party which exists at the time of writing. Nor does the EU seem to be faring too badly amongst the Swedish public, especially considering the hostility felt in former years. While in 1997, 41 per cent of Swedes thought that their country's membership in the EU was 'a bad thing' (Eurobarometer 1997), this had dropped to 36 per cent for data collected in 1998 (Eurobarometer 1999).[22] This is not to imply that Swedes feel any less Swedish today. When asked about their national and European identities in the same Eurobarometer surveys, 57 per cent of Swedes in 1997 said they felt 'Swedish only', while in 1998 this figure had *increased*, albeit only slightly, to 60 per cent.

Just as the heightened awareness of Swedishness includes a greater awareness of language as a marker of national identity, so too the *préférence nationale* in France implies a preference for the national language. The French continue with their attempts to make French one of the languages of Europe — a symbolic means of retaining some sense of dominance in Europe. Even faced with the near reality of English as a European *lingua franca*, it seems unlikely that France will in the near future accept any suggestion that its language be downgraded to quasi-minority status in the EU context. As for Swedes, the minority nature of their language is not so much an issue, since they have already accepted their minority position as a member state. Nonetheless, a positive identity must be maintained and legislation is now being contemplated to guarantee the status of Swedish in the EU (see Sections 6.4 and 7.4). The Swedes have taken the French proposal of a multilingual Europe seriously, but this initiative may yet backfire on the French: stirring up linguistic nationalisms will only hinder efforts to make French a European *lingua franca*, and may even contribute to the further decline of the language in the global arena.

CHAPTER 7

Language and national identity in the global arena

For as long as different peoples in the world have interacted, there can be said to have existed a global arena. Within this arena, international relations have been shaped by two distinct phenomena: internationalisation and globalisation (Giddens 1998: 137). On the one hand, internationalisation implies little more than increased contact between nations and is in no sense a recent phenomenon. Globalisation, on the other hand, is a process of economic, political and cultural convergence or homogenisation which has become particularly prevalent since the late 1980s–early 1990s.[1] While internationalisation brought with it the challenges of greater social comparison and competition between nations, globalisation makes it even more difficult for nations to attain psychological distinctiveness: myths of national superiority are less easily maintained in a world where national cultures become more similar. This loss of psychological distinctiveness often leads to identity crises for many nations, which are forced to consider new strategies for generating positive identities in the global arena.

This chapter examines first the nature of the global arena and considers the emergence of a global culture and identity (Section 7.1). A discussion then follows of English, the language which has come to dominate the global arena and which forms an important element of any global culture or identity to the extent that such can be said to exist (Section 7.2). The cases of France and Sweden are then examined in terms of the particular challenges faced by these countries in the global arena (Sections 7.3 and 7.4 respectively). These two sections pave the way for a final overview which compares past and future French and Swedish identity strategies developed in response to internationalisation and globalisation (Section 7.5).

7.1 A new global culture?

In a post-industrial world, the future role of the nation-state is debated by those who predict its decline and those who emphasise its continual relevance.

Amongst the former are liberals, socialists and Marxists who, despite their ideological differences, have long envisaged the withering away of the nation-state, be it through the spread of universal, humanist values or through the rise of proletarian ideologies (Hobsbawm 1992; cf. also Richmond 1984; Smith 1995: 11). More recently, post-modernists highlight the increasing irrelevance of the nation-state in a world characterised by mass travel and migration, global telecommunication systems, regional power blocs and transnational economic corporations.

> While nations were functional for an industrial world and its technological and market needs, the growth of the 'service society' based on computerised knowledge and communications systems overleapt national boundaries and penetrated every corner of the globe.   (Smith 1991: 155)

In such circumstances, many see individual national identities as being increasingly relegated to the private domain, which is more accepting of cultural diversity (Jenkins and Sofos 1996: 10). Furthermore, it is argued that the role of the nation-state is sure to decline faced with the clear need for global solutions to problems such as environmental pollution, clandestine immigration, disease and drugs (cf. W. Wallace 1991; Hettne, Sörlin and Østergård 1998: 40–1; Nguyen 1998: 77–8). However, just what form of global culture will take over from national cultures is the object of much debate. Holton (1998: 166–85) explains that some observers (e.g. Ritzer 1993) equate globalisation with cultural homogenisation, and in particular Americanisation; others (e.g. Huntington 1996) speak instead of polarisation, such as between the West and an emergent Islamic-Confucian axis; others still (e.g. Hannerz 1992) stress a hybridisation or creolisation of different cultures. What is notable is that all three of these theories of global culture involve some form of convergence.

In the opposing camp are the realists, who not only stress the continual relevance of the nation-state, but also question the existence of a truly global culture. While the post-modern era may be witnessing the convergence or homogenisation of morals and life styles around the globe, this by no means implies the emergence of a world citizen (Nguyen 1998: 80). At the present moment, any sense of a global culture is largely an élite phenomenon which lacks the ethno-historic grounding needed to engage the masses.

> Unlike national cultures, a global culture is essentially memoryless. Where the nation can be constructed so as to draw upon and revive latent popular experiences and needs, a 'global culture' answers to no living needs, no identity-in-the-making. It has to be painfully put together, artificially, out of the many existing folk and national identities into which humanity has been so long divided. There

are no 'world memories' that can be used to unite humanity; the most global experiences to date — colonialism and the World Wars — can only serve to remind us of our historic cleavages. (Smith 1990: 179–80)

While globalisation does exist, this is limited to specialised, usually technological, fields. Moreover, by bringing disparate cultures into close proximity, global interdependence may only serve to emphasise differences and provoke ethnonational reactions to increased external pressures (Smith 1991: 157, 1995: 145; Taguieff 1996; Nguyen 1998: 38). It seems unlikely that the former French prime minister, Édith Cresson, would have expressed such jingoism in 1991 as likening the Japanese to ants (Ardagh 1999: 599), had it not been for world trade and the competition Japan represented at a time of economic crisis in France. In this sense, the hegemony of the nation-state may well be reinforced, rather than undermined, by globalisation and international organisations such as the United Nations (Billig 1996: 191).

While it may be possible to speak of a truly world culture in the future, this book adopts a realist position which assumes that the global arena which exists today is still very much a playing ground for competing nation-states and their identities (Holsti 1985; Hettne, Sörlin and Østergård 1998: 41). Following social identity theory, this arena comprises both subordinate and dominant groups, the most powerful of which is unquestionably the USA. Other nation-states, such as France and Sweden, can be considered more or less as subordinate groups. Whether or not they accept this subordinate status is another matter. Nonetheless, they all engage in the same activity of positive identity production or maintenance through strategies of convergence and/or divergence which often involve language.

7.2 English: A global language?

The use of English as a global language can be traced back to the seventeenth and eighteenth centuries, when Britain was a leading colonial power. In the eighteenth and nineteenth centuries, it was the pre-eminent role taken by this same country in the industrial revolution which assured the success of the language. Today, it is the technological, economic, military and cultural dominance of the USA which has made English such a popular choice for a global language amongst the masses and the élite alike. In addition to the 375 million native speakers, it has been suggested that 1.1 billion people know English as a second or foreign language (Graddol 1998: 29).[2]

Supporters of English as a global language base their arguments on several myths. English is said to be somehow natural, in that it is linked to the inevitable forces of globalisation (see Pennycook 1994: 9). When viewed especially from the perspective of undeveloped countries, it is also claimed to be intrinsically associated with modernisation, defined as 'the transition from traditional to so-called modern principles of economic, political and social organization.' (Phillipson 1992: 43; cf. also Phillipson 1992: 79; 1999: 103). But even in so-called Western countries, an association is often made between English and modernity, which may stem in part from the observation that the language has an extensive vocabulary to cover modern technologies (e.g. computing, aeronautics). English is also considered easy to learn: its vocabulary is a mixture of Germanic and Latin roots, not to mention borrowings from languages such as French; it has no complicated morphology or grammar; and English speakers are generally considered as tolerant of linguistic variation and prepared to accept approximations (Ager 1997: 52). English is regarded as beneficial in so far as it facilitates international communication. Global English is also claimed to be neutral, 'ethnically and ideologically unencumbered' (Fishman 1977b: 118) in that it is far removed from the language spoken by native speakers and can no longer be considered the property of any one country (Crystal 1997: 21). Siguan (1996: 141) describes it as:

> a basic English adapted for the exchange of elementary information such as the English that can be used in a hotel reception, or a very specific English, particular to specialised domains, for example biology or finance. In both of these cases, the cultural and ideological implications are minimal.

Such arguments have however not withstood closer examination (cf. May 2001: 200–4). The ill-founded nature of the claim that English is somehow more 'modern' than other languages serves as an example. English may well have an extensive vocabulary to cover modern technologies, but this is only due to the fact that many of these technologies were developed in English-speaking countries, or designed with the large English-speaking market in mind. In addition, it must be noted that terminology for these same technologies is also coined in other countries, by agencies such as the terminology and neology commissions in France, and the Centre for Technical Terminology in Sweden (see Section 4.4). Nor have the arguments relating to the purported neutrality of English succeeded in convincing scholars and intellectuals with a particular knowledge of the Third World, who instead view the imposition of global English as linguistic imperialism (Phillipson 1992: 35–6). Gandhi (1965) was vehemently opposed to the use of English in India, likening this practice to a form of mental slavery; and in Kenya, Ngũgĩ wa Thiong'o (1986) claims that the use of English is a form of neo-colonialism, serving to maintain the domination of a small élite and their foreign allies.[3] It is this realisation which led Tanzania to elevate Swahili to sole official language in 1967, the same year that the National Language Act in Malaysia stripped English of its co-official status in favour of Malay only (Lowenberg 1988: 162; Crystal 1997: 115). While some other former colonial countries such as Singapore actively encourage their citizens to learn English, authorities are nonetheless aware of the cultural and ideological consequences of adopting English, often compensating by means of cultural divergence on other dimensions (Wardhaugh 1987: 132). The consequences of English being a global language extend far beyond colonialism; the spread of this language involves broader cultural issues and questions of power relationships between and within countries.

> [I]ts widespread use threatens other languages; it has become the language of power and prestige in many countries, thus acting as a crucial gatekeeper to social and economic progress; its use in particular domains, especially professional, may exacerbate different power relationships and may render these domains more inaccessible to many people; its position in the world gives it a role also as an international gatekeeper, regulating the international flow of people; it is closely linked to national and increasingly non-national forms of culture and knowledge that are dominant in the world; and it is also bound up with aspects of global relations, such as the spread of capitalism, development aid and the dominance of North American media. (Pennycook 1994: 13)

Some (e.g. Crystal 1997: 19) claim that the solution to establishing a global means of communication lies not in the outright adoption of English, but in bilingualism: English as a global *lingua franca* would therefore not threaten but complement identity-bearing national languages. However, this view somewhat naively assumes that bilingualism is consistently additive, expanding an individual's linguistic repertoire to include more than one language. Research in a variety of language contact situations around the world reveals that for minority groups, acquiring the language of another ethnic group often results in subtractive bilingualism (Lambert 1975), a transitional stage between two states of monolingualism. Moreover, bilingual policies are costly in time and money, and demand goodwill on the part of the dominant group of the society in question. Even the claimed stability of diglossia is relative (Edwards 1994: 86; cf. also Boyer 1991: 15–36). If the functional differentiation of the two languages breaks down, this may lead to language shift, a condition identified by three main phenomena (Hyltenstam 1996: 14):

- loss of fields or 'domains' of use (e.g. administration, media, education)
- loan words and interference from the dominant language (i.e. code switching with use of elements from the dominant language)
- reductions (e.g. simplified syntax, reduced lexis)

While the introduction of loan words into the minority language is a more frequent cause of concern to its users, the loss of domains to the dominant language and, at a later stage, reductions in the stylistic flexibility, vocabulary and grammatical structure of the minority language are paradoxically more indicative of language shift (Hyltenstam 1996: 14). With this in mind, it seems appropriate to reconsider the growing number of domains where English now enjoys high status, if not complete hegemony, in many non-English-speaking countries: international relations, media and entertainment, communications, science and technology, education, international travel and safety, etc. To take the field of international relations as an example, English plays an official or working role in most international organisations or fora. While it is the sole official language of the European Free Trade Association (EFTA), it is paradoxically the official language of no EFTA member country.[4]

The increasing use of English in the domains mentioned above shows how the global sphere is progressively encroaching on national arenas: national languages are now having to compete with English on their own territory. But the phenomena of internationalisation and globalisation need not entail complete convergence to English and can in fact promote linguistic diversity. It was international cooperation which led to the establishment of protective measures for linguistic minorities such as the United Nations Declaration of the Rights of Persons Belonging to National, Ethnic, Religious and Linguistic Minorities (1992), the Draft Declaration on the Rights of Indigenous Peoples (1993) and the Draft Universal Declaration of Linguistic Rights (1996) (Skutnabb-Kangas and Phillipson 1994; May 2001: 190–1). The very symbol of globalisation — the Internet — has also made it possible for regional minorities to distribute their languages more readily. While in the past, small markets seldom justified the publication of works in these languages, the Internet allows for greater and more rapid distribution, especially amongst the young, where it is feared that regional languages are dying out.[5] Even companies are abandoning their economic rationalistic arguments, realising the potential for offering multilingual products and services in this global era. Such is the rationale behind the decision of one company in Australia — Internet Names WorldWide — to begin registering Internet domain names in Chinese, Arabic,

Japanese, Tamil and a range of European languages. In the words of the company's general manager: 'We are looking at the birth of the first truly international Internet community where language is not a barrier' (*The Age*, 6 July 2000). Far from constituting a threat, globalisation thus offers new opportunities for languages other than English to thrive.

Such examples highlight the compatibility of two ostensibly converse tendencies: ethnic groups can embrace a dominant global culture (convergence) while all the time stressing their localised, ethnic identities (divergence). Many minority groups now combine these strategies of convergence and divergence in order to generate positive identities. Much to the chagrin of the central government, the Basques and Catalans in Spain often use English, as opposed to Castilian, as their means of wider communication. Even for nation-states, it may be that a more effective means of generating a positive national identity in this global era is some degree of convergence. Such an approach was advocated over a decade ago by Minc in the context of the European Union (see Section 6.2). By anticipating and embracing the rise of English as a global language, nation-states can find a new psychological distinctiveness. In what can be termed 'divergence in convergence', acts of convergence can be transformed into acts of national divergence. A good knowledge of English amongst the population may in itself suffice to generate a positive national identity: 'We Swedes are modern because we speak English well' (see Section 7.4). In other cases, divergence in convergence may entail the use of particular national varieties expressed through accent (see Sections 2.3 and 3.2.5.2) and lexical idiosyncrasies: 'Germans will want to sound like Germans when they speak English, not like Britons or Americans' (Graddol 1998: 27). It could be argued that the polycentric nature which already characterises English (cf. Kachru 1982) makes it particularly suited to play the role of an international *lingua franca*; however with their monocentric perspective of the norm, some French commentators claim that this type of 'fragmentation' may yet result in the decline of English for this purpose (cf. de Saint Robert 2000: 25).

As the proponents of Esperanto have long claimed, the choice of English is not the most egalitarian of solutions to the need for a global *lingua franca* (Chiti-Batelli 1987). Yet even Esperanto does not offer a completely democratic alternative. The language is Eurocentric and, with a Latin-based vocabulary, would not be as easily learnt by speakers of non-Romance languages. Nor is Esperanto detached from ideology as some claim. At the height of its popularity, the language was strongly linked to pacifist movements, and was favoured particularly by socialist groups and trade unions (Thiesse 1999: 80; Wright 2000: 246; cf. also Calvet 1998: 199). As well as neglecting the psychological barriers and motivational problems involved with learning an artificial language, the Esperanto argument ignores one of the main assumptions of social identity theory: intergroup relations do not take place on an equitable footing, and groups strive to generate or maintain positive identities by establishing or reinforcing power imbalances (cf. also Pennycook 1994: 9). This is not to say that the power relationships between different groups do not change over time. While English (or rather American English) may be the dominant language in the global arena at the present moment, this situation could change with a radical shift in the balance of economic, political or military power. Such an occurrence is quite possible sometime in the next century, not least because of continual economic growth in Asia. Nonetheless, in the Asian economies which are already highly developed, English seems firmly established as the working language, as seen above in the case of Singapore. Faced with the current hegemony of English as a world language, finding new strategies for maintaining positive national identities will become increasingly important. Some nation-states will succeed by demonstrating creativity in a form of divergence in convergence. Others will find it difficult to change the policies of divergence they have employed in the past. One such country facing this difficulty is France.

7.3 Language and identity in France: The global arena

> It is through our language that we exist in this world other than as a country among so many others. (Georges Pompidou, cited in Deniau 1995: 22)

As is clear from the words of France's former President, Georges Pompidou, language has long been used by the French to attain a state of psychological distinctiveness in the global arena. Yet maintenance of the privileged status which France and its language have enjoyed in the global arena for centuries has become increasingly difficult faced with the rise of the United States and of English as a global language. This section examines the gradual transition which France is having to make from a dominant power to a nation-state which increasingly finds itself in a minority position in the global arena. To a large extent, France persists with strategies typically associated with dominant groups (see Sections 3.2.2 and 3.2.5.1): faced with an insecure identity, the

French authorities continue to stress French independence and cultural difference, what they refer to as the *exception française*. However, more recent years have witnessed the emergence of more effective strategies which take into consideration changing geo-political circumstances in the global arena. Considering that language has a long history with regard to the construction of national identity in France, it is not surprising it figures predominantly in these new, creative strategies.

Perhaps the first sign that France considered that its language needed to be defended in the global arena was the establishment of the *Alliance française* in 1883 and the *Mission laïque française* in 1902 (Gordon 1978: 37).[6] Throughout the nineteenth century, German had been on the rise as a language of thought and science, and France's pre-eminence had been shaken by its defeat in the Franco-Prussian War in 1871. But it was at the beginning of the twentieth century in particular that the French began to notice that their language had progressively lost ground to that of their main colonial rival, the English (Hagège 1987: 187). The presence of the Americans at the Paris Peace Conference in 1919 resulted in the recognition of English as a diplomatic language with the same status as French (Phillipson 1992: 33). Yet, although the resulting Treaty of Versailles can be seen as marking the end of an era of French linguistic pre-eminence in the global arena, French national pride remained largely positive on account of the country's possession of the second greatest empire in the world (Gildea 1996: 17). Not until the late 1930s-early 1940s did France's fortunes begin to change. As Gordon (1978: 11) notes, it was from this time that:

> the French language [...] was challenged by radically new circumstances — among these the Depression, the rise of nationalism in the Third World, the humiliation of World War II, the collapse of Western empires, and the emergence of superpowers to assume the roles Great Britain and France had once played as world leaders. No longer could the defenders of the universal role of French rest on laurels won in the eighteenth century, no longer could they hope to see French remain an important international language without a deliberate effort to defend and diffuse it. (cf. also Deniau 1995: 49)

As an indication of the 'crisis', the French language was granted official status at the founding of the United Nations in 1945 by one vote only (Jacob and Gordon 1985: 118).

As the Cold War gathered momentum, France was increasingly integrated into the edifice of the capitalist bloc. Examples include the Bretton Woods monetary system, the General Agreement on Tariffs and Trade (GATT), the International Monetary Fund (IMF) and the establishment of the North

Atlantic Treaty Organisation (NATO) in 1949 (Jenkins 1990: 158). One condition of Marshall Aid had also been that France remove all barriers to American exports and investment (Gildea 1996: 9). The growing economic and military dependence especially on the United States which such examples entailed was to have significant repercussions for French national identity (Jenkins 1990: 153 and 158).

The optimism surrounding the return of de Gaulle in 1958 was largely a product of his foreign policy of independence (Citron 1991: 184). In particular, de Gaulle succeeded in convincing his compatriots that French sovereignty and greatness rested on the country's nuclear capability (Gildea 1996: 207). It was thus no surprise that in 1960 France tested its first atomic bomb, providing the country with a *force de frappe* and symbolising the strength and resolve of French identity. De Gaulle also tried to capitalise on his country's purported political independence by going further than any other Western government in cultivating links with the Soviet Union, and being the first Western power to recognise communist China in 1965 (Jenkins 1990: 177). Other examples of Gaullist independence include the French withdrawal from the integrated command structure of NATO in 1966, condemnation of American military intervention in Vietnam, support for the Arab cause in the Six Day War in 1967 during which the US supported Israel, and calls for an independent Québec, also in 1967 (Jenkins 1990: 176–7; Gildea 1996: 202). Yet to what extent de Gaulle's nationalism carried any real substance is uncertain; it is sometimes claimed that de Gaulle's stance amounted to no more than self-delusion, or political rhetoric used to disguise the real nature of French dependence on the United States (cf. Jenkins 1990: 178). As Winock (1997: 277–181) points out, France did not hesitate to stand alongside the United States in the second Berlin crisis in 1961, or during the Cuban missile crisis in 1962. In Winock's view, true anti-Americanism has only really emanated from extreme parties such as the French Communist Party (PCF) and the National Front (FN).

Irrespective of its real substance, Gaullist defensiveness towards American influence did exist to some degree. It was even extended to the field of language, in a way which relied heavily on the notions of linguistic determinism and relativity (Ager 1997: 27; see Section 2.4.2). Hagège (1987: 132) shows how acts asserting French independence from the United States have usually been accompanied by publications defending the French language against English (cf. also Flaitz 1988: 104). Of greatest influence was René Etiemble's *Parlez-vous franglais?* (1964), which denounced the 'Atlantic pidgin' (*sabir atlantique*) as a 'cancer'. Etiemble's work was followed by a more concrete manifestation of linguistic anti-Americanism, namely the founding under de Gaulle in 1966 of the *Haut comité pour la défense et l'expansion de la langue française* (see Section 4.4). As part of its work on language corpus planning, this government agency sought to maintain the purity of French and devise new terminology to replace the influx of English loan words (Judge 1993: 18). But as mentioned in Section 7.2, the presence of loan words does not necessarily indicate language shift. This fact is confirmed by the observations of French linguists such as Hagège (1987: 61), who demonstrates that despite the borrowings, English has had no effect on the 'hard core' (Hagège 1987: 30) — i.e. the pronunciation, morphosyntax, etc. — of the French language. Nonetheless, for the purposes of maintaining a positive national identity, the perceived threat which English continues to pose to French is no less real.

> [T]he condemnation of American borrowings, far from being founded on the reality of a threat, is merely the displaced expression of an anti-Americanism fed by nostalgia for the prestige of former times. (Hagège 1987: 134)

The irony is that French has probably never been so widely spoken as it is today (cf. also de Beaucé 1988: 21). The number of 'real' French speakers — defined as those for whom French is a first, second or adopted language — rose by 7.7 per cent from 105 million in 1990 to 112.7 million in 1998 (i.e. 1.9 per cent of the world's population), while the number of 'occasional' Francophones — defined as those for whom 'the use and command of French are limited by circumstances or capacities of expression' — increased by 11.8 per cent from 55 million to 60.6 million (i.e. a further 1 per cent of the world's population) (Haut conseil de la Francophonie 1999: 326 and 345). Nonetheless, French concerns can be explained by the relative *decrease* in numbers of French speakers compared with an increase in speakers of English, Portuguese and Chinese (Guillou 1993: 33).

Nonetheless, former prestige and power cannot be regained by fighting against borrowings from English (Calvet 1998: 187). Pergnier (1989: 203) argues that the use of *franglais* 'satisfies the more or less conscious wish of part of the French population to identify with a mythical and one-dimensional model of modernity' (see also Section 7.2). But the use of English in order to appear more modern is to a large extent a reflection of a desire to embrace modernity on other, non-linguistic dimensions. Hagège (1987: 154) points out that the French equivalents of 'computers' and 'windsurfers' (*ordinateurs* and *planches à voile* respectively) did not really become popular until French-made products dominated the domestic market. The so-called 'war' against English should therefore not be fought on a linguistic battlefield, but rather in terms of economics, politics and other social factors. Not only has traditional French linguistic purism failed to understand this important point, it may even have adverse effects on French, stifling the linguistic creativity necessary to express the social and economic reality of increased modernisation. As argued in the following citation from Hagège (1987: 164), such a restrictive view of language reflects a more general inability of French identity to adapt to changing circumstances.

> The mentality which inspires the overcautious defence of the purity of French is precisely the same as that which causes the weakness of France faced with American vitality: weight of traditions, mistrust, lack of taste for adventure here, and there, dynamism, optimism, passion for risk and creativity.

In addition to language purism, corpus-related language myths of the type which emerged in the seventeenth and eighteenth centuries (see Section 4.2) are often used by those in official circles in order to claim the supposed superiority of the French over the English. Rivarol-inspired claims that French is more clear, precise and elegant than English are frequently heard (e.g. Hagège 1987: 199–200; Lalanne-Berdouticq 1993: 121; Deniau 1995: 21; Haut conseil de la Francophonie 1999: 553–4), such as in the now famous example of United Nations Resolution 242 from 1967. The first paragraph of article 1 of this resolution called for the '[w]ithdrawal of Israel armed forces from territories occupied in the recent conflict' (Djonovich 1989: 42). It has often been claimed that the French version of this text is more precise, demanding the '*retrait des forces armées israéliennes des territoires occupés lors du récent conflit*'. While the French text implies the withdrawal from *all* the territories by making reference to 'the territories', the English version is considered ambiguous, possibly referring only to *some* territories. Advocates of the precision of French are quick to highlight the fact that French makes a distinction between '*de territoires*' (from (some) territories), and '*des territoires*' (from the territories). What appears to have been overlooked is that this distinction can also be made in English, as has just been shown. It is possible that the ambiguity of the English version was merely an oversight on the part of the authors or translators. This explanation would confirm the overall dubious quality of the English text, which also uses the noun 'Israel' instead of the more appropriate adjective 'Israeli'.

Another popular myth concerns the falsely claimed redundant nature of English vocabulary, as demonstrated by the existence of too many synonyms of the type 'to disseminate' and 'to scatter' (de Broglie 1986: 55). Once again, this myth neglects some major differences which exist between these words, namely that of register. While both 'to disseminate' and 'to scatter' refer to the same action, the former is likely to be used in more formal or technical contexts. The former also expresses a more abstract or figurative action: one can 'disseminate information' but cannot 'scatter information'.

In addition to corpus planning, status planning also plays an important role in the 'protection' of French from English in France. Such was the intention behind law no. 75–1349 of 31 December 1975 relative to the use of the French language (a.k.a. the Bas-Lauriol Law), which imposed the use of French in three main domains: in commercial and advertising contexts, as a form of consumer protection; in work contracts, to protect the employee; and in the context of information given to the consumer either by private firms or public bodies (Judge 1993: 21). Yet the Bas-Lauriol Law proved largely ineffective and did not hinder English from gaining ground in certain domains. In 1976, English language papers accounted for 76 per cent of all papers given at natural science conferences sponsored by the state research agency, the *Centre national de la recherche scientifique* (CNRS) (Jacob and Gordon 1985: 119). Half a decade later, in 1980–1, more than 80 per cent of articles by French researchers in periodicals which received government subsidies appeared in English (Hagège 1987: 188). Such observations prompted the French Minister for Research and Technology to threaten to cut off funding for any French scientific journal using English (Jacob and Gordon 1985: 119). However, this did not dissuade the very French Pasteur Institute from changing the name of its journal *Annales de l'Institut Pasteur* to *Research in Microbiology* in 1989 (Siguan 1996: 137).

French is perceived as equally threatened in the field of entertainment. Crystal (1997: 91) notes that even up until 1990, French films continued to attract majority audiences in France. In recent years, such films account for as little as 30 per cent of the national box office. An increased interest in subtitled films — what the French call films in *version originale* — as opposed to dubbed films, has also been observed over the last decade. However as Flaitz (1988: 79–82) points out, this increased popularity need not necessarily reflect an attraction to other languages such as English. Growing audience sophistication and sensitivity towards artistic genres and different cultures could account for the greater number of subtitled films.

After a decade of relative inaction, the 1990s witnessed a wave of renewed efforts to guarantee the status of French in France. Decree no. 90–66 of 17 January 1990 imposed a quota which required that at least 40 per cent of programmes on national television be in French. As it refers to only one language, this legislation can be considered as going substantially further than the European Commission's 1989 directive *Télévision sans frontières*, which laid down that at least 50 per cent of material on each network in a member state should be of European origin (Ardagh 1999: 706). Two years after the French decree, the government took advantage of the constitutional reform following the ratification of the Treaty on European Union, amending article 2 to add the paragraph: 'The language of the Republic is French' (constitutional law no. 92–554 of 25 June 1992). Such a measure had not been deemed necessary for several centuries.

1994 saw the passing of two main laws concerned with status planning. Modifying legislation from 1986, law no. 94–88 of 1 February 1994 imposed a similar quota on the audio sector as was previously applied to television: 40 per cent of material on French radio was to be by French artists singing in French. Yet by far the most important act of language planning was law no. 94–665 of 4 August 1994 relative to the use of the French language (a.k.a. the Toubon Law). Faced with the largely ineffective Bas-Lauriol Law, the Toubon Law sought to extend the scope of the protection of French to cover six main domains: education, commerce, the media, the workplace, the public service and the conference industry (Ager 1997: 40). It was also intended that the Toubon Law would be more rigorously enforced than its precursor: whereas in the past the role of watchdog had been left to private organisations, such as the *Association générale des usagers de la langue française* (AGULF), it would now be one of the responsibilities of the state-run *Délégation générale à la langue française* (DGLF) to draw attention to breaches and present an annual report to parliament on the law's application.

In its decision of 29 July 1994, the *Conseil constitutionnel* (Constitutional Council) rejected some provisions of the proposed law, which it judged contrary to the principles of free thought and expression, as established in article 11 of the Declaration of the Rights of Man and the Citizen. While the legislator could impose official terminology on public servants, it was decided that the general public must be allowed to express themselves as they please (Ager 1996a: 162). In addition, the *Conseil* ruled that the granting of government subsidies to researchers could not be linked to the choice of language of their publications. The Toubon Law eventually came into force, but only after the necessary legal modifications were made, and following a lively debate in the National Assembly. Despite a negative reaction by the press, who likened it to Nazi linguistic purism (cf. Battye and Hintze 1992: 51–2), the Toubon Law appears to have the support of the public at large: 81–93 per cent of those questioned in a SOFRES survey in 1994 approved of the legislation (www.culture.fr/culture/dglf/sondage.htm).

The Toubon Law also represented a change of tactic in the fight against English (see also Section 6.3). In particular, it was hoped that the law would counteract the *de facto* dominance of English in France not through traditional defensive measures, but rather by actively promoting a policy of multilingualism. According to the legislation, public bodies, such as the Parisian transport network (RATP) and the national railways (SNCF), are required to use at least two languages when providing translations for travellers. A similar provision applies to the translations of Internet sites maintained by government ministries and agencies. The incorporation of this new strategy of multilingualism was also made apparent when Philippe Douste-Blazy, the then French Minister of Culture, presented on 20 March 1996 a new language policy with three principal objectives (cf. www.culture.fr/culture/dglf/commin/fich-00.htm):

- to guarantee the presence and *rayonnement* (radiance) of French, the language of the Republic
- to conserve the role of French as language of international communication
- to promote multilingualism

Despite the new tactic, very little has changed: the spread of French abroad and its promotion as an international language remain the key elements of a language policy which seeks to shore up France's position in the world. Under de Gaulle, the number of French teachers abroad increased nearly threefold from 12,362 in 1959–60 to 33,814 in 1968–9, and in 1971, the sum allocated to the *rayonnement* of the French language amounted to 665 million francs (Gordon 1978: 57). With the collapse of Communism in Eastern Europe, the *Alliance française* too lost no time in expanding its operations to cities in Poland, Hungary, Bulgaria, Georgia and other countries (Lalanne-Berdouticq 1993: 147–8).

Yet despite these and other efforts, French continues to decline as an international language. The number of delegations to the United Nations which choose French as a working language has dropped from 31 in 1992 to 27 in 1997 (cf. www.culture.gouv.fr/culture/dglf/lois/onu-2.htm). The corresponding numbers of delegations choosing English as a working language were 74 in 1992 and 99 in 1997. In particular, it has been observed that English is the preferred working language of many of the newer UN member states, such as North and South Korea, Estonia, the Marshall Islands, Latvia, Liechtenstein, Lithuania and Micronesia (Haut conseil de la Francophonie 1999: 37). The role of French within the UN's internal workings has also been reduced to the point where the language is increasingly used for translation rather than for drafting purposes: 90 per cent of all UN documents submitted for translation are drafted in English (Haut conseil de la Francophonie 1999: 38). Hopes of reversing this trend are behind the French government's traditional backing of French-speaking candidates for the positions of Secretary-General. In other international organisations (e.g International Monetary Fund, World Bank), French is also progressively relegated to official circles, whereas it had once dominated even in unofficial contexts (Délégation générale à la langue française 1999: 60–2). After the 'linguistic disaster' of the 1994 Winter Olympics in Lillehammer, Norway, where French was practically absent despite its supposed official status, the French government was determined to make sure that a similar situation did not arise at the 2000 Summer Olympics in Sydney, Australia (Haut conseil de la Francophonie 1999: 41; cf. also www.culture.fr/ culture/dglf/JOlympiques/josydney.htm).

Much of France's efforts to rescue its international standing and that of its language have concentrated on *la Francophonie*, the political association of states which have French in common, be it as an official language, an unofficial *lingua franca*, or as a language which enjoys some symbolic significance. The French are quick to point out that the initiative to bring together the French-speaking world came from African leaders, notably Presidents Senghor of Senegal and Bourguiba of Tunisia. Yet accusations of French neo-colonialism aside (cf. Djité 1992; Calvet 1974), *la Francophonie* does serve to generate a positive French identity in two main respects. First, it serves as a new arena within which France can easily dominate, thus compensating somewhat for the country's decline as a world power. Second, by creating a supranational group of French-speaking states within the global arena, *la Francophonie* increases France's chances of remaining a major player on the world stage and gives a boost to French in the struggle against English. Africa in particular is seen as a potential linguistic market which the French have no intention of ceding to English. In this light, France's involvement in Rwanda in 1990–4 has been described not so much as a humanitarian response as a war against English 'using African "troops"' (Ager 1996b: 61, 136–8, 144). There is also potential for France to generate a positive identity through a role as an international mediator. According to some observers, *la Francophonie* constitutes the key to reaching a mutual understanding between Europe and the Arab world (Guillou 1993: 27).

The benefits of *la Francophonie* are nonetheless of a precarious nature for France. In response to the accusations of neo-colonialism mentioned in the previous paragraph, the country has already bowed to pressure to accept a more polycentric approach to French-speaking culture. In particular, the notion of a *francopolyphonie* has been suggested to emphasise the multilingual nature of the *Francophone* organisation (Ager 1996b: 73). This theme was taken up further at the 1993 summit in Mauritius, which had as its motto 'unity in diversity' (Guillou 1993: 16; Ager 1996b: 187–8). Yet despite this new image, French faces the continual possibility of rejection in many countries. As is the case with English in many former British colonies (see Section 7.2), French is viewed by some not as a source of common consciousness, so much as an obstacle to national or ethnic identity (Gordon 1978: 11). Alternatively, successful attempts to spread the language especially to the masses in Africa could meet resistance from the local élite, who use their knowledge of French as a means of guaranteeing a high social status (Ager 1996b: 51–2). The delicate task of reconciling Western and Islamic values may also prove too difficult for a country such as France, where racism and xenophobia are often problematic (Ager 1996b: 185). Nor is it certain that France will remain the leading economic, political and cultural force in the French-speaking world, when faced with increased competition from Canada, in particular Québec (Ager 1996b: 4). Such potential challenges may well make *la Francophonie* a difficult source of positive identity for the French in the future.

7.4 Language and identity in Sweden: The global arena

Internationalism, together with modernism, have been cornerstones of Swedish identity since the 1950s (Dahlstedt 1976: 25; see also Section 4.3). This is not to say that Swedish identity ceased to exist, simply that it took on a strong international dimension from that time. One area where this change in outlook is quite apparent is in the discourse surrounding the teaching of literature in Swedish schools. Englund (1997: 189–90) shows that while in the 1920s, the literature studied was centred on the nation and cultural heritage, by the 1980s, the emphasis had switched to human relations, pluralism and social education. Texts were no longer chosen because they were written by Swedes or about Swedish life, unlike in France, where Englund shows that the teaching of literature over this same period remained very much centred on national-humanistic discourse.

Swedish internationalism has resulted in the country playing a pro-active role in organisations such as the United Nations, which in turn has earned it the reputation of a responsible world citizen. The success with which Sweden has until now managed to generate a positive national identity in the global arena owes much to the exploitation of its minority status, and in particular its policy of neutrality.

> For the little, but ambitious, Swedish state, neutrality has ultimately been an instrument for political influence. During the Cold War (when in practice Sweden was silently part of the Western alliance), the rhetoric of neutrality fulfilled the same function as talk about the Swedish model: to put Sweden in focus on the international stage. As a 'neutral' state, Sweden lay claim to conveying the voice of the small states in a world characterised by the struggle between two blocks. We sought an identity as the foremost amongst the many small. It was a foreign policy profile which had been developed during the inter-war period and which constituted an ingenious means of adapting Sweden's ambitions to greatness to the nation's limited economic, political and military resources. These deficiencies were compensated for by ideological claims. (Karaveli 1997: 74)

Sweden's policy of non-alliance, which has allowed it to play the role of mediator in many conflicts around the globe, has long been incorporated into social democratic ideology. During the Vietnam War, Swedish neutrality served as a convenient platform from which to attack what was seen as ideologically driven hostility on the part of the US. In response to criticism by the government of Olof Palme towards American action in the so-called 'Christmas bombings' of Vietnam in 1972, the US even took the diplomatically significant step of recalling its ambassador from Stockholm and refused to receive the newly appointed Swedish ambassador to Washington. Some Swedish commentators went as far as to consider American culture in general as a threat (cf. Frykman 1993: 166). Although by no means as widespread or deep-seated as in France, there were fears also that Anglo-American was invading the national language, giving rise to *svengelska* (or Swenglish) which threatened the 'national way of life and identity' (Lundberg 1960: 28). Nonetheless, even the anti-American intellectuals of the 60s and 70s were not immune to the profound influence of American culture and language (Vikør 1993: 145).

These days there is little doubt that Swedish internationalism is more about Anglo-Americanism than anything else (Battail 1994: 12). Indeed 'linguistic internationalization' is the term which has been used to describe the stream of American English loan words into the Swedish language (Dahlstedt 1976: 26). When the Swedish Language Council teamed up with the Swedish postal service in a campaign against Swenglish in the late 1980s, the reactions of the public demonstrated to what extent the use of English borrowings had now become accepted: the calls to purify Swedish of English were rejected by many who claimed that the campaign reflected an unhealthy nationalism or even racism (Vikør 1993: 190 and 193; see also Section 4.3). Research shows that the number of loan words from English in everyday Swedish texts may actually have been overrated (Chrystal 1988). In technical terminologies, however, these words are much more frequent (Vikør 1993: 144). Unlike in France, the use of loan words in scientific domains has been widely encouraged, as clearly seen by the comments of Swedish linguist Erik Wellander.

> Internationally used terms in physics, chemistry, biology, astronomy, etc. must without discussion be welcomed in our language. Practically this inflow of new words will imply that the Swedish language in the field of modern science and technology makes its entrance into the West-European language community. (cited in Selander 1980: 26)

It is unclear just what Wellander meant when he claimed that the entrance of Swedish into the West-European language community was dependent on the use of such terms as *hydrogen, nitrogen* and *oxygen,* instead of the Swedish *väte, kväve* and *syre*. But it is possible that his preference lay with the former, not so much because of their 'international' nature as their use by American scientists.

American culture and language now enjoy high status in Sweden. That watching Donald Duck, albeit in translation, on television every Christmas Eve has become a Swedish tradition is indicative of a very Swedish strategy for generating a positive identity: divergence in convergence (see Section 7.2). While on the surface, such behaviour may have the appearance of convergence to the dominant, American culture, this same culture is used to express an alternative national identity. Moreover, it seems that it is not even necessary to adapt these dominant cultural characteristics to a Swedish reality: the mere fact that traits of the dominant group are embraced seems to suffice to claim Swedish psychological distinctiveness. Much of the positive image of Sweden generated by the pop group ABBA was a function of their singing in international English, not a heavily accented variety thereof. Other research carried out amongst young people confirms that convergence does not necessarily imply loss of national identity: 'modern young people feel themselves to be Danish (Swedish etc.) *as well as* inhabitants of the "world-wide America" of pop culture, films and consumption patterns they have grown up with' (Vikør 1993: 145; cf. also Bojsen 1989: 42).

The high level of proficiency in English which the Swedes enjoy carries immense symbolic value when they compare themselves with other nations such as the French or the Spanish. A sound knowledge of English is what allows the Swedes to compensate for any insecurity about constituting one of the smaller language groups in the world.

> Small linguistic polities such as speakers of Swedish, for example, rely heavily on the use of English as a contact language not only with native speakers of English but with other non-native English speakers. Without the linguistic vehicle offered by English, or any other prominent lingua franca spoken as a second language, the countries represented by these language groups would soon collapse, since it is clear that few power groups would invest the necessary time and energy in so unprofitable a task as learning a little-known language, such as Swedish. (Flaitz 1988: 26)

As extreme as Flaitz' own opinion may be, it does reflect quite well how the Swedes perceive the situation themselves. The comments of one Swedish academic are indicative of the widespread view that, while the national language has a role within Sweden, '[i]n communicating with countries outside Scandinavia Swedish is not, however, suitable' (Selander 1980: 17). Swedish attitudes towards English are so positive that some claim the language has reached as high a status as Swedish (Dahlstedt 1980: 104; Hollqvist 1984: 19–21). Others rate the value accorded to English by the Swedes as surpassing that of Swedish: 'English is considered as more effective, modern, beautiful and better than their own language' (Laureys 1997: 25). Others still suggest that the national language may even be considered by some Swedes as an obstacle to reaching a high level of proficiency in English (Margareta Westman, personal communication). In the hierarchy of language attitudes which can be observed in Sweden, English is thus situated at the top, acting as a sort of linguistic trump card for the purposes of generating a positive social identity.

While the consequences of such positive attitudes towards English may be lost on the average Swede, scholars have begun to point to the potential for language shift. Due to its pervasive nature, English can already be considered a second, rather than foreign, language in Sweden (Phillipson 1992: 25; Siguan 1996: 142; see also footnote 2 in Section 7.2). Indeed, students begin to learn English from the fourth or fifth (sometimes third) year of primary school (Vikør 1993: 142). Moreover, considering the widespread bilingualism at the grassroots level as well as amongst the élite, the potential for language shift to English exists in a unique way in Sweden (Hyltenstam 1996: 30). Not only is knowledge of English fairly widespread throughout the country, the language is progressively dominating key domains such as politics and administration, as has already been seen in the context of the EU (see Section 6.4). Other fields include science and education, business, and culture and entertainment (Teleman 1993).

In the fields of science and education, knowledge of a widely understood language is often considered essential to ensure the spread of experimental results and participate in discussions with researchers in other parts of the world (Hyltenstam 1996: 20). At most Swedish universities, academic theses can be written in one of several European languages: Swedish, English, French or German. Allowance is also made for Danes and Norwegians wishing to write in their mother tongue. Nonetheless, there is an overwhelming preference to use English for this purpose, as witnessed by the results of a survey conducted in Lund in 1991 (see Table 7.1).

These figures are in accordance with those of a similar study conducted at Uppsala university in 1993–4 (Gunnarsson 1999). Here, English was found to be the language of between 89 per cent and 100 per cent of all doctoral theses, conference papers and academic articles written in the fields of technology/science, pharmacology and medicine. Only in law was English not dominant — no doctoral theses and a mere 13 per cent of academic articles were written in that language during the study period — presumably because many aspects of this field are confined to the national context, with the notable exception of international law. In light of such results, it is not difficult to understand the concerns of Westman (1996: 184) and others, who claim that the situation has reached a point where many Swedish scientists have difficulty writing in Swedish because they are not used to explaining and discussing their fields in that language. For this reason, Gunnarsson (1999: 21) suggests the teaching of Swedish terminology in those faculties where the language is under threat.

Table 7.1 Number of doctoral dissertations written in English, Swedish and other languages at Lund University in 1991 according to field of study

Field of study	English	Swedish	Other
Theology	1	1	0
Law	0	4	0
Medicine	60	0	0
Odontology	6	0	0
Technology	14	3	0
Humanities	4	12	0
Social sciences	7	12	3
Mathematical sciences	23	0	0

From Teleman (1993: 134)

English is also increasingly becoming the language of teaching at Swedish universities. Often this situation occurs when there is at least one foreign student in the class and is partly due to a desire to attract overseas students. Since it overtook German in 1946 as the compulsory foreign language learnt by schoolchildren, English has also been gaining ground in Swedish secondary schools (Hyltenstam 1996: 24–8). For example, English is the language of instruction in 75.5 per cent of SPRINT programmes which involve the teaching of school subjects in foreign languages (Nixon 1999: 3).[7] The spread of English into the domain of secondary education is seen as an inevitable consequence of language shift at more advanced levels.

> Actually, it is no wonder that English is trickling down: when science thinks and writes in English, there are in the end no Swedish words to talk about the triumphs of science. It becomes easier to speak English in undergraduate science courses at university and gradually easier to do the same in upper secondary schools. (Teleman 1993: 135)

The use of English in Swedish schools is symptomatic of a functional approach to language learning on the part of the Swedes, which some commentators have referred to as 'pure engineering' (Battail 1994: 11). Even Swedish has not remained immune from this functional reduction of language. As a result of school reforms in the 1960s, Swedish as a subject was transformed into an opportunity for teaching communication, professional skills and citizen education (Thavenius 1995: 474).

In the domain of business, English is also encroaching on Swedish. The Anglicisation of some Swedish company names — such as Skanska and Gotabanken from *Skånska* and *Götabanken* respectively (Svenska språknämnden 1998) — may not constitute a real threat for Swedish; however, the same cannot be said for the many Swedish companies which resort to a 'functional bilingualism', using English as the company's official language, even if duties are performed in both Swedish and English (Hollqvist 1984: 123). In the fields of popular culture and entertainment English is also making its mark. Anglo-American television programmes abound and English is becoming more and more pervasive in Swedish advertising (Hyltenstam 1996: 17). Foreign films in Sweden are subtitled rather than dubbed, as has traditionally been the case in France. Moreover, an increasing number of English-language films on video are appearing without any subtitling at all.

Some researchers have tried to describe the dialectic relationship of English and Swedish in these and other domains of language use. One typology is shown in Figure 7.1.

PRIVATE SPHERE		COMMUNITY SPHERE		GLOBAL SPHERE
Home		School, education		Medicine
Health care		Health care		Technology
Social life	MEDIA	Technology	MEDIA	Academia
Free time		Research		International politics
Work place		Public affairs		Arts industry
		Cultural life		Commercial activity
		Business		
Intimate language		Standard language		

Swedish

English

Figure 7.1 The dialectic relationship of Swedish and English within the private, community and global spheres. (From Teleman and Westman 1997:6)

This figure shows that as well as already dominating fields classified as belonging to the global sphere, English is also gaining ground in the community sphere (as indicated by the dotted line). This has the effect of substantially reducing the potential use of standard Swedish — for which the community sphere is the only real field of expression — since a more informal or intimate style of language dominates the private sphere. Also indicative of the second language function of English is the existence of a second tier of media, as represented by English-speaking TV stations like CNN and BBC World, both of which penetrate into many Swedish homes via cable networks.

In light of the growing amount of academic research into the spread of English in Sweden, Swedish authorities are beginning to take the potential threat to the national language seriously. In 1997, the Swedish Language Council (*Svenska språknämnden*) was given the task of researching whether a government policy to promote Swedish was necessary (Regeringsbeslut 1997-04-30). The plan of action proposed in March 1998 (Svenska språknämnden 1998) included a range of measures to ensure the status of Swedish in certain domains. As mentioned in Section 6.4, some of these measures concerned Sweden's membership in the European Union. Other domains included higher education, where it was suggested that Swedish be the normal language of instruction. By this was intended that university lecturers and students be competent in Swedish, and that academic theses written in foreign languages be accompanied by a summary in Swedish. A similar condition was proposed for primary and secondary education, where teachers should be required to demonstrate a full command of Swedish in order to hold permanent positions.

The report also recommended that no student receive a final pass mark in Swedish without a good mastery of the written and spoken language. In addition, schools which offer bilingual education should be able to guarantee that a student's ability to discuss subject material in Swedish is not neglected.

In the field of media, the Language Council's report stated that television and radio stations should see to it that a sufficient amount of Swedish language material is included in their programming. Subtitling in Swedish should also be of good quality, and journalism courses should be improved to encourage a better awareness of 'correct' Swedish. In the domain of information technology, it was suggested that computer programs which offer language help (e.g. spell checks) be continually monitored for correct use of language, and that language experts be consulted as part of computer program development. Multimedia programs used in schools should also ordinarily be translated into Swedish. A final recommendation envisaged that the existing language-planning agencies play a major role in the realisation of language policies. In May 2000, a parliamentary committee was set up to investigate these proposals further, with the view to formulating a concrete plan of action for the promotion of Swedish. The deliberations of the committee, which comprises language specialists and representatives from all political parties, are expected to be made known around the end of 2001 (Kulturdepartementet, press release, 5 October 2000, see www.kultur.regeringen.se; Olle Josephson, personal communication).

7.5 France and Sweden in the global arena: Past and future challenges

In their attempts to attain national psychological distinctiveness, France and Sweden have both traditionally relied on policies of political and military independence. As these policies were largely geared to the mechanisms of the Cold War, the collapse of the Communist bloc has threatened to undermine the positive national identity which both countries had succeeded in generating. French claims to great-power status are questioned as France can no longer play one superpower off against the other (Gildea 1996: 209; Jenkins and Copsey 1996: 114). Similarly, Sweden has found itself in a foreign policy identity vacuum as one of the cornerstones of Swedish identity — neutrality — becomes increasingly irrelevant. Indeed, Sweden has participated in the NATO-sponsored military cooperation programme know as Partnership for Peace (PFP) from its beginning in 1994; the country has also enjoyed observer status in the Western

European Union (WEU) defence forum since 1995. But the end of the Cold War is not the only hurdle faced by France and Sweden in the global arena. Globalisation is the other main challenge, which unlike the Cold War, reveals the very different identity-generating strategies employed by France and Sweden.

As a country which has traditionally enjoyed dominant status in the global arena, France finds it all the more difficult to accept a globalisation process which relegates it to the status of a minority in the face of American domination. During the 1993–4 Uruguay negotiations of the general agreement on tariffs and trade (GATT), the French government insisted on a cultural exception (*exception culturelle*) in order to 'protect' French cultural industries from their purportedly unsophisticated American equivalents. Soon after his election as president in 1995, Chirac also strove to reassert France's presence in the global arena, for example by resuming nuclear testing in the South Pacific (Ardagh 1999: 27).

Unlike in France, globalisation can be seen as an advantage in Sweden: the country has a long tradition of exploiting its minority status as part of an ideology of internationalism. An important element of the Swedish approach involves a commitment to modern industries. But since the 1980s, Swedish industries have encountered serious difficulties, faced with growing economic competition in particular from Asia. In search of a new niche, Swedish companies now look to the tertiary sector. Indeed, a recent government plan of action shows how Sweden is aspiring to become a leader in the field of knowledge and information technology (*Svenska Dagbladet*, 18 September 1999). As Graddol (1998: 29) points out, this service-orientated sector relies heavily on the use of language. As such, one can only assume that this new focus will contribute to the further spread of English in Sweden.

The differing responses of France and Sweden to the rise of English as an international language are explained by differences in the respective identity-generating strategies of the two countries. English constitutes an important element of a positive Swedish identity in the global arena: far from being perceived a threat, English is considered as an asset. In France, however, the role of the French language in the global arena is seen as a reflection of the role played by the country as a whole in this same arena.

> The role and spread of our language in the world reflects our place and ability to play a major role there. (Guillou 1993: 32)

For some defenders of the French language, the rise of English therefore symbolises a 'dethroning' of their language and of their country's position in the world (Hagège 1987: 287; cf. also Flaitz 1988: 117 and 187). But while implying the superiority of French culture over mass, Americanised culture may have succeeded until now, this strategy may not necessarily continue to serve as an effective means of generating a positive identity for France and *la Francophonie* in the future.

> Francophonie's official disdain for consumerism smacks more of the politics of envy than of sincerity. [...] The defenders of Francophonie do not say why Francophone culture is superior to Americanophone culture, why the American soap opera is to be rejected as an art form, or why the Astérix theme park is preferable to Disneyland Paris. If the future of Francophonie is to rest on its cultural preferences, and at the same time it is to be presented as a universal movement, there will have to be better comparative arguments which can defeat the charge of both xenophobia and elitism. (Ager 1996b: 185 and 187)

It may be that greater flexibility and imagination will be necessary to defend French identity in the long run (Gildea 1996: 227). Indeed, there are signs that, in certain domains, France is already beginning to adopt some form of convergence. The French actor Gérard Depardieu now regularly appears in American films, while most of the films by French director Luc Besson are in English and feature American actors. The latter's recent film *Joan of Arc* constitutes a classic example of what this study has referred to as divergence in convergence (see Section 7.2): in this case, Besson seeks to tell an unquestionably French story (divergence) through the medium of English (convergence). Other signs that there may be some willingness to converge include the suggestion made in 1997 by Claude Allègre, then Education Minister, that the French should 'stop considering English as a foreign language', a remark which not surprisingly caused a storm of protest amongst certain commentators, notably from one Québécois academic (cf. Wright 2000: 9, 244). As seen by the examples of windsurfers, computers and the Internet (see Section 7.3 and this section above), convergence in the global arena can also take place on non-linguistic dimensions, that is to say, while still maintaining the use of the French language. Indeed, one of the aims of the government programme (PAGSI), launched in 1998 to prepare France for its entry into the information age (convergence), is to create new IT terminology in French and ensure the presence of the language on the English-dominated web (divergence) (Délégation générale à la langue française 1999: 107–22). Further strategies of this nature may require that the French language shed some of its strong cultural connotations. Such action may even increase the chances of French becoming a truly global language (Ager 1996b: 53).

But while the French begin the difficult transition to ABBA-like strategies of divergence in convergence in the global arena, the Swedes seem to be considering the traditional protective stance of the French, by contemplating legislation to safeguard Swedish from English. In a global arena undeniably dominated by the United States, it appears that the answer to maintaining positive French and Swedish identities will increasingly depend on finding the right balance between convergence and divergence, on both linguistic and non-linguistic dimensions (see Section 3.2.5.2). Not only will this challenge apply to official circles, but also to the grassroots level. The latter was the focus of the second type of study included in this book, namely the survey, which is discussed in Chapter 8.

CHAPTER 8

Language and national identity in France and Sweden: A survey

In their examination of language attitudes and identity strategies in France and Sweden, Chapters 4, 5, 6 and 7 have made use of a content analysis (see Section 3.1). In accordance with this type of analysis, the primary focus has until now been on the official level, that is on official language policies and the way the state incorporates language into its national identity strategies. Amongst the alternative techniques to the societal analysis is the direct method, which focuses on the grassroots level (see Section 3.1). The present chapter considers a questionnaire on language attitudes and national identity strategies which was distributed amongst upper secondary school students in France and Sweden. An outline of the aims of this survey (Section 8.1) and the particular methodology used (Section 8.2) serves as a backdrop against which to discuss and interpret the results from a comparative perspective (Section 8.3).

8.1 Aims of survey

Unlike the societal analyses of previous chapters which predominantly concentrated on the official level, the survey which is the focus of this chapter sought to measure language attitudes and examine the role of language in national identity strategies specifically at the grassroots level. As seen in Section 2.4.2, the language attitudes which exist at this level can be considered as covert language policies which are the product of folk, as opposed to official, nationalisms. Attitudes and strategies at the official and grassroots levels need not necessarily coincide; indeed, any discrepancies between the two levels could signal that language attitudes and the role played by language in the construction of national identity are possibly in a state of transition. One might expect that the greatest discrepancies are observed between official attitudes and those amongst young people, since the latter are often leaders in change, including that of a linguistic nature (cf. Holmes 1992: 225–6; Wardhaugh 1998: 192). For this reason, this survey focused in particular on upper secondary school children in both France and Sweden.

Amongst the young respondents, the survey sought to test hypotheses which focus on issues of language attitudes and national identity strategies considered in four contexts: a general perspective, the national arena, the European arena and the global arena. These hypotheses are based on the attitudes of official circles, as revealed by the content analyses in Chapters 4, 5, 6 and 7. In the case of France, the hypotheses are also founded on the subjective writings of guardians of the language, and reflect assumptions frequently held in the English-speaking world *vis-à-vis* language attitudes and national identity strategies in that country (cf. Flaitz 1988: 199). The hypotheses which were tested are as follows:

1. Language and national identity: a general perspective
   Hypothesis 1a: There is a high degree of national and linguistic consciousness in France.
   Hypothesis 1b: There is a low degree of national and linguistic consciousness in Sweden.

2. Language and national identity in the national arena
   Hypothesis 2a: In today's France, attitudes towards minority languages remain negative. Linguistic boundaries are still significant when making social comparisons with ethnolinguistic minorities.
   Hypothesis 2b: In today's Sweden, attitudes towards minority languages are positive. Linguistic boundaries are no longer significant when making social comparisons with ethnolinguistic minorities.

3. Language and national identity in the European arena
   Hypothesis 3a: A positive French identity in the European arena is generated through strategies of divergence.
   Hypothesis 3b: A positive Swedish identity in the European arena is generated through strategies of convergence.

4. Language and national identity in the global arena
   Hypothesis 4a: A positive French identity in the global arena is generated through strategies of divergence.
   Hypothesis 4b: A positive Swedish identity in the global arena is generated through strategies of convergence.

In addition, the survey sought to shed some light on the following research questions:

Research question 1: Are there any discrepancies between the grassroots and official levels *vis-à-vis* the role played by language in the construction of French and Swedish identities?

Research question 2: Are the results of the present survey in accordance with those of other studies which focus on the role of language in the construction of French and Swedish identities?

8.2 Methodology

The methodology of the survey discussed here is examined in more detail in Oakes (2000: 167–88). What follows is a brief overview of the main stages in the development of the instrument (Section 8.2.1) and the methodological procedures followed (Section 8.2.2).

8.2.1 Development of the instrument

Of the possible survey methods available, it was decided that the most suitable would be a written questionnaire (cf. Oakes 2000: 167–8). Despite the advantages of this means of inquiry, it was important to keep in mind the major disadvantages which are well discussed in literature on research methodology (e.g. Baker 1992: 19; Vassberg 1993: 101–2). For example, self reports of any kind — be it of an attitude, rating of language proficiency, designation of mother tongue, etc. — must be interpreted with caution; the possibility of certain 'biases' can also affect results (cf. Brislin 1986: 163). Following an overview of previous studies (Section 8.2.1.1), this section examines the particular challenges faced with regard to content validation (Section 8.2.1.2) and translation (Section 8.2.1.3).

8.2.1.1 *Previous studies*

The content and layout of the questionnaire owed much to the following empirical studies of language attitudes in various contexts: Trudgill and Tzavaras (1977) on ethnolinguistic identity amongst Albanian-Greeks, Belazi (1982) on French–Arabic code-switching in Tunisia, Bentahila (1983) on French–Arabic code-switching in Morocco, Edwards and Shearn (1987) on language attitudes in Belgium, Flaitz (1988) on French attitudes to English as a world language, Baker (1992) on attitudes to bilingualism in Wales, Vassberg (1993) on acts of identity in Alsace, and Wingstedt (1998) on language ideology in Sweden. These studies served as models in several respects for the present survey. For example, they led to the adoption for most items of a five-point interval, Likert-like scale (completely agree, partially agree, undecided, don't really agree, don't agree at all); along with Likert (1932: 44–6), they also proved particularly useful in the wording and formulation of the individual questionnaire items (cf. Oakes 2000: 169). The questionnaire as based on these models was then refined as a result of two pilot studies conducted in 1997, one in Australia, the other in France (cf. Oakes 2000: 171). A more in-depth discussion of the aims of individual items can be found in Oakes (2000: 175–83).

Of the above mentioned studies, it was Flaitz (1988) and Wingstedt (1998) which proved particularly beneficial, not least because they focused specifically on French and Swedish identities respectively. The survey discussed here nevertheless differed from these two previous studies in four main respects. First, the perspective or context of study for language attitudes and national identity strategies was different. On the one hand, Flaitz (1988) focuses only on attitudes towards English, a perspective which corresponds to what is considered in the present study as the global arena. On the other hand, Wingstedt (1998), who nevertheless investigates some attitudes towards English in Sweden, concentrates predominantly on attitudes towards ethnic minorities and their languages. This latter context corresponds to what is considered in this book as the national arena. In contrast to both Flaitz (1988) and Wingstedt (1998), the study presented here considers language attitudes and national identity strategies in four contexts: from a general perspective, in the national arena, in the European arena, and in the global arena. In order to obtain a complete picture of language attitudes and national identity strategies in France and Sweden, it was judged necessary to study all of these contexts, not least because the identity of a nation as constructed in one arena can affect the construction of that same nation's identity in another arena (see Section 3.2.5.3).

The second respect in which the present survey differed from those of Flaitz (1988) and Wingstedt (1998) concerns the age of the respondents: those in the former study are aged from 12 years onwards, while those in the latter range from 21 to 71 years. The decision to focus here only on young people was made for two related reasons. First, it is recalled that one of the research questions of the survey was to investigate if any discrepancies in language attitudes and national identity strategies existed between the official and grassroots levels (see Section 8.1). In so far as young people are still in a process of socialisation and have not fully developed adult prejudices (Hudson 1980: 17–18), one might expect that it is the opinions of young people that are most likely to differ from those of the official level.[1] The second reason for deciding to conduct the present study amongst young people only concerned the prospect of European and global identities. While the reality of these identities was questioned in Sections 6.1 and 7.1, one might expect that they are most likely to exist amongst young people, who have grown up in an era characterised by European integration, and by globalisation and modern technologies.

The third way in which the study discussed here differs from those of Flaitz (1988) and Wingstedt (1998) relates to the moment in time when the data was collected. While Wingstedt's (1998) study can still be considered relatively contemporary, it is possible that the results of Flaitz (1988) are no longer valid. Fourth and finally, the present study can be distinguished from the two previous studies on French and Swedish in so far as it adopted a comparative approach. As argued in Section 1.1, such an approach allows for a better understanding of the link between language and national identity, as well as the ethnolinguistic implications of some of the major challenges currently facing France, Sweden, and other European nation-states: regionalism, immigration, European integration and globalisation.

8.2.1.2 Content validation

As mentioned in Section 3.1, the validation of attitude surveys is particularly difficult because there is often a lack of harmony between the three components which make up an attitude: affect, cognition and behaviour. However, as also noted in that section, an argument can be made that in a study which focuses on attitudes and identity strategies of groups, it is the cognitive component of an attitude which is most relevant. Such an argument seems all the more acceptable when the groups concerned are as large as nations, within which individual, personal attitudes are sure to differ greatly (see Section 3.2.4.3). This point was made by Wingstedt (1998: 252) in her study of language ideology in Sweden, where it was suggested that the cognitive dimension of an attitude was even more important than the affective.

> What may be particularly important in the reproduction and propagation of an ideology is perhaps not what people think themselves, but rather what people believe are the norms and values of most other people. (Wingstedt 1998: 252)

In assessing the content validity of items of the present study, clearly what was needed were criteria of a more subjective nature which corresponded to this cognitive dimension of an attitude.

In her study of language attitudes towards English in France, Flaitz (1988: 56) follows the advice of Sax (1968), who suggests the use of judges who can measure each item of the instrument to assess its validity. This model was also followed for the present study. Each questionnaire item was therefore tested with two scholars — one French, the other Swedish — who were well informed about the relevant ethnolinguistic issues, as well as during a work-in-progress seminar held in Sweden. In addition, the researcher was himself required to gain a sound knowledge of issues of language and national identity in France and Sweden, as manifested in the societal analyses of Chapters 4, 5, 6 and 7.

8.2.1.3 *Translation*

One of the major challenges concerning the present survey was the issue of translating the questionnaire which was distributed to students in French and Swedish respectively (cf. appendices). The type of method used here was the direct or one-way method (cf. McKay *et al.* 1996: 93), which consisted of translating from the source language (initially English, but then French) into the target language (Swedish). Once the Swedish version was complete, modification occurred to both the French and Swedish versions through decentring (cf. McKay *et al.* 1996: 94). This process occurred over approximately a year, that is throughout the whole development of the questionnaire. During this time, the advice of a native speaker of French and a native speaker of Swedish was essential to check the stylistic acceptability of the two versions.

The actual type of translation used for the study combined a conceptual translation with a culturally equivalent translation. Unlike a literal translation, which uses dictionary equivalents, a conceptual translation 'uses terms or phrases in the target language that capture the implied associations, or connotative meaning, of the text used in the source language instrument' (McKay *et al.* 1996: 94). The French *se détériorer* (literally 'to deteriorate') in items 43 and 44 of the questionnaire was thus rendered by *påverka negativt* (literally 'to affect negatively') in Swedish (see appendices). It was judged that both these expressions had similar connotative meanings with regard to the effect of other languages on French/Swedish, or the influence of second language varieties of French/Swedish on the standard.

A culturally equivalent translation 'extends the conceptual equivalence of words and phrases in the source instrument to tap equivalent patterns of thought and behaviour in the social world of the target language speakers' (McKay *et al.* 1996: 94). For example, items 38 of the Swedish version asked respondents if they thought it was the responsibility of the Swedish school system to provide home language teaching, that is for regional as well as immigrant languages (see Section 5.4). While most students in Sweden could be expected to have heard of home language tuition, it was judged that most students in France would be more likely to know about the teaching of regional languages, such as through *ikastolas* in the Basque Country or *diwans* in Brittany, than about the teaching of language and cultures of origin (ELCO) programmes (see Sections 5.2.1 and 5.4). For this reason, item 38 of the French instrument made reference only to the teaching of regional languages. The importance of conceptual and culturally equivalent translation techniques is also highlighted by the label used for the middle point on the interval scale used in questions 18 and 19 ('Do you feel French/European?/How Swedish/European do you feel?'). In the French version of the instrument, this point was labelled *moyennement* (literally 'average'), while in the Swedish version, lack of a useable semantic equivalent to *moyennement* led to the use of *ganska mycket* (literally 'quite a lot') to label the same point. The decision to use *moyennement* and *ganska mycket* was made on the advice of the two native speakers mentioned above, who judged that the two terms could be considered conceptual or cultural equivalents.

When translating and decentring the questionnaires, it was also important to ensure that questions and statements were phrased using a similar register in both languages. That one version of the instrument did not require a higher reading level or degree of knowledge than the other was considered an essential criterion for a good translation. As McKay *et al.* (1996: 103) point out, a good translation results in greater validity of the data.

8.2.2 Procedures

This section examines the methodological procedures followed for the study. The selection of schools and respondents is first considered (Section 8.2.2.1). A discussion then follows on how the instrument was administered (Section 8.2.2.2) and which statistical analyses were performed (Section 8.2.2.3).

8.2.2.1 *Selection of the schools and respondents*

Ten schools in total participated in the study: six in France (in Paris, Bayonne and Draguigan) and four in Sweden (in Stockholm, Kiruna and Malmberget) (cf. Oakes 2000: 183). All of these were upper secondary schools, known as *lycées* (or in one case *écoles nationales*) in France, and *gymnasieskolor* in Sweden. In choosing this more advanced level of schooling which is not compulsory, it was hoped that a certain degree of maturity would have been reached amongst the students, whereby some thought had been devoted to questions of language and national identity, as well as issues such as regionalism, immigration, globalisation and European integration. The other two criteria which were initially used to select schools — location (i.e. centre versus periphery) and students' field of study — were later excluded from the analysis. These either proved to have no significant effect on the results or were not of direct relevance to a comparison of language and national identity in France and Sweden (cf. Oakes 2000: 198–200). A final point regarding the selection of schools relates to socio-economic standing. While every effort was made to involve schools in similar types of socio-economic areas, or where students of similar socio-economic backgrounds could be found, no assurance can be given that these efforts were successful, not least because the researcher was largely reliant on the Academy of Paris to suggest schools that might be willing to participate.

Once the schools had been decided on, only one criterion was used to select students to act as respondents: mother tongue, defined here as the first language spoken at home. For the purposes of expressing language attitudes, it was decided that the respondents' backgrounds regarding French and Swedish should be as close as possible. In this way, it was hoped that all respondents would feel some form of sentimental attachment to these languages. Only those students who had French/Swedish as a mother tongue were included, although bilinguals with other mother tongues in addition to French/Swedish were also accepted. In the case of France in particular, it was recognised that the mother tongue criterion also potentially included non-French people who nevertheless had French as a mother tongue (e.g. Maghrebis, West Africans, etc.). Conversely, this criterion excluded those students who did not have French/Swedish as a mother tongue, but who nevertheless enjoyed a sentimental attachment to it because they learnt it at an early age. Far from being unique to the mother tongue criterion, such problems accompany the choice of most selection criteria; they are important factors which need to be considered when interpreting the data.

The methodological problems concerned with defining mother tongue are well-known, especially in the context of population censuses (cf. Fasold 1984: 114–15). As seen in Section 1, the increase in people declaring the use Macedonian and Maltese in the Australian census of 1986 was largely a result of heightened ethnic awareness and did not reflect an increase in real language use (Clyne 1991: 104–5). That similar self-reports were used in the present survey to indicate mother tongue was not considered problematic, considering that the aim was not to examine the use of a certain language, but rather its symbolic value for national identity. Whether French/Swedish was actually a respondent's mother tongue was not as important as whether that person *considered* French/Swedish as her or his mother tongue. In his discussion of the related notion of 'native speaker', Davies (1991: 73) notes that 'individuals can regard themselves (and others) as native speakers for symbolic rather than communicative purposes' (see also Section 1).

Of the 495 questionnaires which were originally distributed (240 in France and 255 in Sweden), a total of 421 students met the mother tongue criterion to participate in the study. The greater number of students in Sweden as seen in Table 8.1 was due to the fact that there were more students in France who did not have French as a mother tongue and who were therefore omitted from the study.

Table 8.1 Number of students (N) selected as respondents in different locations in France and Sweden

France			Sweden	
Location		N	Location	N
Paris (school 1)		28	Stockholm (school 1)	57
Paris (school 2)		26	Stockholm (school 2)	70
Paris (school 3)		21	Kiruna	52
Paris (school 4)		34	Malmberget	55
Bayonne		56		
Draguignan		22		
Total		187		234

8.2.2.2 *Administration of the instrument*

For reasons discussed in Oakes (2000: 186–7), it was decided that the researcher should be present to administer the questionnaire for the present study. The questionnaires were administered between January 1998 and September 1999, to all students in a given class, so as not to exclude anyone. Only at a later stage were those students who did not meet the mother tongue selection criterion (see Section 8.2.2.1) omitted from the corpus.

Ideally, the distribution period should have been much shorter in order to minimise the potential for a change in attitudes over time. However bureaucratic difficulties encountered with many of the schools in France had the effect of prolonging the distribution process (cf. Oakes 2000: 183). Other problems experienced in France included the unwillingness of some schools to have the researcher present. In those cases where school administrators and/or teachers distributed and returned the questionnaires themselves, instructions were provided in addition to those already given on top of every questionnaire (see appendices), so as to reinforce the researcher's wish that students refrain from discussing their responses amongst one another. Another example of the need to adapt the study to the bureaucracy of the French education system was the requirement made by one school head that items 47 ('One must be born in France to be considered French') and 48 ('One must have French parents to be considered French') be omitted from the questionnaire. That these two items were deemed too sensitive underscores once again the key role played by the school system in the French refusal to grant official recognition to alternative ethnic origins (see Sections 5.2.1 and 5.2.2).

8.2.2.3 *Statistical analyses*
Once the questionnaires had been collected, the data were coded and entered into the statistical package SPSS. Due to uneven distributions revealed with regard to sex and parents' place of birth, coupled with the fact that more students in the centres than in the peripheries had at least one parent born abroad (cf. Oakes 2000: 188), a decision was made to perform four-way ANOVAs on the interval (i.e. five-point scale) data, using country, sex, location and parents' place of birth as independent variables. In particular, ANOVA tests were chosen over t-tests so as to avoid any potential for confounding effects. A main effects model was fitted, which did not take into consideration any interactions between the four variables. The decision to exclude interactions from the analysis was made on the basis that the primary focus of the survey was the effect of country (France versus Sweden), while sex, location and parents' place of birth were only of secondary interest.

Items such as 27 ('Do you think that another language/other languages could threaten the future of French/Swedish?') resulted in frequency or nominal data of the type 'yes', 'perhaps', 'no' and 'don't know'. Chi square crosstabulations were performed to test the effect of country and the other independent variables (i.e. sex, location and parents' place of birth) on such data. Correlations were used to test the interdependence of two sets of interval data, e.g. variable 18 ('How French/Swedish do you feel?') by variable 19 ('How European do you feel?'). For all three types of tests — ANOVAs, Chi square crosstabulations and correlations — it was decided to compensate for the relatively large number of tests performed, by adopting a more stringent level of significance: 0.02 as opposed to the frequently used 0.05.

8.3 Results and comparative discussion of the survey

The aim of this section is to present and discuss some of the findings of the survey conducted amongst upper secondary students in France and Sweden. The focus here is limited to the effect of the independent variable country. A more in-depth discussion, including the consideration of other background variables (e.g. sex, location, students' place of birth, parents' place of birth), can be found in Oakes (2000: 189-243).

Following the structures of Chapters 4 to 7, this section is divided into four parts: students' language attitudes and national identity strategies are considered from a general perspective (Section 8.3.1), in the national arena (Section 8.3.2), in the European arena (Section 8.3.3) and in the global arena (Section 8.3.4). Comparisons are also introduced with the results of other studies, in particular the empirical surveys of Flaitz (1988) and Wingstedt (1998), as well as the societal analyses of Chapters 4, 5, 6 and 7. A final section summaries the results of the survey in terms of the hypotheses and research questions posed (Section 8.3.5).

8.3.1 Language and national identity: A general perspective

This section considers the results from a general perspective. By 'general perspective' is meant one which does not make reference to language and national identity as they exist in the particular contexts of the national, global or European arenas. The questionnaire items which could be considered in such a way were grouped according to the following two sub-themes: national consciousness (Section 8.3.1.1) and linguistic consciousness (Section 8.3.1.2).

8.3.1.1 *National consciousness*
National consciousness amongst the respondents was measured predominantly by means of items — or variables (V) — 18 ('How French/Swedish do you feel?') and 42 ('I am proud to be French/Swedish'), but to some extent also by item 26. This latter item asked respondents to draw up a list of ten ideas or things which they considered important for French/Swedish identity or culture, a task with which many of the Swedish respondents had great difficulty. One Swedish student wrote only 'waffles' (!) and added: 'I do not know of any special cultural symbols in Sweden (weak culture)'; another managed to muster a few symbols such as 'democracy' and 'healthcare', but remarked: 'Of course I feel Swedish, but I feel more European, we are all citizens of the world. That is why

I cannot come up with so much.' These comments are classic examples of the myth of 'negative' or 'inverted' Swedish nationalism mentioned in Section 4.4. However, as was also seen in that section, Swedish identity has relied, since the 1930s, not so much on overt as covert symbols which can be thought of as 'unwaved flags' (Billig 1995: 40–1; see Section 2.2.3). Different groups express their identities with different emphasis and by using different cultural registers (Löfgren 1993: 27, 72–3; see Section 4.3). The Swedish respondents may not have thought of their identity in terms of objective symbols like the French, but this does not imply that the former lacked a subjective sense of national identity. Indeed, when more direct means of measurement were used in items 18 and 49, the Swedish respondents were found to report a *stronger* (mean=1.5 for variable 18) and *more positive* (mean=1.6 for variable 49) national identity than their French counterparts (means=2.3 and 2.4 respectively; $p<0.001$; see Table 8.2).

The higher scores observed amongst the French respondents are no doubt partially due to differences in ethnic background amongst the French and Swedish students (cf. Oakes 2000: 195–6). Indeed, when those respondents with at least one foreign-born parent were excluded from the corpus, the French students, as well as their Swedish counterparts, expressed a slightly stronger national identity and pride in that identity: French means=2.1 for both variables 18 and 49; Swedish means=1.4 and 1.5 respectively (cf. Oakes 2000: 203). Far from being unexpected, these results are in agreement with one of the principles of ethnolinguistic identity theory seen in Section 3.2.3: the fewer groups an individual belongs to, the stronger his or her ethnolinguistic identity will be. In other words, the allegiance which many respondents felt to another country — because it was the birthplace of one or both of their parents — had the effect of diluting the strength of their French/Swedish identity and national pride.

Table 8.2 National consciousness according to country

	Country	N	Mean	F	df.	sig.
V18 How French/Swedish do you feel?	France	181	2.3	51.7	1,390	0.000
	Sweden	234	1.5			
V49 I am proud to be French/Swedish	France	185	2.4	50.0	1,394	0.000
	Sweden	234	1.6			

For V18 means: 1=enormously; 2=a lot; 3=average/quite a lot; 4=a bit; 5=not at all. For V49 means: 1=agree totally; 2=agree partially; 3=undecided; 4=don't particularly agree; 5=don't agree at all.

It can be argued that it makes little sense to attribute an absolute value to national consciousness, especially when no assurance could be given that the corpus was truly representative *vis-à-vis* ethnic background (see Section 8.2.2.1). Yet the significance of the present results does not lie in the individual means *per se* so much as in the difference between the French and Swedish means. In other words, it would have been more difficult to draw meaningful conclusions about language attitudes and national identity strategies in France and Sweden had a comparative approach not been used. Indeed, the results for variables 18 and 49 are confirmed by at least two other comparative studies.

When asked about their national and European identities in a recent Eurobarometer survey (1999), 60 per cent of the Swedes questioned said they felt 'Swedish only', while only 35 per cent of the French respondents claimed to feel 'French only' (as opposed to 'French and European', 'European and French' or 'European only'). The present results are also in agreement with the observation made in the societal analysis of Section 4.3: although still clearly an influence on how the Swedes perceive their identity, the widespread Swedish claim to an 'inverted' identity is seen here to be no more than a popular myth. For the moment, this myth still appears to serve a purpose: in light of the negative attitudes associated with nationalism, the Swedish claim to an inverted national identity can itself be considered a means of generating a positive identity. Nonetheless, identity strategies in Sweden seem to be in a state of transition; the current ethnonationalist revival is inciting more overt expressions of Swedish identity (see Section 4.3). If this trend continues, and were the present study repeated in a few years' time, it is quite possible that the Swedish students, like their French counterparts, would have no difficulty in citing symbols of their national identity and culture.

8.3.1.2 *Linguistic consciousness*
The measurement of linguistic consciousness required notably more questionnaire items than was necessary for national consciousness, perhaps confirming the claim made in Section 4.1 that this was not an easy notion to define.

As seen in Section 8.3.1.1, item 26 asked respondents to draw up a list of ten ideas or things which they considered important for French/Swedish identity or culture. As the main aim of this question was to judge the role of language in national identity, student responses were reformulated for coding purposes in terms of a 'yes' or 'no' response to the question 'Was language mentioned in list of important ideas/things for French/Swedish identity or culture?' The ranking given to language was noted, as was the frequency of

Table 8.3 Language as an important idea/thing for French/Swedish identity or culture. Observed numbers (No), expected numbers (Ne), percentages (%) and results of Chi square test

Was language mentioned in list of important ideas/things for French/Swedish identity or culture?

	France			Sweden		
	No	Ne	%	No	Ne	%
Yes	51	55.7	28.3	58	53.3	33.7
No	129	124.3	71.7	114	118.7	66.3
Total	180	180	100	172	172	100

$\chi^2 = 1.19$; df = 1; sig = 0.274; missing cases = 69

other language-related items mentioned. As seen in Table 8.3, only a small percentage of students in France (28.3 per cent) and Sweden (33.7 per cent) mentioned language.

These results may not have been significant but, amongst those who did mention language in their list of ideas/things, this was accorded first place by 31.4 per cent of students in France and 31.6 per cent of those in Sweden. Other language-related items listed included literature, specific books or authors: 17.6 per cent of students in France, 8.1 per cent of those in Sweden (cf. Oakes 2000: 204).

It is difficult to interpret these results since item 26 did not function well methodologically. Despite receiving instructions that their responses should be personal, students did consult one another, in some schools shouting out possible answers which may have influenced the responses of other classmates (cf. Oakes 2000: 205). In a similar question ('Which elements of the French inheritance are the most important?') which was used in a SOFRES opinion poll conducted in April 1988 amongst 1,000 respondents representing the average Frenchman and woman, the number of respondents indicating language and literature was much higher: 51 per cent and 56 per cent respectively (cf. Ager 1990: 224). The results of the SOFRES poll are however not comparable with those of the present survey. While the former used a closed question, i.e. one in which the possible replies (language, literature, customs, cinema, etc.) were provided, the latter used an open-ended question, relying on the initiative of the respondents to suggest possible symbols.

Following the pattern observed for national consciousness (see Section 8.3.1.1), the students did in fact rate language highly when asked to respond to more direct statements in items 28 to 32 (see Table 8.4).

Table 8.4 Linguistic consciousness according to country

		Country	N	Mean	F	df.	sig.
V28	The French/Swedish language is part of French/Swedish cultural heritage	France Sweden	186 233	1.7 1.4	8.6	1,394	0.004
V29	We owe it to our ancestors to speak French/Swedish	France Sweden	185 234	2.4 2.6	6.3	1,394	0.013
V30	French/Swedish is worth knowing	France Sweden	185 233	1.8 1.6	2.6	1,393	0.110
V31	French/Swedish is a language which is well adapted to/can be used in a modern society	France Sweden	183 233	2.4 2.1	6.2	1,391	0.013
V32	French/Swedish is a beautiful language	France Sweden	185 233	1.9 1.9	0.74	1,393	0.392

For means: 1=agree totally; 2=agree partially; 3=undecided; 4=don't particularly agree; 5=don't agree at all

Not surprisingly, the French respondents thought that their language was part of French cultural heritage (mean=1.7 for variable 28); they also judged French beautiful (mean=1.9 for variable 32), worthy of knowing (mean=1.8 for variable 30), and well-suited to a modern society (mean=2.4 for variable 31). What proved more revealing was that the duty they felt to their ancestors to speak French was greater than that felt by their Swedish counterparts (mean=2.4 for variable 29 as opposed to 2.6 in Sweden; $p<0.02$). Despite the strong civic rhetoric which emanates from official circles in France, the French students did not reject the ethnic link between language and national identity which was implied in the reference to ancestors. These results are therefore in agreement with the claim made in the societal analysis of Section 4.2 that many French people perceive their identity in ethnic terms.

An evaluation of the linguistic consciousness amongst the Swedish respondents proved equally revealing. Not only did the Swedes judge their language to be beautiful (mean=1.9 for variable 32) and worthy of knowing (mean=1.6 for variable 30), they also agreed more than their French counterparts that Swedish was an important part of their national culture (mean=1.4 for variable 28, as opposed to 1.7 in France; $p<0.005$), and that it was a language which could be used in a modern society (mean=2.1 for variable 31, as opposed to 2.4 in France; $p<0.02$). These results are compatible with the claim made in Section 4.4 that the traditional, self-evident nature of the link between language and national identity in Sweden does not necessarily imply that language plays less of a role in the construction of Swedish identity than it does in that of French identity. A more adventurous interpretation would be that, like Swedish identity, Swedish linguistic consciousness is also becoming stronger, more overt. However, it would be unwise to draw such a conclusion before examining Swedish attitudes to two of the other possible indicators of linguistic consciousness mentioned in Section 4.1: linguistic prescriptivism and purism (see Table 8.5).

The particular issues concerning linguistic prescriptivism which the survey addressed were youth language and orthography. In light of the age of the respondents, the attitudes towards youth language sought here can be considered self-related (cf. Wingstedt 1998: 191). As such, one would have expected the respondents to rate themselves favourably, or at least not too negatively, when faced with variable 33. That French respondents agreed nonetheless with the statement (mean=2.1) can be explained by the pervasiveness of the language crisis debate and the fact that it is above all the school which upholds the tradition of linguistic prescriptivism (see Sections 4.2 and 4.4). What was more surprising was that the Swedish students also agreed (mean=2.4), despite the strong sense of linguistic democratism which has characterised Sweden especially since the rise of social democracy in that country (see Section 4.4). Nonetheless, the Swedish results appear to be confirmed by those of other studies. In her research on language ideology in Sweden, Wingstedt (1998: 245) found that 67.4 per cent agreed — either 'totally' or 'with hesitation' — with the statement 'The language of young people is getting worse and worse'. The

Table 8.5 Attitudes towards linguistic prescriptivism and purism according to country

		Country	N	Mean	F	df.	sig.
V33	Young people speak worse French/ Swedish nowadays	France Sweden	182 233	2.1 2.4	7.5	1,390	0.006
V34	It is very important to be able to spell correctly in French/Swedish	France Sweden	183 234	1.8 1.7	3.5	1,392	0.063
V35	It is important that French/Swedish is kept as pure as possible from foreign loan words	France Sweden	183 234	3.0 2.7	5.2	1,392	0.022

For means: 1=agree totally; 2=agree partially; 3=undecided; 4=don't particularly agree; 5=don't agree at all

corresponding figure observed in this study was 62.7 per cent. Unlike the present survey, Wingstedt's study included respondents from 21 to 71 years of age. Yet although there appeared to be a vague tendency that the oldest group (59–71 years) were more prescriptively inclined, the differences between this group and the others did not prove significant. Wingstedt (1998: 246) concludes that '[t]he majority of the respondents feel that young people's language is deteriorating, even if it is a "Self-related" phenomena [sic].' This conclusion seems all the more justified considering the results of the present survey.

The attitudes towards the issue of orthography elicited by variable 34 (see Table 8.5) were not so evidently self-related. Again the French responses were not surprising (mean=1.8), considering the strong normative tradition in France concerning spelling reform. Yet in light of the more tolerant approach to linguistic variation generally associated with Sweden, one might have expected the Swedish students not to have agreed as strongly as they did (mean=1.7). It is, however, worth remembering that a more prescriptive view has traditionally been taken in Sweden precisely with regard to spelling reform (see Section 4.4). Indeed, in the study mentioned in the previous paragraph, Wingstedt (1998: 251) found that an astounding 97 per cent of her respondents agreed — either 'totally' or 'with hesitation' — with the same statement as used in this survey, where the corresponding figure observed was 88.1 per cent. The difference in percentage may be due to the fact that the respondents in Wingstedt's study were on the whole much older than those in the present survey. That young people are often less prescriptively inclined would seem logical considering that, within the context of the language crisis debate, it is young people in particular who are accused of not knowing how to spell (see Section 4.4).

In addition to linguistic prescriptivism, language purism with regard to foreign loan words may also be an indicator of a strong linguistic consciousness (see Section 4.1). On this issue, the results of item 35 were revealing in so far as there was a tendency for the Swedish respondents to agree more than their French counterparts (mean=2.7 as opposed to 3.0 in France; see Table 8.5), even if this difference fell just short of the more stringent probability threshold of 0.02 used for the purposes of this survey (see Section 8.2.2.3). The French results are somewhat misleading, since they imply that a majority of French students did not have an opinion on the subject (point 3 on Likert-like scale=undecided). An examination of a collapsed version of the responses to item 35 reveals that in actual fact, a majority of students *disagreed*: 39.9 per cent compared with 37.7 per cent who agreed and 22.4 per cent who were undecided (cf. Oakes 2000: 208).

A possible explanation as to why the French students did not agree as adamantly as expected with the item about language purism concerns their younger age. As seen in Section 3.2.5.1, foreign borrowings are frequent in youth language. Indeed, this is exactly what Hagège (1996: 164–7) found in an interview with young French rappers, who considered loan words as a form of enriching their vocabulary, as a means of allowing language to be dynamic, to reflect the cosmopolitan nature of French society. Similar observations have been made in the French context by Goudaillier (1998: 18–22), who notes that the speech of young people in France's *cités* is characterised by borrowings from Arabic, Berber, English, Gypsy and African languages, as well as from regional languages and dialects. A similar observation is made in Sweden by Kotsinas (1992: 58–9), who notes that immigrant varieties of Swedish, such as that spoken in Rinkeby (see Section 5.3.2), are often appropriated by young Swedes who have no immigrant background whatsoever. This phenomenon observed amongst young people in particular may explain why the 48.3 per cent of Swedish students who were inclined towards linguistic purism (cf. Oakes 2000: 208) fell short of the 65.7 per cent observed by Wingstedt (1998: 259), who used exactly the same item in her survey, but whose respondents ranged from 21 to 71 years in age.

While attitudes towards language prescriptivism and purism offer some insight into the strength of the link between language and ethnic or national identity, it was noted in Section 4.1 that this need not always be the case. The results of a Pearson correlation test revealed nonetheless that, at least in the context of the present study, language prescriptivism and purism could on the

Table 8.6 Correlations between attitudes towards language prescriptivism and purism, and other items concerning ethnolinguistic identity in general in France and Sweden (data combined)

	V33	V34	V35
V33	1.0000	.2341**	.1662**
V34	.2341**	1.0000	.2733**
V35	.1662**	.2733**	1.0000
V18	−.0378	.2008**	.2663**
V49	−.0242	.1467**	.2749**
V28	−.0124	.1337**	.0738
V30	−.0104	.2642**	.2407**
V32	.0725	.1598**	.3057**

**$p<0.01$

whole be used as reliable indicators of a strong link between French, Swedish and the respective national identities (see Table 8.6).

That variable 33 did not on the whole correlate well with other variables was not surprising: as seen in this section above, the self-related nature of the statement 'Young people speak worse French/Swedish nowadays' resulted in partial agreement only. However, the test revealed that variables 34 ('It is very important to be able to spell correctly in French/Swedish') and 35 ('It is important that French/Swedish is kept as pure as possible from foreign loan words') correlated always positively and on the whole fairly well with other variables concerned with ethnolinguistic identity, although notably not with variable 28 ('The French/Swedish language is part of French/Swedish cultural heritage') in the case of variable 35. It can therefore be concluded that, at least in the context of the present survey, the positive attitudes towards linguistic prescriptivism and purism can be considered as reliable indicators of a strong ethnolinguistic identity in both countries, and in particular in Sweden. Nevertheless, two clarifications need to be made. First, prescriptive or purist attitudes at the affective or cognitive level do not necessarily translate into real prescriptivism or purism at the level of behaviour (cf. Wingstedt 1998: 258–9; also Section 3.1). It is quite possible that students would not always use correct spelling or avoid foreign loan words. A good example is provided by the responses given to item 26, which included many spelling mistakes (e.g. *la Tour Effel, Effeil, Eifel* and *Eiffelle, Jeanne d'Arque*) and loan words from English (e.g. *le French kiss, le shopping, skejtboard*). The second point which needs to be clarified is that attitudes towards linguistic prescriptivism and purism frequently change depending on the context or the contact language in question. That student attitudes proved less prescriptive and less puristic when considered in the context of English is seen in Section 8.3.4.

8.3.2 Language and national identity: The national arena

As seen in Chapter 5, the term 'national arena' is used in this study to refer to the territory delimited by the boundaries of a nation-state. The identity which characterises this arena is usually founded on that of the dominant ethnic core. This ethnic core relies on the presence of Others to act as contradistinctions, a role which is played in particular by regional and immigrant minorities. It is therefore these groups and their languages which form the basis of the presentation and discussion of the results here. The section is divided according to two sub-headings: attitudes towards the languages of these minorities (Section 8.3.2.1), and the use of language as a defence mechanism by the dominant ethnic core (Section 8.3.2.2).

8.3.2.1 *Attitudes towards minority languages*
The results of the students' attitudes to minority languages in France and Sweden are shown in Table 8.7.

In order to obtain an overall picture of the attitudes of French and Swedish respondents towards minority languages, it makes sense to begin with an examination of an item, such as variable 42, which was general in outlook. While both groups of students claimed to think that minority languages in their respective countries should be preserved as much as possible, there was a tendency for the French respondents to be more categorical in their opinion: mean=2.3 as opposed to 2.5 for Swedish students, although the level of significance (0.049) fell short of the 0.02 level used for the purposes of this study (see Section 8.2.2.3). What is immediately apparent is that the French results are the reverse of what might have been expected from the societal analyses, where it was seen that French official opinion has traditionally been characterised by a lack of tolerance towards minority languages (see Sections 5.2.1, 5.2.2 and 5.4). The Jacobin ideology which has dominated for so long at

Table 8.7 Attitudes towards minority languages according to country

		Country	N	Mean	F	df.	sig.
V42	Minority languages in France/ Sweden should be preserved as much as possible	France Sweden	186 233	2.3 2.5	3.90	1,394	0.049
V38	Providing teaching in regional languages/home language tuition ought not to be the responsibility of the French/ Swedish school system	France Sweden	181 234	3.0 3.7	33.07	1,390	0.000
V39	Basque/Sámi is a beautiful language	France Sweden	184 234	2.9 3.3	10.11	1,393	0.002
V40	Arabic is a beautiful language	France Sweden	185 234	2.9 3.8	48.38	1,394	0.000

For means: 1=agree totally; 2=agree partially; 3=undecided; 4=don't particularly agree; 5=don't agree at all

the official level in France does not appear to have left much of an impression on the young respondents of this study, who do not view ethnic minorities and their languages as negative Others for the purposes of generating positive national identities.

Unlike for variable 42, a clear difference was revealed between the French and Swedish students on the question of minority language education (variable 38). As seen in Table 8.7, the French students were undecided as to whether the teaching of regional languages ought to be the responsibility of the French school system (mean=3.0), while their Swedish counterparts were fairly resolved that home language tuition *should* be the responsibility of the Swedish school system (mean=3.7; $p<0.001$). When comparing the results of the two groups, it is important to remember that variable 38 was worded in two ways. While in Sweden reference was made to home (i.e. both regional and immigrant) languages, only regional languages were mentioned in France. As discussed in Section 8.2.1.3, this decision was made on the assumption that French students would be unlikely to know about the ELCO programmes for immigrant languages (see Section 5.4). It appears that this assumption was correct, since many French students had not even heard of the regional language schools mentioned as an example in item 38 (e.g. *ikastolas, diwans*) and which are in fact much more widespread, and therefore well-known, than the ELCO programmes. The lack of knowledge about the teaching of regional languages, and in particular private institutions such as the *ikastolas* and *diwans*, was attested by the questions asked of the researcher regarding this item, as well as the high proportion of undecided responses given in France: 34.8 per cent (as opposed to 33.7 per cent who agreed with item 38, and 31.5 per cent who disagreed). This ignorance *vis-à-vis* minority language education is symptomatic of the marginal interest which this issue has traditionally received in France: ELCO programmes for immigrant languages are not funded by the French state, and the teaching of regional languages in state schools is optional, when not left completely to private schools such as the *ikastolas* and *diwans* (see Section 5.4). In addition, the media have paid little attention to minority language issues, at least not until 1999, when the Charter for Regional or Minority Languages became the object of much discussion (see Section 5.4). What proved most telling about the results was that this lack of knowledge about minority language education did not translate into negative attitudes. The results of item 38 thus provide further evidence for the claim made in the previous paragraph that there may be a new tolerance of minority languages amongst young people in France.

In Sweden, the positive attitudes expressed towards state-supported minority education (mean=3.7 for variable 38) must be viewed with some caution, since other studies of attitudes towards home language tuition have not revealed such positive attitudes as observed here. For example, Wingstedt (1998: 308–9) found that the majority of her respondents (51.2 per cent) disagreed with the statement 'Of course the cost of home language teaching should be met with tax revenue' (as opposed to 39.9 per cent who were in favour). The corresponding figures in this study were 64.1 per cent who disagreed with item 38, and 21.0 per cent who agreed. One possible explanation for the positive attitudes observed in the present study concerns the fact that, unlike Wingstedt's study, item 38 made no explicit mention of financial issues. It is quite possible that respondent attitudes would have proven less favourable, had item 38 been worded in a way which more explicitly expressed the suggestion that the state provide financial support to minority language education.

Another possible explanation for the fairly positive Swedish attitudes observed for item 38 concerns the social desirability bias, according to which respondents try to put themselves in the best possible light (cf. Oakes 2000: 168). Sweden has traditionally taken pride in having been one of the first countries to provide minority language education. Moreover, this pride is felt at all levels of society, no doubt because of the extensive coverage which home language tuition has received in the media. The Swedish situation can be compared to a certain extent with that of Canada. While the latter country is generally considered as embracing cultural pluralism (see Section 5.1.3), Edwards (1994: 185) observes that 'the multicultural *symbol* is what appeals, not a reality which might actually alter things.' Similarly in Sweden, the reality may be another behind the liberal façade: ideological pluralism is not matched by real structural pluralism (see Section 5.4), and there is some evidence of a deep-seated intolerance of the ethnic Other, as manifested, for example, by the frequently heard Swedish expression *Jag är inte racist, men* . . . (I am not racist, but . . .) (see Section 5.3.2). Indeed, negative attitudes towards minorities and their languages often surface in more concrete contexts, such as those simulated by items 39 and 40, which made reference to specific minority languages.

The aim of items 39 ('Basque/Sámi is a beautiful language') and 40 ('Arabic is a beautiful language') was to investigate further the pluralistic attitudes which may have been expressed in items 42 and 38. In particular, it was judged that reference to specific languages — in this case, Basque and Sámi to represent regional languages and Arabic to represent immigrant languages (cf. Oakes 2000: 178) — may reveal that attitudes which initially proved positive to linguistic pluralism were in fact little more than lip-service. Empirical research has shown that items such as 39 and 40 do not so much tap aesthetic evaluations of certain languages as the imposed preconceptions about the groups which speak them (see Section 3.1). That Swedish students on the whole did not judge Sámi to be a beautiful language (variable 39: mean=3.3; see Table 8.7) would appear to suggest that the Sámi people play an important role as a negatively-viewed outgroup for the purposes of constructing Swedish national identity. Such a claim cannot be made about the Basque people in France, since French students *agreed*, albeit only very slightly, that Basque was a beautiful language: mean=2.9 ($p<0.005$). Once again, the negative attitudes traditionally associated with regional languages in France were not borne out in the data.

A similar observation was made in relation to Arabic: while French students agreed very slightly with variable 40, their Swedish counterparts were relatively resolved that Arabic was not a beautiful language: mean=3.8 as opposed to 2.9 for French students ($p<0.001$; see Table 8.7). Despite their proclaimed support for minority language preservation and education as demonstrated by attitudes towards items 42 and 38, the young Swedes clearly did not share the pluralistic attitudes of official circles when considered in the context of specific languages. In the particular case of Arabic, a strong, negative correlation was even observed between strength of Swedish identity (item 18) and attitudes towards Arabic as a beautiful language ($r=-0.23$; $n=234$; $p<0.001$). Although a negative correlation was also observed in France between strength of national identity and the belief amongst the French students that Arabic was a beautiful language, this correlation did not prove significant ($r=-0.08$; $n=181$; not significant). Considering the widespread support for the *Front national* and lively debate on immigration in France (see Section 5.2.2), one might have expected more negative attitudes towards Arabic in that country. While the problems which are purportedly caused by immigration continue to be discussed at the official level and in the media, the young French people studied here did not seem to consider immigrants as negative outgroups for the purposes of constructing a positive national identity. It is quite possible that the younger generation in today's France have come to terms with the ethnic diversity of their country. Indeed, immigrant cultures have already been incorporated into aspects of French culture which touch the lives of young people, such as football and rap music (see Section 5.2.2).

8.3.2.2 *Language as a defence mechanism*
As seen in Section 3.2.5.2, language is often used as a defence mechanism by

the dominant ethnic group to protect its socio-economic privileges. It is in this light that one can for example interpret the emergence of the socially constructed Rinkeby Swedish (see Section 5.3.2). The possible use of language as a defence mechanism for the dominant French and Swedish ethnic groups was tested by examining attitudes to two topics: the perceived influence of minorities and their languages on the national language, and the strength of the linguistic boundary between the dominant and minority groups. The first of these topics made use of items 43 and 44, for which the results of the ANOVAs are shown in Table 8.8.

While both groups of students rejected the statements, it was the French students who were more categorical in their rejection: means=3.6 as opposed to 3.1 for Swedish students for both variables 43 and 44 ($p<0.005$). The claim made in Section 5.2.2 that language, and in particular the notion of *sur-norme*, serves as a means of discriminating against immigrants in France is therefore not justified by the student responses. Linguistic prescriptivism in a general sense may still be alive amongst the French respondents (see Section 8.3.1.2), but language does not appear to be an important dimension of social comparison for them in the particular context of majority-minority relations. Once again, these results suggest that ethnolinguistic minorities are readily accepted by young French people. The same cannot be said for the Swedish data.

Although the Swedish respondents rejected the claims in variables 43 and 44, three comments can be made about these results. First, the rejection amongst the Swedish respondents was not convincing (means=3.1; see Table 8.8). Second, the results of the Chi square tests on the distribution of actual (collapsed) responses revealed that although not in a majority, those

Table 8.8 Perceived influence of minorities and their languages on French and Swedish according to country

		Country	N	Mean	F	df.	sig.
V43	French/Swedish is deteriorating/affected negatively because other languages are spoken in France/Sweden	France Sweden	185 234	3.6 3.1	8.47	1,394	0.004
V44	French/Swedish is deteriorating/affected negatively because there are many people who have it as a second language	France Sweden	185 234	3.6 3.1	17.23	1,394	0.000

For means: 1=agree totally; 2=agree partially; 3=undecided; 4=don't particularly agree; 5=don't agree at all

Swedes who agreed with the statements were greater in number than expected: 32.9 per cent for variable 43 ($\chi^2=16.18$; df=2; $p<0.001$) and 27.4 per cent for variable 44 ($\chi^2=23.59$; df=2; $p<0.001$). The third observation which can be made about the Swedish results concerns the location of the school (centre versus periphery) where the study was conducted. When a 3-way ANOVA (i.e. using location, sex, and parents' place of birth) was performed on the Swedish data only, students in Stockholm (i.e. the centre) were actually found to *agree* with variables 43 and 44: means=2.8 in the centre as opposed to 3.5 in the periphery ($F(1,212)=22.84$; $p<0.001$ for variable 43 and $F(1,212)=16.11$; $p<0.001$ for variable 44; cf. Oakes 2000: 215). In other words, Swedish students in the centre *did* think that Swedish was affected negatively because other languages were spoken in Sweden and because many people spoke it as a second language. The results therefore do not so much reject as modify the original claim, by highlighting that it is in the centre as opposed to the periphery that language is employed as a defence mechanism in Sweden. An explanation can be sought in the different types of minority language involved: in the periphery, the Others referred to in variables 43 and 44 are likely to be represented by regional languages and minorities; in the centre, it is immigrants and their languages which probably assume these roles. In other words, the results show that language may be used in Sweden as a defence mechanism against immigrants. This observation is also confirmed by those made in Sections 5.3.1 and 5.3.2, where it was seen that acts of linguistic boundary hardening (e.g. the debates around semilingualism and Rinkeby Swedish) have concerned immigrants and their languages much more than regional minorities and theirs.

The second means of examining the use of language as a defence mechanism consisted of measuring the strength of the linguistic boundary between the dominant and minority groups. The results of variables 41, 45 and 46 which adopted this angle are shown in Table 8.9.

On the issue of whether or not knowledge of French or Swedish should be a prerequisite for gaining French or Swedish citizenship (variable 41), both groups of students appeared at first to be 'undecided' (means=3.0 for French and 3.1 for Swedish students). Closer inspection revealed that the results disguised the fact that opinion was divided both in France and Sweden, as seen by the actual distribution of (collapsed) responses for variable 41 (see Table 8.10).

Although 40.4 per cent of the French respondents agreed that language should be used as a prerequisite for citizenship, a substantial 39.9 per cent did not. These results would appear to indicate that there is significant support in France for a new, multicultural approach to integration, according to which

Table 8.9 Strength of linguistic boundary according to country

		Country	N	Mean	F	df.	sig.
V41	One should not be allowed to become a French/Swedish citizen without knowledge of French/Swedish	France Sweden	183 229	3.0 3.1	1.03	1,387	0.331
V45	I identify strongly with French/Swedish speakers in other countries (e.g. Québec/Finland)	France Sweden	186 232	3.1 2.9	1.22	1,393	0.269
V46	One can be French/Swedish without speaking French/Swedish	France Sweden	186 234	3.3 3.1	4.87	1,395	0.028

For means: 1=agree totally; 2=agree partially; 3=undecided; 4=don't particularly agree; 5=don't agree at all

Table 8.10 Importance of language criterion for French/Swedish citizenship. Observed numbers (No), expected numbers (Ne), percentages (%) and results of Chi square test

V41 One should not be allowed to become a French/Swedish citizen without knowledge of French/Swedish

	France			Sweden		
	No	Ne	%	No	Ne	%
Agree	74	66.6	40.4	76	83.4	33.2
Undecided	36	39.5	19.7	53	49.5	23.1
Disagree	73	76.8	39.9	100	96.2	43.7
Total	183	182.9*	100	229	229.1*	100

χ^2=2.38; df=2; sig.=0.304; missing cases=9
*182.9 and 229.1 are due to rounding to one decimal place

citizens enjoy total linguistic freedom. By contrast in Sweden, although a majority (43.7 per cent) thought that language should not be used as a prerequisite for obtaining Swedish citizenship, a substantial number of students (33.2 per cent) thought it should be, thus endorsing a proposal put forward by the right-wing party *Det nya partiet* (see Section 5.3.2). While these results fell short of those obtained by Wingstedt (1998: 282–3), who found that a majority (50.3 per cent) of her respondents agreed with the statement 'Everyone who applies for Swedish citizenship should take an examination on the Swedish language', the 41.6 per cent who disagreed show that opinion was also fairly divided in her study. The results of another item from Wingstedt's study (1998: 282–3) nonetheless underscores the complexity of the issue at hand. In a more strongly formulated claim ('Only immigrants who speak Swedish with their family members and raise their children in Swedish should be allowed to become Swedish citizens'), respondents were seen to shy away from what Wingstedt describes as the 'high degree of nationalistic and assimilatory expectations on citizenship' reflected by this statement: the percentage of respondents who agreed with this claim dropped notably to 18.5 per cent.

Granting citizenship is one thing; accepting minority group members as truly French or Swedish is another. In Section 5.2.2, it was seen that linguistic boundaries were used in France to distinguish the French not only from speakers of other languages, but also from native speakers of French from other countries (e.g. in the Maghreb, Africa, etc.). However, the results of the present survey did not reveal a strong linguistic boundary with regard to other speakers of French. Indeed, students in France disagreed only slightly with the statement in item 45 ('I identify strongly with French-speakers in other countries, e.g. Québec'[2]): mean=3.1 (see Table 8.9). The results suggest once again that there may be a softening of the linguistic boundaries which delimit French identity. This softening process also seems to apply to speakers of languages other than French. Although the respondents in France rejected item 46 ('One can be French/Swedish without speaking French/Swedish'), their rejection (mean=3.3; see Table 8.9) was not as categorical as expected considering that language has traditionally constituted a core value of French identity.

By contrast, no evidence was found for a softening of linguistic boundaries in Sweden. The Swedish respondents identified, although only slightly, with native Swedish speakers in other countries (mean=2.9 for variable 45; see Table 8.9). They also rejected the claim, although equally as slightly, that one could be Swedish without speaking Swedish (mean=3.1 for variable 46; see Table 8.9), thereby showing that language is not totally insignificant when it comes to distinguishing Swedes from non-Swedes. As argued by ethnolinguistic identity theory, the perception of a boundary as hard and impermeable leads to a heightened identity (see Section 3.2.3). While Swedish linguistic boundaries cannot be described as hard, neither can they said to be soft, as one may have expected considering that the link between language and national identity has traditionally been self-evident in Sweden (see Section 4.4). In so far as linguistic boundaries may be in the process of hardening in Sweden, the results observed here are compatible with those discussed in Section 8.3.1.2, which pointed to an increase in the strength of linguistic consciousness in Sweden.

Table 8.11 Non-linguistic criteria in definition of French and Swedish identity according to country

		Country	N	Mean	F	df.	sig.
V47	One must be born in France/Sweden to be considered French/Swedish	France Sweden	158 233	3.9 3.6	0.41	1,366	0.523
V48	One must have French/Swedish parents to be considered French/Swedish	France Sweden	158 234	3.8 3.8	0.98	1,367	0.324

For means: 1=agree totally; 2=agree partially; 3=undecided; 4=don't particularly agree; 5=don't agree at all

Two additional variables (47 and 48) sought reactions to criteria other than language in the definition of Frenchness and Swedishness. The results are shown in Table 8.11.

That French students rejected variable 47 (mean=3.9), which defined French identity in terms of birthplace or the principle of *jus soli*, confirms the observation made in Section 5.2.2 that the French model of integration or myth of inclusion is 'today less supremely self-confident than it was' (Ager 1999: 87), especially when considered at the grassroots level. Obversely, that the Swedish respondents rejected variable 48 (mean=3.8), which made reference to ancestry or the principle of *jus sanguinis*, highlights the possibility of a non-ethnic definition of Swedish identity. It is quite possible that young people readily employ a whole range of ethnic and civic criteria (e.g. language, birthplace, ancestry, self-ascription) when judging whether an individual belongs to the dominant group. This apparently flexible view of national identity contrasts with that of official circles which tend to adopt more polarised definitions. A good example of the latter is the French principal who requested that variables 47 and 48 be omitted from the questionnaire in his school (see Section 8.2.2.2). While these items were deemed too sensitive, no doubt because of a belief in the French model of integration or myth of inclusion, the headmaster of the school in question did not object to variables 41 and 46, which used the French language as a criterion of French identity.

8.3.3   Language and national identity: The European arena

The construction of national identity is not limited to the context of the nation-state and Others such as regional and immigrant minorities. As seen in

Chapter 6, national identity is also constructed in the context of the European arena which has developed in particular because of the European Union (EU). This section presents and discusses the results of the survey items which dealt with language attitudes and national identity strategies within this arena. Three main sub-themes serve as a framework for the discussion: European identity (Section 8.3.3.1), the role of French and Swedish in the EU (Section 8.3.3.2), and attitudes towards an official language for the EU (Section 8.3.3.3).

8.3.3.1 *European identity*

It was seen in Chapter 6 that, to a certain extent, the European arena generates its own identity. Two of the questionnaire items sought to measure the strength and feasibility of this identity. First, variable 19 ('How European do you feel?') used the same five-point scale to measure European identity as was used to measure national identity (see Section 8.3.1.1). The results of the ANOVAs are shown in Table 8.12.

Table 8.12 Strength of European identity according to country

		Country	N	Mean	F	df.	sig.
V19	How European do you feel?	France	178	3.0	0.86	1,387	0.356
		Sweden	234	3.1			

For means: 1=enormously; 2=a lot; 3=average/quite a lot; 4=a bit; 5=not at all

The analysis of variable 19 showed that there was no significant difference between the two groups with regard to strength of European identity: both reported an average degree of Europeanness: means=3.0 in France and 3.1 in Sweden. As mentioned in Section 8.2.1.3, these results must be interpreted cautiously, because of the slightly different translations used in the two versions of the questionnaire to describe point 3 on the scale: 'average' in French and 'quite a lot' in Swedish. This difference in translation may explain why the results of this survey did not correspond to those of Eurobarometer (1999), which showed that while 65 per cent of respondents in France felt European to some degree, this was the case of only 39 per cent of those in Sweden. Indeed, in variable 51 ('The EU countries are too different to create a European identity'), which sought attitudes to the perceived feasibility of European identity and where the problem of translation did not arise, the ANOVAs produced the results expected from the societal analysis of Chapter 6 (see Table 8.13).

Table 8.13 Perceived feasibility of European identity according to country

	Country	N	Mean	F	df.	sig.
V51 The EU countries are too different to create a European identity	France Sweden	184 229	3.3 2.5	42.62	1,388	0.000

For means: 1=agree totally; 2=agree partially; 3=undecided; 4=don't particularly agree; 5=don't agree at all

While French students did not think that the EU countries were too different to create a European identity (mean=3.3), Swedish students clearly did believe this was the case (mean=2.5; $p<0.001$). These results raise once again the question posed in Section 6.1: is a European identity possible? On the one hand, the French results do not necessarily provide an affirmative response to this question. As mentioned in Section 6.3, European integration has traditionally been viewed as an extension of French official nationalism, as part of the construction and strengthening of the French nation-state (Hettne, Sörlin and Østergård 1998: 26). In this light, it is no wonder that the French respondents had no difficulty in conceiving a European identity. Yet it remains an open question whether or not this will continue to be French opinion when the nature of the EU changes in the future. Further enlargement eastwards to countries which have traditionally looked to Germany as their European role model will surely have the effect of changing the function of the EU so that it no longer clearly corresponds to French national interests. On the other hand, the Swedish results do not necessarily provide a negative response to the question of whether a European identity is possible. While the results of this survey correspond to the anti-European backlash observed in Sweden (see Section 6.4), the country is relatively new to the European Union, having only become a member state in 1995. It is quite possible that a sense of European identity will in fact develop over time.

Further analyses were conducted to investigate the effect of national identity on European identity. The results of the Pearson correlation test performed on variables 18 ('How French/Swedish do you feel?'), 19 ('How European do you feel?') and 51 ('The EU countries are too different to create a European identity') are shown in Table 8.14.

As might have been expected, a strong, negative correlation (-.2599) was observed between variables 19 and 51: the stronger the European identity reported, the more likely respondents were to agree that the creation of a European identity was possible. What proved more revealing, however, were

Table 8.14 Correlations between items concerning national and European identity in France and Sweden (data combined).

	V18	V19	V51
V18	1.0000	.2517**	.1338**
V19	.2517**	1.0000	−.2599**
V51	.1338**	−.2599**	1.0000

**$p<0.01$

the strong, positive correlations observed between variable 18, which measured strength of national identity, and the two variables concerned with European identity: variables 19 and 51. As for the relationship between variables 18 and 19, the strong, positive correlation (.2517) addresses one of the major problems associated with European identity as discussed in Section 6.1: national and European identities need not be mutually exclusive. It is, of course, possible that the students reported a European identity by geopolitical default: French and Swedes are European in so far as France and Sweden are both countries in the geographical region known as Europe, as well as member states of the European Union (cf. Chryssochoou 1996: 307–8). Nonetheless, the results show that the young respondents of this study had no difficulty in managing multiple identities. Although national identity was clearly stronger than European identity, the two were obviously considered complementary. As for the relationship between variables 18 and 51 ('The EU countries are too different to create a European identity'), the strong, positive correlation observed (.1338) is difficult to interpret, especially since it appears to contradict the results of the ANOVAs for variable 51 (see Table 8.13). In particular, the French rejection of this variable would have led one to expect a negative correlation between variables 18 and 51. Indeed, this observation was made when a correlational analysis was performed on the French data separately (−.0354). The corresponding correlation coefficient for the same analysis conducted on the Swedish data was .0881. Although neither of these coefficients was significant, they nevertheless confirm the tendency that the French students could conceive a European identity, while their Swedish counterparts could not. To attempt to understand this difference, it is necessary to investigate how the French and Swedish respondents perceive the role of their respective countries in the EU, as symbolised by the perceived role of their respective national languages in the EU.

8.3.3.2 *The role of French and Swedish in the EU*

Two items related to the role which respondents perceived for their respective languages in the EU: items 36 ('The possibilities for the use of French/Swedish *have increased* because of the EU') and 37 ('The possibilities for the use of French/Swedish *will increase* because of the EU'). It was envisaged that attitudes towards these two statements would provide some information as to whether strategies of divergence were used to generate a positive identity in the European arena. The focus on language does not limit the strategies to those of a linguistic nature; just as the definition of language attitudes is usually broadened to include attitudes towards speakers of a particular language (Fasold 1984: 148), so too can the attitudes towards items 36 and 37 be considered as indications of more general, non-linguistic strategies of divergence. The purpose of two statements, one which focused in the past situation, one on the future, was to investigate the possibility of any diachronic variation. Further data relating to the role which respondents perceived for their respective languages in the EU were elicited with the aid of item 56 ('The linguistic diversity in the EU ought to be preserved as much as possible'). The results of the ANOVAs for all three of these variables are shown in Table 8.15.

In their attitudes to variable 36, both groups of students were pessimistic. In Sweden, the belief that the EU had not increased the possibilities of use of Swedish was nevertheless stronger than in France: mean=3.5 as opposed to 3.2 in France ($p<0.005$). The differences between the French and Swedish results for both these variables do not necessarily indicate that the French respondents were less pessimistic than their Swedish counterparts *vis-à-vis* the role of their language. It is possible that the responses for these variables reflect more

Table 8.15 Attitudes towards the role of French and Swedish in the EU according to country

		Country	N	Mean	F	df.	sig.
V36	The possibilities for the use of French/ Swedish *have increased* because of the EU	France Sweden	184 234	3.2 3.5	8.58	1,393	0.004
V37	The possibilities for the use of French/ Swedish *will increase* because of the EU	France Sweden	184 232	3.1 3.4	12.73	1,391	0.000
V56	The linguistic diversity of the EU ought to be preserved as much as possible	France Sweden	186 230	1.8 2.0	2.27	1,391	0.133

For means: 1=agree totally; 2=agree partially; 3=undecided; 4=don't particularly agree; 5=don't agree at all

factually-based attitudes. On the one hand, French is a major European language which was one of the original official languages of the EEC and the preferred choice of working language in all institutions before the adhesion of the United Kingdom in 1973 (see Section 6.3). On the other hand, Swedish has only been an official language of the EU since 1995, and is one of Europe's less widely spread languages, a status which the Swedes have long accepted (see Section 6.4).

The difference between the French and Swedish students for variable 36 was echoed in relation to variable 37, which revealed that both groups of students were also pessimistic to the increased use of their language in the EU *in the future*: mean=3.1 in France and 3.4 in Sweden ($p<0.001$; see Table 8.15). The Swedish results for variables 36 and 37 came as little surprise, considering the strategies of convergence which Sweden has traditionally used in the global arena (see Section 7.4), and which it later sought to employ in the European arena (see Section 6.4). What proved more telling were the French results, which were not in accordance with the strategies of divergence which have long been used by France to generate a positive identity within the European arena. These traditional strategies of divergence were seen in Section 6.3 and are clearly evident in the results of a SOFRES opinion poll conducted in 1988 before the introduction of the single market: amongst the 1,000 respondents questioned, 44 per cent thought that '1992 and the Single European Market' was good for the French language, because it would increase French influence in Europe (cf. Ager 1990: 224–6).

But while the French respondents may not have demonstrated the expected signs of divergence in the European arena for variables 36 and 37, they did so for variable 56, by expressing a desire that the linguistic diversity in the EU be preserved as much as possible (mean=1.8; see Table 8.15). However, the Swedish students also judged linguistic diversity in the EU of importance (mean=2.0), indicating that Swedish identity strategies in the European arena may also include some form of divergence alongside the more traditional convergence. There are several possible reasons for these results. First, the interest in linguistic diversity in the EU is certainly encouraged by a strong linguistic consciousness which has developed in Sweden over the last decade (see Sections 4.4 and 8.3.1.2). Second, as argued in Section 6.1, the bringing together of nation-states in a new European arena has increased the opportunities for social comparison and competition between nations. The heightened sense of national identity which this comparison and competition entails is likely to be accompanied by an assertion of national symbols, including language. Third, any pressure upon nations such as Sweden to converge, for example to a European culture or single European language, paradoxically also encourages divergence, as the reinforcement of individual national (and linguistic) identities becomes all the more important in order to maintain psychological distinctiveness. In light of the Swedish students' proclaimed concern for linguistic diversity in the EU, it is more than likely that the parliamentary committee set up to formulate a plan of action for the promotion of Swedish will suggest measures to protect its status in the EU (see Section 6.4).

8.3.3.3 Attitudes towards an official language for the EU

The remaining items which covered questions of language and national identity in the European arena focused not on strategies of divergence, but rather on those concerned with convergence, by seeking attitudes towards an official language for the EU. Once again, the interpretation of the results need not be limited to the linguistic dimension, but can also be used to make inferences about attitudes to convergence on more general, non-linguistic dimensions. The results of variables 52 to 55 are shown in Table 8.16.

In response to the suggestion that a single official language was needed in the EU for a European identity to be created (variable 52), both French and Swedish students disagreed (means=3.5 in France and 3.2 in Sweden; not significant). In light of these results, and those of variable 56 (see Table 8.15), any attempt to introduce an official EU language can be expected to be met with resistance, at least if French and Swedish are not amongst the proposed languages.

Table 8.16 Attitudes towards an official language for the EU according to country

		Country	N	Mean	F	df.	sig.
V52	A single official language is needed in the EU for a European identity to be created	France Sweden	186 231	3.5 3.2	2.67	1,392	0.103
V53	An artificial language (e.g. Esperanto) ought to be the EU's official language	France Sweden	186 231	4.0 4.3	4.32	1,392	0.038
V54	English ought to be the EU's official language	France Sweden	186 231	3.8 2.4	119.53	1,392	0.000
V55	English is the most important language in the EU	France Sweden	183 230	2.6 1.9	34.87	1,389	0.000

For means: 1=agree totally; 2=agree partially; 3=undecided; 4=don't particularly agree; 5=don't agree at all

Variables 53 and 54 went one step further than variable 52, by suggesting specific examples for an official EU language. In the first case, the proposed language was the artificial language Esperanto. It is not surprising that both groups of students rejected this suggestion: the psychological barriers and motivational problems involved with learning an artificial language like Esperanto are well known (cf. Chiti-Batelli 1987). However, it is open to speculation just why it was the Swedish respondents who tended to be more opposed to Esperanto (mean=4.3 compared with 4.0 for French students; see Table 8.16), even if the level of significance (0.038) fell just short of the 0.02 used for this study. In Section 7.4, it was claimed that Swedes often adopt an instrumental or functional approach to language learning which has been described by one commentator as 'pure engineering' (Battail 1994: 11). It is therefore possible that the Swedes are on the whole not so much interested in so-called egalitarian languages such as Esperanto (see Section 7.2) as those which are likely to provide them with the best possible means of generating a positive national identity. In order to attain such a positive identity in an Esperanto-dominated EU, Swedes would have to learn the language from scratch, and reach a degree of proficiency superior to that of citizens of other EU member states. Such a feat would prove all the more difficult considering that the vocabulary of Esperanto is Latin-based, and would therefore be more easily learnt by speakers of Romance languages such as French (see Section 7.2).

When it comes to generating a positive identity through knowledge of a foreign language, the Swedes are on much safer ground with English (see Section 7.4). Indeed, the Swedish respondents reported a higher proficiency in their first foreign language (which was English for 87.8 per cent of them) than did their French counterparts: mean=2.9 as opposed to 2.4 in Sweden ($p<0.001$; cf. Oakes 2000: 194).[3] The Swedish method of learning English relies heavily on osmosis: most Swedes acquire a high degree of competence in English not by learning the language at school, but rather by being constantly surrounded by it due to an abundance of Anglo-American programmes and films on Swedish television, the use of English in Swedish advertisements, etc. As attested by the fact that the Swedish respondents of the present survey reported a lower degree of proficiency than their French counterparts in their second foreign language (cf. Oakes 2000: 194), the Swedes are not particularly better than other Europeans at learning other languages, such as Esperanto. It therefore came as no surprise to learn that the Swedish respondents agreed with variable 54, which proposed English as the EU's official language (mean=2.4; see Table 8.16). Nor was it surprising that, unlike their Swedish counterparts, the French students rejected the same proposal (mean=3.8; $p<0.001$; see Table 8.16). As seen in Section 7.3, the French have traditionally constructed a positive identity in the European arena through strategies of linguistic divergence, that is to say by using the French language to attain psychological distinctiveness. Nonetheless, the French respondents recognised the *de facto* importance of English in the EU (mean=2.6 for variable 55; see Table 8.16), even if it was the Swedish students who were most categorical in their agreement (mean=1.9; $p<0.001$). This recognition of the importance of English amongst the French respondents perhaps constitutes what Minc refers to as an anticipation of the rise of English in Europe (see Section 6.2). In other words, the attitudes observed here could signal a change in French identity strategies, whereby strategies of convergence are beginning to be employed in conjunction with the more traditional strategies of divergence. Further evidence for this claim emerges in the analysis of French attitudes towards English as a global language in the following section.

8.3.4 Language and national identity: The global arena

As seen in Chapter 7, the dominant Other or outgroup in the global arena speaks English. The goal of the questionnaire items which considered language and national identity in the global arena was therefore to tap attitudes specifically towards this language. In so far as English is also becoming a European *lingua franca* (see Section 6.2), the items studied here can also be considered as an extension of those examined in the previous section. The presentation and discussion of the results of the variables which follow is divided into two sub-themes: attitudes towards English (Section 8.3.4.1) and the perceived threat from English (Section 8.3.4.2).

8.3.4.1 *Attitudes towards English*

The results of the ANOVAs performed on variables 58 to 64, which sought student attitudes towards English, are shown in Table 8.17.

As seen in Section 7.2, supporters of English as a global language often make the claim that English is linked to the inevitable forces of globalisation and intrinsically associated with modernity (cf. Phillipson 1999: 103–4). This belief does not reflect reality so much as the power relations between the ingroup and English-speaking outgroups. In an attempt to understand these relations in the context of French and Swedish identities, variable 58 sought student reactions to the claim that English was well adapted to a modern society. Not surprisingly, it was the Swedish respondents who agreed most with this suggestion (mean=1.3 as opposed to 2.1 for their French counterparts; $p<0.001$). Nor was it surprising to learn that Swedes rated English better adapted to a modern society than they did for their own language, as measured by variable 31: mean=2.1 (see Section 8.3.1.2).[4] As seen in Section 7.4, many Swedes consider English as 'more effective, modern, beautiful and better than their own language' (Laureys 1997: 25). This belief, coupled with the relatively high proficiency in English observed amongst many Swedes, has constituted an important means of generating a positive Swedish identity, especially since the 1950s–1960s. What was more interesting was that the French respondents also appeared to rate English more 'modern' than they did their national language, as measured by variable 31: mean=2.4 (see Section 8.3.1.2).[5] It was seen in Section 7.3 that stressing the virtues of French (e.g. its purported clarity, logic and overall superiority) has traditionally formed one of the strategies of

Table 8.17 Attitudes towards English according to country

		Country	N	Mean	F	df.	sig.
V58	English is a language which is well adapted to a modern society	France Sweden	186 232	2.1 1.3	114.67	1,393	0.000
V59	English is a beautiful language	France Sweden	185 233	2.4 1.8	38.09	1,393	0.000
V60	English is difficult to learn	France Sweden	185 233	3.0 3.8	40.99	1,393	0.000
V61	Knowing English will help to find work	France Sweden	185 233	1.6 1.5	0.88	1,393	0.349
V62	Learning English broadens my general knowledge	France Sweden	186 232	2.0 1.5	33.79	1, 394	0.000
V63	The more educated one is, the better one speaks English	France Sweden	186 232	3.9 3.1	38.74	1,394	0.000
V64	Children ought to learn English at rimary school/at school from an early age	France Sweden	186 231	2.1 1.8	10.14	1,393	0.002

For means: 1=agree totally; 2=agree partially; 3=undecided; 4=don't particularly agree; 5=don't agree at all

linguistic divergence employed by France in the global arena to achieve the necessary psychological distinctiveness to generate a positive identity. The French results nonetheless confirm those of Flaitz (1988: 166), whose respondents were found to be of a similar opinion regarding the related suggestion that English had all the qualities to be a world language (mean=2.3 on the same five-point scale as used for the present survey).

Positive attitudes are also expressed in the perceived beauty of a language: as seen in Section 3.1, evaluations of languages on dimensions such as aesthetic quality reflect 'the levels of status and prestige that [these languages] are *conventionally* associated with in a particular community' (Giles and Coupland 1991: 37–8). Accordingly, Flaitz also found that the French respondents of her survey gave a high rating to the British variety of English — but not the American one — with regard to elegance (mean=1.90 on a similar five-point scale). These results were in agreement with those of variable 59 of the present study ('English is a beautiful language'): mean=2.4 (see Table 8.17). Nonetheless, it was the Swedish respondents who once again rated English more highly for perceived beauty: mean=1.8 ($p<0.001$). The results also indicate that while the Swedes rated English more highly in terms of aesthetics than their own language (compare mean=1.9 for variable 32; see Section 8.3.1.2), this was not the case for the French respondents (compare mean=1.9 for variable 32).[6]

Supporters of English also claim that it is an easy language to learn and therefore well-suited to become a global language (see Section 7.2). Respondent attitudes to this claim were sought by means of item 60 ('English is difficult to learn'), which was rejected by the Swedish students more than their French counterparts: mean=3.8 as opposed to 3.0 for French students ($p<0.001$; see Table 8.17). These results were to be expected, considering that Swedes have an advantage when it comes to learning English due to the omnipresence of the language in their country (see Section 7.4). It must also be said that the Swedish respondents reported a greater proficiency in their first foreign language (which was English for 87.8 per cent of them) than did their French counterparts (amongst whom English was the first foreign language for 72.0 per cent): mean=2.9 as opposed to 2.4 in Sweden ($p<0.001$; cf. Oakes 2000: 194).[7] Indeed, a strong, negative correlation was observed between variable 60 and 1st foreign language proficiency: -.4510 ($p<0.01$).

No significant difference was found between the French and Swedish students with regard to variable 61: both groups considered that English was instrumental in their finding employment (mean=1.6 in France and 1.5 in

Sweden; see Table 8.17). If no significant difference was observed between the groups with regard to variable 61, this was not the case for variable 62 ('Learning English broadens my general knowledge'); to this suggestion, the Swedish students were found to agree more than their French counterparts: mean=1.5 as opposed to 2.0 in France ($p<0.001$; see Table 8.17). On the one hand, the student responses to this statement can be considered to some extent as factually-based: the learning of any language contributes to broadening one's general knowledge. On the other hand, the results can also be considered indicative of more subjective attitudes, in so far as the claim in variable 62 could be seen to suggest that it is English, perhaps more than other languages, which represents the key to knowledge, to being considered worldly. The positive Swedish attitudes are understandable, considering that it is through English that Sweden has traditionally generated a positive identity in the global arena (see Section 7.4). However, the results also show that English was far from lacking in value in the eyes of the French respondents. This observation was further reinforced by the results of attitudes towards variable 64. Both groups of students thought that children ought to learn English at school from an early age, even if it was the Swedish students who agreed more: mean=1.8 as opposed to 2.1 for French students ($p<0.005$; see Table 8.17). Clearly, the French respondents considered English a useful tool. In this respect, the present results confirm those of Flaitz (1988: 175), whose French respondents claimed overwhelmingly that they had learnt or were learning English because it was a 'useful' language: mean=1.2 on a similar five-point scale.

Despite the positive French attitudes observed towards English so far, some evidence was found of those attitudes which correspond to the defensive posture normally associated with attitudes to English in France. The French respondents rejected variable 63, which suggested that proficiency in English was somehow associated with a higher degree of education: mean=3.9 (see Table 8.17). The results can be explained in terms of the distinction between high and low culture as discussed in Section 7.5. In France, particular prestige is attached to high culture, which can be considered as a mark of education. An individual's knowledge of classical languages (e.g. Latin and Greek) is therefore likely to be much more highly regarded than that of English. Indeed, the French authorities and defenders of the national language have long scorned English as a global language because of its purported link to American mass culture. Considering the positive attitudes observed in her study, Flaitz (1988: 187 and 199) concludes that the negative posture towards English normally associated with France originates from an élite, whose defensive reactions can be explained in terms of perceived threats. This negative posture is propagated through institutions like the French school system, which considers that it has a duty to uphold the values of high culture, as manifested accordingly in the French respondents' rejection of variable 63.

By contrast, so-called low culture is not the object of such disdain in Sweden, as witnessed by the omnipresence of American mass culture in that country (see Section 7.4). It is in this light that one can understand the less vehement Swedish rejection of the suggestion that proficiency in English was linked to one's level of education: mean=3.1 for variable 63 ($p<0.001$; see Table 8.17). Despite this mean score, 32.3 per cent of the Swedish respondents *did* think that knowledge of English was a mark of education (as opposed to the mere 12.4 per cent who were of the same opinion in France). This percentage of Swedish respondents who claimed that proficiency in English was higher than expected, as shown by the results of a Chi square test for the collapsed responses to variable 63 ($\chi^2=42.67$; df=2; sig.=0.000; cf. Oakes 2000: 229). Clearly for a large number of the Swedish respondents, English can be considered as a trump card, the key to being better educated (see Section 7.4), perhaps also to social mobility both at home and in the global arena.

8.3.4.2 *Perceived threat from English*

In addition to the general attitudes sought towards English, five items aimed to measure reactions to the claim that the widespread use of English threatened the future of French or Swedish respectively (see Section 7.2). The most direct form of measurement was used in item 27 ('Do you think that another language/other languages could threaten the future of French/Swedish?'). The results of the Chi square test are shown in Table 8.18.

As seen in this table, the distribution of French and Swedish students answering 'yes', 'no', 'perhaps' and 'don't know' to this question was highly significant ($p<0.001$). A majority of students in both countries agreed that there was no threat to their national language (32.3 per cent in France and 42.9 per cent in Sweden). Those who did perceive a definite threat were relatively few in Sweden (9.9 per cent), and more numerous in France (29.0 per cent). As for those who were unsure and answered 'perhaps', this was the case for roughly a third of the Swedes (30.9 per cent), but less than one fifth of the French (18.3 per cent). In short, the majority of French students answered 'no', followed by 'yes', 'don't know' and 'perhaps'; in Sweden, the pattern observed was 'no', 'perhaps', 'don't know' and 'yes', which matched exactly

Table 8.18 Threat to future of French/Swedish. Observed numbers (No), expected numbers (Ne), percentages (%) and results of Chi square test

V27 Do you think that another language/other languages could threaten the future of French/Swedish?

	France			Sweden		
	No	Ne	%	No	Ne	%
Yes	54	34.2	29.0	23	42.8	9.9
Perhaps	34	47.1	18.3	72	58.9	30.9
No	60	71.0	32.3	100	89.0	42.9
Don't know	38	33.7	20.4	38	42.3	16.3
Total	186	186	100	233	233	100

$\chi^2 = 31.22$; df=3; sig=0.000; missing cases=2

that observed by Wingstedt (1998: 261), who posed the question: 'Do you think that Swedish will die out in 100 years?' By way of response to this question, 1.8 per cent answered 'yes', 3.0 per cent answered 'don't know', 20.1 per cent 'perhaps' and an overwhelming 75.1 per cent responded 'no'. The higher percentage of 'no' responses observed by Wingstedt may be due to the slightly different question asked. The question posed in the present study ('Do you think that another language/other languages could threaten the future of French/Swedish?') did not so much suggest that these languages may not exist in the future, as propose that they may not have the same status, may exist in a different form, etc. This distinction surely addresses the hypothesis of Wingstedt (1998: 261) that 'most laypeople of the linguistic majority find it inconceivable that their mother tongue would die in a foreseeable future, in spite of the fact that Swedish — albeit an official majority language in a politically autonomous state — could be characterized as a "lesser used language" onto which English is encroaching at a seemingly accelerating pace.' While the results of Wingstedt verify her claim, those of the present study would seem to indicate that young Swedes more readily envisage changes to their language's status and form.

The second part of item 27 asked those students who answered 'yes' or 'perhaps' to state which language or languages they considered threatening. As expected, the language mentioned most often was English: in 75 out of a potential 88 'yes' and 'perhaps' responses in France (85.2 per cent), and in 71 out of 95 cases (74.7 per cent) in Sweden. The other languages mentioned were as follows: in France, Spanish in seven cases, German in five cases, Arabic in four, Basque in three cases, Chinese in two, and Breton, Japanese, Tamil and the 'languages of the south [sic]' in one case each; in Sweden, German in eight cases, French in six cases, Arabic and a 'European/EU language' in four cases each, Turkish in three cases, Danish, Norwegian and Spanish in two cases each, a 'computer language', Finnish, a 'global language', 'immigrant languages', Rinkeby Swedish, Russian, Syrian, 'something foreign' and 'other cultures' in one case each. In France, other EU languages were therefore mentioned by 13.6 per cent of the students who answered 'yes' or 'perhaps', immigrant languages by 6.8 per cent and regional languages by 4.5 per cent; in Sweden, other EU languages were represented by 23.2 per cent of the responses, immigrant languages by 10.5 per cent and other Nordic languages by 5.3 per cent.[8] The Swedish results are confirmed by those of Wingstedt (1998: 261), who found that a majority (68.5 per cent) of respondents claimed the principal threat was from English, followed by 'Swenglish', German and French (2.9 per cent of responses each), and a variety of other languages including Arabic, Euro-English and some form of Nordic language.

In particular, the Swedish results of the present survey merit further comment. Some Swedish respondents seemed to welcome the possibility of Swedish giving way to English: one student remarked 'It doesn't matter if English/American takes over Sweden'; another who claimed that English *did* pose a threat to Swedish added 'Not that I care'. However, many of the students who mentioned English clarified that they did not really consider the language to be a threat. The extra comments made by the Swedish respondents to this effect were as follows:

- To threaten is the wrong word.
- But I do not see it as a threat.
- What do you mean 'a threat'?
- Perhaps not threaten but influence the language's development. English of course. American English.
- Our language is simply developing. English has a clear influence, but only for the better.
- I am totally sure that Swedish will survive, but other languages will no doubt become more important. I do not see it as a threat, but rather it is good to be able to communicate with people.
- Perhaps English, but I do not think it will take over the whole Swedish language.

From the above comments, it can be clearly seen that, on the whole, the Swedish respondents did not consider English as a threat to their national language. This observation confirms the suggestion made above in this section, that the question posed in the present study was asking something different from that posed by Wingstedt (1998). No extra comments were made by the French respondents.

That the French and Swedish respondents did not perceive a strong threat from English was also confirmed by the rejection by both groups of variables 50, 57, 65 and 66. The results of the ANOVAs are shown in Table 8.19.

The results of the item which focused on mixing in English words when speaking French or Swedish were particularly revealing for two main reasons. First, both groups rejected variable 50, indicating that they considered it acceptable to use English words in their national languages: mean=3.4 in France and 3.1 in Sweden. In this sense, the results of variable 50 contrast with those of variable 35 (see Section 8.3.1.2). For this latter variable, Swedish students agreed that it was important that their national language be kept as pure as possible from foreign loan words (mean=2.7), while their French counterparts were undecided on the matter (mean=3.0), although notably not in favour of linguistic purism. The main difference between variables 35 and 50 is, of course, that the latter sought reactions to the use of loan words specifically from English. Comparison of the two sets of results confirms the claim made in Section 7.4 that, as far as language attitudes are concerned, English is situated at the top of the hierarchy in Sweden, thus making borrowings from that language more acceptable than those from other

Table 8.19 Perceived threat from English according to country

	Country	N	Mean	F	df.	sig.
V50 One should not mix in/use English words when one speaks French/Swedish	France Sweden	187 234	3.4 3.1	4.92	1,396	0.027
V57 Knowing English is detrimental to knowledge of French/Swedish	France Sweden	186 232	3.6 4.4	58.97	1,393	0.000
V65 Knowing English threatens one's French/Swedish identity	France Sweden	185 232	3.8 4.3	23.96	1,393	0.000
V66 There are too many English-language films at the cinema and on TV in France/Sweden	France Sweden	186 232	3.4 3.7	2.98	1,394	0.085

For means: 1=agree totally; 2=agree partially; 3=undecided; 4=don't particularly agree; 5=don't agree at all

languages. The results also suggest that a similar language hierarchy exists in France. Second, the results of the analysis of variable 50 revealed a slight tendency whereby the French respondents rejected the suggestion more than their Swedish counterparts, although the level of significance (0.027) fell just short of the 0.02 used in this study. The results observed here would appear to *confirm* those of variable 35, in so far as it was the French respondents who were less inclined towards linguistic purism. As mentioned in Section 8.3.1.2, one reason for this lack of purist approach to the national language amongst the French (and the Swedish) respondents of this study may be their young age. Indeed, while opinion was divided as to whether the use of English and American words was 'a bad thing' (50 per cent) or 'a good thing' for the French language (45 per cent) in a SOFRES poll of 1988, Ager (1990: 225) points out that the latter view was supported particularly among respondents aged between 18 and 24 years. An alternative, or more likely additional, reason is that already mentioned in Section 8.3.4.1 and confirmed by the observations of Flaitz (1988) and others (e.g. Ager 1999: 111): the general public is more accepting than the intellectual élite of English and American borrowings into French, which lead to the emergence of hybrid languages such as *franglais* and Swenglish (see Sections 7.3 and 7.4).

Item 57 ('Knowing English is detrimental to knowledge of French/ Swedish') went one step further, in suggesting that the acquisition of English may lead to subtractive as opposed to additive bilingualism (see Section 7.2). As expected, it was the Swedish students who rejected this statement more (mean=4.4 as opposed to 3.6 in France; $p<0.001$; see Table 8.19). Similar results were found for item 65 ('Knowing English threatens one's French/ Swedish identity'), which extended Lambert's (1975) additivity-subtractivity theory of bilingualism from language to identity (cf. Hamers and Blanc 2000: 214): mean=4.3 in Sweden as opposed to 3.8 in France; $p<0.001$; see Table 8.19). Nonetheless, the differences between the groups should not detract from the fact that the French respondents still rejected these claims. Similar observations were made in France by Flaitz (1988: 166–71), whose respondents disagreed with the statements 'The American influence on French culture worries me' (mean=3.3 on the same five-point scale as used for this study) and 'If we French begin to speak English, we will adopt American values' (mean=3.4). As for the Swedish results, they too show that convergence towards English as a global language does not necessarily entail a threat to their national identities or knowledge of their national languages, thus confirming the observation made by Vikør (1993: 145) cited in Section 7.4: 'modern young people feel themselves to be Danish (Swedish etc.) *as well as* inhabitants of the "world-wide America" of pop culture, films and consumption patterns they have grown up with.' Further evidence for this claim is provided by the results of variable 66, which revealed that both groups rejected the suggestion that there were too many English-language films at the cinema and on television in France and Sweden: means=3.4 in France and 3.7 in Sweden (not significant; see Table 8.19). The French results are particularly revealing, considering the efforts of France to 'protect' French identity by insisting on a cultural exception (*exception culturelle*) during the 1993–4 Uruguay round of the general agreement on tariffs and trade (GATT) talks (see Section 7.5).

8.3.5 Summary of survey results

In this final section, the results of the survey are summarised first according to the four sets of hypotheses and two research questions set out in Section 8.1.

> Hypothesis 1a: There is a high degree of national and linguistic consciousness in France.
>
> Hypothesis 1b: There is a low degree of national and linguistic consciousness in Sweden.

As expected, the French respondents reported a positive national identity and pride in that identity (see Section 8.3.1.1). Nonetheless, French national consciousness was perhaps not as strong as might have been predicted. Some explanation can be found in the large number of French students in the survey with at least one foreign-born parent. But while it is true that these students had the effect of weakening French national identity and pride in that identity, the fact remained that national consciousness was not as strong amongst the French respondents as it was amongst their Swedish counterparts. The very strong and positive national identity reported amongst the Swedish respondents was especially interesting considering the widespread myth amongst Swedes that they have an 'inverted nationalism' or somehow lack a sense of national identity (see Section 4.3).

Considering the long history of language constituting a core value of national identity in France (see Section 4.2), it was not surprising to learn that the relatively strong national consciousness observed amongst the French students was also translated into a strong linguistic consciousness (see Section 8.3.1.2). This linguistic consciousness was demonstrated by positive attitudes expressed towards French (e.g. that it was a beautiful language, worthy of knowing, and well-suited to a modern society). As argued before (e.g. Section 3.1), such judgements are not based on any inherent value of a particular language, but rather on imposed societal norms or mainstream beliefs which, in this case, reflect national consciousness. Particularly noteworthy was the observation that the respondents did not reject the suggested link between language and an ethnic conception of French identity. These results thus provide evidence for the observation made in Section 4.2 that for most French people, national identity is composed of both an ethnic and a civic dimension. Nonetheless, there was some evidence that linguistic consciousness, like national consciousness, was not as strong amongst the French respondents as might have been expected. In particular, attitudes towards the quality of French and the importance of correct spelling were not as prescriptive as those which dominate at the official level and amongst some intellectual élites (see Section 4.4). Most noteworthy, however, was the observation that opinion was divided on the issue of language purism, with a majority (39.9 per cent) claiming that it was *not* important that French be kept as pure as possible from foreign loan words.

By contrast, the Swedish respondents *did* on the whole think that it was important to preserve the purity of Swedish as much as possible. This observation was indicative of the unexpectedly high degree of linguistic consciousness reported by the Swedish students (see Section 8.3.1.2). Not only did they affirm that it was important to spell correctly, and that Swedish was a beautiful language worthy of knowing, the Swedes were even more categorical than their French counterparts in their opinion that Swedish was an important part of Swedish heritage which could also be used in a modern society. These findings are particularly revealing considering that the positive attitudes observed in Sweden towards English have traditionally been understood in terms of the Swedes regarding that language as 'more effective, modern, beautiful and better than their own language' (Laureys 1997: 25). While these results do not imply that attitudes towards English were not even more positive than those towards Swedish (see Section 8.3.4.1), they do indicate that language is far from an insignificant part of Swedish identity.

On the basis of the results of the survey in this study, hypothesis 1a is therefore accepted, but it is noted that national and linguistic consciousness amongst the young respondents in France was perhaps not as strong as at the official level. By contrast, hypothesis 1b is rejected, on the grounds that the Swedish respondents reported a high degree of national and linguistic consciousness which in many cases even surpassed that of their French counterparts.

Hypothesis 2a: In today's France, attitudes towards minority languages remain negative. Linguistic boundaries are still significant when making social comparisons with ethnolinguistic minorities.

Hypothesis 2b: In today's Sweden, attitudes towards minority languages are positive. Linguistic boundaries are no longer significant when making social comparisons with ethnolinguistic minorities.

Contrary to expectations, attitudes in France *vis-à-vis* regional and immigrant languages were not shown to be negative (see Section 8.3.2.1). The French respondents agreed that minority languages in their country should be preserved as much as possible. Similarly, attitudes towards state-supported teaching of regional languages did not prove to be as unfavourable as expected: while it was true that 33.7 per cent thought that the teaching of these languages was not the responsibility of the French school system, 31.5 per cent thought that it was. Even the fact that a majority (34.8 per cent) were undecided on this matter could be interpreted positively: the lack of knowledge about regional languages which this figure may represent did not translate into negative attitudes formed out of ignorance. A more direct formulation, which made reference to specific languages, proved even more revealing: French students were seen to agree that both Basque and Arabic were beautiful languages. Some explanation for these relatively positive attitudes towards Arabic — and by extension towards the immigrant languages it symbolised — can be found in the large number of students in France with at least one foreign-born parent (cf. Oakes 2000: 195–6). Nonetheless, the fact remains that the attitudes in France were still more positive — or less negative — than those observed amongst the Swedish students. The positive attitudes observed towards Arabic are particularly significant, since they appear to be at odds with the support for extreme right-wing parties observed amongst some French people and the lively debate on immigration in France (see Section 5.2.2).

Similar observations were not made in Sweden (see Section 8.3.2.1). Although the Swedish respondents claimed to be positive towards minority language preservation and tuition, they nevertheless expressed negative attitudes towards Sámi and Arabic, the languages chosen to represent regional and immigrant languages respectively. A strong, negative correlation was even observed between strength of Swedish identity and attitudes towards Arabic as a beautiful language. These results appear to confirm the claim made in

Section 5.3.2, that the Swedish multicultural policies introduced from the 1960s–1970s at the official level have not filtered down to the grassroots level, where there is evidence of negative attitudes towards ethnolinguistic groups, especially of the immigrant kind.

In accordance with the observation made in the previous section, language was also found to play a significant role in the definition of Swedishness as constructed in the national arena (see Section 8.3.2.2). The Swedish respondents rejected the claims that Swedish was affected negatively, both because it was spoken by many people as a second language and because other languages were spoken in Sweden. Nonetheless, this rejection was not convincing; more importantly, respondents in Stockholm were actually found to agree with these claims, albeit only slightly. The existence of a linguistic boundary which delimits Swedish identity was also supported by some evidence of solidarity-related attitudes towards Swedish speakers in other countries. An albeit only slight belief that one should not be able to become a citizen without speaking Swedish and could not be considered truly Swedish without speaking this language also showed that the linguistic dimension was not totally insignificant when it came to distinguishing Swedes from non-Swedes. These observations are in accordance with those made in the content analysis of Section 5.3.2, where it was seen that language is used in Sweden as a politically correct means of distinguishing the Other (e.g. in debates on semilingualism and Rinkeby Swedish). Indeed, the Swedish respondents reported much softer non-linguistic boundaries — in this case place of birth and ethnic background — possibly for fear of being accused of racism.

The non-linguistic boundaries were not reported as hard in France either, but in this country, neither were the linguistic boundaries (see Section 8.3.2.2). Much more than their Swedish counterparts, the French respondents rejected the claims that the quality of French was deteriorating as a result of it being spoken by many people as a second language, or because other languages were spoken in France. The French students were not as categorical as might have been expected in their rejection of the suggestion that one could be French without speaking French; nor did they appear to identify strongly with French speakers in other countries. In addition, they were divided on the issue of whether knowledge of French should constitute a prerequisite for obtaining French citizenship. The dominant ethnic group may have a long history of using language to construct its identity in the national arena (see Sections 5.2.1, 5.2.2 and 5.4); nonetheless, in the context of majority-minority relations, language does not appear to be as important a dimension of social comparison and psychological distinctiveness for the young French respondents studied here.

Hypothesis 2a is rejected, on the grounds that very little evidence was found of negative attitudes towards minorities in France; nor did linguistic boundaries appear to be hardened in social comparisons with ethnolinguistic minorities. Hypothesis 2b is also rejected. Not only did the Swedish results reveal negative attitudes *vis-à-vis* ethnolinguistic minorities behind a multicultural façade, they also provided some evidence for the claim that language is used as a politically correct means of distinguishing between Swedes and non-Swedes.

Hypothesis 3a: A positive French identity in the European arena is generated through strategies of divergence.

Hypothesis 3b: A positive Swedish identity in the European arena is generated through strategies of convergence.

Although notably weaker than national identity, the European identity reported by respondents in both countries was stronger than expected — 'average' or 'quite a lot', depending on the translation used (see Section 8.3.3.1) — thus providing some evidence of convergence in the European arena. Surprisingly, no significant difference emerged between the strength of identity reported by the two groups, despite the fact that France has long been involved in the process of European integration, while Sweden's participation is relatively new, having joined the EU as recently as 1995. A significant difference was observed, however, on the question of whether EU countries were too different to create a European identity: while the French claimed that such an identity was feasible, the Swedes thought that it was not. This is not to say that the opinion of the Swedish respondents will not become more favourable over time; nor is it to say that the view of the French students will not become more negative, if further enlargement results in the EU no longer corresponding as well as it does at the time of writing to French national interests. However, at the time of this study, national and European identities are considered by the respondents not as mutually exclusive, but rather as complementary concepts. The strong, positive correlation observed between the strength of national identity and that of European identity thus addresses one of the major questions associated with the creation of the latter: can European identity be reconciled with national identities (see Section 6.1)?

Albeit notably more so in Sweden, respondents in both countries were pessimistic with regard to the role played by their language in the EU (see Section 8.3.3.2). Moreover, the future prospects of this role were not considered much better. The French and Swedish students nonetheless both stressed, to a relatively equal degree, the importance of maintaining linguistic diversity in the EU. These results indicate that, while the respondents did not stress an important role in the EU for their respective languages, they nevertheless thought that their linguistic identities ought not to be compromised. This latter observation was also confirmed by the French and Swedish negative attitudes towards the idea of a single European language (see Section 8.3.3.3). But while both groups fiercely rejected the suggestion that Esperanto play this role, the Swedish respondents reacted positively to the proposal of English as the EU's official language. As expected, the French students were negative towards the idea that English be accorded this official status, but notably, they did recognise the *de facto* importance which English has already acquired in the European arena.

Hypothesis 3a is therefore rejected on the grounds that, alongside the traditional strategies of divergence, the French respondents demonstrated some evidence both of linguistic and non-linguistic convergence in the European arena. Hypothesis 3b is also rejected. Although they showed clear signs of convergence, in particular of a linguistic nature towards English, the young Swedes did not think that their Swedish linguistic identity should be jeopardised in the EU.

> Hypothesis 4a: A positive French identity in the global arena is generated through strategies of divergence.
>
> Hypothesis 4b: A positive Swedish identity in the global arena is generated through strategies of convergence.

As expected, it was the Swedish respondents who expressed the most positive attitudes towards English (see Section 8.3.4.1). Not only did they think that it was a beautiful language which was not difficult to learn, the Swedes also thought that knowing English would broaden their general knowledge and contribute to their finding employment. It was also thought that English lent itself well to use in a modern society and should be taught at school from an early age. What proved more interesting was that positive attitudes, albeit slightly weaker, were also observed in France. Evidence was found nonetheless of the defensive attitudes towards English normally professed by guardians of the language in France. In particular, the French respondents rejected the suggestion that knowledge of English was a sign of education. These results are in accordance with the view of many members of the intellectual élite in France that English is associated with mass culture (see Section 7.3). While the Swedish respondents also rejected the same suggestion, they did so less vehemently, and it was found that 32.3 per cent actually thought that knowledge of English *was* a marker of one's level of education.

A majority in both countries (42.9 per cent in Sweden and 32.3 per cent in France) perceived no definite threat to the future of their language (see Section 8.3.4.2). Analysis of the responses of those respondents who did, however, indicated that English was clearly the most threatening language. Yet the Swedish results required further comment: many of those who mentioned English felt it necessary to clarify that they did not really consider the language as a threat, but merely an influence, which some even saw as beneficial. Both groups of respondents also rejected the suggestions that knowledge of English was detrimental to French/Swedish, that it threatened one's French/Swedish identity, and that there were too many English-language films at the cinema or on TV in France/Sweden. Not surprisingly, it was the Swedish students who, on the whole, proved more categorical in their rejection of these three suggestions. However, there was an unexpected tendency amongst the French students to disagree most with the claim that one should not mix in English words when one speaks French. These results are particularly significant considering the long tradition of linguistic purism observed at the official level and amongst guardians of the language in France. Moreover, they are supported by the results of Section 8.3.1.2, where a tendency was noted for Swedish students to agree more than their French counterparts that it was important to preserve the purity of their national language.

Hypothesis 4a is therefore rejected on the grounds that attitudes towards English amongst the young French respondents proved positive. English was not perceived as a threat by the majority and there was evidence of a willingness to converge towards English as a global means of communication. By contrast, hypothesis 4b is accepted since attitudes towards English proved reasonably strong and positive amongst the Swedish respondents. The language was not perceived as a threat by the majority, and there was much evidence to support the claim that the Swedes use strategies of convergence in the global arena to generate a positive identity.

> Research question 1: Are there any discrepancies between the grassroots and official levels *vis-à-vis* the role played by language in the construction of French and Swedish identities?

In so far as the hypotheses were largely based on the attitudes traditionally associated with official circles, the findings of the survey, which was conducted at the grassroots level, reveal a major schism between the two levels in both France and Sweden. Regional and immigrant minorities continue to pose problems for the French model of integration or myth of inclusion which has dominated at the official level since the French Revolution (see Sections 5.2.1, 5.2.2 and 5.4). However, the young French people studied here clearly did not consider ethnolinguistic minorities of any type as negative outgroups for the purposes of constructing a positive national identity (see Sections 8.3.2.1 and 8.3.2.2). Despite the many attempts of their successive governments to bolster the status of French in the EU (see Section 6.3), the French respondents did not stress the role of their language to the same extent (see Section 8.3.3.2), and even recognised the *de facto* importance which English has already acquired in the European arena (see Section 8.3.3.3). Nor did the French respondents uphold the negative, defensive attitudes towards English normally associated with official circles and especially guardians of the language in France (see Section 7.3): English was viewed positively and not considered a threat to the French language or identity, thereby indicating that there may be a willingness to converge towards English as a global means of communication (see Sections 8.3.4.1 and 8.3.4.2). Only with regard to national and linguistic consciousness when viewed from a general perspective could there be claimed to be any degree of similarity between the official and grassroots levels in France (see Sections 4.2, 4.4, 8.3.1.1 and 8.3.1.2).

By contrast, the high degree of national consciousness reported by the Swedish respondents (see Section 8.3.1.1) was not in agreement with the widespread myth, originating largely from the social democratic ideology of official circles, that Swedish identity is weak, or somehow 'tamer' than other national identities (see Section 4.3). Considering the relative absence to date of official policy regarding the Swedish language, it was also surprising that the respondents in Sweden expressed such a strong linguistic consciousness (see Section 8.3.1.2). In addition, the Swedish students showed evidence of negative attitudes towards ethnolinguistic minorities, especially those of the immigrant type (see Section 8.3.2.1). These attitudes were found to be at odds with the official multicultural policies which have existed in Sweden since the 1960s–1970s (see Section 5.3.2). Although there was evidence of divergence in convergence strategies traditionally used by Sweden to generate a positive identity in international fora (see Sections 6.4 and 7.4), the young Swedes did not think that their linguistic identity in the EU should be compromised (see Section 8.3.3.2). There was clear evidence of convergence, however, with regard to using English as a means of generating a positive Swedish identity in the global arena (see Sections 8.3.4.1 and 8.3.4.2).

Research question 2: Are the results of the present survey in accordance with those of other studies on the role of language in the construction of French and Swedish identities?

The findings of the survey were in accordance with those of the two other empirical studies which examined language and national identity in France and Sweden at the grassroots level, even if not amongst young people in particular. As mentioned in Section 8.2.1.1, Flaitz (1988) focuses only on attitudes towards English, a perspective which corresponds to what is considered in the present study as the global arena. She notes that attitudes towards English amongst the general public in France are essentially positive, and concludes that the unfavourable posture towards English normally associated with France originates from a certain élite or intelligentsia, who have a vested interest in maintaining negative attitudes towards the English-speaking world.

> [T]his group has found success in convincing much of the English-speaking world that the majority of French men and women find English and its native speakers offensive. The data reported in this study suggest this to be a conclusion of questionable validity. Moreover, there is no hard evidence available from other studies which would suggest that average French citizens share the perspective of their power elite. In a word, the English-speaking world has drawn its conclusions from the subjective literature of France's guardians of the language from heresay [*sic*] and anecdote. (Flaitz 1988: 199)

The findings of the present study are thus in accordance with those of Flaitz, even if the latter was conducted over ten years earlier.

In Sweden, Wingstedt (1998) also investigates attitudes towards English to some extent, although the primary focus of her study is on attitudes towards ethnic minorities and their languages. She observes signs of a heightened linguistic consciousness similar to that noted in this survey and manifested by an inclination amongst her respondents towards language purism and prescriptivism (Wingstedt 1998: 245 and 259). In addition, she reports that two competing language ideologies currently exist in Sweden: on the one hand, the linguistic and cultural pluralism which is embraced in official policies; on the other hand, 'the assimilationist, monolingualist ideology which is deeply rooted in the "naturalized" conception of the nation state, [and which] still lingers on in large segments of the population' (Wingstedt 1998: 341). These competing ideologies reflect the same lack of cohesion between 'official and "folk"/popular ideologies' (Wingstedt 1998: 341) which was noted in the present study. Finally, the use of language as a metaphor or politically correct means of distinguishing between Swedes and non-Swedes was equally confirmed by Wingstedt (1998: 344), who points to the disproportionate attention placed on language in the debates on the status and rights of minorities in Sweden.

Further confirmation of the survey results was provided by the societal analyses of Chapters 4 to 7, in so far as these also focused, to some degree, on the grassroots level. In particular, the suggestion that young French people may be coming to terms with the ethnic diversity of their country is supported by the observation that many elements of immigrant culture have already been incorporated into aspects of French culture which are of particular relevance to young people, such as football and rap music (see Section 5.2.2). The English-language films of French director Luc Besson also served as an example of the observation that some French people are turning to strategies of divergence in convergence in order to generate a positive identity in the global arena (see Section 7.5). The societal analyses of Sweden showed that the rise of neo-Nazism and emergence of mainstream extreme right-wing parties still only concerned a small minority; however, the less pernicious expressions of Swedish nationalism that were observed in the form of a heightened interest in Swedish history and popularity of folk-rock groups such as Nordman (see Section 7.4) nonetheless support the survey findings which indicate that Swedish identity may have become more overt in recent years. Language was also seen to play a major role in that identity, especially in the national arena, where it served as a defence mechanism, as manifest in the debates on semilingualism and Rinkeby Swedish (see Section 5.3.2). Finally, the societal analyses also noted concern amongst some scholars in Sweden that there is a potential risk for language shift unless efforts are made to guarantee the use of Swedish in certain domains (see Sections 6.4 and 7.4). While these concerns were not observed to the same extent amongst the young Swedish respondents, the latter nevertheless attached some importance to protecting their linguistic identity in fora like the EU.

Chapter 9

Conclusion

At various points throughout this book, it has been argued that the topic of language and national identity benefits from using both a comparative perspective, and several contexts or arenas of investigation. A case has also been made for the advantages of using theoretical insights from a range of disciplines, and employing a variety of methods of inquiry. Despite the difficulties in managing the scale of such an approach, the present study has nevertheless sought to provide an original insight into language attitudes and national identity strategies amongst young people in France and Sweden. It has also aimed to contribute to the extensive body of literature on the topic of language and national identity in general.

This study would certainly not have come close to achieving its goals without the aid of a sound theoretical paradigm. In the present case, a combination of language attitude theory and social/ethnolinguistic identity theory provided an excellent point of departure. Of particular benefit, however, were the three additions which were made to this framework. First, the notions of convergence and divergence proved helpful in describing and understanding language attitudes and national identity strategies, especially in the European and global contexts where France and Sweden are in a minority. Second, the recognition of non-linguistic as well as linguistic boundaries allowed the author to study the negotiation process which takes place between different dimensions of national identity. In other words, the theoretical framework also considered the role of extra-linguistic factors in determining the importance attributed to language. Third and finally, the concept of different arenas was necessary to take into account how the construction of national identity in one arena is affected by the state of national identity as it exists in another arena.

In this final chapter, the same theoretical framework is used to summarise the current state of language attitudes and national identity strategies in France and Sweden. The results of both the societal analyses and the empirical study are brought together in a summary of the overall findings of the book (Section 9.1). A final section identifies some key areas for future research (Section 9.2).

9.1 Summary of findings

Following the convention of previous chapters, the overall findings of the study are summarised here first from a general perspective (Section 9.1.1), then according to the national (Section 9.1.2), European (Section 9.1.3) and global (Section 9.1.4) arenas.

9.1.1 Language and national identity in France and Sweden: A general perspective

As seen in Chapter 4, the construction of linguistic and national consciousness in Sweden mirrored that in France for many centuries: François I's Edict of Villers-Cotterêts of 1539 was followed, albeit over a century later, by guidelines in 1661 reinforcing the use of Swedish in diplomatic correspondence; the Swedish Academy set up in 1786 modelled itself on the French equivalent established in 1635; and the effect of nineteenth-century Romanticism in Sweden resulted in similar efforts to consolidate national identity as those observed under the Third Republic in France. It is not until World War II that a clear divergence between the two countries can be observed: while French identity continued to be overtly promoted by the Vichy government and afterwards, Swedish national consciousness went underground in reaction to Nazi racial theories and social democratic ideology.

At the official level, this dichotomy remains more or less valid today. While a strong linguistic and national consciousness continues to emanate from official circles in France, few overt references to linguistic and national identity are made by the authorities in Sweden. However, this scenario appears reversed at the grassroots level. The results of the direct survey conducted amongst young people in France revealed that not only was national consciousness weaker than in Sweden (see Section 8.3.1.1), the respondents did not share the prescriptive and purist attitudes normally associated with linguistic consciousness in France (see Section 8.3.1.2). By contrast, the high degree of national consciousness reported by the Swedish respondents was not in agreement with the widespread myth, originating largely from the social democratic ideology of official circles, that Swedish identity is weak, or somehow more subdued than other national identities (see Section 4.3). Considering the lack to date of official policy regarding the Swedish language, it was also surprising that the respondents in Sweden expressed such a strong linguistic consciousness (see Section 8.3.1.2).

Two interpretations are possible for the Swedish results. First, it could be claimed that linguistic and national consciousness have always been as strong as observed in the empirical study, but that they were expressed in a covert fashion. Indeed, Löfgren (1993: 27, 72–3) has observed that Swedish identity does not manifest itself in the same overt manner as American or even French identity, while Teleman and Westman (1999) claim that '[t]he status of the Swedish language in Sweden has long gone without saying' (see Section 4.3). Without denying the validity of these observations, a more adventurous interpretation for the results of the survey is that Swedish linguistic and national consciousness is becoming stronger, and the link between language and national identity more overt. This latter interpretation is supported by the observations of the societal analysis (see Sections 4.3 and 4.4), which indicated that Sweden is currently in the midst of an ethnonationalist revival, which may have linguistic implications. The ultimate test in determining whether linguistic and national consciousness are currently in a state of transition in Sweden must nevertheless lie in future research of an empirical nature (see Section 9.2).

9.1.2 Language and national identity in France and Sweden: The national arena

In sixteenth- and seventeenth-centuries France and Sweden, the state was not interested in which languages were spoken by the masses (see Sections 5.2.1 and 5.3.1). Of greater concern was that those in the peripheries were loyal to the state and to religion. This 'indifferent tolerance' (Wingstedt 1998: 78) of linguistic diversity came to an end with the consolidation of national identity which followed the Revolution in France and the Romanticist movement in Sweden, and which carried on into the twentieth century. Regional languages were denigrated or denied in the name of national unity and cohesion. From the 1950s–1960s, a change in policy began to emerge in both countries. But while in France, the Deixonne Law of 1951 remained largely symbolic, the Home Language Reform of 1977 constituted a real, albeit ill-conceived attempt at multiculturalism on the part of the Swedish authorities (see Section 5.4). The new Swedish approach was driven by a search for a solution to the ethnic diversity which resulted from post-World War II immigration (see Section 5.3.2). No such change of policy greeted the arrival of immigrants in France, where the French model of integration or myth of inclusion was seen as the only legitimate means of reconciling French and immigrant identities (see Section 5.2.2).

At the official level, regional and immigrant minorities continue to challenge this uniquely French solution to ethnic diversity. The problems which are purportedly caused by immigration are systematically discussed at the official level and in the media (see Section 5.2.2), while France's refusal to ratify the Charter for Regional or Minority Languages is indicative of the official denial of minorities within the *Hexagone* (see Sections 5.2.1 and 5.4). However, at the grassroots level, the young French respondents of the direct study clearly did not regard ethnic minorities as significant negatively-viewed outgroups for the purposes of constructing a positive French identity (see Section 8.3.2.1). Nor did the students in France, unlike the French authorities, have recourse to language when making social comparisons of themselves with ethnic minorities (see Section 8.3.2.2).

By contrast, there was some evidence that linguistic boundaries were used by the young Swedish respondents in Stockholm as a politically correct means of excluding immigrant minorities. Indeed, the Swedish respondents reported much softer boundaries of a non-linguistic nature (i.e. birth place, ethnic background), possibly for fear of being accused of racism. As seen in the societal analysis (see Section 5.3.2), language is used as a symbol for majority-minority relations in Sweden, giving rise, for example, to the debates on semilingualism and Rinkeby Swedish. In the same way that the French official myth of inclusion conceals *de facto* inequalities behind a superficial homogenous front (see Section 5.2.2), the social democratic ideology which emanates from official circles in Sweden surreptitiously encourages uniformity behind an egalitarian façade (see Section 5.3.1). It is perhaps not so surprising then, that official multicultural policies have not filtered down to the grassroots level, and in particular to the young Swedes who participated in the empirical study. Whether language will come to play an even greater role in the construction of Swedish identity in the national arena as a result of the ethnonationalist revival is a question for future research (see Section 9.2). Similarly, further studies would be required to determine if the tolerance of ethnolinguistic minorities observed amongst the young respondents in France represents a transition in language attitudes and national identity strategies.

9.1.3 Language and national identity in France and Sweden: The European arena

As demonstrated by de Gaulle's call for a *Europe des patries*, successive French governments have long employed policies of divergence to generate a positive national identity in the European arena (see Section 6.3). Moreover, these strategies of divergence have only become more pronounced over time, as French influence in the EU has become less assured. Considering the inextricable link between language and national identity in France, it is not surprising that the French form of divergence has included efforts to ensure the status of French in the European Union and in Europe at large (see Section 6.3). By contrast, such clear acts of linguistic divergence were not adopted by Sweden when it entered the EU in 1995. Instead, the Swedish authorities opted for strategies which can be described as 'divergence in convergence' (see Section 7.2). While at the same time converging towards a common European project, especially on linguistic dimensions through the use of English as a European *lingua franca*, Sweden hoped to attain psychological distinctiveness by becoming the new 'intellectual force' (Karaveli 1997: 76) which would help the EU run more efficiently (see Section 6.4).

As also seen in the societal analysis, the Swedish strategies of divergence in convergence have not proven as great a success as expected, and some anti-EU sentiment has emerged (see Section 6.4). The young Swedes of the empirical study did not express such negative attitudes towards Europe, demonstrating as they did some degree of convergence to a European identity (see Section 8.3.3.1). Nonetheless, there was some unexpected evidence of divergence, as the young Swedes felt that their linguistic and national identity should not be jeopardised in the European arena (see Section 8.3.3.2). The results of the French respondents were also revealing in so far as they also showed some degree of convergence to a European identity (see Section 8.3.3.1). In addition, the young French students did not stress the role of their language in the EU to the same extent as do official circles in France (see Section 8.3.3.2), and even recognised the *de facto* importance which English has already acquired in the European arena (see Section 8.3.3.3). Whether one can speak of a transition in the use of language to construct French and Swedish national identities in the European arena cannot be confirmed without conducting further research (see Section 9.2). However, in Sweden, a transition seems all the more likely, considering the observation made in the societal analysis that the Swedish authorities are at the time of writing contemplating legislation to protect the official status of Swedish in the EU (see Section 6.4).

9.1.4 Language and national identity in France and Sweden: The global arena

Throughout the Cold War, France and Sweden both relied on policies of independence to attain psychological distinctiveness in the global arena (see

Section 7.5). Yet while these policies may have been similar on the surface, they formed part of very different overall identity-generating strategies which continue to prevail today. In France, the approach is one of divergence, of stressing France's differences, or what the French call the *exception française*. As in the European arena, language plays a key role in the French acts of divergence. Through corpus and status planning, the French authorities seek to 'protect' their language from the influence of English, and reinforce its position both at home and in the global arena (see Section 7.3).

In Sweden, the policies of independence have formed part of a more complex strategy which, as in the European arena, can be categorised as divergence in convergence (see Section 7.2). Sweden has transformed its engagement with the international community and its commitment to global issues (convergence) into a distinctly Swedish form of foreign policy (divergence). By exploiting its minority status, Sweden has managed to play a key role in the global arena not normally associated with a country of its size (see Section 7.4). The convergence element of the Swedish strategy is particularly apparent in relation to language. But there are signs that linguistic divergence is becoming more important. Encouraged by some Swedish scholars who point to the potential for a more extensive language shift to English, the Swedish authorities are considering measures similar to those used in France in order to guarantee the status of Swedish at least at home, even if not in the global arena at large (see Section 7.4).

This new emphasis on linguistic divergence at the official level and amongst a certain élite does not seem to have reached the young Swedes who participated in the direct study. Attitudes to English were very positive and indicated that the respondents thought that English was well-suited to serve as a global language (see Section 8.3.4.1). But the strategy of convergence to English was not absolute: many participants explained that they did not consider English as a threat so much as an influence on Swedish; and there was a tendency for the Swedish respondents to be less negative than their French counterparts towards the idea of language purism *vis-à-vis* English borrowings (see Section 8.3.4.2). Clearly, the strategies employed by the young Swedes continue to constitute some form of divergence in convergence.

By contrast, the French respondents did not uphold the negative, defensive attitudes towards English normally associated with official circles and especially guardians of the language in France: English was viewed relatively positively and not considered a threat to the French language or identity (see Sections 8.3.4.1 and 8.3.4.2). The French results signal that there is a willingness at the grassroots level to engage in some degree of convergence towards English in the global arena. Whether these strategies of convergence will eventually filter upwards to official circles in France remains as uncertain as whether the new emphasis on linguistic divergence amongst some Swedish scholars will become more widespread at the grassroots level. These are two questions for future research (see Section 9.2).

9.2 Future research

While the present study has provided insights into the link between language and national identity in France and Sweden, there is room for further studies building on the findings presented here. Of the issues which are worthy of greater attention, five immediately come to mind.

First, it is important to remember that the results of the present study reflect the situation amongst a relatively small number of respondents: a total of 421 students (187 in France and 234 in Sweden). In order to make more confident generalisations, further studies need to be conducted amongst a greater number and variety of students. Extending the study to more schools would, for example, be one means of ensuring that the data were truly representative *vis-à-vis* socio-economic background (see Section 8.2.2.1).

The second area for future research has already been alluded to in Sections 9.1.1 to 9.1.4. Sociolinguists are well aware that the use of a particular linguistic form by younger people does not necessarily signal language change in progress; this phenomenon could instead be the result of what has been termed age-grading (Hockett 1950), that is, the use of speech forms appropriate to one's age group (cf. Holmes 1992: 186–8; Wardhaugh 1998: 192). There is no reason why the same distinction could not apply to the field of language attitudes and national identity strategies. In other words, do the differences which were observed between the young respondents and official circles in France and Sweden signal a transition? Or are these differences merely attributable to age, in so far as the young respondents studied here will grow up to have similar language attitudes and national identity strategies as those observed at the official level? While the results of the content analysis would appear to point to the first scenario, at least in Sweden, such conclusions cannot be drawn in full confidence without further empirical research of a longitudinal nature. Alternatively, a real-time approach to change could be simulated by using a combination of general descriptions of the ethnolinguistic situation previously and the so-called apparent time model, which would widen the scope of study to include a range of different age groups (Eckert 1997: 152–4; cf. also Holmes 1992: 226).

The third possible area for future research concerns the effect of other independent variables. While the major findings of the survey related to country differences, a limited number of tendencies were observed in relation to the effect of sex, location and ethnic background. For example, are those in peripheral regions more tolerant of ethnic minorities? Or are they merely untouched by the issue of immigration? For reasons of space and given the primary focus of this book, such questions were not investigated and discussed in detail here. Even some cases of non-significant differences would benefit from further examination. For example, why did ethnic background not prove to be a significant factor with regard to the survey items which dealt with the national arena? Could it be that immigrant minorities in France and Sweden have internalised the attitudes of the surrounding dominant group?

The fourth prospect for future research is of a theoretical nature. The three additions made to theoretical paradigm would benefit from further development. First, what are the benefits and implications of simultaneously employing strategies of convergence and divergence, what this book has referred to as 'divergence in convergence'? Does divergence in convergence represent a viable means of managing multiple identities at both the official and grassroots level? Second, to what extent can the negotiation between linguistic and non-linguistic dimensions of identity be exploited to generate a positive identity? How far can a group compromise on its linguistic identity in order to reap non-linguistic benefits? Third, what is the degree of overlap between different arenas which act as construction sites for national identity? Can the debate on immigration in the national arena be explained predominantly in terms of difficulties in generating a positive national identity in the European and global arenas?

The fifth and final area which would benefit from future research involves the extension of the study to countries other than France and Sweden. As noted in Section 6.1, the European arena represents an especially worthy context for the study of identity-construction strategies, not least because the power relationships between competing European nation-states are still in the process of being determined. As such, it is the European arena which should perhaps constitute the point of departure for any extension of the study to other countries. Studies of a similar type as this one conducted in other countries would provide additional data on the many manifestations of the link between language and national identity. They would also benefit from employing a comparative perspective such as that used here, in order to understand more comprehensively the diverse range of ethnolinguistic implications of and responses to some of the major challenges facing countries in Europe and around the world: regionalism, immigration, European integration and globalisation.

Notes

Chapter 1

1. The number of self-reported Irish speakers increased from 789,429 in the census of 1971 to 1,095,830 in that of 1991, the latter representing 31.6 per cent of the total population (Williams 1999:271).

Chapter 2

1. With his ethnic view of the nation, Connor (1993:374) argues that patriotism and nationalism are different phenomena: patriotism, on the one hand, is essentially of a civic nature, denoting 'an emotional attachment to one's state or country and its political institutions'; nationalism, on the other hand, is a product of the ethnic characteristics of the nation (cf. also Kymlicka 1995:13). However, Connor fails to point out the obvious genealogical overtones of the word 'patriotism' (from the Latin *patria* or father's country). Unlike Connor, many researchers who advocate the civic model of the nation (e.g. Nguyen 1998:30) choose to regard nationalism and patriotism as synonymous.

2. However, even sporting events are not immune from nationalist violence, as witnessed by the spate of football hooliganism seen in Europe in the years prior to the time of writing.

3. The reader is reminded of the discussion in Section 2.1, whereby it was argued that even dominant groups had ethnic identities. The 60 groups examined in Krejčí and Velímský's study therefore also included French, Swedish and other dominant *ethnies*.

4. A new term was developed in the mid-1960s to refer to a non-Basque speaker or immigrant who voluntarily learns *euskara*. An *euskaldunberri* (new Basque-speaker) is thus clearly distinguished from an *euskaldunzaharra* (old Basque-speaker) who has spoken the language since birth (Conversi 1997:67). Svonni (1996:118–19) notes a semantic change in Sámi too, concerning the disappearance of one of the meanings of the word *sápmi*: a person who has mastered the Sámi language. Due to language shift amongst many Sámi today, this meaning has given way to one which denotes a person of Sámi ethnicity, irrespective of whether she or he speaks Sámi.

Chapter 3

1. Which level of a person's identity — individual, group, human — is emphasised at any given moment can be determined with the help of the later developed self-categorisation theory (Turner *et al.* 1987).

2. *Verlan* is a type of lexical transformation whereby the order of syllables is reversed. This process is demonstrated by the word *verlan* itself, which has been formed by reversing the order of syllables of the word *l'envers* ('backwards' in English).

Chapter 4

1. In contrast to the republican interpretations of Brunot (1967) and Chaurand (1969), Balibar (1985:24–9) maintains that Charles was in fact not a speaker of *lingua romana* himself, but this remains largely debatable.

2. Although these works were predated by John Palsgrave's grammar *L'Esclaircissement de la langue françoyse* (1530), the latter was intended for speakers of English, and did not serve the same function of enriching the French language to allow it to compete with Latin.

3. The continuity of this myth is revealed by the fact that Rivarol's *Discours* has remained popular enough to be reprinted as recently as 1998.

4. Set up in 1792, the Convention was the third revolutionary assembly, which comprised committees such as the Committee of Public Instruction established previously in 1791, and the Committee of Public Safety which came into being in 1793.

5. Jacobins is the name given to the ardent revolutionaries who met in Paris in the old Jacobin convent. While the Girondins, a group of moderate bourgeois deputies from the department of Gironde, dominated the Convention in its beginnings, the Jacobins took control from the summer of 1793 until the summer of 1794, and contributed to the Terror (see this section below) and concentration of power around a small handful of men.

6. The Gauls remained largely unknown before the second half of nineteenth century; until then, the history of France had 'begun' in fifth century, with Clovis, king of the Franks (Walter 1988:32). Part of the construction of the new myth of origin involved the martyrisation of the Gauls, who were claimed to have been oppressed by the Frankish invaders (Jenkins and Sofos 1996:16; Thiesse 1999:51).

7. Alfred Dreyfus was a Jewish officer in the French army who, accused of passing secrets to the Germans, was convicted of spying on evidence which later proved to be highly dubious. The campaign for his release received public prominence in 1898, with Emile Zola's famous open letter *J'accuse*. The affair provoked a debate on who was considered French, and revealed an 'ideological hostility to any distinction between citizenship and nationality' (Safran 1989:115).

8. This book was written in the Latin script, which was introduced to Sweden around 1225. Yet even before this, in the eleventh and twelfth centuries, a literature existed in the form of runestone inscriptions (Bergman 1984:20).

9. The influence of the Gustav Vasa Bible lasted until 1917, when a new translation appeared which is sometimes referred to as the Gustav V Bible. The Gustav II Adolf Bible and Karl XII Bible of 1618 and 1703 respectively were not newly translated, the latter containing merely a somewhat modernised orthography (Bergman 1984:93). A totally new translation of the New Testament from the Greek appeared in 1999 under the title *Bibel 2000*.

10. Notably, Stiernhielm had nothing against German loan words. In his view, Swedish and German were 'two completely related sisters' (Bergman 1984:126).

11. Like the French Academy, which did not start to publish its dictionary until 1694, work was also slow to emanate from the Swedish equivalent. A grammar appeared in 1836, but the dictionary did not begin to be published until 1893 (Bergman 1984:157). At the time of writing, work is being undertaken on the letter T of the dictionary (Söhrman 1997:32), while Teleman et al. (1999) recently published a new *Svenska akademiens grammatik*.

12. The French marshal Jean Bernadotte, who was at the time in conflict with Napoléon Bonaparte, was chosen to succeed Karl XIII, who had no heir of his own. On ascending to the throne in 1810, Bernadotte adopted the Swedish name Karl.

13. It is worth noting that, in encouraging Swedes to purify their language of foreign words, Tegnér himself uses words of Low-German origin — *ära* (honour), *hjältar* (heroes), *språk* (language), *ädelt* (noble) — which later became accepted Swedish words (Bergman 1973:86).

14. It was Gustav II Adolf (1594–632) who built up a Swedish empire that included Finland, the Baltic states, parts of western Russia and northern Germany (Pomerania and Bremen). He also led Sweden into the Thirty Year War, in which he himself died fighting on the side of the Protestants. Today, neo-Nazis in Sweden look with nostalgia to this period of Swedish history, in particular to the so-called war-king Karl XII, whose death in battle signalled the end of the Sweden's age of greatness.

15. Norway was in a union with Sweden until 1905 when it became independent.

16. Another example of the relative lack of concern for Swedish culture demonstrated by successive governments relates to the poor funding given to universities for the study of the humanities: 'The humanities and civics in Sweden only received about a half of the relative resources which are allocated to the same fields in other Nordic countries' (Ohlander and Torstendahl 1998).

17. Despite accusations that they are sometimes xenophobic and play on a longing for a great Swedish past, Nordman's lyrics are described by Lilliestam (1996:129) as a reflection of the times in Sweden.

18. Phonetic spellings are, however, widely accepted in foreign loan words (e.g. *tejp*=tape, *hajk*=hike). They can also be observed in 'casual forms' (e.g. *mej* (=me) instead of *mig*, *dom* (=them) instead of *de*, etc.), but in this case represent as much a change in pronunciation (e.g. from [miːg] to [mej]) as a change in orthography (Vikør 1993:189–92).

19. Originating only in the 1970s, the myth of 1832–5 appears to correspond to two events which did actually occur: the Guizot Law concerning elementary education in 1833, and the publication in 1832–5 of the sixth edition of the Academy's dictionary in which the spelling *ai* finally replaced *oi* in words such as *français*, *j'avais*, etc. (Catach 1991; Schiffman 1996:119; Ager 1996a:120).

Chapter 5

1. Unlike genocide, ethnocide seeks to destroy the ethnic element of a group, without

actually physically killing its members (Smith 1991:32). Linguicide can be considered one part of this process (Breton 1993:231–2).

2. The term 'denizen' has been used to describe an intermediary category between foreigner and citizen. Although of foreign citizenship, denizens enjoy permanent residence, but rarely political rights (Hammar 1990).

3. Depending on the definition used, not all scholars would classify Québec as a nation (see Section 2.2.2). However, all would appear to agree that there is a definite Québec nationalism which has a founding myth and which implements certain ideological policies *vis-à-vis* ethnic minorities.

4. Distinction is sometimes made between two main Germanic dialects in the Alsace/Lorraine area: Alsatian, an Alemannic dialect distributed throughout southern and central Alsace, and Lorrain, a Franconian dialect spoken in Lorraine, the northern part of Alsace, and in Luxembourg, where it is known as Lëtzeburgesch (Walter 1988:134; Ager 1990:55).

5. A prime example of a member of the regional élite who turned his back on his regional identity is Renan who was Breton (see Section 2.2.1 and this section below).

6. It was not only the French who engaged in the linguistic oppression of Alsace. Similar bans and restrictions were imposed on the use of French during those periods when Alsace was under German rule (1871–1918 and 1940–5) (Ager 1990:53–4; Vassberg 1993:17–21).

7. While independence was never granted to regional minorities in France, it is an irony that at the same point in time, France was actively supporting the aspirations of French-speaking minorities abroad. In a speech given from the balcony of Montréal town hall in 1967, de Gaulle famously exclaimed 'Vive le Québec libre!' (Jacob and Gordon 1985:125).

8. The dilemma is even more clearly demonstrated in the United Kingdom, where devolution has resulted in an identity crisis on the part of the dominant (English) ethnic group. As the notion of Britishness becomes increasingly irrelevant, this group has been forced to rethink its English identity, which many had long conflated with British identity.

9. The so-called 'Islamic headscarf affair' refers to the expulsion by a college headmaster in Creil (near Paris) of three Muslim girls who refused to remove their headscarves. The headmaster claimed that the scarves were contrary to the principle that the French republican school system should remain secular. Lionel Jospin, then Minister of Education, overturned the headmaster's decision and the wearing of headscarves was again accepted. The affair re-emerged in 1994, when the new, right-wing government took a tougher stance on 'ostentatious' religious symbols (as opposed to more discrete crucifixes). Around 80 girls were expelled, but many were reinstated after the intervention of the *Conseil d'Etat* (Council of State) (Ardagh 1999:231).

10. *Habitations à loyer modéré* (or HLMs) are the French equivalent of council flats or public sector housing.

11. The term *Beur* was formed by reversing the syllables of *Arabe* (Goudaillier 1998:57–8). As seen in Section 3.2.5.1, this process is known as *verlan* and is practised frequently amongst the young inhabitants of the *cités* which exist on the outskirts of large cities in France.

12. Finland was part of the Swedish empire from the sixteenth century until 1809, when it became an autonomous Grand Duchy within the Russian empire until independence in 1917.

13. Joik is Sámi folk song; one of its notable features is that its lyrics are improvised.

14. The Hanseatic League was a trading organisation founded by north German towns and German commercial groups abroad. From the thirteenth to the fifteenth century, it was an important economic and political force in northern Europe, in particular in the Baltic region.

15. However, it must be noted that Sweden later gave into Soviet pressure in 1946 and deported 146 Baltic soldiers who had served under the Germans during the war.

16. On a more positive note, the multicultural policies of the 1970s led to the granting of the right to vote in local elections for denizens (see Section 5.1.3; Bernard 1998:101).

17. Another politically correct means of distinguishing ethnic Swedes from immigrants relies on the concept of citizenship. For example, when the media report a crime, the criminal is almost certainly of immigrant background if he or she is referred to as a 'Swedish citizen' (Söhrman 1997:175).

18. Reference to this proposed linguistic criterion of Swedish citizenship has strangely disappeared from the updated version of the website of *Det nya partiet* (www.detnyapartiet. com/dhtm/dpolitik/kultur/fornuft.htm). It is unknown whether this omission represents a change in policy, or merely some issue regarding the design of the web pages.

19. Only an oral examination is available for Alsatian and Lorrain. As for Gallo, only an oral examination exists at *baccalauréat* level (Ager 1996a:69).

20. With the break-up of Yugoslavia, Serbo-Croat was divided into Serbian and Croatian for teaching purposes. However, it appears that interest has declined to the point that these languages are no longer part of the ELCO programme (Ager 1996a:69; Délégation générale à la langue française 1999:101–2).

21. Sámi, Tornedalian and Rom children requesting home language instruction are exempt from the following conditions: the language must be the daily language of communication in the home; there must be a least five students requesting instruction; and a student can only have home language instruction outside normal class times for a maximum of seven years (Hyltenstam 1999a:15–16; Hyltenstam, Stroud and Svonni 1999:56).

22. Another language which could have been included is Swedish sign language, which was declared the mother tongue of deaf people in 1981 (Bergman and Nilsson 1999:337).

23. Another national minority which could have been included are the Finland Swedes (*finlandssvenskar*). This group may not always think of themselves as speaking a separate language to the Swedes (as opposed to Swedish Finns–or *sverigefinnar*–who speak Finnish), but they certainly do consider themselves as having a unique identity, distinct from that of both the Swedes and the Finns (Herberts 1991).

24. The *Commissariat général de la langue française* and the *Comité consultatif pour la langue française* have since been replaced by the *Délégation générale de la langue française* and the *Conseil supérieur de la langue française* respectively (see Section 4.4).

25. The observation could also be made that official awards are often granted to non-linguists (e.g. Durand 1997) for works which praise the French language and defend it in particular against English.

Chapter 6

1. The EU was born out of the Treaty on European Union (TEU), a.k.a. the Maastricht Treaty, which came into force in November 1993. This brought together three previously unrelated organisations: the European Coal and Steel Community (ECSC), founded in 1951, as well as the European Atomic Energy Community (Euratom) and the European Economic Community (EEC), both of which were the result of treaties signed in Rome in 1957. At the time of writing, the members of the EU are: Austria, Belgium, Denmark, Finland, France, Germany, Greece, Ireland, Italy, Luxembourg, the Netherlands, Portugal, Spain, Sweden and the United Kingdom.

2. The term 'democratic deficit' is used to refer to insufficient provision for democratic control (Bainbridge 1998:119). It is most commonly used to support increased powers to the European Parliament, which comprises the directly elected representatives of citizens in members states. Many nation-states which promote an official nationalism that does not correspond to that observed at the grassroots level can also suffer from a democratic deficit (Hettne, Sörlin and Østergård 1998:425; Section 2.2.3). Nevertheless, the EU has much ground to cover if it wishes to obtain a similar degree of legitimacy as that held by nation-states: at the time of writing, it offers limited political transparency and, although the members of the European parliament (MEPs) have been directly elected since 1979, this is still not the case for the president and members of the Commission, the only truly supranational institution.

3. The difficulty in overcoming local ethnonationalisms has contributed to the failure of other pan-movements in the past (e.g. pan-Slavism, pan-Arabism, pan-Turkism) (Smith 1991:171–2).

4. Although strictly not a member state of the EU, Iceland nevertheless belongs to the European Free Trade Association (EFTA) which for many nation-states has served as a first step towards EEC, then EU membership (see also footnote 4 in Section 7.2).

5. As an attempt to dampen fears that too much power was being transferred to Brussels, the TEU saw the introduction of the principle of subsidiarity, which stipulates that decisions should be made as close as possible to the citizen. While the principle is usually considered as guaranteeing the sovereignty of national governments, it can also be interpreted as paving the way for increased political regionalisation or devolution within the individual member states (cf. Wright 2000:180).

6. In addition to the increased support given to Le Pen's *Front national* in France, recent victories of extreme right-wing political parties in Europe include that of the Swiss People's Party, the Progress Party in Norway, and the Freedom Party in Austria (*The Guardian*, 22 October 1999). It is interesting to note that some of these parties (e.g. the Progress Party in Norway) also attack indigenous minorities, in this case the Sámi (*Le Monde*, 12 August 1999).

7. The Treaty on European Union gave issues of immigration and asylum the status of 'questions of common interest'. Although these are still discussed within an intergovernmental framework, the Commission now has right of initiative in such matters and the European Parliament must be consulted. The Treaty of Amsterdam goes further in

requiring that by 2004, all decisions relating to the free circulation of people (formerly managed largely by the intergovernmental Schengen agreement), immigration and asylum will be made by the Council of Ministers by majority voting and not unanimously (Bernard 1998:206).

8. It has often been claimed that Turkey's application for membership of the EU has been rejected on numerous occasions in part because the country is by nature, although not officially, a Muslim state (cf. Eriksen 1993:75; Schlesinger 1994:324).

9. Implementation of Council Regulation No. 1 can vary slightly on account of institutions being allowed to stipulate, in their rules of procedure, which of the languages are to be used in specific cases (article 6). As for the European Court of Justice, it is free to determine itself the languages used in proceedings (article 7).

10. While not an official language, Irish is commonly referred to as a treaty language (Labrie 1993:67), since it is used for important documents such as treaties. Council Regulation No. 1 also enshrines the right of individuals to use any of the official languages in their dealings with EU institutions and be answered in the same language (article 2). The Treaty of Amsterdam extends this right to Irish Gaelic (article 21, Consolidated Version of the Treaty Establishing the European Community; www.europa.eu.int/eur-lex/en/treaties/index.html).

11. This question arose in the *Anita Groener v Minister for Education and City of Dublin Vocational Education Committee* case (case 371/87) (de Witte 1991:168–70; Boch 1998:391–3).

12. Recognition of the importance of cultural diversity was first introduced with the Treaty of European Union in 1993: 'the Community shall contribute to the flowering of cultures of the Members States, while respecting their national identities and regional diversity' (article 128). This notion was reinforced in 1999 by the Treaty of Amsterdam (article 6, Consolidated Version of the Treaty on European Union; www.europa.eu.int/eur-lex/en/treaties/index.html).

13. Despite its 6 million speakers, Catalan is denied official status, unlike Danish which only has 5 million speakers.

14. Gordon (1978:67) notes that in 1962, 85% of the then EEC's business was conducted in French.

15. Such problems have not plagued the Toubon Law of 1994 (see Section 7.3), presumably because the *Délégation générale à la langue française* took the precaution of consulting the Commission in 1993 (Ager 1996a:156).

16. More recently, in a survey conducted in 1998, it was found that the majority of documents sent to French government agencies from the Commission and Council of Ministers (although not the European Parliament or the Court of Justice) were in a foreign language (presumably the majority in English), and that translations of documents in French often arrived after the original version (Délégation générale à la langue française 1999:62–7).

17. Indeed, such is already the conclusion reached by Maria Ridelberg-Lemoine of the Swedish Cultural Centre in Paris, as a result of her dealings with French government agencies (personal communication).

18. This motivation explains the ostensibly atypical behaviour for a conservative party accused of turning its back on the interests of the Swedish nation-state (Karaveli 1997:18).

19. A recent example of Swedish inability to change the ways of Brussels relates to the accusations of fraud and financial mismanagement directed at the Commission in early 1999. In a letter of protest, the Swedish Prime Minister Göran Persson wrote to the then President of the Commission Jacques Santer, calling for increased political transparency. The press was quick to pick up on the war of words which broke out between the two parties, especially since, in line with the Swedish tradition of transparency, the reply sent by Jacques Santer was made public. Sweden's efforts have, however, not all been in vain, and some of its concerns have been incorporated into the Treaty of Amsterdam (Svenska institutet 1998).

20. Such streamlining may include a change in the number of commissioners per country. At the time of writing, the five largest member-states (France, Germany, Italy, Spain and the United Kingdom) have two commissioners each, while all other member-states only have one (Bainbridge 1998:180). Another example of possible measures is the weighting accorded to member-states under the system of qualified majority voting (QMV) used in the Council of Ministers (cf. Bainbridge 1998:410–15).

21. While often quoted for their praise of civic principles (see Section 2.2.1), the words of Renan have not been heeded regarding the relationship between the nation-state and Europe: 'Nations are not something eternal. They had their beginnings and they will end. A European confederation will very probably replace them' (Renan 1990:20).

22. The corresponding figures for those who thought that Sweden's membership in the EU was 'a good thing' were 27 per cent in 1997 and 35 per cent in 1998 (Eurobarometer 1997 and 1999 respectively).

Chapter 7

1. Giddens (1998:28) notes that as recently as around 1988, the word globalisation was rarely used in academic or media circles.

2. 'A second language is a language that the individual must learn to master on top of his/her mother tongue in order to fulfil all desired functions in his/her daily life (within and outside work life). A foreign language is a language which is used by the individual for limited communication needs, e.g. during trips abroad or in conversations with foreign visitors in his/her home country' (Hyltenstam 1996:16).

3. Unlike Ngũgĩ and others, however, Pennycook (1998:216) argues that the colonial discourses which are associated with English can only effectively be confronted through English, the language in which they were constructed.

4. EFTA came into existence with the Stockholm convention of 1960 signed by Austria, Denmark, Norway, Portugal, Sweden, Switzerland and the United Kingdom. It offered a more intergovernmental alternative to the then EEC, which was considered by the above states as too supranational in nature. As most of these countries have since moved on and joined what is now the EU, EFTA is left with only four members: Iceland, Liechtenstein,

Norway and Switzerland. For a discussion of the use of English in some other organisations, see Crystal (1997:78–110).

5. A list of websites for European regional languages is available from the Euromosaic homepage: www.uoc.es/euromosaic.

6. The *Alliance française* is a private organisation — albeit with support from the state — which provides language courses, libraries, cinema clubs, cultural events and theatre groups through a network of 1,085 associations in 138 countries around the world. The *Mission laïque française* is an association of 74 French schools in more than 30 countries (Haut conseil de la Francophonie 1999:78–9).

7. SPRINT is an abbreviation of *språk- och innehållsintegrerad inlärning och undervisning* (content and language integrated learning and teaching) and exists in over 20 per cent of upper secondary schools. Other languages of instruction used are German (8 per cent), French (6 per cent), Spanish (4 per cent), Finnish (2 per cent) and others (4.5 per cent).

Chapter 8

1. Attention is drawn here to the suggestion that young people have not *fully* developed adult prejudices. Indeed, research has shown that many children hold some degree of language and ethnic attitudes from as early as the age of three (cf. Hudson 1980:210–14; Day 1982).

2. Québec was used as an example here because it could be roughly considered equivalent to Finland, the only other country where Swedish is spoken as a native language by a significant proportion of the population. Mention of other French-speaking countries, such as those in Africa, would have introduced other factors (e.g. issues concerning immigration, differences in religion, etc.) which would have potentially reduced the comparability of the results in the two countries (cf. Oakes 2000:179).

3. The five-point interval scale used to measure proficiency was: 1=perfectly; 2=well; 3=quite well; 4=not very well; 5=not at all.

4. The difference in means for variables 31 and 58 has, however, not been statistically proven.

5. Once again, this difference has not been proven statistically.

6. As with variables 31 and 58, the difference in means between variables 32 and 59 has not been statistically proven.

7. It is recalled that the five-point interval scale used to measure proficiency was: 1=perfectly; 2=well; 3=quite well; 4=not very well; 5=not at all.

8. The figure for immigrant languages in France includes the one case of Tamil and that of 'languages of the south', a term which at a guess might refer to African languages spoken amongst immigrants in France. Not included in this figure is Chinese; it was judged that any perceived threat from this language would surely have been seen as originating from China, rather than from Chinese immigrants in France. As for the figure for immigrant languages in Sweden, this includes Rinkeby Swedish.

Appendix A

Questionnaire in French

L'IDENTITÉ ETHNOLINGUISTIQUE FRANÇAISE

Le questionnaire qui suit fait partie d'une étude dont le but est de déterminer l'importance de la langue dans l'identité ethnique, cela à deux niveaux: français et européen. Tes réponses seront une contribution précieuse à cette étude. Il n'y a pas de bonnes ou de mauvaises réponses; ce sont tes expériences et tes impressions personnelles qui nous intéressent. C'est pourquoi il est important que tu remplisses le questionnaire tout(e) seul(e), afin que tes réponses reflètent ton point de vue à toi. Tes réponses resteront anonymes.

À PROPOS DE TOI-MÊME

D'abord quelques questions générales.

1. En quelle année es-tu? (première, terminale, etc.) _____

2. Quel bac prépares-tu/as-tu l'intention de préparer? (littéraire, scientifique, etc.)
   _____

3. Quel âge as-tu? _____ ans

4. Sexe: M ❏   F ❏

5. Où es-tu né(e)? (précise le village ou la ville, le département et le pays si ce n'est pas la France) _____

6. Quelle est ta langue maternelle? (c'est-à-dire la première langue parlée à la maison)

   français ❏   autre (préciser): _____

7. Quelle était ta première langue étrangère?

   anglais ❏   espagnol ❏   autre (préciser): _____

8. Quelle était ta deuxième langue étrangère?

   anglais ❏   allemand ❏   espagnol ❏

   je n'en ai pas ❏   autre (préciser): _____

9. As-tu visité des pays étrangers? Non ❏   Oui ❏
   Si oui, lesquels? _____

_____

Pour les questions 10–17, on te demande de juger ton degré de compétence dans les langues que tu connais (aptitude à comprendre, parler, lire, écrire). Mets une croix dans la case qui selon toi correspond le mieux ta compétence.

	Parfaitement	Bien	Assez bien	Pas très bien	Pas du tout
10. Je comprends ma première langue étrangère (voir question 7) ...	❏	❏	❏	❏	❏
11. Je parle ma première langue étrangère ...	❏	❏	❏	❏	❏
12. Je lis ma première langue étrangère ...	❏	❏	❏	❏	❏
13. J'écris ma première langue étrangère ...	❏	❏	❏	❏	❏
14. Je comprends ma deuxième langue étrangère (voir question 8) ...	❏	❏	❏	❏	❏
15. Je parle ma deuxième langue étrangère ...	❏	❏	❏	❏	❏
16. Je lis ma deuxième langue étrangère ...	❏	❏	❏	❏	❏
17. J'écris ma deuxième langue étrangère ...	❏	❏	❏	❏	❏

Avec la construction de l'Europe en cours, on parle de plus en plus aujourd'hui d'une identité européenne, c.-à-d. d'un sentiment d'appartenance à l'Europe et de solidarité avec les autres Européens. Mets une croix dans la case qui décrit le mieux tes sentiments d'appartenance.

	Énormement	Beaucoup	Moyennement	Un peu	Pas du tout
18. Est-ce que tu te sens français(e)?	❏	❏	❏	❏	❏
19. Est-ce que tu te sens européen(ne)?	❏	❏	❏	❏	❏

À PROPOS DE TES PARENTS

20. Où est né ton père? (précise le village ou la ville, le département et le pays si ce n'est pas la France)

   _____

21. Où est née ta mère ? (précise le village ou la ville, le département et le pays si ce n'est pas la France)

   _____

22. Quelle est la langue maternelle de ton père?
    français ❏   autre (préciser): _____

23. Quelle est la langue maternelle de ta mère?
    français ❏   autre (préciser): _____

24. Quelle est la profession de ton père? _____

25. Quelle est la profession de ta mère? _____

À PROPOS DES SYMBOLES FRANÇAIS

26. Nomme 10 idées ou choses que tu considères comme importantes pour l'identité ou la culture françaises. Parmi celles que tu as nommées, donne un numéro d'ordre aux trois plus importantes (1=la première en importance, 2=la seconde en importance, 3=la troisième en importance).

   _____   _____

   _____   _____

   _____   _____

   _____   _____

   _____   _____

À PROPOS DE LA LANGUE FRANÇAISE

27. Penses-tu qu'une autre langue/d'autres langues peut/peuvent menacer l'avenir du français?

    Oui ❑   Peut-être ❑   Non ❑   Je ne sais pas ❑

    Si tu as répondu oui ou peut-être, quelle(s) langue(s)? S'il y en a plusieurs, essaie de les ranger par ordre décroissant d'importance (1=la plus menaçante, 2=un peu moins menaçante, etc.).

Voici quelques remarques sur la langue française. Pour chaque phrase, dis si tu es d'accord ou non en mettant une croix dans la case qui correspond le mieux à ton point de vue.

	Tout à fait d'accord	Plutôt d'accord	Indécis(e)	Pas tellement d'accord	Pas du tout d'accord
28. La langue française fait partie de l'héritage culturel français.	❑	❑	❑	❑	❑
29. Nous devons à nos ancêtres de parler français.	❑	❑	❑	❑	❑
30. Il vaut la peine de savoir le français.	❑	❑	❑	❑	❑
31. Le français est une langue qui est bien adaptée à la vie moderne.	❑	❑	❑	❑	❑
32. Le français est une belle langue.	❑	❑	❑	❑	❑
33. Les jeunes d'aujourd'hui parlent le français de plus en plus mal.	❑	❑	❑	❑	❑
34. Il est très important de bien savoir l'orthographe du français.	❑	❑	❑	❑	❑
35. Il est important de préserver la pureté du français en évitant les emprunts aux langues étrangères.	❑	❑	❑	❑	❑
36. Les possibilités d'utilisation du français <u>ont augmenté</u> avec la formation de l'Union européenne.	❑	❑	❑	❑	❑
37. Les possibilités d'utilisation du français <u>augmenteront</u> avec la formation de l'Union européenne.	❑	❑	❑	❑	❑

À PROPOS DES MINORITÉS EN FRANCE ET DE LEURS LANGUES

Voici quelques remarques sur les minorités en France — aussi bien sur des groupes autochtones que sur les immigrés — ainsi que sur leurs langues. Pour chaque phrase, dis si tu es d'accord ou non en mettant une croix dans la case qui correspond le mieux à ton point de vue.

	Tout à fait d'accord	Plutôt d'accord	Indécis(e)	Pas tellement d'accord	Pas du tout d'accord
38. Ce n'est pas à l'école française de prendre la responsabilité de dispenser un enseignement dans les langues régionales (comme on fait par exemple dans les *ikastola* au Pays Basque, les *diwan* en Bretagne, etc.)	❏	❏	❏	❏	❏
39. Le basque est une belle langue.	❏	❏	❏	❏	❏
40. L'arabe est une belle langue.	❏	❏	❏	❏	❏
41. On ne doit pas pouvoir acquérir la citoyenneté française si on ne sait pas le français.	❏	❏	❏	❏	❏
42. On devrait préserver le plus possible les langues minoritaires en France.	❏	❏	❏	❏	❏
43. Le français se détériore parce qu'on parle d'autres langues en France.	❏	❏	❏	❏	❏
44. Le français se détériore en France parce que pour beaucoup de gens c'est seulement une deuxième langue.	❏	❏	❏	❏	❏

À PROPOS D'ÊTRE FRANÇAIS(E)

Voici quelques remarques sur le fait d'être Français(e). Pour chaque phrase, dis si tu es d'accord ou non en mettant une croix dans la case qui correspond le mieux à ton point de vue.

		Tout à fait d'accord	Plutôt d'accord	Indécis(e)	Pas tellement d'accord	Pas du tout d'accord
45.	Je m'identifie fortement avec les francophones dans d'autres pays (par ex. au Québec).	❏	❏	❏	❏	❏
46.	On peut être Français sans parler le français.	❏	❏	❏	❏	❏
47.	Il faut être né en France pour être considéré comme Français.	❏	❏	❏	❏	❏
48.	Il faut avoir des parents français pour être considéré comme Français.	❏	❏	❏	❏	❏
49.	Je suis fier/fière d'être Français(e).	❏	❏	❏	❏	❏
50.	On ne devrait pas employer des mots anglais quand on parle français.	❏	❏	❏	❏	❏

À PROPOS DE L'IDENTITÉ EUROPÉENNE ET DE LA SITUATION LINGUISTIQUE DE L'UNION EUROPÉENNE

Voici quelques remarques sur l'identité européenne et la situation linguistique de l'Union européenne (UE). Pour chaque phrase, dis si tu es d'accord ou non en mettant une croix dans la case qui correspond le mieux à ton point de vue.

	Tout à fait d'accord	Plutôt d'accord	Indécis(e)	Pas tellement d'accord	Pas du tout d'accord
51. Les pays membres de l'UE sont trop différents pour pouvoir forger une identité européenne.	❏	❏	❏	❏	❏
52. Pour pouvoir forger une identité européenne, il faut une seule langue officielle au sein de l'UE.	❏	❏	❏	❏	❏
53. Une langue artificielle comme par ex. l'espéranto devrait devenir la langue officielle de l'UE.	❏	❏	❏	❏	❏
54. L'anglais devrait devenir la langue officielle de l'UE.	❏	❏	❏	❏	❏
55. L'anglais est la langue la plus importante de l'UE.	❏	❏	❏	❏	❏
56. On devrait préserver le plus possible la variété linguistique au sein de l'UE.	❏	❏	❏	❏	❏

À PROPOS DE L'ANGLAIS COMME LANGUE INTERNATIONALE

Voici quelques remarques sur l'anglais comme langue mondiale. Pour chaque phrase, dis si tu es d'accord ou non en mettant une croix dans la case qui correspond le mieux à ton point de vue.

	Tout à fait d'accord	Plutôt d'accord	Indécis(e)	Pas tellement d'accord	Pas du tout d'accord
57. La connaissance de l'anglais nuit à la connaissance du français.	❏	❏	❏	❏	❏
58. L'anglais est une langue qui est bien adaptée à la vie moderne.	❏	❏	❏	❏	❏
59. L'anglais est une belle langue.	❏	❏	❏	❏	❏
60. L'anglais est difficile à apprendre.	❏	❏	❏	❏	❏
61. La connaissance de l'anglais m'aidera à trouver un emploi.	❏	❏	❏	❏	❏
62. Apprendre l'anglais élargit mes connaissances générales.	❏	❏	❏	❏	❏
63. Plus on est instruit, mieux on parle anglais.	❏	❏	❏	❏	❏
64. Les enfants devraient apprendre l'anglais dès l'école primaire.	❏	❏	❏	❏	❏
65. Connaître l'anglais menace l'identité française.	❏	❏	❏	❏	❏
66. On présente beaucoup trop de films anglophones à la télévision et au cinéma en France.	❏	❏	❏	❏	❏

Appendix B

Questionnaire in Swedish

SPRÅK OCH ETNISK IDENTITET BLAND SVENSKAR

Följande enkät ingår i en undersökning som syftar till att utröna vilken betydelse språket har för etnisk identitet på två plan: svensk och europeisk. Genom att fylla i enkäten ger du ett viktigt bidrag till denna undersökning. Det bör påpekas att inga svar är rätt eller fel; dina erfarenheter och åsikter är det enda som är av intresse. Därför är det viktigt att fylla i enkäten själv, så att svaren speglar din egen uppfattning. Du besvarar frågorna anonymt.

OM DIG SJÄLV

Först några allmänna frågor om din bakgrund.

1. Vilken årskurs går du i? _____

2. Vilket program går du på? _____

3. Hur gammal är du? _____ år

4. Kön: Man ❏ Kvinna ❏

5. Var är du född? (stad eller by, landskap och land, om annat än Sverige) _____

6. Vilket är ditt modersmål? (språk som du lärde dig först/från början hemma)

    svenska ❏   annat (ange vilket): _____

7. Vilket var ditt första främmande språk?

    engelska ❏   annat (ange vilket): _____

8. Vilket var ditt andra främmande språk?

    tyska ❏   franska ❏   spanska ❏

    har ej ❏   annat (ange vilket): _____

9. Har du någonsin varit utomlands? Nej ❏ Ja ❏

Om ja, i vilket land/vilka länder? _____

_____

I frågorna 10–17 ska du bedöma hur du behärskar de språk du kan (muntligt, skriftligt, o.s.v.). Sätt ett kryss i den ruta som bäst motsvarar hur du skulle bedöma din kompetens.

	Utmärkt	Bra	Ganska bra	Inte så bra	Inte alls
10. Hur bra förstår du ditt första främmande språk (i fråga 7)?	❏	❏	❏	❏	❏
11. Hur bra talar du ditt första främmande språk?	❏	❏	❏	❏	❏
12. Hur bra läser du ditt första främmande språk?	❏	❏	❏	❏	❏
13. Hur bra skriver du ditt första främmande språk?	❏	❏	❏	❏	❏
14. Hur bra förstår du ditt andra främmande språk (i fråga 8)?	❏	❏	❏	❏	❏
15. Hur bra talar du ditt andra främmande språk?	❏	❏	❏	❏	❏
16. Hur bra läser du ditt andra främmande språk?	❏	❏	❏	❏	❏
17. Hur bra skriver du ditt andra främmande språk?	❏	❏	❏	❏	❏

Till följd av integrationssträvandena mellan EU-länderna talas det alltmer om en europeisk identitet, d.v.s. en känsla av tillhörighet med Europa och samhörighet med andra européer. Sätt ett kryss i den ruta som motsvarar din uppfattning om dina tillhörigheter.

	Väldigt mycket	Mycket	Ganska mycket	Lite grann	Inte alls
18. Hur mycket känner du dig som svensk?	❏	❏	❏	❏	❏
19. Hur mycket känner du dig som europé?	❏	❏	❏	❏	❏

OM DINA FÖRÄLDRAR

20. Var är din pappa född? (stad eller by, landskap och land, om annat än Sverige)

    _____

21. Var är din mamma född? (stad eller by, landskap och land, om annat än Sverige)

    _____

22. Vilket är din pappas modersmål?
    svenska ❑   annat (ange vilket): _____

23. Vilket är din mammas modersmål?
    svenska ❑   annat (ange vilket): _____

24. Vilket är din pappas yrke? _____

25. Vilket är din mammas yrke? _____

OM SVENSKA SYMBOLER

26. Ange 10 företeelser som du anser vara viktiga för den svenska kulturen eller identiteten. Rangordna bland dem du har nämnt de tre viktigaste (1=viktigast, 2=näst viktigast, 3=näst näst viktigast).

    _____   _____
    _____   _____
    _____   _____
    _____   _____
    _____   _____

OM SVENSKA SPRÅKET

27. Tror du att något annat/några andra språk kan hota svenskans framtid?

    Ja ❑   Kanske ❑   Nej ❑   Vet ej ❑

    Om ja eller kanske, vilket/vilka språk? Om fler, försök rangordna dem (1=största hotet, 2=näst största hotet, o.s.v.).

    _____

Här följer några påståenden om svenska språket. För varje påstående, ange om du är överens eller ej genom att sätta ett kryss i den ruta som passar bäst med din uppfattning.

		Helt överens	Delvis överens	Osäker	Inte särkilt överens	Inte alls överens
28.	Svenska språket ingår i det svenska kulturarvet.	❏	❏	❏	❏	❏
29.	Vi är skyldiga våra förfäder att tala svenska.	❏	❏	❏	❏	❏
30.	Svenska är värt att kunna.	❏	❏	❏	❏	❏
31.	Svenska är ett språk som kan användas i ett modernt samhälle.	❏	❏	❏	❏	❏
32.	Svenska är ett vackert språk.	❏	❏	❏	❏	❏
33.	Ungdomar talar allt sämre svenska nuförtiden.	❏	❏	❏	❏	❏
34.	Det är mycket viktigt att kunna stava rätt på svenska.	❏	❏	❏	❏	❏
35.	Det är viktigt att svenskan bevaras så ren som möjligt från utländska lånord.	❏	❏	❏	❏	❏
36.	Svenskans användningsmöjligheter har ökat p.g.a. EU.	❏	❏	❏	❏	❏
37.	Svenskans användningsmöjligheter kommer att öka p.g.a. EU.	❏	❏	❏	❏	❏

OM MINORITETER I SVERIGE OCH DERAS SPRÅK

Här följer några påståenden om minoriteter i Sverige — såväl inhemska som invandrargrupper — och deras språk. För varje påstående, ange om du är överens eller ej genom att sätta ett kryss i den ruta som passar bäst med din uppfattning.

		Helt överens	Delvis överens	Osäker	Inte särkilt överens	Inte alls överens
38.	Den svenska skolan bör inte ta ansvar för hemspråksundervisning.	☐	☐	☐	☐	☐
39.	Samiska är ett vackert språk.	☐	☐	☐	☐	☐
40.	Arabiska är ett vackert språk.	☐	☐	☐	☐	☐
41.	Man borde inte få bli svensk medborgare utan att kunna svenska.	☐	☐	☐	☐	☐
42.	Minoritetsspråk i Sverige bör bevaras så mycket som möjligt.	☐	☐	☐	☐	☐
43.	Svenska språket påverkas negativt av att det också talas andra språk i Sverige.	☐	☐	☐	☐	☐
44.	Svenska språket påverkas negativt av att de finns många som har svenska som andra språk.	☐	☐	☐	☐	☐

OM ATT VARA SVENSK

Här följer några påståenden om att vara svensk. För varje påstående, ange om du är överens eller ej genom att sätta ett kryss i den ruta som passar bäst med din uppfattning.

		Helt överens	Delvis överens	Osäker	Inte särkilt överens	Inte alls överens
45.	Jag identifierar mig starkt med svensktalande i andra länder (t.ex. i Finland).	☐	☐	☐	☐	☐
46.	Man kan vara svensk utan att tala svenska.	☐	☐	☐	☐	☐
47.	Man måste vara född i Sverige för att kunna räknas som svensk.	☐	☐	☐	☐	☐
48.	Man måste ha svenska föräldrar för att kunna räknas som svensk.	☐	☐	☐	☐	☐
49.	Jag är stolt över att vara svensk.	☐	☐	☐	☐	☐
50.	Man bör inte blanda in engelska ord när man talar svenska.	☐	☐	☐	☐	☐

OM EUROPEISK IDENTITET OCH EU:S SPRÅKLIGA SITUATION

Här följer några påståenden om europeisk identitet och EU:s språkliga situation. För varje påstående, ange om du är överens eller ej genom att sätta ett kryss i den ruta som passar bäst med din uppfattning.

		Helt överens	Delvis överens	Osäker	Inte särkilt överens	Inte alls överens
51.	EU-länderna är för olika för att en europeisk identitet ska kunna skapas.	❏	❏	❏	❏	❏
52.	Man behöver ett enda officiellt språk inom EU för att kunna skapa en europeisk identitet.	❏	❏	❏	❏	❏
53.	Ett konstgjort språk som t.ex. esperanto borde bli EU:s officiella språk.	❏	❏	❏	❏	❏
54.	Engelska borde bli EU:s officiella språk.	❏	❏	❏	❏	❏
55.	Engelska är det viktigaste språket i EU.	❏	❏	❏	❏	❏
56.	Den språkliga mångfalden inom EU borde bevaras så mycket som möjligt.	❏	❏	❏	❏	❏

OM ENGELSKA SOM VÄRLDSSPRÅK

Här följer några påståenden om engelska som världsspråk. För varje påstående, ange om du är överens eller ej genom att sätta ett kryss i den ruta som passar bäst med din uppfattning.

	Helt överens	Delvis överens	Osäker	Inte särkilt överens	Inte alls överens
57. Att kunna engelska inverkar negativt på kunskaper i svenska.	❑	❑	❑	❑	❑
58. Engelska är ett språk som kan användas i ett modernt samhälle.	❑	❑	❑	❑	❑
59. Engelska är ett vackert språk.	❑	❑	❑	❑	❑
60. Engelska är svårt att lära sig.	❑	❑	❑	❑	❑
61. Att kunna engelska kommer att hjälpa mig att hitta arbete.	❑	❑	❑	❑	❑
62. Genom att lära mig engelska blir jag mer allmänbildad.	❑	❑	❑	❑	❑
63. Ju mer välutbildad man är, desto bättre talar man engelska.	❑	❑	❑	❑	❑
64. Barn borde lära sig engelska i skolan från tidig ålder.	❑	❑	❑	❑	❑
65. Att kunna engelska hotar den svenska identiteten.	❑	❑	❑	❑	❑
66. Engelskspåkiga filmer dominerar TV- och filmutbudet alltför mycket i Sverige.	❑	❑	❑	❑	❑

Bibliography

Note: In the bibliography the Nordic letters å, ä, ö and ø have been treated as English 'a' and 'o' respectively, rather than as separate characters which appear at the end of the alphabet. For example, the name Østerud is placed under 'o', and not at the end of the bibliography as it would be according to Nordic custom.

Abrams, D. 1990. "How do group members regulate their behaviour? An integration of social identity and social-awareness theories." In *Social Identity Theory — Constructive and Critical Advances*, D. Abrams and M. A. Hogg (eds), 89–112. Hemel Hempstead: Harvester Wheatsheaf.

Abrams, D. 1992. "Processes of social identification." In *Social Psychology of Identity and the Self Concept*, G. Breakwell (ed.), 57–99. Surrey: Surrey University Press/Academic Press.

Achard, P. 1987. "Un idéal monolingue." In *France, pays multilingue*, vol. 1, G. Vermes and J. Boutet (eds), 38–57. Paris: L'Harmattan.

Acton, Lord. 1967. *Essays in the Liberal Interpretation of History*. Edited by W. H. Neill. Chicago: University of Chicago Press.

Ager, D. E. 1990. *Sociolinguistics and Contemporary French*. Cambridge: Cambridge University Press.

Ager, D. E. 1993. "Identity, community and language policies in contemporary France." In *Language Education for Intercultural Communication*, D. Ager, G. Muskens and S. Wright (eds), 71–90, Clevedon: Multiligual Matters.

Ager, D. E. 1995. "Immigration and language policy in France." *Journal of Intercultural Studies* 15 (2): 35–52.

Ager, D. E. 1996a. *Language Policy in Britain and France: The Processes of Policy*. London/New York: Cassell.

Ager, D. E. 1996b. *'Francophonie' in the 1990s: Problems and Opportunities*. Clevedon: Multilingual Matters.

Ager, D. E. 1997. *Language, Community and the State*. Exeter: Intellect.

Ager, D. E. 1999. *Identity, Insecurity and Image: France and Language*. Clevedon: Multilingual Matters.

Ager, D. E. 2001. *Motivation in Language Planning and Language Policy*. Clevedon: Multilingual Matters.

Agheyisi, R. and Fishman, J. A. 1970. "Language attitude studies: A brief survey of methodological approaches." *Anthropological Linguistics* 12 (5): 137–57.

Ajzen, I. 1988. *Attitudes, Personality and Behaviour*. Milton Keynes: Open University Press.

Allardt, E. 1979. *Implications of the Ethnic Revival in Modern Industrial Society: a Comparative Study of the Linguistic Minorities in Western Europe*. [Commentationes Scientiarum Socialium 12]. Helsinki: Societas Scientiarum Fennica.

Allardt, E. and Starck, C. 1981. *Språkgränser och samhällsstruktur.* Stockholm: Almqvist & Wiksell.
Alsmark, G. 1984. "Landet lagom: Några aspekter på svensk kultur." In *Är Lagom bäst?: Om kulturmöten i Sverige,* 133–53. Norrköping: Statens invandrarverk.
Anderson, A. B. 1979. "The survival of ethnolinguistic minorities." In *Language and Ethnic Relations,* H. Giles and B. Saint-Jacques (eds), 67–85. Oxford: Pergamon Press.
Anderson, B. 1983. *Imagined Communities: Reflections on the Origin and Growth of Nationalism.* London: Verso.
Andersson, L.-G. 1979. "Dialekt, skola och betyg." In *Dialekt og riksspråk i skulen: Rapport frå eit Nordisk symposium på Lysebu 2–5 april, 1979.* Oslo: Oslo universitet.
Andersson, L.-G. 1985. *Fult språk: Svordomar, dialekter och annat ont.* Stockholm: Carlssons.
Andolf, G. 1985. "Nationalism och objektivitet i historieböckerna." In *Att vara svensk. Föredrag vid Vitterhetsakademiens symposium 12–13 april, 1984,* 3–22. Stockholm: Kungliga Vitterhets-, historie- och antikvitetsakademien.
Anglejan, A. d' and Tucker, G. R. 1973. "Sociolinguistic correlates of speech styles in Quebec." In *Language Attitudes: Current Trends and Prospects,* R. W. Shuy and R. W. Fasold (eds), 1–27. Washington: Georgetown University Press.
Appel, R. and Muysken, P. 1987. *Language Contact and Bilingualism.* London: Edward Arnold.
Ardagh, J. 1999. *France in the New Century: Portrait of a Changing Society.* London: Viking.
Armstrong, J. A. 1982. *Nations before Nationalism.* Chapel Hill: University of North Carolina Press.
Arnstberg, K.-O. 1989. *Svenskhet: Den kulturförnekande kulturen.* Stockholm: Carlssons.
Arnstberg, K.-O. and Ehn, B. 1976. *Etniska minoriteter i Sverige förr och nu.* Lund: LiberLäromedel.
Asher, R. E. (ed.). 1994. *The Encyclopedia of Language and Linguistics.* Oxford: Pergamon Press.
Australian Concise Oxford Dictionary. 1997. 3rd edition. Oxford: Oxford University Press.
Ayres-Bennett, W. 1987. *Vaugelas and the Development of the French Language.* London: The Modern Humanities Research Association, King's College.
Baggioni, D. 1987. *Francophonie et multiculturalisme en Australie.* Paris: L'Harmattan.
Baggioni, D. 1997. *Langues et nations en Europe.* Paris: Éditions Payot.
Bainbridge, T. 1998. *The Penguin Companion to the European Union.* 2nd edition. Harmondsworth: Penguin.
Baker, C. 1992. *Attitudes and Language.* Clevedon: Multilingual Matters.
Balakrishnan, G. (ed.). 1996. *Mapping the Nation.* London: Verso.
Balibar, R. 1985. *L'Institution du français: Essai sur le colinguisme des Carolingiens à la république.* Paris: Presses Universitaires de France.
Balibar, R. 1987. "Préface." In *France, pays multilingue,* vol. 1, G. Vermes and J. Boutet (eds), 9–20. Paris: L'Harmattan.
Balibar, R. and Laporte, D. 1974. *Le Français national: Politique et pratiques de la langue nationale sous la Révolution française.* Paris: Hachette.
Balous, S. 1970. *L'Action culturelle de la France dans le monde.* Paris: Presses Universitaires de France.

Balwin, P. 1990. *The Politics of Social Solidarity: Class Bases of the European Welfare State 1875–1975*. Cambridge: Cambridge University Press.

Banton, M. 1983. *Racial and Ethnic Competition*. Cambridge: Cambridge University Press.

Barbour, S. 1996. "Language and national identity in Europe; Theoretical and practical problems." In *Language, Community and Communication in Contemporary Europe*, C. Hoffmann (ed.), 28–46. Clevedon: Multilingual Matters.

Barker, E. 1927. *National Character and the Factors in its Formation*. London: Methuen.

Baron, S. 1947. *Modern Nationalism and Religion*. New York: Harper.

Barth, F. (ed.). 1969. *Ethnic Groups and Boundaries*. Boston: Little, Brown and Company.

Battail, J.-F. 1994. "Särart och internationalisering — några reflektioner utifrån." In *Statens Offentliga Utredningar (SOU) 1994: 9*, 9–17. Stockholm: Kulturdepartementet.

Battye, A. and Hintze, M.-A. 1992. *The French Language Today*. London: Routledge.

Bauer, L. and Trudgill, P. 1998. *Language Myths*. Hamondsworth: Penguin.

Beaucé, T. de 1988. *Nouveau discours sur l'universalité de la language française*. Paris: Gallimard.

Belazi, H. M. 1982. *Multilingualism in Tunisia and French/Arabic Code Switching among Educated Tunisian Bilinguals*. Ph.D diss., Cornell University.

Bennett, J. W. (ed.). 1975. *The New Ethnicity: Perspectives from Ethnology*. St. Paul: West Publishing.

Bentahila, A. 1983. *Language Attitudes among Arabic-French Bilinguals in Morocco*. Clevedon: Multilingual Matters.

Bergman, B. and Nilsson, A.-L. 1999. "Teckenspråket." In *Sveriges sju inhemska språk — ett minoritetsperspektiv*, K. Hyltenstam (ed.), 329–51. Lund: Studentlitteratur.

Bergman, G. 1973. *A Short History of the Swedish Language*. Translated and adapted by F. P. Magoun and H. Kökeritz. Lund: Berlingska Boktryckeriet.

Bergman, G. 1984. *Kortfattad svensk språkhistoria*. Stockholm: Prisma Magnum.

Bergström, O. 1907. *Lärobok i Sveriges historia för folkhögskolan*. 3rd edition. Stockholm: J. Beckamns Förlag.

Berlin, I. 1976. *Vico and Herder: Two Studies of the History of Ideas*. New York: The Viking Press.

Bernard, P. 1998. *L'Immigration: Les Enjeux de l'intégration*. Paris: Le Monde/Éditions Marabout.

Berry, J. W. 1980. "Acculturation as varieties of adaption." In *Acculturation: Theory and Models and some New Findings*, A. Padilla (ed.), 9–25. Boulder: Westview Press/ American Association for the Advancement of Science.

Bhabha, H. K. 1990. "DissemiNation: Time, narrative and the margins of the modern nation." In *Nation and Narration*, H. K. Bhabha (ed.), 1–7. London: Routledge.

Bildt, C. 1991. *Hallänning, svensk, europé*. Stockholm: Bonniers.

Billig, M. 1995. *Banal Nationalism*. London: Sage Publications.

Billig, M. 1996. "Nationalism as an international ideology: Imagining the nation, others and the world of nations." In *Changing European Identities: Social Psychological Analyses of Social Change*, G. Breakwell and E. Lyons (eds), 181–94. Oxford: Butterworth-Heinemann.

Blackburn, R. 1992. "The ruins of Westminster." *New Left Review* 191: 5–35.

Blanchet, P. 1994. "Problèmes méthodologiques de l'évaluation des pratiques sociolinguistiques en langues 'régionales' ou 'minoritaires': L'Exemple de la situation en France." *Langage et société* 69 (septembre): 93–106.

Blanchet, P. 2000. "Les cultures régionales et l'extrême-droite en France: Entre manipulations et inconscience." *Les Temps modernes* 608: 100–16.

Blomqvist, J. and Teleman, U. (eds). 1993. *Språk i världen: Broar och barriärer*. Lund: Studentlitteratur.

Boch, C. 1998. "Language protection and free trade: The triumph of the Homo McDonaldus?" *European Public Law* 4 (3): 379–402.

Bojsen, E. 1989. "Dansk under engelsk-amerikansk fortryllelse?" *Språk i Norden*: 39–46.

Bonnemason, J. 1993. *Les Langues de France*. Mouans Sartoux: Publications de l'École Moderne Française.

Boulot, S. and Boizon-Fradet, D. 1987. "Un siècle de réglementation des langues à l'école." In *France, pays multilingue*, vol. 1, G. Vermes and J. Boutet (eds), 163–87. Paris: L'Harmattan.

Bourdieu, P. 1991. *Language and Symbolic Power*. Edited by J. B. Thompson; translated by G. Raymond and M. Adamson. Cambridge: Polity Press.

Bourhis, R. Y. 1982. "Language policies and language attitudes: Le Monde de la francophonie." In *Attitudes towards Language Variation*, E. B. Ryan and H. Giles (eds), 34–62. London: Edward Arnold.

Bourhis, R. Y., Giles, H. and Rosenthal, D. 1981. "Notes on the construction of a 'Subjective Vitality Questionnaire' for ethnolinguistic groups." *Journal of Multilingual and Multicultural Development* 2: 145–55.

Boyer, H. 1991. *Langues en conflit: Études sociolinguistiques*. Paris: L'Harmattan.

Brass, P. R. 1991. *Ethnicity and Nationalism*. New Dehli: Sage Publications.

Breakwell, G. (ed.). 1992. *Social Psychology of Identity and the Self Concept*. Surrey: Surrey University Press/Academic Press.

Breakwell, G. 1996. "Identity processes and social change." In *Changing European Identities: Social Psychological Analyses of Social Change*, G. Breakwell and E. Lyons (eds), 13–27. Oxford: Butterworth-Heinemann.

Breakwell, G. and Lyons, E. (eds). 1996. *Changing European Identities: Social Psychological Analyses of Social Change*. Oxford: Butterworth-Heinemann.

Breton, R. 1988. "From ethnic to civic nationalism." *Ethnic and Racial Studies* 11 (1): 85–102.

Breton, R. 1993. "Linguicide et ethnocide: Pourquoi et comment tuer les langues?" In *Les Minorités ethniques en Europe*, A.-L. Sanguin (ed.), 231–8. Paris: L'Harmattan.

Breton, R. 1994. "L'approche géographique des langues d'Europe." In *Le Plurilinguisme européen*, C. Truchot (ed.), 41–68. Paris: Champion.

Brislin, R. W. 1986. "The wording and translation of research instruments." In *Field Methods in Cross-Cultural Research*, W. J. Loner and J. W. Berry (eds), 137–64. Beverly Hills: Sage.

Brodow, B., Ehrlin, A., Holmberg, O., Ljung, P.-E., Malmgren, G., Malmgren, L.-G., Nilsson, S., Ottosson, S., Svenonius, I. and Thavenius, J. 1976. *Svenskämnets kris*. Lund: LiberLäromedel.

Broglie, G. de 1986. *Le Français pour qu'il vive*. Paris: Gallimard.

Brown, R. J., Hinkle, S., Ely, P. G., Fox-Cardamone, L., Maras, P. and Taylor, L. A. 1992. "Recognizing group diversity: Individualist-collectivist and autonomous-relational social orientations and their implications for intergroup processes." *British Journal of Social Psychology* 31: 327–42.

Brunot, F. 1967. *Histoire de la langue française des origines à nos jours.* 13 vols. Paris: Librairie Armand Colin.

Caldwell, J. 1994. "Provision for minority languages in France." *Journal of Multilingual and Multicultural Matters* 15 (4): 293–310.

Calvet, L.-J. 1974. *Linguistique et colonialisme: Petit traité de glottophagie.* Paris: Payot.

Calvet, L.-J. 1987. *La Guerre des langues et les politiques linguistiques.* Paris: Payot.

Calvet, L.-J. 1998. *Language Wars and Linguistic Politics.* Translated by M. Petheram. Oxford: Oxford University Press.

Caput, J.-P. 1972. *La Langue française: Histoire d'une institution.* 2 vols. Paris: Larousse.

Carcassonne, G. 1998. *Étude sur la compatibilité entre la Charte européenne des langues régionales ou minoritaires et la Constitution.* Available at: www.ladocfrancaise.gouv.fr/cgi-bin/multitel/CATALDOC/accueil_df

Carranza, M. A. 1982. "Attitudinal research on Hispanic language varieties." In *Attitudes towards Language Variation*, E. B. Ryan and H. Giles (eds), 63–83. London: Edward Arnold.

Castles, S., Cope, B., Kalantzis, M. and Morrissey, M. 1992. *Mistaken Identity: Multiculturalism and the Demise of Nationalism in Australia.* 3rd edition. Sydney: Pluto Press.

Catach, N. 1991. *L'Orthographe en débat: Dossiers pour un changement.* Paris: Éditions Nathan.

Cerquiglini, B. 1991. *La Naissance du français* [Que sais-je? 2576]. Paris: Presses Universitaires de France.

Cerquiglini, B. 1999. *Les Langues de la France. Rapport au Ministre de l'Education Nationale, de la Recherche et de la Technologie, et à la Ministre de la Culture et de la Communication.* Available at: www.ladocfrancaise.gouv.fr/cgi-bin/multitel/CATALDOC/accueil_df

Certeau, M. de, Julia, D. and Revel, J. 1975. *Une Politique de la langue: La Révolution française et les patois.* Paris: Gallimard.

Chaurand, J. 1969. *Histoire de la langue française* [Que sais-je? 167]. Paris: Presses Universitaires de France.

Chaurand, J. (ed.). 1999. *Nouvelle Histoire de la langue française.* Paris: Seuil.

Chiti-Batelli, A. 1987. *Communication internationale et avenir des langues et des parlers en Europe.* Nice: Presses d'Europe.

Chryssochoou, X. 1996. "How group membership is formed: Self categorisation or group beliefs? The construction of a European identity in France and Greece." In *Changing European Identities: Social Psychological Analyses of Social Change*, G. Breakwell and E. Lyons (eds), 297–313. Oxford: Butterworth-Heinemann.

Chrystal, J.-A. 1988. *Engelskan i dagpress.* [Skrifter utgivna av Svenska språknämnden 74]. Stockholm: Esselte.

Cinnirella, M. 1996. "A social identity perspective on European integration." In *Changing European Identities: Social Psychological Analyses of Social Change*, G. Breakwell and E. Lyons (eds), 253–74. Oxford: Butterworth-Heinemann.

Citron, S. 1991. *Le Mythe national.* 2nd edition. Paris: Les Éditions Ouvrières/Études et Documentation Internationales.

Claude, I. 1955. *National Minorities: An International Problem.* Cambridge: Harvard University Press.
Clément, R. and Noels, K. A. 1999. "Langage et communication intergroupe." In *Stéréotypes, discrimination et relations intergroupes,* R. Y. Bourhis and J.-P. Leyens (eds), 233–59. Sprimont: Mardaga.
Clerico, G. 1999. "Le français au XVIe siècle." In *Nouvelle Histoire de la langue française,* J. Chaurand (ed.), 145–224. Paris: Seuil.
Club de l'Horloge (ed.). 1985. *L'Identité de la France.* Paris: Éditions Albin Michel.
Clyne, M. 1991. *Community Languages: The Australian Experience.* Cambridge: Cambridge University Press.
Clyne, M. 1995. *The German Language in a Changing Europe.* Cambridge: Cambridge University Press.
Cohen, A. (ed.). 1974a. *Urban Ethnicity.* London: Tavistock.
Cohen, A. (ed.). 1974b. *The Two-Dimensional Man.* London: Tavistock.
Connor, W. 1972. "Nation-building or nation-destroying?" *World Politics* 24: 319–50.
Connor, W. 1978. "A nation is a nation, is a state, is an ethnic group is a ... ." *Ethnic and Racial Studies* 1 (4): 377–400.
Connor, W. 1990. "When is a nation?" *Ethnic and Racial Studies* 13 (1): 92–103.
Connor, W. 1993. "Beyond reason: The nature of the ethnonational bond." *Ethnic and Racial Studies* 16 (3): 373–189.
Conversi, D. 1997. *The Basques, the Catalans and Spain: Alternative Routes to Nationalist Mobilisation.* London: Hurst and Company.
Corder, S. P. 1973. *Introducing Applied Linguistics.* Harmondsworth: Penguin.
Coulmas, F. 1988. "What is a national language good for?" In *With Forked Tongues,* F. Coulmas (ed.), 1–24. Singapore: Karoma Publishers.
Coulmas, F. 1991a. "European integration and the idea of a national language: Ideological roots and economic consequences." In *A Language Policy for the European Community: Prospects and Quandries,* F. Coulmas (ed.), 1–42. Berlin/New York: Mouton de Gruyter.
Coulmas, F. (ed.). 1991b. *A Language Policy for the European Community: Prospects and Quandries.* Berlin/New York: Mouton de Gruyter.
Coulmas, F. 1999. "The Far East." In *Handbook of Language and Ethnic Identity,* J. A. Fishman (ed.), 399–413. Oxford: Oxford University Press.
Council of Europe. 1992. *European Charter for Regional or Minority Languages.* [European Treaty Series 148]. Strasbourg: Council of Europe.
Council of Ministers. 1958. "Regulation no. 1 determining the languages to be used by the European Economic Community." *Official Journal of the European Communities* 17 (6.10.58): 385.
Crawford, J. 1989. *Bilingual Education: History, Politics, Theory and Practice.* Trenton: Crane Publishing.
Crystal, D. 1997. *English as a Global Language.* Cambridge: Cambridge University Press.
Dalin, O. von 1910. "Then Swänska Argus, XLV." In *Then Swänska Argus,* vol. 1, B. Hesselman and M. Lamm (eds), 340–6. Stockholm: Albert Bonniers Förlag.
Dahlstedt, K.-H. 1976. "Societal ideology and language cultivation: The case of Swedish." *International Journal of the Sociology of Language* 10: 17–50.

Dahlstedt, K.-H. 1980. "Språksituationen in Norden." In *Språken i vårt språk*, I. Jonsson (ed.), 102–18. Stockholm: PAN/Norstedt.

Daoust, D. 1997. "Language planning and language reform." In *The Handbook of Sociolinguistics*, F. Coulmas (ed.), 436–52. Oxford: Blackwell.

Daun, Å. 1988. "Svenskhet." In *Det mångkulturella Sverige: En handbok om etniska grupper och minoriteter*, I. Svanberg and H. Runblom (eds), 411–15. Stockholm: Gidlunds Bokförlag.

Daun, Å. 1989. *Svensk mentalitet*. Stockholm: Rabén & Sjögren.

Daun, Å. 1992. *Den europeiska identiteten: Bidrag till samtal om Sveriges framtid*. Stockholm: Rabén & Sjögren.

Daun, Å. 1996. *Swedish Mentality*. Translated by J. Teeland; foreword by D. Cooperman. University Park: Pennsylvania State University Press.

Davies, A. 1991. *The Native Speaker in Applied Linguistics*. Edinburgh: Edinburgh University Press.

Day, R. R. 1982. "Children's attitudes towards language." In *Attitudes towards Language Variation*, E. B. Ryan and H. Giles (eds), 116–31. London: Edward Arnold.

Délégation générale à la langue française (DGLF). 1998. *Rapport au parlement sur l'application des dispositions des conventions ou traités internationaux relatives au statut de la langue française dans les institutions internationales*. Paris: Ministère de la Culture et de la Communication.

Délégation générale à la langue française (DGLF). 1999. *Rapport au parlement sur l'application de la loi du 4 août 1994 relative à l'emploi de la langue française*. Paris: Ministère de la Culture et de la Communication.

Deniau, X. 1995. *La Francoponie* [Que sais-je? 2111]. 3rd edition. Paris: Presses Universitaires de France.

Deprez, K. and Persoons, Y. 1984. "On the ethnolinguistic identity of Flemish high school students in Brussels." *Journal of Language and Social Psychology* 3 (4): 273–96.

Désirat, C. and Hordé, T. 1976. *La Langue française au XXème siècle*. Paris: Bordas.

Deutsch, K. 1942. "The trend of European nationalism — the language aspect." *American Political Science Review* June: 533–41.

Djité, P. 1990. "The place of African languages in the revival of the Francophone movement." *International Journal of the Sociology of Language* 86: 87–102.

Djité, P. 1992. "The French revolution and the French language: A paradox?" *Language Problems and Language Planning* 16 (2): 163–77.

Djonovich, D. J. (ed.). 1989. *United Nations Resolutions. Series II: Resolutions and Decisions of the Security Council*. Vol. 4, 1966–7. New York: Oceana Publications.

Doob, L. W. 1964. *Patriotism and Nationalism*. New Haven: Yale University Press.

Dornyei, Z. 1990. "Conceptualising motivation in foreign-language learning." *Language Learning* 40: 45–78.

Driedger, L. 1996. *Multi-Ethnic Canada: Identities and Inequalities*. Toronto: Oxford University Press.

Duhamel, A. 1993. *Les Peurs françaises*. Paris: Flammarion.

Durand, C. 1997. *La Langue française: Atout ou obstacle?* Toulouse: Presses Universitaires du Mirail.

Durand, J. 1993. "Sociolinguistic variation and the linguist." In *French Today: Language in its Social Context*, C. Sanders (ed.), 257–85. Cambridge: Cambridge University Press.

Dutourd, J. 1998. "Préface." In *L'Universalité de la langue française*, A. de Rivarol. Paris: Arléa.

Eastman, C. 1984. "Language, ethnic identity and change." In *Linguistic Minorities, Policies and Pluralism*, J. Edwards (ed.), 259–76. London: Academic Press.

Eckert, P. 1997. "Age as a sociolinguistic variable." In *The Handbook of Sociolinguistics*, F. Coulmas (ed.),151–67. Oxford: Blackwell.

Edgren, H. 2000. "Hot och verklighet. Om EU-svenskan som hotbild." In *Svenskan som EU-språk*, B. Melander (ed.), 77–99. Uppsala: Hallgren & Fallgren Studieförlag AB.

Edwards, J. 1977. "Ethnic identity and bilingual education." In *Language, Ethnicity and Intergroup Relations*, H. Giles (ed.), 253–82. London: Academic Press.

Edwards, J. (ed.). 1984. *Linguistic Minorities, Policies and Pluralism*. London: Academic Press.

Edwards, J. 1985. *Language, Society and Identity*. Oxford: Basil Blackwell.

Edwards, J. 1992. "Language in group and individual identity." In *Social Psychology of Identity and the Self Concept*, G. Breakwell (ed.), 129–46. Surrey: Surrey University Press/ Academic Press.

Edwards, J. 1994. *Multilingualism*. London: Routledge.

Edwards, J. and Shearn, C. 1987. "Language and identity in Belgium: Perceptions of French and Flemish students." *Ethnic and Racial Studies* 10 (2): 135–48.

Ehn, B. 1975. *Sötebrödet. En etnologisk skildring av jugoslaver i ett dalsländskt pappersbrukssamhälle*. Stockholm: Stockholm Tiden-Institut för folklivsforskning.

Ehn, B. 1986. *Det otygliga kulturmötet: Om invandrare och svenska på ett daghem*. Malmö: LiberFörlag.

Ehn, B. 1993. "Nationell inlevelse." In *Försvenskningen av Sverige: Det nationellas förvandlingar*, B. Ehn, J. Fyrkman and O. Löfgren, 204–71. Stockholm: Natur och Kultur.

Ehn, B., Fyrkman, J. and Löfgren, O. 1993. "Inledning." In *Försvenskningen av Sverige: Det nationellas förvandlingar*, B. Ehn, J. Fyrkman and O. Löfgren, 8–21. Stockholm: Natur och Kultur.

Ekerot, L.-J. 2000. "Klar komplexitet. Om språk och begriplighet vid översättning av författningstexter." In *Svenskan som EU-språk*, B. Melander (ed.), 46–76. Uppsala: Hallgren & Fallgren Studieförlag AB.

Englund, B. 1997. *Skolans tal on litteratur: om gymnasieskolans litteraturstudium och dess plats i ett kulturellt åter-skapande med utgångspunkt i en jämförelse av texter för litteraturundervisning i Sverige och Frankrike*. Stockholm: HLS.

Eriksen, T. H. 1990. "Linguistic diversity and the quest for national identity: The case of Mauritius." *Ethnic and Racial Studies* 13 (1): 1–24.

Eriksen, T.H. 1993. *Ethnicity and Nationalism*. London: Pluto Press.

Espaces 89 (ed.). 1985. *L'Identité française*. Paris: Éditions Tierce.

Etiemble, R. 1964. *Parlez-vous franglais?* Paris: Gallimard.

Eurobarometer. 1995. *Eurobarometer 44*. Available at: www.europa.eu.int/comm/dg10/epo/ eb/eb44/index.html

Eurobarometer. 1997. *Eurobarometer 47*. Available at: www.europa.eu.int/comm/dg10/ epo/eb/eb47/eb47.html

Eurobarometer. 1999. *Eurobarometer 50*. Available at: www.europa.eu.int/comm/dg10/epo/eb/eb50/eb50.html

European Bureau for Lesser Used Languages. (no date specified). *Call for Linguistic Rights in European Fundamental Rights Charter. Statement of the European Bureau for Lesser Used Languages on European Languages in the Charter of Fundamental Rights for the European Union*. Dublin: European Bureau for Lesser Used Languages. Available at: www.eblul.org/gp/call-en.htm

European Parliament. 1981. "Resolution on a Community charter of regional languages and cultures and on a charter of rights of ethnic minorities." *Official Journal of the European Communities* C287 (9.11.81): 106–7.

European Parliament. 1983. "Resolution on measures in favour of minority languages and cultures." *Official Journal of the European Communities* C68 (14.3.83): 103–4.

European Parliament. 1987. "Resolution on the languages and cultures of regional and ethnic minorities of the European Community." *Official Journal of the European Communities* C318 (30.11.87): 160–4.

European Parliament. 1991. "Resolution on languages in the Community and the situation of Catalan." *Official Journal of the European Communities* C19 (28.1.91): 42–3.

European Parliament. 1994. "Resolution on linguistic and cultural minorities in the European Community." *Official Journal of the European Communities* C61 (28.2.94): 110–13.

Eurostat. 1998. "Women achieve more than men (Major report on education)." *Report no. 0998, 12 February 1998*. Available at: www.europa.eu.int/comm/eurostat

EU-sekretariatet. 1996. *Cirkulär 6: Riktlinjer för att främja svenska språkets ställning i EU-arbetet*. Stockholm: Utrikesdepartementet.

Evans, M. 1996. "Languages of racism within contemporary Europe." In *Nation and Identity in Contemporary Europe*, B. Jenkins and S. A. Sofos (eds), 33–53. London/New York: Routledge.

Fasold, R. 1984. *The Sociolinguistics of Society*. Oxford: Basil Blackwell.

Fasold, R. 1990. *The Sociolinguistics of Language*. Oxford: Basil Blackwell.

Fichte, J. G. 1968. *Addresses to the German Nation*. Edited and annotated by G. A. Kelly; translated by R. F. Jones and G. H. Turnbull. New York: Harper and Row.

Fishman, J. A. 1966. *Language Loyalty in the United States: The Maintenance and Perception of Non-English Mother Tongues by American Ethnic and Religious Groups*. The Hague: Mouton.

Fishman, J.A. 1971a. "The impact of nationalism on language planning." In *Can Language be Planned? Sociolinguistic Theory and Practice for Developing Nations*, J. Rubin and B. H. Jernudd (eds), 3–20. Honolulu: East-West Center/University Press of Hawaii.

Fishman, J.A. 1971b. "The sociology of language: An interdisciplinary social science approach to language in society." In *Advances in the Sociology of Language*, vol. 1, J. A. Fishman (ed.), 217–404. The Hague: Mouton.

Fishman, J.A. 1977a. "Language and ethnicity." In *Language, Ethnicity and Intergroup Relations*, H. Giles (ed.), 15–57. London: Academic Press.

Fishman, J.A. 1977b. "The spread of English as a new perspective for the study of 'language maintenance and language shift'." In *The Spread of English: The Sociology of English as an Additional Language*, J. A. Fishman, R. L. Cooper and A. W. Conrad (eds), 109–33. Rowley: Newbury House.

Fishman, J.A. 1988. "'English only': Its ghosts, myths, and dangers." *International Journal of the Sociology of Language* 74: 125–40.
Fishman, J.A. 1989. *Language and Ethnicity in Minority Sociolinguistic Perspective.* Clevedon: Multilingual Matters.
Fishman, J.A. 1997. "Language and ethnicity: The view from within." In *The Handbook of Sociolinguistics,* F. Coulmas (ed.), 327–43. Oxford: Blackwell.
Fishman, J.A. (ed.). 1999. *Handbook of Language and Ethnic Identity.* Oxford: Oxford University Press.
Fishman, J. A., Gertner, M. H., Lavy, E. G. and Milán, W. G. 1985. *The Rise and Fall of the Ethnic Revival.* Berlin: Mouton de Gruyter.
Flaitz, J. 1988. *The Ideology of English: French Perceptions of English as a World Language.* Berlin/New York/Amsterdam: Mouton de Gruyter.
Fosty, A. 1985. *La Langue française dans les institutions communautaires de l'Europe.* Québec: Conseil de la langue française.
Frykman, J. 1993. "Nationella ord och handlingar." In *Försvenskningen av Sverige: Det nationellas förvandlingar,* B. Ehn, J. Fyrkman and O. Löfgren, 121–203. Stockholm: Natur och Kultur.
Fysh, P. 1997. "Gaullism and liberalism." In *Political Ideologies in Contemporary France,* C. Flood and L. Bell (eds), 73–102. London: Cassell.
Gal, S. 1979. *Language Shift: Social Determinants of Linguistic Shift in Bilingual Austria.* New York: Academic Press.
Gandhi, M. 1965. *Our Language Problem.* Edited by A. T. Hingorani. Bombay: Bhartiya Vidya Bhavan.
Gans, H. 1979. "Symbolic ethnicity: The future of ethnic groups and culture in America." *Ethnic and Racial Studies* 2 (1): 1–20.
García, S. 1993. "Europe's fragmented identities and the frontiers of citizenship." In *European Identity and the Search for Legitimacy,* S. Garciá (ed.), 1–29. London/New York: Pinter.
Gardner, R. C. and Lambert, W. E. 1972. *Attitudes and Motivation in Second-Language Learning.* Rowley: Newbury House.
Garmadi, J. 1981. *La Sociolinguistique.* Paris: Presses Universitaires de France.
Gaunt, D. and Löfgren, O. (eds). 1985. *Myter om svensken.* Stockholm: Liber.
Geer, E. de and Wande, E. 1988. "Finnar." In *Det mångkulturella Sverige: En handbok om etniska grupper och minoriteter,* I. Svanberg and H. Runblom (eds), 94–109. Stockholm: Gidlunds Bokförlag.
Geertz, C. 1994. "Primordial and civic ties." In *Nationalism,* J. Hutchinson and A. D. Smith (eds), 29–34. Oxford: Oxford University Press.
Gellner, E. 1964. *Thought and Change.* London: Weidenfeld and Nicolson.
Gellner, E. 1983. *Nations and Nationalism.* Oxford: Basil Blackwood.
Gibbons, J. 1990. "Applied linguistics in court." *Applied Linguistics* 11 (3): 229–137.
Giddens, A. 1994. "The nation as power-container." In *Nationalism,* J. Hutchinson and A. D. Smith (eds), 34–5. Oxford: Oxford University Press.
Giddens, A. 1998. *The Third Way: The Renewal of Social Democracy.* Cambridge: Polity Press.
Gildea, R. 1996. *France since 1945.* Oxford: Oxford University Press.

Giles, H. 1973. "Accent mobility: A model and some data." *Anthropological Linguistics* 15: 87–105.
Giles, H. (ed.). 1977. *Language, Ethnicity and Intergroup Relations*. London: Academic Press.
Giles, H. 1979. "Ethnicity markers in speech." In *Social Markers in Speech*, K. R. Scherer and H. Giles (eds), 251–89. Cambridge: Cambridge University Press.
Giles, H. and Coupland, N. 1991. *Language: Contexts and Consequences*. Milton Keynes: Open University Press.
Giles, H. and Johnson, P. 1981. "The role of language in ethnic group relations." In *Intergroup Behaviour*, J. C. Turner and H. Giles (eds), 199–243. Oxford: Basil Blackwell.
Giles, H. and Johnson, P. 1987. "Ethnolinguistic identity theory: A social psychological approach to language maintenance." *International Journal of the Sociology of Language* 68: 69–99.
Giles, H and Niedzielski, N. 1998. "Italian is beautiful, German in ugly." In *Language Myths*, L. Bauer and P. Tudgill (eds), 85–93. Hamondsworth: Penguin.
Giles, H. and Saint-Jacques, B. (eds). 1979. *Language and Ethnic Relations*. Oxford: Pergamon Press.
Giles, H., Bourhis, R. Y. and Davies, A. 1979. "Prestige speech styles: The imposed norm and inherent value hypotheses." In *Language in Anthropology IV: Language in Many Ways*, W. McCormack and S. Wurm (eds), 589–96. The Hague: Mouton.
Giles, H., Bourhis, R. Y. and Taylor, D. M. 1977. "Towards a theory of language in ethnic group relations." In *Language, Ethnicity and Intergroup Relations*, H. Giles (ed.), 307–48. London: Academic Press.
Giles, H., Bourhis, R. Y., Trudgill, P. and Lewis, A. 1974. "The imposed norm hypothesis: a validation." *Quarterly Journal of Speech* 60: 405–10.
Giles, H., Mulac, A., Bradac, J. J. and Johnson, P. 1987. "Speech accommodation theory: The next decade and beyond." In *Communication Yearbook*. Vol. 10. Newbury Park: Sage.
Giordan, H. 1982. *Démocratie culturelle et droit à la différence: Rapport au Ministre de la Culture*. Paris: La Documentation Française.
Giordan, H. 1984. "Du folklore au quotidien." In *Par les langues de France*, vol. 1, H. Giordan (ed.), 5–12. Paris: Centre Georges Pompidou.
Giordan, H. 1992a. "Droits des minorités, droits linguistiques, Droits de l'Homme." In *Les Minorités en Europe: Droits linguistiques et Droits de l'Homme*, H. Giordan (ed.), 9–39. Paris: Éditions Kimé.
Giordan, H. 1992b. "Les langues de France: De l'hégémonie républicaine à la démission de l'État." In *Les Minorités en Europe: Droits linguistiques et Droits de l'Homme*, H. Giordan (ed.), 129–44. Paris: Éditions Kimé.
Giordan, H. 1994. *Les Langues régionales et/ou minoritaires de l'Union européenne*. Commission européenne. Taskforce «Ressources humaines, éducation, formation et jeunesse».
Glazer, N. and Moynihan, D. A. 1963. *Beyond the Melting Pot*. Cambridge: Massachusetts Institute of Technology Press.
Glazer, N. and Moynihan, D.A. (eds). 1975. *Ethnicity: Theory and Experience*. Cambridge: Harvard University Press.
Goldstein, J. and Bienvenue, R. (eds). 1985. *Ethnicity and Ethnic Relations in Canada*. Toronto: Butterworth.

Goody, J. and Watt, I. 1963. "The consequences of literacy." *Comparative Studies in Society and History* 5: 304–45.

Gordon, D. C. 1978. *The French National Language and National Identity (1930–1975)*. The Hague: Mouton Publishers.

Goscinny, R. and Uderzo, A. 1969. *Asterix the Gaul*. Translated by A. Bell and D. Hockridge. London: Hodder Dargaud.

Goudaillier, J.-P. 1998. *Comment tu tchatches! Dictionnaire du français contemporain des cités*. Paris: Maisonneuve et Larose.

Graddol, D. 1998. "Will English be enough?" In *Where are we Going with Languages?*, A. Moys (ed.), 24–32. London: Nuffield Foundation.

Grau, R. 1987. "Les langues face aux institutions et aux juridictions." In *France, pays multilingue*, vol. 1, G. Vermes and J. Boutet (eds), 143–62. Paris: L'Harmattan.

Grau, R. 1992. "Le statut juridique des droits linguistiques en France." In *Les Minorités en Europe: Droits linguistiques et Droits de l'Homme*, H. Giordan (ed.), 93–112. Paris: Éditions Kimé.

Gravier, J.-F. 1972. *Paris et le désert français en 1972*. Paris: Flammarion.

Gray, C. D. and Kinnear, P. R. 1998. *SPSS for Macintosh Made Simple*. Hove: Psychology Press.

Greenfield, L. 1994. "Types of European nationalism." In *Nationalism*, J. Hutchinson and A. D. Smith (eds), 165–71. Oxford: Oxford University Press.

Grillo, R. D. 1989. *Dominant Languages: Language and Hierarchy in Britain and France*. Cambridge: Cambridge University Press.

Gueunier, N. 1985. "La crise du français en France." In *La Crise des langues*, J. Maurais (ed.), 3–38. Québec: Conseil de la langue française.

Guillou, M. 1993. *La Francophonie: Nouvel enjeu mondial*. Paris: Hatier.

Gunnarsson, B.-L. 1999. "Svenska, English eller Deutsch — om språksituationen vid de svenska universiteten." *Språkvård* 4/99: 11–22.

Haarmann, H. 1986. *Language in Ethnicity: A View of Basic Ecological Relations*. Berlin/New York/Amsterdam: Mouton de Gruyter.

Haberland, H. 1991. "Reflections about minority languages in the European Community." In *A Language Policy for the European Community: Prospects and Quandries*, F. Coulmas (ed.), 179–94. Berlin/New York: Mouton de Gruyter.

Haberland, H. and Henriksen, C. 1991. "Dänisch — eine kleine Sprache in der EG." *Sociolinguistica* 5: 85–98.

Habermas, J. 1996. *Between Facts and Norms: Contributions to a Discourse Theory of Law and Democracy*. Translated by William Rehg. Cambridge: Polity Press.

Hagège, C. 1987. *Le Français et les siècles*. Paris: Éditions Odile Jacob.

Hagège, C. 1996. *Le Français, histoire d'un combat*. Paris: Éditions Michel Hagège.

Halliday, M. A. K. 1976. "Anti-languages." *American Anthropologist* 78: 570–84.

Hamers, J. and Blanc, M. 2000. *Bilinguality and Bilingualism*. 2nd edition. Cambridge: Cambridge University Press.

Hammar, T. 1990. *Democracy and the Nation State*. Aldershot: Averbury.

Hannerz, U. 1992. *Cultural Complexity*. New York: Columbia University Press.

Hansegård, N. 1968. *Tvåspråkighet eller halvspråkighet?* Stockholm: Bokförlaget Aldus/Bonniers.

Hansegård, N. 1997. "En återblick på begreppet halvspråkighet." In *Mer än ett språk. En antologi om två- och flerspråkigheten i norra Sverige*, E. Westergren and H. Åhl (eds), 178–201. Stockholm: Nordstedts Förlag AB.
Harouel, J.-L. 1985. "La société pluriculturelle: Une illusion suicidaire." In *L'Identité de la France*, Club de l'Horloge (ed.), 199–209. Paris: Éditions Albin Michel.
Haselhuber, J. 1991. "Erste Ergebnisse einer empirischen Untersuchung zur Sprachensituation in der EG-Kommission." *Sociolinguistica* 5: 37–50.
Haugen, E. 1959. "Planning for a standard language in modern Norway." *Anthopolgical Linguistics* 1 (3): 8–21.
Haugen, E. 1966a. "Dialect, language, nation." *American Anthropologist* 68: 922–35.
Haugen, E. 1966b. *Language Conflict and Language Planning: The Case of Modern Norwegian*. Cambridge: Harvard University Press.
Haugen, E. 1972. *The Ecology of Language*. Stanford: Stanford University Press.
Haugen, E. 1981. "Language fragmentation in Scandinavia: Revolt of the minorities." In *Minority Languages Today*, E. Haugen, J. D. McClure and D. Thomson (eds), 100–19. Edinburgh: Edinburgh University Press.
Haugen, E. 1985. "The language of imperialism: Unity or pluralism?" In *Language of Inequality*, N. Wolfson and J. Manes (eds), 3–17. Berlin/New York/Amsterdam: Mouton.
Haugen, E., McClure, J. D. and Thomson, D. (eds). 1981. *Minority Languages Today*. Edinburgh: Edinburgh University Press.
Haut conseil de la Francophonie. 1999. *État de la Francophonie dans le monde: Données 1997–1998 et 6 études inédites*. Paris: La Documentation Française.
Hayes, C. 1964. "Carlton J. H.: The major types of nationalism, 1931." In *The Dynamics of Nationalism*, L. Snyder (ed.), 51–2. London: D. Van Nostrand Company.
Hechter, M. 1975. *Internal Colonialism: The Celtic Fringe in British National Development, 1536–1966*. London: Routledge.
Hechter, M. 1986. "A rational choice approach to race and ethnic relations." In *Theories of Race and Ethnic Relations*, D. Mason and J. Rex (eds), 264–79. Cambridge: Cambridge University Press.
Hechter, M. and Levi, M. 1994. "Ethno-Regional Movements in the West." In *Nationalism*, J. Hutchinson and A. D. Smith (eds), 184–95. Oxford: Oxford University Press.
Héraud, G. 1993. *L'Europe des ethnies*. Paris: Bruylant.
Herberts, K. 1991. "Finlands svenskar — missförstådd minoritet?" In *Nationella identiteter i Norden — ett fullbordat projekt?*, A. Linde-Laursen and J. O. Nilsson (eds), 239–56. Stockholm: Nordiska rådet/Allmänna Förlaget.
Herder, J. G. 1881. *Herders sämmtliche Werke*. Berlin: Weidmannsche Buchhandlung.
Herder, J.G. 1969. *J. G. Herder on Social and Political Culture*. Translated, edited and with introduction by F. M. Barnard. Cambridge: Cambridge University Press.
Herlitz, G. 1995. *Swedes: What we are like and why we are as we are*. Uppsala: Konsultförlaget i Uppsala AB.
Hettne, B., Sörlin, S. and Østergård, U. 1998. *Den globala nationalism*. Stockholm: SNS Förlag.
Hilton, D. J., Erb, H.-P., Dermot, M. and Molian, D. J. 1996. "Social representations of history and attitudes to European unification in Britain, France and Germany." In *Changing European Identities: Social Psychological Analyses of Social Change*, G. Breakwell and E. Lyons (eds), 275–95. Oxford: Butterworth-Heinemann.

Hjelmskog, S. 2000. "Regional och inomregional bosättning i Sverige." In *Hemort Sverige*. Stockholm: Integrationsverket.

Hobsbawm, E. 1992. *Nations and Nationalism since 1780*. 2nd edition. Cambridge: Cambridge University Press.

Hobsbawm, E. and Ranger, T. 1984. *The Invention of Tradition*. Cambridge: Cambridge University Press.

Hockett, C. F. 1950. "Age-grading and linguistic continuity." *Language* 26: 449–59.

Hoffmann, S. 1987. "France and Europe: The dichotomy of autonomy and cooperation." *Contemporary France: A Review of Interdisciplinary Studies* 1: 46–54.

Hollqvist, H. 1984. *The Use of English in Three Large Swedish Companies*. Stockholm: Almqvist & Wiksell International.

Holmes, J. 1992. *An Introduction to Sociolinguistics*. Harlow: Longman.

Holsti, K. J. 1985. *The Dividing Discipline*. Boston: Allen and Unwin.

Holton, R. J. 1998. *Globalization and the Nation-State*. Houdsmills: Macmillan Press.

Hudson, R. 1980. *Sociolinguistics*. Cambridge: Cambridge University Press.

Huguenin, J. and Martinat, P. 1998. *Les Régions: Entre l'Etat et l'Europe*. Paris: Le Monde/ Éditions Marabout.

Humboldt, W. von 1988. *On Language: The Diversity of Human Language-Structure and its Influence on the Mental Development of Mankind*. Translated by P. Heath; introduction by H. Aarsleff. Cambridge: Cambridge University Press.

Huntington, S. 1996. *The Clash of Civilizations and the Remaking of World Order*. New York: Simon and Schuster.

Husband, C. and Saifullah Khan, V. 1982. "The viability of ethnolinguistic vitality: Some creative doubts." *Journal of Multilingual and Multicultural Development* 3 (3): 193–205.

Huss, L. and Lindgren, A.-R. 1999. "Scandinavia." In *Handbook of Language and Ethnic Identity*, J. A. Fishman (ed.), 300–18. Oxford: Oxford University Press.

Hutchinson, J. 1994. "Cultural nationalism and moral regeneration." In *Nationalism*, J. Hutchinson and A. D. Smith (eds), 122–31. Oxford: Oxford University Press.

Hutchinson, J. and Smith, A. D. (eds). 1994. *Nationalism*. Oxford: Oxford University Press.

Hutchinson, J. and Smith, A.D. (eds). 1996. *Ethnicity*. Oxford: Oxford University Press.

Hyltenstam, K. 1985. "Minoritetsspråk och svenska." *Språkvård* 4/85: 14–21.

Hyltenstam, K. 1996. "Svenskan, ett minoritetsspråk i Europa — och i världen?" In *Svenskans beskrivning 21: Förhandlingar vid tjugoförsta sammankomsten för svenskans beskrivning*, A.-M. Ivars, A.-M. London, L. Nyholm, M. Saari and M. Tandeflt (eds), 9–33. Lund: Lund University Press.

Hyltenstam, K. 1997. "Diskussion av begreppen språk och dialekt — med resonemang om meänkielis status som eget språk." In *Steg mot en minoritetspolitik. Europarådets konvention om historiska minoritetsspråk. Statens Offentliga Utredningar (SOU) 1997: 192*: 351–88. Stockholm: Jordbruksdepartementet.

Hyltenstam, K. 1999a. "Inledning: Ideologi, politik och minoritetsspråk." In *Sveriges sju inhemska språk — ett minoritetsperspektiv*, K. Hyltenstam (ed.), 11–40. Lund: Studentlitteratur.

Hyltenstam, K. 1999b. "Begreppen språk och dialekt — om meänkielis status som eget språk." In *Sveriges sju inhemska språk — ett minoritetsperspektiv*, K. Hyltenstam (ed.), 98–137. Lund: Studentlitteratur.

Hyltenstam, K. 1999c. "Svenskan i minoritetsperspektiv." In *Sveriges sju inhemska språk — ett minoritetsperspektiv*, K. Hyltenstam (ed.), 205–40. Lund: Studentlitteratur.

Hyltenstam, K. and Arnberg, L. 1988. "Bilingualism and education of immigrant children and adults in Sweden." In *International Handbook of Bilingualism and Bilingual Education*, C. B. Paulston (ed.), 475–513. New York: Greenwood Press.

Hyltenstam, K. and Stroud, C. 1982. "Halvspråkighet — ett förbrukat slagord." *Invandrare och minoriteter* 3:10–13.

Hyltenstam, K. and Stroud, C. 1991. *Språkbyte och språkbevarande. Om samiskan och andra minoritetsspråk.* Lund: Studentlitteratur.

Hyltenstam, K., Stroud, C. and Svonni, M. 1999. "Språkbyte, språkbevarande, revitalisering. Samiskas ställning i svenska Sápmi." In *Sveriges sju inhemska språk — ett minoritetsspråksperspektiv*, K. Hyltenstam (ed.), 41–97. Lund: Studentlitteratur.

Jacob, J. E. and Beer, W. R. (eds). 1985. *Language Policy and National Unity*. Totowa: Rowman and Allanheld.

Jacob, J. E. and Gordon, D. C. 1985. "Language policy in France." In *Language Policy and National Unity*, J. E. Jacob and W. R. Beer (eds), 106–33. Totowa: Rowman and Allanheld.

Janson, T. 1997. *Språken och historien*. Stockholm: Nordstedts.

Jenkins, B. 1990. *Nationalism in France: Class and Nation since 1789*. London: Routledge.

Jenkins, B. and Copsey, N. 1996. "Nation, nationalism and national identity in France." In *Nation and Identity in Contemporary Europe*, B. Jenkins and S. A. Sofos (eds), 101–24. London/New York: Routledge.

Jenkins, B. and Sofos, S. A. 1996. "Nation and nationalism in contemporary Europe: A theoretical perspective." In *Nation and Identity in Contemporary Europe*, B. Jenkins and S. A. Sofos (eds), 9–32. London/New York: Routledge.

Jerab, N. 1988. "L'arabe des Magrébins. Une langue, des langues." In *Vingt-cinq communautés linguistiques en France*, vol. 2, G. Vermes (ed.), 31–59. Paris: L'Harmattan.

Jernudd, B. H. 1989. "The texture of language purism: An introduction." In *The Politics of Language Purism* [Contributions to the Sociology of Language 54], B. H. Jernudd and M. J. Shapiro (eds), 1–19. Berlin: Mouton de Gruyter.

Johnson, D. 1993. "The making of the French nation." In *The National Question in Europe in Historical Context*, M. Teich and R. Porter (eds), 35–62. Cambridge: Cambridge University Press.

Johnsson, H.-I. 1995. *Sverige i fokus*. Stockholm: Svenska institutet.

Jones, W. R. 1949. "Attitude toward Welsh as a second language. A preliminary investigation." *British Journal of Educational Psychology* 19 (1): 44–52.

Jones, W.R. 1950. "Attitude toward Welsh as a second language. A further investigation." *British Journal of Educational Psychology* 20 (2): 117–32.

Judge, A. 1993. "French: A planned language?" In *French Today: Language in its Social Context*, C. Sanders (ed.), 7–26. Cambridge: Cambridge University Press.

Judge, A. 2000. "France: 'One state, one nation, one language'?" In *Language and Nationalism in Europe*, S. Barbour (ed.), 44–82. Oxford: Oxford University Press.

Kachru, B. (ed.). 1982. *The Other Tongue: English across Cultures*. Urbana: University of Illinois Press.

Karaveli, M. 1997. *Blågul framtid: En essä om nationen och det svenska*. Stockholm: Arena.

Keating, M. 1996. *Nations against the State*. Houndmills: Macmillan Press.

Kedourie, E. 1966. *Nationalism*. 2nd edition. Oxford: Blackwell.
Kelman, H. C. 1972. "Language as aid and barrier to involvement in the national system." In *Advances in the Sociology of Language*, vol. 2, *Selected Studies and Applications*, J. A. Fishman (ed.), 185–212. The Hague/Paris: Mouton.
Kessel, P. 2000. "La République menacée." *Libération*, 24 July. Available at: www.liberation.fr/quotidien/debats/juillet00/20000724a.html.
Kloss, H. 1969a. *Grundfragen der Ethnopolitik im 20. Jahrhundert. Die Sprachgemeinschaften zwischen Recht und Gewalt*. Vienna/Stuttgart: Braumüller.
Kloss, H. 1969b. *Research Possibilities on Group Bilingualism: A Report*. Québec: Université Laval.
Kloss, H. 1978. *Die Entwicklung neuer germanischer Kultursprache von 1800–1950*. 2nd edition. Düsseldorf: Schwann.
Kohn, H. 1955. *Nationalism: Its Meaning and History*. Princeton: Van Nostrand.
Kohn, H. 1961. *The Idea of Nationalism: A Study in its Origins and Background*. New York: Macmillan.
Kohn H. 1968. "Nationalism." *1968 International Encyclopedia of the Social Sciences*, vol. 11, 63–70. New York: Crowell, Collier and Macmillan.
Kotsinas, U.-B. 1992. "Immigrant adolescents' Swedish in multicultural areas." In *Ethnicity in Youth Culture. Report from a Symposium in Stockholm, Sweden, June 3–6, 1991*, C. Palmgren, K. Lövgren and G. Bolin (eds), 43–62. Stockholm: Youth Culture at Stockholm University.
Kotzé, E. F. 1994. "Ethnicity." In *The Encyclopedia of Language and Linguistics*, R. E. Asher (ed.), 1151–6. Oxford: Pergamon Press.
Krejči, J. and Velímský, V. 1996. "Ethnic and political nations in Europe." In *Ethnicity*, J. Hutchinson A. D. and Smith (eds), 209–21. Oxford: Oxford University Press.
Kristeva, J. 1988. *Etrangers à nous-mêmes*. Paris: Fayard.
Kymlicka, W. 1995. *Multicultural Citizenship: A Liberal Theory of Minority Rights*. Oxford: Oxford University Press.
Labov, W. 1966. *The Social Stratification of English in New York City*. Washington: Center for Applied Linguistics.
Labrie, N. 1993. *La Construction linguistique de la Communauté européenne*. Paris: Champion.
Labrune, G. and Toutain, P. 1986. *L'Histoire de France*. Paris: Nathan.
Lafont, R. 1967. *La Révolution régionaliste*. Paris: Gallimard.
Lafont, R. 1968. *Sur la France*. Paris: Gallimard.
Lafont, R. 1992. "La situation sociolinguistique de la France." In *Les Minorités en Europe: Droits linguistiques et Droits de l'Homme*, H. Giordan (ed.), 145–63. Paris: Éditions Kimé.
Lainio, J. 1999. "Språk, genetik och geografi — om kontinuitetsproblematiken och debatten om finska som minoritetsspråk." In *Sveriges sju inhemska språk — ett minoritetsperspektiv*, K. Hyltenstam (ed.), 138–204. Lund: Studentlitteratur.
Lalanne-Berdouticq, P. 1993. *Pourquoi parler français?* Paris: Éditions Fleurus.
Lambert, W. E. 1975. "Culture and language as factors in learning and education." In *Education of Immigrant Students*, A. Wolfgang (ed.), 55–83. Toronto: Ontario Institute for Studies in Education.

Lambert, W. E., Hodgson, R., Gardner, R. C. and Fillenbaum, S. 1960. "Evaluation reactions to spoken languages." *Journal of Abnormal and Social Psychology* 60: 44–51.
Lamy, P. 1979. "Language and ethnolinguistic identity: The bilingual question." In *Language Planning and Identity Planning.* [International Journal of the Sociology of Language 20], P. Lamy (ed.), 23–36. The Hague: Mouton.
Landry, R. and Bourhis, R. Y. 1997. "Linguistic landscape and ethnolinguistic vitality: An empirical study." *Journal of Language and Social Psychology* 16 (1): 23–49.
Lange, A. and Westin, C. 1981. *Etnisk diskriminering och social identitet.* Stockholm: LiberFörlag.
Läroplan för grundskolan. 1980. *Allmän del: mål och riktlinjer, kursplaner, timplaner.* Stockholm: LiberLäromedel/Utbildningsförlaget.
Laroussi, F. and Marcellesi, J.-B. 1993. "The other languages of France." In *French Today: Language in its Social Context,* C. Sanders (ed.), 85–104. Cambridge: Cambridge University Press.
Lartichaux, J.-Y. 1977. "Linguistic politics during the French revolution." *Diogènes* 97: 65–84.
Laureys, G. 1997. "Mellan nationalstat och europeisk union. En jämförelse mellan Norden och Benelux." In *Norden i Europa: Brott eller kontinuitet? Föredrag vid ett Erasmusseminarium för skandinavister, Helsingfors universitet 16–21.9.1996,* M. Fremer, P. Lilius and M. Saari (eds), 16–26. Helsinki: Helsinki University Press.
Lavenir de Buffon, H. 1995. "Pour l'Europe, choisir le français." *Le Figaro,* 12 October.
Le Page, R. B. 1964. *The National Language Question: Linguistic Problems of Newly Independent States.* London: Oxford University Press.
Le Page, R. B. and Tabouret-Keller, A. 1985. *Acts of Identity: Creole-Based Approaches to Language and Ethnicity.* Cambridge: Cambridge University Press.
Liebkind, K. 1996. "Social psychology and contact linguistics." In *Contact Linguistics. An International Handbook of Contemporary Research,* vol. 1, H. Goebl, P. Nelde, Z. Stary and W. Wölck (eds), 41–8. Berlin/New York: Walter de Gruyter.
Liebkind, K. 1999. "Social psychology." In *Handbook of Language and Ethnic Identity,* J. A. Fishman (ed.), 140–51. Oxford: Oxford University Press.
Likert, R. 1932. *A Technique for the Measurement of Attitudes.* [Archives of Psychology 140]. New York.
Lilliestam, L. 1996. "Nordman och 'det svenska'." In *Tyst, nu tala jag! Tradition, information och humanister. Populärvetenskapliga föreläsningar hållna under Humanistdagarna den 12–13 oktober 1996.* Göteborg: Humanistiska fakultetsnämnden, Göteborgs universitet.
Linde-Laursen, A. 1995. "Small differences — large issues: The making and remaking of a national border." *South Atlantic Quarterly* 94 (4): 1123–44.
Ljung, M. 1988. *Skinheads, hackers and lama ankor: Engelskan i 80-talets svenska.* Stockholm: Trevi.
Loden, M. and Rosener, J. 1991. *Workforce America! Managing Employee Diversity as a Vital Resource.* Homewood: Business One Irwin.
Lodge, A. R. 1993. *French: From Dialect to Standard.* London/New York: Routledge.
Lodge, A.R. 1998. "French is a logical language." In *Language Myths,* L. Bauer and P. Tudgill (eds), 23–31. Hamondsworth: Penguin.

Löfgren, O. 1985. "Hur tillverkar man kulturarv?" In *Myter om svensken*, D. Gaunt and O. Löfgren (eds), 11–27. Stockholm: Liber.

Löfgren, O. 1989. "The nationalisation of culture." *National Culture as Process*. Re-edition of *Ethnologica Europea* 19 (1): 5–25.

Löfgren, O. 1993. "Nationella arenor." In *Försvenskningen av Sverige: Det nationellas förvandlingar*, B. Ehn, J. Fyrkman and O. Löfgren, 21–118. Stockholm: Natur och Kultur.

Loman, B. 1974. "Till frågan om tvåspråkighet och halvspråkighet i Tornedalen." In *Språk och samhälle 2. Språket i Tornedalen*, B. Loman (ed.), 43–79. Lund: CWK Gleerup.

Lowenberg, P. 1988. "Malay in Indonesia, Malaysia, and Singapore: Three faces of a national language." In *With Forked Tongues*, F. Coulmas (ed.), 146–79. Singapore: Karoma Publishers.

Lundberg, A. 1960. "Om bruket av fula ord." *Industria* 10/1960: 24–8.

McDonald, M. 1989. *'We are not French!': Language, Culture and Identity in Brittany*. London: Routledge.

Macdonald, S. (ed.). 1993. *Inside European Identities*. Providence/Oxford: Berg.

McKay, R. B., Breslow, M. J., Sangster, R. L., Gabbard, S. M., Reynolds, R. W., Nakamoto, J. M. and Tarnai, J. 1996. "Translating survey questionnaires: Lessons learned." In Advances in Survey Research [New Directions for Evaluation 70], M. T. Braverman and J. K. Slater (eds), 93–104. San Francisco: Jossey-Bass.

Macnamara, J. 1971. "Successes and failures in the movement for the restoration of Irish." In *Can Language be Planned? Sociolinguistic Theory and Practice for Developing Nations*, J. Rubin and B. H. Jernudd (eds), 65–94. Honolulu: East-West Center/University Press of Hawaii.

McNamara, T. F. 1988. "Language and social identity." In *Language and Ethnic Identity*, W. B. Gudykunst and K. L. Schmidt (eds), 59–72. Clevedon: Multilingual Matters.

McNamara, T.F. 1997. "What do we mean by 'social identity'? Competing frameworks, competing discourses." *TESOL Quarterly* 31 (3): 561–7.

McNeill, W. H. 1994. "Reasserting the polyethnic nation." In *Nationalism*, J. Hutchinson and A. D. Smith (eds), 300–5. Oxford: Oxford University Press.

Macquarie Dictionary. 1997. 3rd edition North Ryde: Macquarie Library.

Mansour, G. 1993. *Multilingualism and Nation Building*. Clevedon: Multilingual Matters.

Martel, P. 1987. "Vingt-cinq ans de luttes identitaires." In *France, pays multilingue*, vol. 1, G. Vermes and J. Boutet (eds), 125–42. Paris: L'Harmattan.

Mårtensson, E. 1986. "Det nya niandet." *Nordlund* 10: 35–79.

Martinet, G. 1994. *Le Réveil des nationalismes français*. Paris: Seuil.

Maslow, A. 1954. *Motivation and Personality*. New York: Harper and Row.

Mason, D. and Rex, J. (eds). 1986. *Theories of Race and Ethnic Relations*. Cambridge: Cambridge University Press.

Maurais, J. 1985. "Introduction." In *La Crise des langues*, J. Maurais (ed.), 1–2. Québec: Conseil de la langue française.

May, S. 2001. *Language and Minority Rights: Ethnicity, Nationalism and the Politics of Language*. London: Longman.

Méla, V. 1997. "Verlan 2000." *Langue française* 114, June: 16–34.

Melander, B. 2000a. "EU och svenskan — fördärv eller chans?" In *Svenskan som EU-språk*, B. Melander (ed.), 7–12. Uppsala: Hallgren & Fallgren Studieförlag AB.

Melander, B. 2000b. "EU:s språkpolitik — en månfasetterad fråga." In *Svenskan som EU-språk*, B. Melander (ed.), 13–28. Uppsala: Hallgren & Fallgren Studieförlag AB.

Melander, B. 2000c. "Politikersvenska men tjänstemannaengelska." In *Svenskan som EU-språk*, B. Melander (ed.), 100–43. Uppsala: Hallgren & Fallgren Studieförlag AB.

Miguet, A. 1996. "Francophonie et Europe." In *Francophonie: Mythes, masques et réalités: Enjeux politiques et culturels*, B. Jones, A. Miguet and P. Corcoran (eds), 67–90. Paris: Publisud.

Mill, J. S. 1910. *Utilitarianism, Liberty, Representative Government.* London: J. M. Dent and Sons.

Miller, R. A. 1982. *Japan's Modern Myth: The Language and Beyond.* New York/Tokyo: Weatherhill.

Milroy, L. 1982. "Language and group identity." *Journal of Multilingual and Multicultural Development* 3 (3): 207–16.

Milroy, J. and Milroy, L. 1985. *Authority in Language.* London: Routledge/Kegan Paul.

Milward, A. 1992. *The European Rescue of the Nation State.* London: Routledge.

Minc, A. 1992. *The Great European Illusion: Business in the Wider Community.* Forward by R. Lessem; translated by L. Jones. Oxford: Blackwell.

Mitchell, C. R. 1981. *The Structure of International Conflict.* London: Macmillan.

Moberg, L. and Westman, M. (eds). 1996. *Svenskan i tusen år: Glimtar ur svenska språkets utveckling.* Stockholm: Nordstedts.

Molde, B. 1992. *Svenska i dag: svar på språkfrågor.* Stockholm: Prisma.

Molde, B. 1997. *Mera svenska i dag: svar på språkfrågor.* Stockholm: Rabén Prisma.

Muchnick, A. G. and Wolfe, D. E. 1982. "Attitudes and motivations of American students of Spanish." *The Canadian Modern Language Review* 38: 262–81.

Municio, I. 1993. "Svensk skolpolitik under intryck av två diskurser: nationell självförståelse och demokratiskt credo." In *Invandring, forskning, politik. En vänbok till Tomas Hammar.* Stockholm: Centrum för invandrarforskning, Stockholms universitet.

Nelde, P., Strubell, M. and Williams, G. 1996. *Euromosaic: The Production and Reproduction of the Minority Language Groups in the European Union.* Luxembourg: Office for the Official Publications of the European Union.

Netterstad, M. 1982. *Så sjöng barnen förr.* Stockholm: Rabén & Sjögren.

Ngũgĩ wa Thiong'o. 1986. *Decolonising the Mind: The Politics of Language in African Literature.* London: James Currey.

Nguyen, E. 1998. *Les Nationalismes en Europe: Quête d'identité ou tentation de repli?* Paris: Le Monde/Éditions Marabout.

Nilsson, J. O. 1991. "Modernt, allt för modernt: Speglingar." In *Nationella identiteter i Norden — ett fullbordat projekt?*, A. Linde-Laursen and J. O. Nilsson (eds), 59–99. Stockholm: Nordiska rådet/Allmänna Förlaget.

Nilsson, S. and Thavenius, J. 1976. "Svenskämnets kris — från borgerlig bildning till abstrakt färdighetsträning." In *Svenskämnets kris*, B. Brodow, A. Ehrlin, O. Holmberg, P.-E. Ljung, G. Malmgren, L.-G. Malmgren, S. Nilsson, S. Ottosson, I. Svenonius and J. Thavenius (eds), 10–35. Lund: LiberLäromedel.

Nixon, J. 1999. *SPRINT: Språk- och innehållsintegrerad inlärning och undervisning. Rapport på uppdrag av skolverket.* Stockholm: Skolverket. Available at: www.skolverket.se/pdf/sprintsv.pdf

Noiriel, G. 1988. *Le Creuset français*. Paris: Seuil.

Norrby, C. 1997. "Kandidat Svensson, du eller ni — om utvecklingen av tilltalsskicket i svenskan." In *Svenska som andraspråk och andra språk. Festskrift till Gunnar Tingbjörn*, A.-B. Andersson, I. Enström, R. Källström and K. Nauclér (eds), 319–28. Göteborg: Institutionen för svenska språket, Göteborgs universitet.

Nyborg, K. 1982. *Report on the Multilingualism of the European Community*. European Parliament Working Documents, Doc1–306/82.

Nyström, K. 1993. "Språket som barriär i det forna Jugoslavien." In *Språk i världen: Broar och barriärer*, J. Blomqvist and U. Teleman (eds), 33–42. Lund: Studentlitteratur.

O'Brien, O. 1993. "Good to be French? Conflicts of identity in Northern Catalonia." In *Inside European Identities*, S. Macdonald (ed.), 98–117. Providence/Oxford: Berg.

O Riagáin, P. 1997. *Language Policy and Social Reproduction: Ireland 1893–1993*. Oxford: Clarendon.

Oakes, L. 2000. *Astérix and ABBA: Language and National Identity in France and Sweden*. Ph.D diss., The University of Melbourne.

Ohlander, A.-S. and Torstendahl, R. 1998. "Vem får plats vid Thams universitet?" *Svenska Dagbladet*, 29 May.

Ohlsson, S. Ö. 1978. *Skånes språkliga försvenskning*. Lund: Ekstrand.

Olsson, L. 1980. "La politique culturelle de la France à l'égard de ses minorités linguistiques." *Moderna Språk* 3/1980: 237–54.

Olsson, L. 1981. "La situation linguistique et culturelle des Basques de France I." *Moderna Språk* 4/1981: 373–89.

Olsson, L. 1982. "La situation linguistique et culturelle des Basques de France II." *Moderna Språk* 1/1982: 57–72.

Oscarson, M. 1984. *Self-Assessment of Foreign Language Skills: A Survey of Research and Development Work*. Strasbourg: Council of Europe.

Østerud, Ø. 1997. *Vad är nationalism?* Translated by M. C. Karlsson. Stockholm: Universitetsforlaget.

Østerud, Ø. 1998. "Är nationen inte mer än så?" *Svenska Dagbladet*, 9 May.

Oxford English Reference Dictionary. 1996. 2nd edition. Oxford: Oxford University Press.

Paltridge, J. and Giles, H. 1984. "Attitudes towards speakers of regional accents of French: Effects of regionality, age and sex of listeners." *Linguistische Berichte* 90: 71–85.

Paulston, C. B. 1994. *Linguistic Minorities in Multilingual Settings: Implications for Language Policies*. Amsterdam/Philadelphia: John Benjamins.

Pennycook, A. 1994. *The Cultural Politics of English as an International Language*. London/New York: Longman.

Pennycook, A. 1998. *English and the Discourses of Colonialism*. London: Routledge.

Pergnier, M. 1989. *Les Anglicismes: Danger ou enrichissement pour la langue française?* Paris: Presses Universitaires de France.

Perret, M. 1998. *Introduction à l'histoire de la langue française*. Paris: SEDES.

Peterson, W. 1980. "Concepts of ethnicity." In *Concepts of Ethnicity*, W. Petersen, M. Novak and P. Gleason, 1–26. Cambridge: Harvard University Press.

Peyre, H. 1933. *La Royauté et les langues provinciales*. Paris: Les Presses Modernes.

Phillips-Martinsson, J. 1981. *Svenskarna som andra ser dem*. Lund: Studentlitteratur.

Phillipson, R. 1992. *Linguistic Imperialism*. Oxford: Oxford University Press.

Phillipson, R. 1999. "Political science." In *Handbook of Language and Ethnic Identity,* J. A. Fishman (ed.), 94–108. Oxford: Oxford University Press.

Picoche, J. and Marchello-Nizia, C. 1994. *Histoire de la langue française.* 3rd edition. Paris: Nathan.

Pinker, S. 1994. *The Language Instinct.* New York: William Morrow and Company.

Planze, O. 1966. "Characteristics of nationalism in Europe, 1848–1871." *Review of Politics* 28: 129–43.

Pocock, J. G. A. 1991. "Deconstructing Europe." *The London Review of Books* 13 (24): 6–10.

Poignant, B. 1998. *Langues et cultures régionales. Rapport de Monsieur Bernard Poignant, Maire de Quimper, à Monsieur Lionel Jospin, Premier ministre.* Paris: La Documentation Française. Available at: www.ladocfrancaise.gouv.fr/cgi-bin/multitel/CATALDOC/accueil_df

Pool, J. 1979. "Language planning and identity planning." In *Language Planning and Identity Planning.* [International Journal of the Sociology of Language 20], P. Lamy (ed.), 5–21. The Hague: Mouton.

Propositions du government soumises aux représentants des élus de la Corse. 2000. Available at: www.premier-ministre.gouv.fr/GOUV/CORSE210700.HTM

Raag, R. 1988. "Ester." In *Det mångkulturella Sverige: En handbok om etniska grupper och minoriteter,* I. Svanberg and H. Runblom (eds), 57–70. Stockholm: Gidlunds Bokförlag.

Regeringsbeslut 1997-04-30. *Uppdrag till Svenska spraknämnden att utarbeta förslag till handlingsprogram för att främja svenska språket.* Stockholm: Riksdagen.

Renan, E. 1990. "What is a nation?" Translated and annotated by M. Thom. In *Nation and Narration,* H. K. Bhabha (ed.), 1–22. London: Routledge.

Rex, J. 1996. "Multiculturalism in Europe." In *Ethnicity,* J. Hutchinson and A. D. Smith (eds), 241–5. Oxford: Oxford University Press.

Richmond, A. 1984. "Ethnic nationalism and postindustrialism." *Ethnic and Racial Studies* 7 (4): 4–18.

Rickard, P. 1989. *A History of the French Language.* 2nd edition. London: Unwin Hyman.

Ritzer, G. 1993. *The McDonaldization of Society.* Thousand Oaks: Pine Forge Press.

Rivarol, A. de 1998. *L'Universalité de la langue française.* Paris: Arléa.

Rosenberg, M. and Simmons, R. 1972. *Black and White Self-Esteem: The Urban Schoolchild.* Washington: American Sociological Association.

Ross, J. A. 1979. "Language and the mobilization of ethnic identity." In *Language and Ethnic Relations,* H. Giles and B. Saint-Jacques (eds), 1–13. Oxford: Pergamon Press.

Rossillion, P. (ed.). 1995. *Atlas de la langue française.* Paris: Bordas.

Rouland, N. 1991. *Aux Confins du droit: Anthropologie juridique de la modernité.* Paris: Éditions Odile Jacob.

Royce, A. 1982. *Ethnic Identity.* Bloomington: Indiana University Press.

Runblom, H. 1995. "Immigration to Scandinavia after World War II." In *Ethnicity and Nation Building in the Nordic World,* S. Tägil (ed.), 282–324. London: Hurst and Company.

Runblom, H. 1998. *La Suède, société multiculturelle.* [Actualités suédoises 418]. Stockholm: Svenska institutet.

Ruong, I. 1975. "Historisk återblick rörande samerna." In *Samerna i Sverige. Stöd åt språk och kultur. Betänkande av sameutredningen. Bilagor. Statens Offentliga Utredningar (SOU) 1975: 100*: 375–433.

Ruong, I. 1982. *Samerna i historien och nutiden*. Stockholm: BonnierFakta.

Ryan, E. B., Giles, H. and Hewstone, M. 1987. "The measurement of language attitudes." In *Sociolinguistics: An International Handbook of the Science of Language and Society*, vol. 2, U. Ammon, N. Dittmar and K. J. Mattheier (eds), 1068–81. Berlin: Walter de Gruyter.

Ryan, E. B., Giles, H. and Sebastian, R. J. 1982. "An integrative perspective for the study of attitudes toward language variation." In *Attitudes towards Language Variation*, E. B. Ryan and H. Giles (eds), 1–19. London: Edward Arnold.

Rydberg, V. 1873. "Tysk eller nordisk svenska?" *Svensk tidskrift för litteratur, politik och ekonomi* 1873: 489–530.

Sachdev, I. and Bourhis, R. Y. 1990. "Language and social identification." In *Social Identity Theory: Constructive and Critical Advances*, D. Abrams and M. Hogg (eds), 211–29. New York: Harvester Wheatsheaf.

Safran, W. 1989. "The French state and ethnic minority cultures: policy dimensions and problems." In *Ethnoterritorial Politics, Policy, and the Western World*, J. R. Rudolph, Jr. and R. J. Thompson (eds), 115–57. Bouldon/London: Lynne Rienner Publishers.

Safran, W. 1991. "State, nation, national identity, and citizenship: France as a test case." *International Political Science Review* 12 (3): 219–38.

Safran, W. 1992. "Pluralisme, démocratie et droits linguistiques aux États-Unis." In *Les Minorités en Europe: Droits linguistiques et Droits de l'Homme*, H. Giordan (ed.), 537–56. Paris: Éditions Kimé.

Safran, W. 1999a. "Nationalism." In *Handbook of Language and Ethnic Identity*, J. A. Fishman (ed.), 77–93. Oxford: Oxford University Press.

Safran, W. 1999b. "Politics and language in contemporary France: Facing supranational and infranational challenges." *International Journal of the Sociology of Language* 137: 39–66.

Said, E. 1978. *Orientalism*. New York: Pantheon Books.

St Clair, R. N. 1982. "From social history to language attitudes." In *Attitudes towards Language Variation*, E. B. Ryan and H. Giles (eds), 164–74. London: Edward Arnold.

Saint Robert, M.-J. de 2000. *La Politique de la langue française* [Que sais-je? 3572]. Paris: Presses Universitaires de France.

Salvesen, H. 1995. "Sami ædnan: four states — one nation?" In *Ethnicity and Nation Building in the Nordic World*, S. Tägil (ed.), 106–44. London: Hurst and Company.

Sanguin, A.-L. 1993. *Les Minorités ethniques en Europe*. Paris: L'Harmattan.

Sax, G. 1968. *Foundations of Educational Research*. Englewood Cliffs: Prentice Hall.

Scherer, K. R. and Giles, H. (eds). 1979. *Social Markers in Speech*. Cambridge: Cambridge University Press.

Schiffman, H. F. 1996. *Linguistic Culture and Language Policy*. London: Routledge.

Schlesinger, P. 1994. "Europeaness: A new cultural battlefield?" In *Nationalism*, J. Hutchinson and A. D. Smith (eds), 316–25. Oxford: Oxford University Press.

Schnapper, D. 1991. *La France de l'intégration: Sociologie de la nation en 1990*. Paris: Gallimard.

Schnapper, D. 1994. *La Communauté des citoyens: Sur l'idée moderne de nation.* Paris: Gallimard.
Schnapper, D. 1998a. "La préférence civique." *Cultures en mouvement* 10, août-septembre: 34–8.
Schnapper, D. 1998b. *La Relation à l'autre: Au Coeur de la pensée sociologique.* Paris: Gallimard.
Schulze, H. 1996. *States, Nations and Nationalism: From the Middle Ages to the Present.* Translated by W. E. Yuill. Cambridge, MA: Blackwell.
Sekretariatet för Europainformation. 1994. *EU och Sverige.* Stockholm: Utrikesdepartementet.
Selander, E. 1980. "Language for professional use from the Swedish point of view." *International Journal of the Sociology of Language* 23: 17–28.
Seton-Watson, H. 1981. "Language and national consciousness." *Proceedings of the British Academy.* Oxford: Oxford University Press.
Seurujärvi-Kari, I., Pedersen, S. and Hirvonen, V. 1997. *The Sámi: The Indigenous People of Northernmost Europe.* Brussels: European Bureau of Lesser Used Languages.
Shapiro, M. J. 1989. "A political approach to language purism." In *The Politics of Language Purism*, B. H. Jernudd and M. J. Shapiro (eds), 21–9. Berlin: Mouton de Gruyter.
Shelly, S. L. 1999. "Une certaine idée du français: the dilemma for French language policy in the twenty-first century." *Language and Communication* 19: 305–16.
Siguan, M. 1996. *L'Europe des langues.* Sprimont: Mardaga.
Simpson, J. M. Y. 1981. "The challenge of minority languages." In *Minority Languages Today*, E. Haugen, J. D. McClure and D. Thomson (eds), 235–41. Edinburgh: Edinburgh University Press.
Sjögren, A. 1996. "Språket, nykomlingens nyckel till samhället, men också en svensk försvarsmekanism." In *En "bra" svenska? Om språk, kultur och makt*, A. Sjögren, A. Runfors and I. Ramberg (eds): 19–40. Tumba: Mångkulturellt centrum.
Sjögren, A., Runfors, A. and Ramberg, I. (eds). 1996. *En "bra" svenska? Om språk, kultur och makt.* Tumba: Mångkulturellt centrum.
Skolverket. 2000. *Barnomsorg och skola i siffror 2000: Del 1. Skolverkets rapport nummer 181.* Stockholm: Skolverket. Available at: www.skolverket.se/fakta/statistik/sos/sos001/index.shtml
Skutnabb-Kangas, T. 1981. *Tvåspråkighet.* Lund: Liber Läromedel.
Skutnabb-Kangas, T. and Phillipson, R. 1994. *Linguistic Human Rights: Overcoming Linguistic Discrimination.* Berlin/New York: Mouton de Gruyter.
Smith, A. D. 1971. *Theories of Nationalism.* London: Duckworth.
Smith, A.D. 1986. *The Ethnic Origin of Nations.* Oxford: Blackwell.
Smith, A.D. 1988. "The myth of the 'modern nation' and the myth of nations." *Ethnic and Racial Studies* 11 (1): 1–26.
Smith, A.D. 1990. "Towards a global culture?" *Theory, Culture and Society* 7: 171–91.
Smith, A.D. 1991. *National Identity.* London: Penguin.
Smith, A.D. 1994. "The problem of national identity: Ancient, medieval and modern?" *Ethnic and Racial Studies* 17 (3): 375–99.
Smith, A.D. 1995. *Nations and Nationalism in a Global Era.* Cambridge: Basil Blackwell.
Smolicz, J. 1981. "Core values and cultural identity." *Ethnic and Racial Studies* 4 (1): 75–90.

Snyder, L. 1954. *The Meaning of Nationalism.* New Brunswick: Rutgers University Press.
Snyder, L. (ed.). 1964. *The Dynamics of Nationalism.* London: D. Van Nostrand Company.
Söhrman, I. 1997. *Språk, nationer och andra farligheter.* Stockholm: Arena.
SOU. 1975a. *Samerna i Sverige. Stöd åt språk och kultur. Betänkande av sameutredningen. Statens Offentliga Utredningar (SOU) 1975: 99.* Stockholm: LiberFörlag/Allmänna Förlaget.
SOU. 1975b. *Samerna i Sverige. Stöd åt språk och kultur. Betänkande av sameutredningen. Bilagor. Statens Offentliga Utredningar (SOU) 1975: 100.* Stockholm: LiberFörlag/Allmänna Förlaget.
SOU. 1990. *Samerätt och samiskt språk. Slutbetänkande från samerättsutredningen. Statens Offentliga Utredningar (SOU) 1990: 91.* Stockholm: Allmänna Förlaget.
SOU. 1997a. *Steg mot en minoritetspolitik. Europarådets konvention om historiska minoritetsspråk. Statens Offentliga Utredningar (SOU) 1997: 192.* Stockholm: Fritze.
SOU. 1997b. *Steg mot en minoritetspolitik. Europarådets konvention för skydd av nationella minoriteter. Statens Offentliga Utredningar (SOU) 1997: 193.* Stockholm: Fritze.
SOU. 1998. *Svenskan i EU. Hur vi kan främja kvaliteten på de svenska EU-texterna. Betänkande av utredningen om svenskan i EU. Statens Offentliga Utredningar (SOU) 1998: 114.* Stockholm: Fritze.
Srivastava, R. N. 1984. "Linguistic minorities and national languages." In *Linguistic Minorities and Literacy*, F. Coulmas (ed.), 99–114. Berlin/New York/Amsterdam: Mouton.
Stephens, M. 1976. *Linguistic Minorities in Western Europe.* Llandysul: Gomer Press.
Stroud, C. 1978. "The concept of semilingualism." *Working Papers* 16: 153–72. Lund: Department of General Linguistics, Lund Univesrity.
Stroud, C. and Wingstedt, M. 1989. "Språklig chauvinism?" *Invandrare and minoriteter* 4–5: 5–8.
Sundbärg, G. 1911. *Det svenska folklynnet.* Stockholm: Norstedt & Söners.
Svenska institutet. 1998. *La Suède dans l'Union européenne.* [Feuillet de documentation sur la Suède 94]. Stockholm: Svenska institutet.
Svenska språknämnden. 1998. *Förslag till handlingsprogram för att främja svenska spårket.* Available at: www.spraknamnden.se/SSN/handl.htm
Svensson, S. 1994. *Swedes Vote Yes to Membership in the EU.* [Current Sweden 408]. Stockholm: Svenska institutet.
Svonni, M. 1996. "Saami language as a marker of ethnic identity amongst the Saami." In *Essays of Indigenous Identity and Rights*, I. Seurujärvi-Kari and U.-M. Kulonen (eds), 105–25. Helsinki: Helsinki University Press.
Svonni, M. 1997. "Att lära sig samiska — ett minoritetsspråk." In *Mer än ett språk. En antologi om två- och flerspråkigheten i norra Sverige*, E. Westergren and H. Åhl (eds), 130–52. Stockholm: Nordstedts Förlag AB.
Taboada-Léonetti, I. 1998. "La nation: Le civique et l'ethnique." *Cultures en mouvement* 10, août-septembre: 30–3.
Tabouret-Keller, A. 1991. "Factors of constraints and freedom in setting a language policy for the European Community: A sociolinguistic approach." In *A Language Policy for the European Community: Prospects and Quandries*, F. Coulmas (ed.), 45–57. Berlin/New York: Mouton de Gruyter.
Tabouret-Keller, A. 1999. "Western Europe." In *Handbook of Language and Ethnic Identity*, J. A. Fishman (ed.), 334–49. Oxford: Oxford University Press.

Tägil, S. 1995. "Ethnic and national minorities in the Nordic nation-building process: Theoretical and conceptual premises." In *Ethnicity and Nation Building in the Nordic World*, S. Tägil (ed.), 8–32. London: Hurst and Company.
Taguieff, P.-A. 1996. *La République menacée*. Paris: Textuel.
Tajfel, H. 1974. "Social identity and intergroup behaviour." *Social Science Information* 13: 65–93.
Tajfel, H. 1978. *The Social Psychology of Minorities*. [Minority Rights Group Report 38]. London: Minority Rights Group.
Tajfel, H. and Turner, J.C. 1986. "The social identity theory of intergroup behaviour." In *Psychology of Intergroup Relations*, revised edition of *The Social Psychology of Intergroup Relations*, 1979, S. Worchel and W.G. Austin (eds), 7–24. Chicago: Nelson-Hall Publishers.
Taylor, C. 1991. "Shared and divergent values." In *Options for a New Canada*, R. Watts and D. Brown (eds), 53–76. Toronto: University of Toronto Press.
Taylor, D.M., Meynard, R. and Rheault, E. 1977. "Threat to ethnic identity and second language learning." In *Language, Ethnicity and Intergroup Relations*, H. Giles (ed.), 99–118. London: Academic Press.
Tegnér, E. 1959. *Smärre samlade dikter*. Lund: Gleerups Förlag.
Tegnér, E. d.y. 1922. "Om språk och nationalitet." *Ur språkens värld*, vol. 1, 95–164 Stockholm: Albert Bonniers Förlag.
Teleman, U. 1993. "Det svenska rikspråkets utsikter i ett integrerat Europa." In *Språk i världen: Broar och barriärer*, J. Blomqvist and U. Teleman (eds), 127–41. Lund: Studentlitteratur.
Teleman, U. and Westman, M. 1997. "Behöver vi en nationell språkpolitik?" *Språkvård* 2/97: 5–16.
Teleman, U. and Westman, M. 1999. "Länge leve svenska språket?" *Svenska Dagbladet*, 17 August.
Teleman, U., Hellberg, S. and Andersson, E. 1999. *Svenska akademiens grammatik*. Stockholm: Svenska akademien/Nordstedts ordbok.
Thavenius, J. 1995. "Svenska som läroämne." In *Nationalencyclopedin* 17: 475.
Thérive, A. 1923. *Le Français, langue morte?* Paris: Plon-Nourrit.
Thiesse, A.-M. 1999. *La Création des identités nationales: Europe XVIIIe-XXe siècle*. Paris: Éditions du Seuil.
Thompson, J.B. 1991. "Editor's introduction." In *Language and Symbolic Power*, P. Bourdieu, edited by J.B. Thompson; translated by G. Raymond and M. Adamson, 1–31. Cambridge: Polity Press.
Tilly, C. 1994. "Europe and the international state system." In *Nationalism*, J. Hutchinson and A.D. Smith (eds), 251–4. Oxford: Oxford University Press.
Tocqueville, A. de 1875. *Democracy in America*. Vol. 1. Translated by H. Reeve. London: Longmans, Green and Company.
Tollefson, J.W. 1986. "Language planning and the radical left in the Philippines: The New People's Army and its antecedents." *Language Problems and Language Planning* 12 (1): 30–42.
Tollefson, J.W. 1991. *Planning Language, Planning Inequality: Language Policy in the Community*. Harlow: Longman.

Truchot, C. 1991. "Towards a language policy for the European Union." In *Language Planning: Focusschrift in Honour of Joshua A. Fishman on the Occasion of his 65th Birthday*, D. Marshall (ed.), 87–104. Amsterdam/Philadelphia: John Benjamins.
Trudeau, P. 1990. "The values of a just society." In *Towards a Just Society*, T. Axworthy (ed.), 357–404. Toronto: Viking Press.
Trudgill, P. and Giles, H. 1978. "Sociolinguistics and linguistic value judgements: Correctness, adequacy and aesthetics." In *The Functions of Language and Literature Studies*, F. Coppiertiers and D. Goyvaerts (eds), 167–90. Ghent: Storia Scientia.
Trudgill, P. and Tzavaras, G. A. 1977. "Why Albanian-Greeks are not Albanians: Language shift in Attica and Biotia." In *Language, Ethnicity and Intergroup Relations*, H. Giles (ed.), 171–84. London: Academic Press.
Turner, J. C., Hogg, M. A., Oakes, P. J., Reicher, S. D. and Wetherell, M. 1987. *Rediscovering the Social Group*. Oxford: Blackwell.
Uppman, B. 1978. *Samhället och samerna 1870–1925*. Umeå: Umeå universitetsbibliotek.
Uibopuu, V. 1988. *Finnougrierna och deras språk*. Lund: Studentlitteratur.
Utrikesdepartementet. 1994. *EU-avtalet: Sveriges avtal med Europeiska Unionen*. Stockholm: Utrikesdepartementet, Handelsavdelningen.
Varro, G. 1992. "Les 'langues immigrées' face à l'école française." *Language Problems and Language Planning* 16 (2): 137–62.
Vassberg, L. M. 1993. *Alsatian Acts of Identity: Language Use and Language Attitudes in Alsace*. Clevedon: Multilingual Matters.
Vaugelas, C. V. de 1970. *Remarques sur la langue française*. Edited by J. Streicher. Geneva: Slatikine Reprints.
Vermes, G. and Boutet, J. 1987. "Introduction." In *France, pays multilingue*, vol. 1, G. Vermes and J. Boutet (eds), 21–37. Paris: L'Harmattan.
Vermeulen, H. and Govers, C. (eds). 1994. *The Anthropology of Ethnicity*. Amsterdam: Het Spinhuis.
Vikør, L. 1993. *The Nordic Languages: Their Status and Interrelations*. Oslo: Novus Press.
Voltaire, F. M. A. de 1953–65. *Voltaire's Correspondance*. Edited by T. Besterman. Genève: Institut et Musée Voltaire.
Wallace, H. 1991. "The Europe that came in from the cold." *International Affairs* 67 (4): 661–4.
Wallace, W. 1991. "Foreign policy and national identity in the United Kingdom." *International Affairs* 67 (1): 66–7.
Walter, H. 1988. *Le Français dans tous les sens*. Paris: Robert Laffont.
Walter, H. 1994. *L'Aventure des langues en Occident*. Paris: Robert Laffont.
Wande, E. 1977. "Hansegård är ensidig." *Invandrare och minoriteter* 3–4: 44–51.
Wande, E. 1988. "Språk och invandrare." In *Det mångkulturella Sverige: En handbok om etniska grupper och minoriteter*, I. Svanberg and H. Runblom (eds), 402–8. Stockholm: Gidlunds Bokförlag.
Wardhaugh, R. 1987. *Languages in Competition*. Oxford: Basil Blackwell.
Wardhaugh, R. 1998. *An Introduction to Sociolinguistics*. 3rd edition. Oxford: Blackwell Publishers.
Wartburg, W. von 1946. *Évolution et structure de la langue française*. Berne: Franke.

Waterman, J. 1966. *A History of the German Language.* Seattle: University of Washington Press.
Weber, E. 1977. *Peasants into Frenchmen: The Modernization of Rural France, 1870–1914.* London: Chatto and Windus.
Weber, M. 1968. *Economy and Society.* New York: Bedminster.
Weinstein, B. 1989. "Francophonie: purism at the international level." In *The Politics of Language Purism,* B. H. Jernudd and M. J. Shapiro (eds), 53–79. Berlin: Mouton de Gruyter.
Westergren, E. and Åhl, H. (eds). 1997. *Mer än ett språk. En antologi om två- och flerspråkigheten i norra Sverige.* Stockholm: Nordstedts Förlag AB.
Westman, M. 1996. "Har svenska språket en framtid?" In *Svenskan i tusen år: Glimtar ur svenska språkets utveckling,* L. Moberg and M. Westman (eds), 182–94. Stockholm: Nordstedts.
Williams, C. 1999. "The Celtic world." In *Handbook of Language and Ethnic Identity,* J. A. Fishman (ed.), 267–85. Oxford: Oxford University Press.
Wilson T. M. and Smith M. E. (eds). 1993. *Cultural Change and the New Europe: Perspectives on the European Community.* Boulder/San Francisco/Oxford: Westview Press.
Wingstedt, M. 1996. *Language Ideology and Minority Language Policies: A History of Sweden's Educational Policies towards the Saami, including a Comparison to the Tornedalians.* [Rapporter om tvåspråkighet 11]. Stockholm: Centrum för tvåspråkighetsforskning, Stockholm University.
Wingstedt, M. 1998. *Language Ideologies and Minority Language Policies in Sweden: Historical and Contemporary Perspectives.* Ph.D diss., Stockholm University.
Winock, M. 1982. *Nationalisme, antisémitisme et fascisme en France.* Paris: Éditions du Seuil.
Winock, M. 1996. "Qu'est-ce qu'une nation?" *L'Histoire* 201, juillet-août: 8–13.
Winock, M. 1997. *Parlez-moi de la France.* Paris: Seuil.
Wise, H. 1997. *The Vocabulary of Modern French.* London/New York: Routledge.
Witte, B. de 1991. "The impact of European Community rules on linguistic policies of the Member States." In *A Language Policy for the European Community: Prospects and Quandries,* F. Coulmas (ed.), 163–77. Berlin/New York: Mouton de Gruyter.
Witte, B. de 1993. "Cultural legitimation: Back to the language question." In *European Identity and the Search for Legitimacy,* S. García (ed.), 154–71. London: Pinter Publishers.
Wright, S. 2000. *Community and Communication: The Role of Language in Nation State Building and European Integration.* Clevedon: Multilingual Matters.
Yinger, J. M. 1994. *Ethnicity: Source of Strength? Source of Conflict?* Albany: State University of New York Press.

Index of subjects

2 thermidor an II 61
8 pluviôse an II 61

ABBA 1, 165, 173
Académie française *see* French Academy
accent 20, 46, 153
acculturation 10, 41, 42
affirmative action 99
Africa 56, 61, 65, 97, 102, 104, 119, 162, 163, 201, 247
Afrikaans 120
Albanian 120, 177
Albigensian crusades 55
Algeria 104, 117
Algerians 85
Alliance française 155, 161, 247
Alsace/Lorraine 13, 93, 177, 242
Alsatian:
 language 4, 20, 89, 117
 people 13, 80, 107
American English 20, 138, 154, 157, 164–5, 168, 209, 212, 216, 218
American Revolution 15
Americanisation 128, 148
 in France 172, 213, 218
 in Sweden 164–5, 209, 214
Americans 31, 70, 137, 153, 231
Amish 45
Anglo-conformity 86
Anita Groener v Minister for Education and City of Dublin Vocational Education Committee 144, 245
anti-Americanism 156–7, 164, 172
anti-language 44
anti-Semitism 84, 100
anti-traditionalism 70
Arabic 44, 52, 102, 119, 132, 138, 152, 177, 192, 196, 197, 215, 216, 221
Armenians 100, 104
assimilation(ism) 11, 36, 41, 42, 81–2, 85–7, 88
 in France 87, 97–8, 100, 115, 119
 in Sweden 105, 107–8, 109, 111, 112, 115, 227
Association générale des usagers de la langue française (AGULF) 160
associative schools 118
Assyrians 115

Australia 3, 12, 46, 53, 85–6, 87, 102, 152, 162, 182
Australian English 19
Austria 2, 133, 244, 246
Austrians 133
Austro-Hungarian empire 82

banal nationalism 17
Bas-Lauriol Law 95, 138, 159, 160
Basque:
 language 27, 46, 60, 81, 89, 92, 94, 117, 118, 181, 196–7, 215, 221, 239
 people 15, 27, 80, 81, 153, 197, 239
 political activism in France 94
Basque Country 81, 83, 94, 123
Belgians 97
 see also Flemish and Walloon people
Belgium 25–6, 36, 61, 177, 244
Berber 102, 192
Berlin crisis 156
Beur identity 102
Bible 9, 21, 56, 65, 67
bicultural(ism) 40, 41, 42, 44, 102, 218
bilingual(ism) 24, 25, 40, 86, 177
 additive versus subtractive bilingualism 151, 218
 in France 63, 103, 118
 in Sweden 107, 166, 168, 170
Bilingual Education Act 86
Bohuslän 66
bondekultur (peasant culture) 68
Bosnian 44
bourgeoisie 15, 91, 94
Bremen 241
bressolas 94
Breton:
 language 20, 46, 60, 81, 89, 92, 93, 94, 117, 118, 181, 215
 people 15, 80, 81, 122
 political activism 93, 94
Britain *see* United Kingdom
British English 212
British people 14, 38, 129, 137, 153, 242
Brittany 81, 94, 121
Buddhism 113
Bulgaria 161
Bulgarian 23

Cabo Corso 65
calandretas 94
California 86
Canada 45, 56, 83, 85–6, 87, 163, 196
Canadians 41, 45
  see also Québécois people
Carolingian Renaissance 54
Catalan 80, 245
  in France 81, 89, 94, 117
Catalans 47, 50, 53, 153
  in France 122
Catalonia 130
Catholic(ism) 2, 44, 65, 97, 113
Centre for Technical Terminology 72, 150
Centre national de la recherche scientifique (CNRS) 123, 159
Chanson de Roland 54
Charter of Fundamental Rights of the European Union 135
China 156, 247
Chinese:
  language(s) 132, 152, 157, 215
  people 19, 247
citizenship 12, 24, 240, 242, 243
  in the Baltic states 47
  European 128, 131
  French 13, 63, 95, 98, 100, 101–2, 199–201, 222
  German 13
  Swedish 116, 199–201
Club de l'Horloge 100
Cold War 34, 130, 155, 164, 170, 171, 233
colonialism 65, 83, 100, 149, 151, 162, 163
  neocolonialism 162
Colorado 86
Comett 134
Comité international pour le français, langue européenne 138
Committee of Public Instruction 60, 240
Committee of Public Safety 60, 240
Committee of the Regions 130, 143
Common Agricultural Policy (CAP) 136
Common Foreign and Security Policy (CFSP) 128
communautarisation 99
communism 17, 34, 100, 146, 156, 161, 170
Conseil constitutionnel 95, 122, 160
Conseil supérieur de la langue française (CSLF) 72
constitutional patriotism 129
convergence 41–4, 46, 127, 147, 148, 149, 152, 153, 165, 207, 208, 229
  in France 91, 172, 210, 223, 225, 226, 235
  in Sweden 143, 145, 165, 207, 218, 223, 225, 226, 233, 234
core value theory 2–3
Corsica 81, 95, 96, 118, 123
  language 81, 89, 96, 117, 118, 123

people 15, 95, 122
political activism 94
Council of Europe 120, 121, 127, 132, 136
Council of Ministers 131, 132, 133, 137, 139, 140, 245, 246
Council Regulation No. 1 131, 132, 245
Council of Tours 54
Croatian 44, 243
Creole 50
Cuban missile crisis 156
cultural pluralism see multicultural(ism)

Danish:
  language 44, 64, 132, 140, 216
  people 165, 167, 219
Darwinism 73, 107
decentralisation 62, 94, 120, 242, 244
Declaration of the Rights of Man and the Citizen 59, 160
Declaration of the Rights of Persons Belonging to National, Ethnic, Religious and Linguistic Minorities 152
decolonisation 63
Defferre Law 94
Deixonne Law 84, 93, 117, 118, 231
Delaware 65
Délégation générale à la langue française (DGLF) 72, 118, 119, 124, 139, 160, 162, 172, 243, 245
democratic deficit 128, 244
democratisation of language 72–6
democratism 70, 73, 190
denizens 85, 242, 243
Denmark 14, 15, 17, 43, 65, 66, 81, 113, 137, 244, 246
det nya niandet see ni revival
Det nya partiet see New Party, the
diglossia 151
divergence 41–4, 46, 149, 151, 153, 206, 208, 229
  in France 91, 172, 207, 210, 212, 232, 234
  in Sweden 143, 233, 234, 235
divergence in convergence 44, 153, 154, 236
  in France 172, 228
  in Sweden 165, 226, 233, 234
diwans 94, 181, 195
DOM-TOM (French overseas departments and territories) 88, 104
Draft Declaration on the Rights of Indigenous Peoples 152
Draft Universal Declaration of Linguistic Rights 152
Dreyfus Affair 63, 84
droit à la différence 94, 98, 101, 111, 113
du reform 77
Dutch:
  language 21, 52, 131, 140
  people 52, 140

Index of subjects

Eastern Europe 1, 11, 15, 16, 82, 130, 133, 161
ecolinguistic revolution:
   first 21, 65
   second 23, 67, 82, 107
Economic and Social Committee 143
ELCO (enseignement des langues et cultures d'origine) 117, 119–20, 181, 195, 243
élite(ism) 14–15, 16, 21, 23, 39, 58, 81, 128, 148, 149, 151, 163, 172
   in France 54, 55, 59, 91, 213, 218, 220, 224, 227
   in Sweden 142, 166, 234
   see also intellectuals, intelligentsia
England 14, 15, 57, 66, 81, 137
   see also United Kingdom
English 3, 9, 12, 18, 23, 31, 46, 51, 53, 153, 163, 176
   in Europe 132–5, 137–40, 146, 209–10, 216, 224, 226, 233
   in France 95, 156–9, 161, 171–2, 177, 178, 192, 193, 209–19, 224–5, 226, 227, 228, 233, 234
   as a global language 4, 32, 58, 139, 149–54, 155, 157, 161, 162, 210–19, 224–5, 226, 227, 234–5
   in Ireland 3, 140
   language myths 150–1, 158–9, 166
   in Sweden 1, 31, 143, 144, 153, 164–70, 171, 173, 178, 193, 209–19, 220, 224–5, 227, 233, 234
   in Switzerland 27
   in the United States 24–5, 86; see also American English
English people 45, 58, 129, 155, 158, 242
   see also British people
English-only movement 24–5, 86
Enlightenment 22, 58, 81, 92, 128
Eritrea 112
Espaces 89 100
Esperanto 153–4, 209, 224
Estonia 47, 112, 142, 143, 161
   language 112
   people 112
Ethiopia 112
ethnic revival 11
ethnicity:
   content versus boundaries 10
   definition 10
   objective versus subjective characteristics 10
   primordialism versus situationalism 10
   symbolic 11
ethnocentric(ism) 35, 70, 102, 108
ethnocide 82, 241
ethnolinguistic vitality (ELV) 37, 47
Euratom 138, 244
Eurobarometer 116, 133, 134, 136, 146, 187, 203, 246

Euromosaic 136, 247
European Bureau for Lesser Used Languages (EBLUL) 135
European Charter for Regional or Minority Languages 95, 120–4, 136, 195, 232
European Commission 128, 132, 133, 136, 138, 159
European Court of Justice (ECJ) 131, 133, 245
European Free Trade Association (EFTA) 152, 244, 246
European identity 6, 38, 127–31, 135, 136, 138, 142, 179, 187, 203–5, 208, 223, 233
European integration 4, 47, 64, 103, 127–31, 134, 136, 144, 146, 179, 182, 204, 223, 237
European Parliament 122, 132, 135, 143, 244, 245
European Year of Languages 2001 124
Euroregions 130
Eurostat 134
exception culturelle 171, 219
exception française 103, 124, 155, 234

Faroe Islands 80
Faroese 80
fascism 17, 75
Félibrige 93
feminisation of profession names 76
Finland 15, 16, 51, 82, 105, 113, 139, 141, 143, 241, 242, 244, 247
   Swedish-speaking 20, 243
Finnish:
   language 23, 50, 132, 133, 216, 247
   language in Sweden 19, 104–11, 115, 121
   people 19, 105, 111, 115, 133; see also Swedish Finns
Flanders 25, 84
Flemish:
   language in France 89
   people 25, 36
   political activism in France 93
Florida 86
Framework Convention for the Protection of National Minorities 120–1, 122, 124, 136
Francophobia 22, 61
Francophonie 26, 31, 142, 162–3, 172
Franco-Provençal 89
franglais 156, 157, 218
Franks 62, 240
French:
   in Italy 81
   in Québec 4, 45, 51, 80
French Academy 56–7, 59, 64, 72, 74, 76, 123, 241
French model of integration 15, 98–100, 108, 116, 122, 124, 199–202, 226, 231, 232

French Revolution 15, 21, 50, 59–61, 62, 74, 81, 88, 91–2, 94, 101, 108, 226, 231
Front national *see* National Front

Gaelic *see* Irish language
Galician 81
Gallo 92, 117, 118, 243
Gastarbeiter 85, 87
Gaul 1, 54
Gauls 1, 62, 67, 240
General Agreement on Tariffs and Trade (GATT) 155, 171, 219
Georgia 161
German:
    language 21–3, 25, 46, 52, 58, 60, 67, 68, 93, 131, 133, 134, 139, 140, 144, 155, 167, 168, 215, 216, 247
    people 13, 22–3, 44, 46, 52, 97, 111, 112, 129, 133, 137, 153, 240, 242
Germany 12, 13, 15, 16, 22–3, 57, 58, 61, 84, 85, 87, 93, 97, 204, 241, 244, 246
ghetto(isation) 88, 99
Girondins 240
Giscardists 100
globalisation 1, 4, 6, 47, 103, 147–9, 150, 152, 171, 179, 182, 210, 237
Great Britain *see* United Kingdom
Greece 85, 244
Greek:
    language 9, 58, 132, 139, 213
    people 112, 113, 177
Guizot Law 241
Gypsies 84, 100, 120, 121

habitus 17
Hanseatic League 111, 243
Haut comité pour la défense et l'expansion de la langue française 72, 138, 157
Haut conseil de la Francophonie 76, 103, 121, 123, 157, 158, 161, 247
Hinduism 113
Holland 14, 81
Home Language Reform 110, 113, 117, 231
home language tuition 117, 120, 180, 195, 196
human rights 82, 87, 88, 95, 124
Hungary 82, 112, 161
Hutterites 45

Iceland 15, 113, 244, 246
Icelanders 68, 129
ikastolas 94, 181, 195
imaginary decree of 1832–1835 75
imagined community 18, 52
immigration 1, 4, 24, 84–8, 131, 148, 179, 182, 236, 237, 244, 247
    in France 64, 97–104, 197, 221, 232
    in Sweden 110, 111–16, 231
India 30, 56, 150

Indochina 61
Indonesians 85
industrialisation 16, 63, 108
Institut national de la language française (INaLF) 123
Institut Pasteur 159
integration 40, 42, 88, 98, 100
intellectuals, intelligentsia 23, 34, 52, 58, 83, 150, 227
    in France 12, 56, 57, 123
    in Sweden 164
    see also élite(ism)
internal colonialism 83–4
International Monetary Fund (IMF) 155, 162
internationalisation 1, 6, 147, 152
internationalism 70, 74, 163, 164, 171
Internet 152, 153, 161, 172
Iran 85, 112
Iraq 85, 112
Ireland 3, 137, 140, 244
Irish:
    language 2–3, 46, 140, 239
    people 2, 45
Islam 34, 44, 98, 113, 119, 131, 148, 163, 242, 245
Islamic headscarf affair 98
Israel 156, 158
Italian:
    language 52, 53, 56, 57, 58, 60, 119, 131
    people 14, 53, 97, 104, 129
Italy 14, 17, 56, 57, 84, 85, 117, 244, 246
    French in 81

Jacobin(ism) 60, 62, 93, 96, 98, 100, 194, 240
Japan 15, 46, 130, 132, 149
Japanese:
    language 46, 138, 153, 215
    people 46, 114, 149
Jews 84, 100, 104, 112, 113, 121
jus sanguinis 12, 13, 101, 202
jus soli 12, 101, 122, 202

Kabyle 104, 119
Kalevala 16
Kalmar Union 65
Kenya 151
Korea 161
Kosovo 142

langage maternel françois 55
language:
    symbolic versus communicative functions 2–3, 183
    system versus use 52
language attitudes:
    definition 29
    instrumental versus integrative 31–2
    matched-guise technique 20, 31, 32
    measurement techniques 30–1

Index of subjects   297

language change 64, 72–7, 235
language ideology 30
language myths 52, 71
  about English 150–1, 158–9
  about French 52, 56–9, 158–9, 211
  about Japanese 46, 114
  about Swedish 66, 114
language planning 51, 65, 72, 160
  corpus 51, 57, 59, 66, 77, 144, 157, 159, 234
  covert 25, 82, 86, 133, 175
  overt 25, 82, 124, 134
  status 51, 59, 65, 66, 79–80, 91, 94, 117, 124, 132, 136, 142–4, 146, 151, 155
language purism 49, 52–3, 77
  in France 71, 158, 160, 191–3, 217–18, 220, 225, 234
  in Sweden 65, 67, 71, 73, 191–3, 217–18, 227, 234
language shift 31, 110, 143, 151, 152, 157, 166, 168, 228, 234, 239
langue d'oc 54, 55
  see also Occitan language
langue d'oïl 55, 89
Lappish see Sámi language
Lapps see Sámi people
Läroplan för grundskolan 73
Latin 1, 12, 21, 23, 54, 55, 56, 58, 63, 65, 66, 68, 69, 73, 74, 91, 145, 150, 153, 209, 213, 239, 240
Latvia 47, 142, 161
lexical transparency 73
liberalism 17, 49, 82, 124
Liechtenstein 161, 246
Lingua 134
lingua franca 6, 63, 66, 135, 146, 151, 153, 162, 166, 233
lingua romana 54, 240
linguicide 82
linguistic culture 30
linguistic determinism and relativity 27, 156
linguistic imperialism 150
linguistic normativism see linguistic prescriptivism
linguistic pluralism see multilingual(ism)
linguistic prescriptivism 49, 51–2
  in France 56, 74, 102, 190–1, 192–3, 198
  in Sweden 72, 190–1, 192–3, 227
linguistic variation 5, 9, 18–21, 49, 51, 73, 75, 150, 191
Lithuania 142, 161
Lorrain 89, 117
Luxembourg 242, 244
Luxembourg Compromise 137

Macedonian 3, 182
Maghreb(i) 97, 98, 99, 100, 101, 102, 104, 182, 201
Malaysia 151

Maltese 3, 182
Marshall Aid 156
Marxism 148
masses 15, 16, 54, 81, 90, 91, 116, 148, 149, 163, 231
Mauritius 12, 85
May 1968 63, 77
Meän Kieli 19, 40, 50, 110, 121
Melanesian languages 117
melting pot 24, 86
Mercator 136
Merovingians 54
Minority Language Committee 120, 121
Mission laïque française 155, 247
modernisation 16, 45, 107, 150, 158
modernism 70, 92, 150, 157, 163, 210
monolingual(ism) 25, 111, 115, 151, 227
Morocco 117, 177
Mouvement national 146
multicultural(ism) 25, 81, 84, 85–8, 196
  in France 98–100, 115, 199
  in Sweden 87, 109, 111, 112–13, 115, 116, 125, 163, 196, 222, 226, 227, 231, 232
multilingual(ism) 25, 31, 84, 152
  in France 59, 88, 111, 123, 196–7
  new French policy 139–40, 146, 161
  in Sweden 116, 227, 196–7
multiple identities 11, 37, 40–1, 129, 141, 205, 236
Muslim see Islam
myth of inclusion see French model of integration

nation:
  definition 14
  ethnic versus civic 12–14, 85–7, 98–100
National Front 71, 100, 116, 146, 156, 197, 244
nationalism:
  inverted or negative 69, 186, 187, 219
  as a movement 16
  official versus folk 16, 25, 175, 228
  philological 52
  as a right wing ideology 17
  as a sentiment 16
nation state:
  definition 15
native speaker 183
Nazi(ism) 69, 84, 93, 160, 230
  neoNazi(ism) 71, 228, 241
Neapolitan 119
Netherlands 52, 84, 244
  see also Holland
neutrality 112, 141, 164, 170
New Democracy 71, 146
New Left 130
New Party, the 71, 116, 146, 200
New Zealanders 128

ni revival 77
Nice 90
North Atlantic Treaty Organisation (NATO) 156, 170
Norway 15, 19, 43, 66, 69, 70, 82, 105, 113, 142, 162, 241, 244, 246, 247
Norwegian
    language(s) 3, 19, 23, 44, 216
    people 43, 167

Occitan 81, 89, 94, 117, 118
    see also langue d'oc
Occitania 83
officialese 73, 74
Olympics 162
Ordinance of Villers-Cotterêts 55, 61, 91, 230
Orientalism 34

Pakistanis 85
patois 19, 43, 59, 61, 63, 92
patriotism 17, 104, 129, 239
Peace of Roskilde 66
periphery 16, 60, 83–4, 100, 108, 141, 182, 199, 236
Philippines 33
Picard 55, 92
Pléiade 56
Polish:
    language 2, 47
    people 2, 97
Pomerania 241
Portugal 14, 15, 81, 85, 117, 244, 246
Portuguese
    language 119, 132, 138, 140, 157
    people 97, 98, 104
post-modernism 148
principle of nationality 16
print-capitalism 16, 21
Proposition 63 86
Prussia 2, 22, 58, 62, 84, 155
psychological distinctiveness 6, 35, 36, 46, 47, 114, 127, 135, 141, 147, 153, 154, 165, 170, 208, 210, 212, 223, 233

qualified majority voting (QMV) 246
Québec 45, 51, 80, 87, 123, 156, 163, 201, 242, 247
Québécois:
    language 4, 45, 51, 80
    people 45, 83, 172
queer theory 36

racism 13, 17, 25, 43, 47, 63, 103, 115, 116, 130, 163, 165, 222, 232
rap music 104, 197, 228
rational choice theory 11
rationalism 22, 70, 128
Reformation 21, 65, 105

regionalism 1, 4, 83, 179, 182, 237
    see also decentralisation
Renaissance 21, 128
Rinkeby Swedish 114, 115, 192, 198, 199, 216, 222, 228, 232, 247
Rom see Gypsies
Romani 84, 121, 192
Romanian 23
Romanticism 12, 16, 22, 62, 67, 68, 93, 104, 128, 230, 231
Russia 2, 105, 107, 241, 242
Russian:
    language 132, 139, 216
    people 47
Rwanda 162

Samerättsutredningen 110
Sametinget 110
Sameutredningen 110
Sámi:
    language 105–11, 121, 196–7, 221, 239
    people 74, 105–11, 120, 121, 197, 239, 243, 244
Sapir-Whorf hypothesis 27
    see also linguistic determinism and relativity
sápmi 74, 105
Savoy 90
Schengen 245
Scottish people 15
segregation(ism) 24, 43, 75, 88, 107, 108, 119
semi-lingualism 103, 109–10, 114–15, 199, 222, 228, 232
Serbian 44, 243
sign language 243
Singapore 151, 154
Six Day War 156
Skåne (Scania) 66
social competition 6, 36
social comparison 6, 35, 36, 38, 44, 46, 141, 147, 198, 207, 222, 223, 232
social creativity 36, 42, 91, 94, 102, 110
social democracy 69, 70, 77, 109, 116, 125, 141, 164, 190, 226, 230, 232
social identity:
    definition 35
    secure versus insecure 18, 35–6, 43, 68, 154
social mobility 36, 37, 41, 42, 63, 91, 108, 214
Socrates 134
SOFRES 160, 188, 207, 218
Sorbonne 55, 104
South Africa 81
Soviet Union 34, 47, 112, 156
Spain 14, 15, 81, 85, 117, 134, 153, 244, 246
Spanish (Castilian):
    language 3, 24, 53, 132, 138, 153, 247
    people 53, 129, 165
spelling reform 49, 51, 73, 74–6, 191
sport 17, 43, 98, 104, 162, 197, 228

Sprachnation 23
SPRINT (språk- och innehållsintegrerad inlärning och undervisning) 168, 247
standardisation 19–20, 44, 49, 50–2, 73, 92
state-nation:
  definition 15
Strasbourg Oaths 54
sur-norme 51, 56, 102, 198
Svenska språknämnden *see* Swedish Language Council
Swahili 151
Swedish Academy 67, 230
Swedish Finns 121, 243
Swedish Language Council 72, 77, 144, 146, 164, 169
Swenglish 164, 216, 218
Swiss 25–7, 45, 46
Switzerland 12, 25–7, 46, 61, 85, 246, 247
symbol(ism) 2–3, 24, 27, 33, 36, 37, 43–4, 47, 50, 152, 183, 196, 205, 207
  in France 1, 59, 60, 64, 74, 91, 102, 136, 146, 171
  of ethnic or national identity 2, 13, 17
  of European identity 128, 129
  in Sweden 107, 125, 165, 185, 232
symbole 93
symbolic power 91, 94
Syrian 216

Tahitian 117
Tamil 153, 215, 247
Tanzania 151
Tekniska nomenklaturcentralen (TNC) *see* Centre for Technical Terminology
terminology commissions 72, 76, 150
Terror, the 60, 61, 93, 240
teudesca lingua 54
theory of economic underdevelopment 83
Third Republic 61, 62, 63, 74, 97, 230
Thirty Year War 241
Tornedalian Finnish *see* Meän Kieli
Tornedalians 19, 40, 105–11, 120, 121, 243
Toubon Law 76, 95, 160, 161, 245
Treaty of Amsterdam 130, 244, 245, 246
Treaty on European Union (TEU) 127, 128, 130, 133, 160, 244, 245
Treaty of Paris 58
Treaty of Rastatt 58
Treaty of Rome 131, 133
Treaty of Utrecht 58

Treaty of Verdun 54
Treaty of Versailles 16, 95, 155
Trente Glorieuses 63, 97
Tunisia 117, 162, 177
Turkey 82, 85, 117, 131, 245
Turkish 23, 216
Turks 85, 112

Ukrainian 23
United Kingdom 37, 38, 43, 50, 84, 129, 130, 134, 137, 149, 155, 163, 207, 242, 244, 246
United Nations 15, 95, 129, 132, 149, 152, 155, 158, 161, 163
United Nations Resolution 242 158
United States 3, 11, 12, 24–5, 30, 32, 34, 43, 45, 65, 68, 83, 85, 86, 130, 132, 137, 143, 145, 149, 154–6, 158, 164, 165, 171, 173
Universal Declaration on Human Rights 95
unwaved flag 17, 77, 186
Uppsala University 105, 167
US English *see* English-only movement

Val d'Aoste (Aosta Valley) 81
verlan 44, 240, 242
vernacular(s) 16, 21, 23, 54–5, 65, 119
Vichy 63, 230
Vietnam War 164
Vietnam 156, 164
Vikings 67
Villers-Cotterêts *see* Ordinance of Villers-Cotterêts

Wales 83, 177
Walloon 25–6, 36, 111
welfare 24, 70, 101, 109, 141
Welsh 4, 177
Western European Union (WEU) 171
World War I 63, 69, 93
World War II 63, 82, 85, 92, 93, 97, 105, 112, 155, 230, 231

xenophobia 163, 172
Xhosa 120

Yiddish 84, 121
Yoruba 120
youth language 44, 104, 190, 192
Yugoslavia 11, 44, 85, 117, 129, 243
Yugoslavs 112, 114

Index of names

Aasen, I. 44
Abrams, D. 38
Achard, P. 90
Acton, Lord 82
Ager, D. E. 3, 18, 25, 27, 38, 39, 52, 54, 72, 74, 76, 77, 81, 82, 84, 92, 93, 95, 97, 98, 99, 100, 101, 117, 118, 119, 137, 138, 139, 140, 145, 150, 156, 160, 162, 163, 172, 188, 202, 207, 218, 241, 242, 243, 245
Agheyisi, R. 30
Ahtisaari, M. 142
Ajzen, I. 29
Allardt, E. 83
Allègre, C. 172
Alsmark, G. 71
Anderson, B. 16, 18, 20, 21, 52, 114
Andersson, L.-G. 73, 108
Andolf, G. 69
Anglejan, A. d' 4
Appel, R. 2, 32
Ardagh, J. 64, 94, 98, 99, 104, 137, 146, 149, 160, 171, 242
Armstrong, J. A. 21
Arnberg, L. 117
Arnstberg, K.-O. 51, 71, 107, 111, 112
Astérix 1, 62, 172
Aurivillius, E. 66
Ayres-Bennett, W. 57
Azeglio, M. d' 14

Baggioni, D. 21, 23, 25, 44, 47, 54, 65, 66, 67, 118
Bainbridge, T. 128, 137, 244, 246
Baker, C. 4, 29, 30, 31, 177
Balibar, R. 53, 54, 61, 76, 240
Balous, S. 138
Banton, M. 11, 44
Barbour, S. 18
Barère de Vieuzac, B. 60, 61, 62, 91
Barrès, M. 63
Barth, F. 10
Battail, J.-F. 164, 168, 209
Battye, A. 57, 160
Bayrou, F. 76
Beaucé, T. de 157
Belazi, H. M. 177
Bellay, J. du 56
Bellman, C. M. 66

Bennett, J. W. 11
Bentahila, A. 177
Bentham, J. 101
Bergman, G. 64, 65, 66, 67, 240, 241
Bergström, O. 69
Berlin, I. 22
Bernadotte, J. 241
Bernard, P. 76, 97, 98, 99, 100, 101, 102, 103, 116, 122, 123, 243, 245
Berry, J. W. 41
Besson, L. 172, 228
Bhabha, H. K. 34
Bildt, C. 140, 141
Billig, M. 17, 34, 40, 44, 149, 186
Blackburn, R. 128
Blair, T. 130
Blanc, M. 41, 218
Boch, C. 134, 245
Boileau, N. 57
Boizon-Fradet, D. 118
Bojsen, E. 165
Bolingbroke, H. St John 14
Bonnemason, J. 63
Bossuet, J.-B. 57
Boulot, S. 118
Bourdieu, P. 17, 91, 135
Bourguiba, H. 162
Bourhis, R. Y. 27, 31, 32, 35, 37, 41, 45, 87
Boutet, J. 124
Boyer, H. 151
Brass, P. R. 10
Braudel, F. 64
Breakwell, G. 39
Breton, R. 81, 87
Brislin, R. W. 177
Broglie, G. de 75, 76, 123, 158
Brown, R. 38
Bruno, G. 63, 68
Brunot, F. 53, 56, 59, 60, 61, 93, 240

Caesar, J. 62
Caldwell, J. 124
Calvet, L.-J. 60, 154, 157, 162
Caput, J.-P. 53, 57, 58, 59, 60
Carcassonne, G. 122, 123
Carlsson, I. 114
Carranza, M. A. 31
Cartier, J. 56

Index of names

Casanova, G. 57
Castles, S. 86, 88
Catach, N. 75, 241
Cerquiglini, B. 54, 55, 123
Certeau, M. 53, 59, 60, 61
Charlemagne 54
Chaurand, J. 53, 240
Chevènement, J.-P. 96, 146
Chirac, J. 96, 121, 124, 171
Chiti-Batelli, A. 140, 153, 209
Chryssochoou, X. 128, 129, 137, 205
Chrystal, J.-A. 165
Cinnirella, M. 38, 39, 129
Citron, S. 61, 62, 63, 64, 96, 100, 156
Claude, I. 83
Clément, R. 37
Clerico, G. 56
Clovis 240
Clyne, M. 2, 3, 26, 44, 46, 53, 77, 84, 182
Cohen, A. 10
Columbus, S. 66
Connor, W. 12, 15, 23, 82, 239
Conversi, D. 239
Copsey, N. 34, 63, 170
Corder, S. P. 20
Corneille, P. 57
Coulmas, F. 19, 23, 27, 132
Coupland, N. 41, 42, 212
Crawford, J. 25
Cresson, E. 149
Crystal, D. 150, 151, 159, 247

Dahlstedt, K. H. 65, 70, 72, 73, 74, 163, 164, 166
Dalin, O. von 66, 67
Daoust, D. 51
Daun, Å. 69, 70, 71, 77, 108
Davies, A. 183
Day, R. R. 247
Deniau, X. 123, 138, 154, 155, 158
Depardieu, G. 172
Déroulède, P. 63
Descartes, R. 57
Désirat, C. 62
Diderot, D. 58
Djité, P. 162
Djonovich, D. J. 158
Donald Duck 165
Dornyei, Z. 31
Douste-Blazy, P. 161
Driedger, L. 86
Drumont, E. 63
Dubois, J. 56
Duhamel, A. 64, 137
Dumas, A. 16
Durand, C. 243

Eckert, P. 236

Edwards, J. 2, 4, 10, 19, 24, 29, 30, 45, 81, 82, 83, 86, 96, 114, 151, 177, 196
Ehn, B. 71, 107, 111, 112, 113, 114
Ekerot, L.-J. 144
Englund, B. 163
Erasmus 134
Eriksen, T. H. 10, 17, 43, 85, 245
Estienne, H. 56
Estienne, R. 56
Etiemble, R. 156
Evans, M. 34, 100

Fasold, R. 29, 32, 182, 206
Ferry, J. 62
Fichte, J. G. 16, 22, 23, 52
Fishman, J. A. 2, 3, 9, 10, 15, 24, 27, 30, 53, 130, 150
Flaitz, J. 4, 156, 159, 166, 172, 176, 177, 178, 179, 185, 212, 213, 218, 227
Flaubert, G. 92
Forcadel, E. 56
Fosty, A. 138
Franco, F. 47, 62, 155
François I 55, 230
Frykman, J. 164

Gandhi, M. 150
Gans, H. 11
García, S. 128
Gardner, R. C. 31
Garmadi, J. 51
Gaulle, C. de 72, 136, 137, 156, 157, 161, 232, 242
Geer, E. de 111
Geertz, C. 10
Gellner, E. 13, 14, 16, 68, 81
Gibbon, E. 57
Gibbons, J. 46, 102
Giddens, A. 147, 246
Gildea, R. 34, 100, 155, 156, 170, 172
Giles, H. 2, 20, 29, 30, 32, 35, 37, 40, 41, 42, 44, 45, 52, 212
Giordan, H. 84, 91, 92, 94, 95, 99, 103, 108, 111, 132
Glazer, N. 86
Goethe, J. W. von 16
Goody, J. 76
Gordon, D. C. 62, 88, 92, 93, 94, 95, 118, 137, 138, 155, 159, 161, 163, 242, 245
Goscinny, R. 1
Goudaillier, J.-P. 44, 104, 192, 242
Graddol, D. 149, 153, 171
Grau, R. 95, 99, 118
Gravier, J. F. 94
Grégoire (Abbé) 59, 60, 61, 91
Grillo, R. D. 81, 83, 84, 90, 91, 92
Grimm brothers 16
Groener, A. 144, 245

Index of names

Gueunier, N. 64, 75, 76
Guillou, M. 123, 157, 162, 163, 171
Gunnarsson, B.-L. 167
Gustav II Adolf 69, 240, 241
Gustav III 67
Gustav Vasa 65, 240

Haberland, H. 132
Habermas, J. 129
Hagège, C. 56, 57, 58, 59, 60, 61, 92, 96, 104, 123, 137, 138, 155, 156, 157, 158, 159, 172, 192
Halliday, M. A. K. 44
Hamers, J. 41, 218
Hammar, T. 85, 242
Hannerz, U. 148
Hansegård, N. 109, 110
Harouel, J.-L. 100
Haselhuber, J. 133
Haugen, E. 19, 25, 44, 51, 56
Hazelius, A. 69
Heath, E. 137
Hechter, M. 11, 83, 84
Henri II 56
Henriksen, C. 132
Héraud, G. 130
Herberts, K. 20, 243
Herder, J. G. 22
Herlitz, G. 69
Hettne, B. 11, 12, 14, 16, 24, 25, 26, 64, 101, 105, 109, 127, 129, 131, 136, 148, 149, 204, 244
Hewstone, M. 30
Hilton, D. J. 69
Hintze, M.-A. 57, 160
Hobsbawm, E. 13, 23, 27, 34, 52, 59, 148
Hockett, C. F. 235
Hoffmann, S. 145
Hollqvist, H. 166, 168
Holmes, J. 175, 235, 236
Holsti, K. J. 149
Holton, R. 148
Hordé, T. 62
Hudson, R. 92, 178, 247
Huguenin, J. 81
Humboldt, W. von 22, 23
Huntington, S. 148
Husband, C. 39, 40
Huss, L. 110, 111, 115
Hutchinson, J. 129
Hyltenstam, K. 19, 40, 50, 66, 81, 84, 104, 107, 108, 109, 110, 111, 115, 117, 120, 133, 142, 143, 151, 152, 166, 167, 168, 243, 246

Jacob, J. E. 62, 88, 92, 93, 94, 95, 118, 155, 159, 242
Janson, T. 64, 65, 66

Jenkins, B. 34, 61, 63, 137, 148, 156, 170, 240
Jerab, N. 102
Jernudd, B. H. 20
Joan of Arc 172, 193
Johnson, P. 37, 40
Johnsson, H.-I. 65, 112, 113
Jones, W. R. 31
Jospin, L. 96, 121, 122, 124, 139, 242
Judge, A. 118, 157, 159

Kachru, B. 153
Kant, I. 16
Karaveli, M. 71, 87, 113, 141, 142, 164, 233, 246
Karl XI 66
Karl XII 240, 241
Karl XIV 67
Karlfeldt, E. A. 68
Kedourie, E. 12, 16, 22, 27
Kellgren, J. H. 66
Kelman, H. C. 32
Kennedy, J. F. 40
Kessel, P. 96
Kloss, H. 23, 51
Kohl, H. 130
Kohn, H. 12, 15
Kotsinas, U.-B. 114, 115, 192
Krejči, J. 27, 239
Kristeva, J. 34, 102
Kymlicka, W. 45, 82, 84, 86, 87, 88, 239

Labrie, N. 135, 245
Lafont, R. 27, 83, 94
Lagerlöf, S. 68
Lainio, J. 109, 110, 114, 120
Lalanne-Berdouticq, P. 67, 123, 137, 139, 140, 158, 161
Lambert, W. E. 31, 32, 151, 218
Lancelot, C. 57
Lang, J. 94
Lange, A. 36
Laporte, D. 53, 61
Laroussi, F. 93
Lartichaux, J.-Y. 59, 90, 92
Laureys, G. 166, 211, 220
Lavenir de Bouffon, H. 139
Le Pen, J.-M. 71, 146, 244
Le Page, R. B. 50
Lefèvre d'Étaples, J. 56
Liebkind, K. 3, 41, 45
Liebniz, G. W. 57
Likert, R. 178, 191
Lilliestam, L. 69, 71, 241
Linde-Laursen, A. 17
Lindgren, A.-R. 110, 111, 115
Lindqvist, H. 71
Lodge, A. R. 50, 51, 52, 54, 55, 57, 61, 63, 74, 76, 92

Löfgren, O. 43, 66, 68, 69, 70, 108, 109, 186, 231
Loman, B. 109
Lönnrot, E. 16
Louis XIV 15, 57
Lowenberg, P. 151
Lundberg, A. 164
Luther, M. 21

McDonald, D. 93
McKay, R. B. 180, 181
McNamara, T. F. 32, 36
McNeill, W. H. 85
Malherbe, F. 57
Marcellesi, J.-B. 93
Marchello-Nizia, C. 59
Martel, P. 94
Mårtensson, E. 77
Martinat, P. 81
Maslow, A. 39
Maupassant, G. de 92
Maurais, J. 75
Maurras, C. 63
May, S. 82, 87, 150, 152
Medici, C. of 56
Mégret, B. 146
Meigret, L. 56
Méla, V. 44
Melander, B. 133, 134, 142, 143, 144
Mill, J. S. 82
Miller, R. A. 46, 47
Milroy, J. 52
Milroy, L. 52
Milton, J. 14
Milward, A. 129
Minc, A. 133, 135, 153, 210
Mistral, F. 93
Mitterrand, F. 94, 98, 104, 130, 137
Molde, B. 72
Molière 57
Montesquieu, C. de Secondat, baron de 14
Moscovici, P. 136
Moynihan, D. A. 86
Muchnick, A. G. 31
Municio, I. 112
Muysken, P. 2, 32

Napoléon 22, 61, 241
Nelde, P. 80, 136
Netterstad, M. 69
Ngũgĩ wa Thiong'o 151
Nguyen, E. 13, 18, 25, 87, 94, 95, 97, 99, 101, 130, 146, 148, 149
Nguyen, E. 16, 239
Niedzielski, N. 52
Nilsson, A.-L. 243
Nixon, J. 168
Noels, K. A. 37

Nordman 71, 228, 241
Norrby, C. 77
Nyborg, K. 132

O Riagáin, P. 3
Oakes, L. 177, 178, 181, 182, 183, 184, 185, 186, 188, 191, 192, 196, 199, 209, 212, 214, 221, 247
Ohlander, A.-S. 241
Ohlsson, S. Ö. 66
Østergård, U. 11, 12, 14, 16, 24, 25, 26, 64, 101, 105, 109, 127, 129, 131, 136, 148, 149, 204, 244
Østerud, Ø. 13, 17, 62, 63, 69, 128

Palme, O. 164
Palsgrave, J. 240
Paltridge, J. 20
Pascal, B. 57
Pasqua, C. 13, 101, 146
Paulston, C. B. 112, 114, 115
Payne, T. 101
Pennycook, A. 33, 34, 150, 151, 154, 246
Pergnier, M. 157
Perret, M. 54, 56, 57, 58, 63
Persson, G. 142, 246
Péry, N. 121
Petri, L. 65
Peyre, H. 91
Phillips-Martinsson, J. 71
Phillipson, R. 133, 137, 150, 152, 155, 166, 210
Picoche, J. 59
Pinker, S. 27
Pocock, J. G. A. 128
Poignant, B. 122
Pompidou, G. 137, 140, 154
Pool, J. 27

Raag, R. 112
Racine, J. 57
Ramus, P. 56
Ranger, T. 13
Renan, E. 12, 92, 96, 242, 246
Rex, J. 88
Richelieu (Cardinal) 56
Richmond, A. 148
Rickard, P. 53
Ridelberg-Lemoine, M. 245
Ritzer, G. 148
Rivarol, A. de 58–9, 138, 158, 240
Robespierre, M. 60, 61
Rosenberg, M. 36
Ross, J. A. 10, 45, 80
Rouland, N. 88, 99
Rousseau, J.-J. 12, 58
Royce, A. 9
Rudbeck, O. 66

Runblom, H. 105, 112, 113
Ruong, I. 105
Ryan, E. B. 29, 30
Rydberg, V. 67, 68
Rydqvist, J. E. 67

Sachdev, I. 27, 37, 45
Safran, W. 23, 24, 25, 62, 86, 94, 97, 98, 100, 101, 240
Said, E. 34
Saifullah Khan, V. 39, 40
Saint Robert, M.-J. de 44, 153
Salvesen, H. 105
Sand, G. 92
Santer, J. 246
Sax, G. 179
Scherer, K. R. 2
Schiffman, H. F. 24, 25, 30, 54, 59, 75, 86, 93, 241
Schiller, F. von 101
Schlesinger, P. 6, 34, 87, 129, 130, 245
Schnapper, D. 12, 13, 15, 60, 87, 95, 98, 100, 101, 104, 123, 129
Schröder, G. 130
Schulze, H. 14
Sebastian, R. J. 29, 30
Séguin, P. 146
Selander, E. 165, 166
Senghor, L. S. 162
Sevigné, Mme de 57
Shakespeare, W. 14
Shapiro, M. 53
Shearn, C. 177
Shelly, S. L. 123
Sibelius, J. 17
Siguan, M. 150, 159, 166
Simmas, P. A. 110
Simmons, R. 36
Simpson, J. M. Y. 80
Sjögren, A. 111, 114
Skutnabb-Kangas, T. 109, 152
Smith, A. D. 10, 12, 13, 14, 16, 17, 24, 62, 63, 81, 82, 83, 84, 86, 128, 129, 130, 148, 149, 242, 244
Smolicz, J. 2, 3
Snyder, L. 14
Sofos, S. A. 148, 240
Söhrman, I. 241, 243
Sörlin, S. 11, 12, 14, 16, 24, 25, 26, 64, 101, 105, 109, 127, 129, 131, 136, 148, 149, 204, 244
Srivastava, R. N. 80, 81
St. Clair, R. N. 6
Stendhal 92
Stiernhielm, G. 66, 241
Strindberg, A. 68
Stroud, C. 32, 81, 107, 108, 109, 110, 111, 115, 120, 243

Sundbärg, G. 68
Svensson, S. 141
Svonni, M. 107, 109, 110, 111, 120, 239, 243

Taboada-Léonetti, I. 12, 101
Tabouret-Keller, A. 25, 50, 117
Tägil, S. 113
Taguieff, P. A. 149
Tajfel, H. 34, 35, 36
Taylor, C. 45
Taylor, D. M. 35, 37, 41
Tegnér, E. 67, 241
Teleman, U. 70, 76, 142, 143, 166, 168, 231, 241
Thavenius, J. 69, 168
Thérive, A. 63
Thiesse, A. M. 14, 21, 62, 63, 69, 154, 240
Thompson, J. B. 17
Tiällman, N. 66
Tilly, C. 81
Tocqueville, A. de 43
Tollefson, J. W. 24, 33
Torstendahl, R. 241
Trautmann, C. 124
Trudeau, P. 87
Trudgill, P. 32, 177
Tucker, G. R. 4
Turner, J. C. 34, 35, 36, 239
Tzavaras, G. A. 177

Uderzo, A. 1
Uppman, B. 105

Varro, G. 98, 99, 102, 103, 117, 119
Vassberg, L. M. 4, 20, 177, 242
Vaugelas, C. V. de 57
Velímský, V. 27, 239
Vercingétorix 62
Verdi, G. 17
Vermes, G. 124
Vikør, L. 49, 72, 73, 74, 111, 164, 165, 166, 218, 241
Villiers, P. de 146
Voltaire, F. M. A. de 58

Wagner, R. 17
Wallace, H. 128
Wallace, W. 148
Wallenberg, R. 112
Walter, H. 55, 56, 59, 62, 63, 75, 76, 240, 242
Wande, E. 107, 109, 111, 115, 117, 120
Wardhaugh, R. 12, 25, 32, 93, 151, 175, 235
Wartburg, W. von 53, 54
Washington, G. 101
Watt, I. 76
Weber, E. 63, 91
Weinstein, B. 53, 75

Wellander, E. 165
Westin, C. 36
Westman, M. 70, 76, 166, 167, 231
Wilberforce, W. 101
Williams, C. 3, 239
Wingstedt, M. 4, 30, 32, 47, 88, 105, 107, 108, 109, 110, 111, 114, 115, 177, 178, 179, 185, 190, 191, 192, 193, 196, 200, 215, 216, 217, 227, 231

Winock, M. 13, 16, 18, 62, 63, 94, 156
Wise, H. 54, 57, 74
Witte, B. de 133, 245
Wolfe, D. E. 31
Wright, S. 25, 63, 92, 123, 133, 135, 154, 172, 244

Zidane, Z. 104
Zola, E. 240

In the series IMPACT: STUDIES IN LANGUAGE AND SOCIETY the following titles have been published thus far or are scheduled for publication:

1. PÜTZ, Martin (ed.): *Language Choices. Conditions, constraints, and consequences.* 1997.
2. KIBBEE, Douglas A. (ed.): *Language Legislation and Linguistic Rights. Selected Proceedings of the Language Legislation and Linguistic Rights Conference, the University of Illinois at Urbana-Champaign, March, 1996.* 1998.
3. LINELL, Per: *Approaching Dialogue. Talk, interaction and contexts in dialogical perspectives.* 1998.
4. OWENS, Jonathan: *Neighborhood and Ancestry. Variation in the spoken Arabic of Maiduguri, Nigeria.* 1998.
5. ANDREWS, David R.: *Sociocultural Perspectives on Language Change in Diaspora. Soviet immigrants in the United States.* 1999.
6. RICENTO, Thomas (ed.): *Ideology, Politics and Language Policies. Focus on English.* 2000.
7. McCAFFERTY, Kevin: *Ethnicity and Language Change. English in (London)Derry, Northern Ireland.* 2001.
8. ARMSTRONG, Nigel: *Social and Stylistic Variation in Spoken French. A comparative approach.* 2001.
9. HELLINGER, Marlis and Hadumod BUßMANN (eds.): *Gender Across Languages. The linguistic representation of women and men: Volume I.* 2001.
10. In preparation.
11. In preparation.
12. OKITA, Toshie: *Invisible Work. Bilingualism, language choice and childrearing in intermarried families.* n.y.p.
13. OAKES, Leigh: *Language and National Identity. Comparing France and Sweden.* 2001.
14. WEBB, Vic: *Language in South Africa. The role of language in national transformation, reconstruction and development.* n.y.p.
15. BOXER, Diana: *Applying Sociolinguistics. Domains and face-to-face interaction.* n.y.p.